How genes influence behavior

How genes influence behavior

Jonathan Flint
Wellcome Trust Centre for Human
Genetics, University of Oxford, UK

Ralph J. Greenspan
The Neurosciences Institute, San Diego, USA

Kenneth S. Kendler
Virginia Institute of Psychiatric
and Behavioral Genetics,
Virginia Commonwealth University, USA

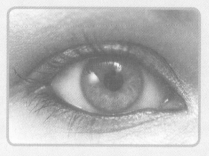

OXFORD
UNIVERSITY PRESS

OXFORD

UNIVERSITY PRESS

Great Clarendon Street, Oxford ox2 6DP

Oxford University Press is a department of the University of Oxford.
It furthers the University's objective of excellence in research, scholarship,
and education by publishing worldwide in

Oxford New York

Auckland Cape Town Dar es Salaam Hong Kong Karachi
Kuala Lumpur Madrid Melbourne Mexico City Nairobi
New Delhi Shanghai Taipei Toronto

With offices in

Argentina Austria Brazil Chile Czech Republic France Greece
Guatemala Hungary Italy Japan Poland Portugal Singapore
South Korea Switzerland Thailand Turkey Ukraine Vietnam

Oxford is a registered trade mark of Oxford University Press
in the UK and in certain other countries

Published in the United States
by Oxford University Press Inc., New York

British Library Cataloguing in Publication Data

Data available

Library of Congress Cataloging in Publication Data
Flint, Jonathan.

How genes influence behavior / Jonathan Flint, Ralph Greenspan, Kenneth Kendler.
   p. cm.

ISBN 978–0–19–955990–9
1. Behaviorism (Psychology) 2. Genetics. 3. Genomic imprinting.
I. Greenspan, Ralph J. II. Kendler, Kenneth S., 1950- III. Title.
BF199.F55 2010
155.7—dc22

2009042123

Typeset by MPS Limited, A Macmillan Company
Printed in Italy by Lego S.p.A.

ISBN 978–0–19–955990–9

1 3 5 7 9 10 8 6 4 2

Thanks

This book was long in the making. We want to express our thanks to Jonathan Crowe, our editor at Oxford University Press. His vision of this project was wonderfully close to our own and he was supportive of our efforts at every turn.

Each of us (J.F., R.J.G. and K.S.K.) has, during our long professional careers, been blessed by many stimulating and supportive colleagues and students. This is not the place to list them all. However, we do want to acknowledge here the depth of our gratitude.

We dedicate this book to our wives, Alison, Dani, and Susan, for their love, support and tolerance.

Figure acknowledgements

Figure 2.1 Courtesy of the National Library of Medicine. **Figure 2.2** Reproduced with kind permission from Henry Boxer Gallery. **Figure 2.3** Kendler, K.S. *et al.*, The Roscommon Family Study. II. The risk of nonschizophrenic nonaffective psychoses in relatives. *Arch Gen Psychiatry*. 1993. 50(8):645–52. **Figure 2.4** © Michael Walsh/istockphoto. **Figure 2.5** Kendler, K.S. *et al.*, The Roscommon Family Study. II. The risk of nonschizophrenic nonaffective psychoses in relatives. *Arch Gen Psychiatry*. 1993. 50(8):645–52. **Figure 2.7** Courtesy of the National Library of Medicine. **Figure 3.1** Reprinted by permission of Macmillan Publishers Ltd: Gusella, J. *et al.*, A polymorphic DNA marker genetically linked to Huntington's disease. *Nature* 306: 234–238, copyright 1983. **Figure 3.2** Hurst, J.A *et al.* 1990. An extended family with a dominantly inherited speech disorder. *Developmental Medicine and Child Neurology* 32: 347–355. **Figure 3.3** Reprinted by permission of Macmillan Publishers Ltd: R.E. Straub *et al.*, Genome-wide scans of three independent sets of 90 Irish multiplex schizophrenia families and follow-up of selected regions in all families provides evidence for multiple susceptibility genes. *Mol. Psychiatry* 7 (6):542–559, copyright 2002. **Figure 4.3** Old Man in Sorrow (On the Threshold of Eternity) 1890 (oil on canvas) by Gogh, Vincent van. Reproduced with permission from The Bridgeman Art Library Nationality. **Figure 4.5** Reproduced with data from K.S. Kendler, C.A. Prescott, J. Myers, and M.C. Neale. The structure of genetic and environmental risk factors for common psychiatric and substance use disorders in men and women. *Arch Gen Psychiatry*, 60 (9):929–937, 2003. **Figure 4.6** Data from from K.S. Kendler and C.A. Prescott. *Genes, Environment, and Psychopathology: Understanding the Causes of Psychiatric and Substance Use Disorders*, New York: Guilford Press, 2006. **Figure 4.7** Data from K.S. Kendler and C.A. Prescott. *Genes, Environment, and Psychopathology: Understanding the Causes of Psychiatric and Substance Use Disorders*, New York: Guilford Press, 2006. **Figure 4.8** With kind permission from Springer Science + Business Media: R. J. Cadoret, 1983, Evidence for gene–environment interaction in the development of adolescent antisocial behavior. *Behav Genet* 13(3):301–10. **Figure 4.9** Adapted from Kendler, *et al.*, (1995). Stressful life events, genetic liability, and onset of an episode of major depression in women. *American Journal of Psychiatry* 152:833–842. **Figure 4.10** Adapted from Kendler, *et al.*, (2008). A developmental twin study of symptoms of anxiety and depression: evidence for genetic innovation and attenuation, *Psychological Medicine* 38:1567–75 © Cambridge Journals, published by Cambridge University Press, reproduced with permission. **Figure 5.2** Gratacos, M., Nadal, M., Martin-Santos, R., Pujana, M.A., Gago, J., Peral, B., Armengol, L., Ponsa, I., Miro, R., Bulbena, A. *et al.*, 2001. A polymorphic genomic duplication on human chromosome 15 is a susceptibility factor for panic and phobic disorders. *Cell* 106: 367–379. **Figure 5.4** Reprinted by permission from Macmillan Publishers Ltd. Munafo, *et al.*, Association of the DRD2 gene Taq1A polymorphism and alcoholism: a meta-analysis of case-control studies and evidence of publication bias. *Molecular Psychiatry* 12: 454–461, copyright 2007. **Figure 5.5** From Lesch, *et al.*, Association of Anxiety-Related Traits with a polymorphism in the Serotonin Transporter Gene Regulatory Region. 1996. *Science* 274: 1527–1530. Reprinted with permission from AAAS. **Figure 5.6** Reproduced by permission from Macmillan Publishers Ltd. Meyer-Lindenberg, A. and Weinberger, D.R. Intermediate phenotypes and genetic mechanisms of psychiatric disorders. *Nat Rev Neurosci* 7: 818–827. Copyright 2006. **Figure 6.1** Hirschhorn, J.N. and Daly, M.J. 2005. Genome-wide association studies for common diseases and complex traits. *Nat Rev Genet.* 6:95–108. **Figure 6.2** © Wellcome Trust Case Control Consortium, 2007. **Figure 6.3** Hindorff LA, Sethupathy P, Junkins HA, Ramos EM, Mehta JP, Collins FS, and Manolio TA. 2009, Potential etiologic and functional implications of genome-wide association loci for human diseases and traits. *Proc Natl Acad Sci USA,* 106: 9362–9367. **Figure 7.2** With kind permission from Springer Science and Business Media: DeFries, J.C., Gervais, M.C., and Thomas, E.A. (1978). Response to 30 generations of selection for open field activity in laboratory mice. *Behavior Genetics,* 8, 3–13. **Figure 7.4** Reproduced from Singer, J.B., *et al. Genetics* 169: 855–862. **Figure 8.1** With kind permission from Springer Science and, Business Media:Ricker, J.P., and Hirsch, J. (1988). Genetic changes occurring over 500 generations in lines of *Drosophila melanogaster* selected divergently for geotaxis. *Behavior Genetics,* 18, 13–25. **Figure 8.3** Reprinted by permission from Macmillan Publishers Ltd. Toma, D.P., White, K.P., Hirsch, J. and Greenspan, R.J. Identification of genes involved in *Drosophila melanogaster* geotaxis, a complex behavioral trait. *Nature Genetics* 31: 349–353.Copyright 2002. **Figure 8.4** Reprinted by permission from Macmillan Publishers Ltd. Dierick, H.A. and Greenspan, R.J. Molecular analysis of flies selected for aggressive behavior. *Nature Genetics* 38: 1023–1031. Copyright 2006. **Figure 8.5** Reprinted by permission from Macmillan Publishers Ltd. Dierick, H.A. and Greenspan, R.J. Molecular analysis of flies selected for aggressive behavior. *Nature Genetics* 38: 1023–1031. Copyright 2007. **Figure 8.6** White, J.G., Southgate, E., Thomson, J.N., and Brenner, S. 1986. The Structure of the Nervous System of the Nematode *Caenorhabditis elegans. Philosophical Transactions of the Royal Society of London B*: 314:1–340. **Figure 8.7** From *C. elegans* Sequencing Consortium. (1998) Genome sequence of the nematode *C. elegans*: a platform for investigating biology. *Science.* 282, 2012–8. With permission from AAAS. **Figure 8.8** Reproduced from de Bono, M., Bargmann, C. I. (1998) Natural Variation in a Neuropeptide Y Receptor Homolog Modifies Social Behavior and Food Response in *C. elegans. Cell*, Vol. 94, Issue 5, pp. 679–689. With permission from Elsevier. **Figure 8.9** Brunner, H.G., Nelen, M., Breakefield, X.O., Ropers, H.H., and van Oost, B.A. 1993. Abnormal behavior associated with a point mutation in the structural gene for monoamine oxidase A. *Science* 262: 578–580. Reprinted with permission from AAAS. **Figure 9.1** Courtesy of the National Library of Medicine. **Figure 9.2** Courtesy of the National Library of Medicine. **Figure 9.3** Reprinted from Hyun *et al.*, *Drosophila* GPCR Han Is a Receptor for the Circadian Clock Neuropeptide PDF. 2005, *Neuron*, 48:267–78. With permission from Elsevier. **Figure 9.4** Reproduced from Konopka, RJ, Benzer, S. (1971). *Clock* mutants of *Drosophila melanogaster.* PNAS 68:2112–6. **Figure 9.7** Reproduced from Konopka, RJ, Benzer, S. (1971). *Clock* mutants of *Drosophila melanogaster.* PNAS 68:2112–6. **Figure 9.8** Zerr, D.M., Hall, J.C., Rosbash, M., and Siwicki, K.K. 1990. Circadian fluctuations of period protein immunoreactivity in the CNS and the visual system of *Drosophila. J Neurosci* 10: 2749–2762. **Figure 9.9** Hardin, P.E., Hall, J.C., and Rosbash, M. 1990. Feedback of the *Drosophila* period gene product on circadian cycling of its messenger RNA levels. *Nature* 343: 536–540. **Figure 9.10** Hardin, P.E., Hall, J.C., and Rosbash, M. 1990. Feedback of the *Drosophila* period gene product on circadian cycling of its messenger RNA levels. *Nature* 343: 536–540. **Figure 9.11** Hardin, PE, 2005. The circadian timekeeping system of *Drosophila. Current Biology*, 15: R714–R722. With permission from Elsevier. **Figure 9.12** Hardin, P.E. 2005. The circadian timekeeping system of *Drosophila. Current Biology* 15: R714–722. With permission from Elsevier. **Figure 9.13** Young, M.W. 1998. The molecular control of circadian behavioral rhythms and their entrainment in *Drosophila. Annu Rev Biochem* 67: 135–152. **Figure 9.14** With kind permission from Springer Science+Business Media: Costa, R., Peixoto, A.A., Thackeray, J.R., Dalgleish, R., and Kyriacou, C.P. 1991.

Length polymorphism in the threonine-glycine-encoding repeat region of the period gene in *Drosophila*. *J Mol Evol* 32: 238–246. **Figure 9.15** Reproduced from Costa, R., Peixoto, A.A., Barbujani, G., and Kyriacou, C.P. 1992. A latitudinal cline in a *Drosophila clock* gene. *Proc Biol Sci* 250: 43–49. **Figure 9.16** Sawyer, L.A., Hennessy, J.M., Peixoto, A.A., Rosato, E., Parkinson, H., Costa, R., and Kyriacou, C.P. 1997. Natural variation in a *Drosophila clock* gene and temperature compensation. *Science* 278: 2117–2120. **Figure 9.17** Reproduced with kind permission from Professor Charalambos P. Kyriacou. **Figure 9.18** Reproduced with kind permission from Professor Charalambos P. Kyriacou. **Figure 9.19** Toh, K.L., Jones, C.R., He, Y., Eide, E.J., Hinz, W.A., Virshup, D.M., Ptacek, L.J., and Fu, Y.H. 2001. An hPer2 phosphorylation site mutation in familial advanced sleep phase syndrome. *Science* 291: 1040–1043. **Figure 10.1** Kandel, E.R. 2001. *Science* 294: 1030–1038. © Dr Eric Kandel. **Figure 10.2** Kandel, E. R. 1976. *Cellular Basis of Behavior: An Introduction to Behavioral Neurobiology.* San Fransisco: W.H. Freeman and Company. © Dr Eric Kandel. **Figure 10.3** Reproduced from Frost WN, Castellucci VF, Hawkins RD, Kandel ER., 1985, Monosynaptic connections made by the sensory neurons of the gill- and siphon-withdrawal reflex in *Aplysia* participate in the storage of long-term memory for sensitization. *PNAS* 23:8266–8269. © Dr Eric Kandel. **Figure A11** Adapted from Matsuzaki, H. *et al.* (2004). Parallel genotyping of over 10,000 SNPs using a one-primer assay on a high-density oligonucleotide array. *Genome Res* 14: 414–425. **Figure A12** © Affymetrix 2004. **Figure A14** Bradley, A. *et al.* (1984) Formation of germ-line chimaeras from embryo-derived teratocarcinoma cell lines. *Nature* 309: 255–256.

Contents

Introduction

The library of the Institute of Psychiatry in London extends over two floors, roughly dividing the collection into the old and the new. The former consists of back issues of the psychiatric profession's trade magazines, as well as books that describe seminal studies, many of which were carried out by the Institute's staff: George Brown's work on depressed women in Camberwell for instance, Michael Rutter's survey of all children living on the Isle of Wight, Hans Eysenck's work on personality. Much of the subject matter, the language it is written in, and the questions being asked are familiar and comprehensible: How common is schizophrenia? Does head injury make it more likely you will develop a mental illness? What is autism? How can a stressful life event be defined and does it increase risk for depression? The methods used are also intelligible; most of the research was carried out by talking to patients and their relatives. Browse the shelves and you'll get the gist of most of what you pick up.

Upstairs, in the newer collection, things are different. Here you will find journals, current issues of the many volumes of *Schizophrenia Research*, *Behavior Research and Therapy* and *Psychological Medicine* from the floor below. But here too there are newer titles, with no forebears, whose meaning, if not relevance, is not immediately obvious. What could *Molecular Psychiatry* be about? And if *Neuron* is clearly a journal

about cells that make up the brain, its contents equally clearly are meant only for the specialist to understand ('SynGAP–MUPP1–CaMKII synaptic complexes regulate p38 MAP kinase activity and NMDA receptor-dependent synaptic AMPA receptor potentiation', for example). Persist a little, despite the incomprehensibility, and one thing does gradually emerge: everywhere you see the importance of genetics, molecular genetics in particular.

Genetics: the universal research language

Genetics has dominated all of biomedical research for some time now. From the 1980s onwards, there has been a steady increase in the number of diseases subjected to molecular genetic analysis, but things have really taken off with the completion of the human genome project, and sequencing of the genomes of apparently innumerable other model organisms (most of which have unpronounceable Latin names together with lifestyles and appearances so alien, if not unfriendly, to our own as to make their relevance to humanity impenetrable, except to an enlightened few).

These prodigious achievements are expected to be succeeded by equally prodigious advances in medicine. Enormous numbers of people, half a million in one study in the UK alone, a planned 1 million in the USA, are being enrolled in studies of genetic effects on health. In the course of these studies, all of our 23,000 or so genes, including hundreds of known variations in them, will be examined and have their DNA sequence determined, so that soon (some believe) doctors will be prescribing medicines based on the specific genetic composition of their patients. It's hard to argue with science on this scale: billions of dollars, touching the lives of millions of people.

Psychiatry, always the Cinderella, came late to the genetics ball, but, if anything, it has been embraced with even more enthusiasm than earlier arrivals. (This owes as much to the despair of those in the profession at the difficulty of finding scientifically rational approaches to the treatment of psychiatric patients as it does to the boundless optimism of molecular biologists.) Media reports provide a stream of apparent successes for genetic assaults: not just genes that make you depressed but happiness genes, gay genes, God genes, and, from a newspaper headline from 2004: '*Britain's biggest study into the* **genetic basis** *of promiscuity... One in five women cheat—and it's* **genetic**... **Infidelity** *linked to* **genetic** *make-up.*'

On the other hand, there has been, and still is, strong opposition to geneticists' claims to understand and explain human behavior. *The Bell Curve*, a book about the genetics of intelligence, aroused such passion that protestors picketed book stores as if the volume were as dangerous as the *Satanic Verses* and could be subject to a *fatwah* issued by the community of sociologists (although those who got round to reading it found the book wasn't nearly as exciting as the public disputes, a common

feature of banned books, including those written by Salman Rushdie). *Not in our Genes* (a title that makes its point so well you scarcely have to read much more to work out what it's about) is one of a number of books arguing that heritability (a measure of the extent to which behavior and other traits are genetically influenced) is not only a flawed concept but one that is ideologically suspect, developed by conservative academics and seized on by right-wing politicians. Genes get political because if genes could be shown to have important effects on behavior, for example on criminality, there would be no point in rehabilitation programs. As criminals are genetically programmed to be criminals, incarceration would be the only thing we can do for them. The same would be true for drug addicts, although perhaps once we know which genes makes a person devote his or her entire life to the pursuit of drug-induced euphoria, we would then be able to manufacture a *biological* therapy (no point obviously in changing the environment, if the disorder is due to faulty genes).

Disagreements in part reflect a division in the genetics community. Despite the late arrival of molecular biology to psychiatry, genetics was important in psychiatric research for many years BC (before cloning). Genetics before DNA, before PCR (a technique invented in the 1980s that greatly facilitated analysis of DNA sequences; see Appendix, p. 226), before a host of other acronyms was, and still largely is, 'quantitative' genetics: the study of families, twins, and adoptees, pursued primarily by talking to patients and their relatives. This is clearly very different from the laboratory-based high-technology discipline that grabs media attention. Unfortunately, although the material of quantitative genetics research is accessible to the non-specialist (such things as questionnaires and diagnostic categories), the methodology is not. Structural equation modeling is not for the faint-hearted, so that many of its insights remain obscure and easy to misinterpret: the concept of heritability, for example, still gets a lot of flak (it was called—with a hint of the improper if not the obscene—'the H word' at one scientific meeting).

So, writing about genes and behavior promises to be controversial. Although controversy is not something that any of us willingly seeks out (so it's unlikely that reading this book will ever be construed as an illicit intellectual activity), it would be disingenuous to ignore the contentious nature of psychiatric genetics and simply sanctimonious to assert that all we want to do is educate our readers. In fact, it is the elusive but irresistible nature of the quest, and the stages of understanding that it has led us through, that provide the motivation and framework for this book.

What will you get in the subsequent pages?

This book is a collaboration from three scientists who have spent a good proportion of their adult lives trying to understand how genes influence behavior. We joined up in this effort because we enjoy talking to each other about our mutual interests, which we approach from complementary areas of expertise. Two of us, Kenneth S. Kendler and Jonathan Flint, are trained in medicine and psychiatry but have taken rather different career paths: K.S.K. focusing on psychiatric genetic studies in humans and J.F. spending most of his time examining the impact of genes on behavior in mice. Ralph J. Greenspan, by contrast, works on the genetics of behavior in the common fruit fly (*Drosophila melanogaster*, an organism that seems to devote its life to hovering around fruit bowls and wine glasses).

We wanted to write a book on the genetics of behavior for non-specialists. Collectively, we've spent many decades writing hundreds of scientific papers in order to communicate with academic colleagues. We wanted this book to be different. We set ourselves the task of making it accurate, accessible, self-critical, and (above all) entertaining. We were, to different degrees, motivated to write the book for three inter-related reasons. Firstly, we think this area of research is of general interest: it is an area of science that teaches us some fundamental things about what it means to be human.

Secondly, we are concerned at how widely misunderstood are the methods and results of psychiatric and behavioral genetics. This is in part because the methods *are* complicated and involve statistical concepts that are not readily accessible to many well-educated individuals. But it is also motivated by what happens when behavior genetics gets into the headlines, which it does more than most research; the desire for a quick or sensationalist story sacrifices accuracy. In some instances, several of which have been very high profile, the findings of these loudly trumpeted studies failed to stand up to further scrutiny. Notable in this category are an early study of bipolar disorder (manic depression) (Egeland *et al.*, 1987) and the claim of a gene for homosexual orientation in men (Hamer *et al.*, 1993). People should be cautious about any initial report of controversial findings, and no study is perfect, but all of the potential problems can, at least in part, be addressed by empirical studies. Too often the importance of these studies is ignored; they are carefully carried out but they are less glamorous than the discovery of a gene for *being gay*.

Thirdly, we were uncomfortable with many of the prior efforts, some written by journalists, some by scientists, to communicate our field to the general public. We were tired of the misrepresentations, the misunderstandings, calumnies even, inflicted on psychiatric and behavioral genetics by the media. We would like to put the record straight. We don't intend to prove that the media reporting is wrong; we won't give you a list of misrepresented scientific reports and their correct interpretation. After all, science depends on questioning the veracity of every finding, so we don't expect things to stay the same for long, not in a fast-moving field like genetics. But there is a clear need for a better effort in this realm.

Our goal is to illustrate the key issues and results, and to describe how they were obtained. Along the way, we hope to convey a feel for the chase and how the search for these elusive genetic influences has changed the way scientists think about the relationship between genes and behavior. We do not strive for encyclopedic coverage and we are judicious in our use of references. There are enough to allow any interested reader to follow up on his or her interests. But we avoid the dense referencing common in more academically oriented works.

We're not relating a story, so you can, if you like, read at random (relatively speaking at least). Nevertheless, the book is structured, going from the more complicated and poorly understood organism (that is, humans) to the less complicated (but still very complex) organisms like *Drosophila*. We describe how we know schizophrenia is heritable and what we know of the condition's genetic basis; we take some time to present the concept of heritability and what it means, introducing you to quantitative genetics (if you come to this book with strong hereditarian or anti-hereditarian views, then here's a section you might want to miss: either it will tell you nothing new, or you won't believe us whatever we say).

Convincing evidence that schizophrenia is, in part, a heritable condition is the premise that spurred attempts to identify the molecular nature of the condition; in other words, to find out which genes are at fault. We'll show you how the molecular genetic research was carried out, but don't expect a dramatic story of scientists grappling to make a breakthrough. The discoveries have not yet provided unambiguous answers to questions about the cause of the disorder.

Learning through hard experience

Back in the 1980s, when human molecular genetics emerged as a discipline, finding the gene for a human genetic disease was glamorous: young post-docs would be working through the night, and what they found was clear-cut, important, clinically useful (cystic fibrosis is not an easy disease to diagnose without a DNA test), and potentially lucrative (at least for the venture capitalists who set up the biotech companies). In the 1990s, when molecular genetics turned its attention to psychiatry, high expectations of success only exacerbated the dissatisfaction with what was revealed, although anyone familiar with quantitative genetics would probably not be surprised at the findings molecular genetics turned up.

If our sole interest in this book had been psychiatric genetics, we would get you as far as describing how scientists found, and some then tried to sell to a drug company, the schizophrenia gene. We would go on to list genomic regions and even a few genes that might be involved in depression, anxiety, and so on. It's an interesting enough story, with a few characters whose company you'll enjoy, the usual larger-than-life crowd. But if that were all, it would neither be the whole nor the most interesting part of the story. Much more intriguing are the attempts now underway to understand how genes have an influence on behavior, studies that were launched with no obvious connection to psychiatry but whose results have now dovetailed with those of psychiatric genetics, which are likely to inform it more in the future. To do this requires that we expand our field of vision beyond humans to other organisms.

A pharmaceutical company executive was once approached by two well-known schizophrenia researchers. The academics laid out their terms: they each wanted vice-presidential status (and appropriate salaries) in the company; they wanted a multi-million dollar donation to their research programs. And in exchange they offered the name of a single gene, a gene for schizophrenia. The executive mused:

> **The mystery to me is why they thought the discovery, even if it were true, would have been of any value to us at all. There are a small number of gene products, cell surface receptors primarily, that are potential drug targets. Otherwise, we have to know about mechanism. A gene name is just that, a gene name. It won't tell me how to cure schizophrenia.**

It surely won't. And getting at the mechanism is hard enough even when you are dealing with a disorder whose physiology is relatively well understood, like diabetes. What do you do if you're dealing with behavioral disorders?

The role of animal models

A molecular geneticist has a simple answer: knock out the gene in a mouse, in a fly, or even in a worm. The ability to turn genes on and off as we wish, even in specific regions of the brain, is one of the most extraordinary accomplishments of molecular genetics. It provides a way of finding out what a gene does, as you can compare an organism with the gene with one without it: by keeping all other genes identical, whatever differences you see must arise from the artificially induced gene mutation. The problem is that worms, flies, and mice do not have schizophrenia; they may possess the candidate schizophrenia gene, but how do we know that the gene does the same thing in a fly or mouse as it does in our brain? Or that knocking out a gene is actually a good way to ask about its normal function? How do we even know that genetic effects on behavior are comparable between humans and other animals? Perhaps the pathways are completely different; after all, one thing that marks out our species is behavioral flexibility, an apparent freedom from biological determination that indicates we are not ruled by our genes. This seems like a rather obvious problem, one that should stymie much genetic research, but you would not think so from the number of schizophrenic mice, flies, and, yes, worms that have been reported. What on earth is going on here? As for humans, there are both quantitative and molecular approaches to how genes influence behavior in rodents, insects, and nematodes. We'll describe their application to the genetic basis of anxiety in mice, since it's easier to argue that a mouse can be anxious than psychotic.

Experiments by humans carried out on mice turn out, in the *Hitch Hiker's Guide to the Galaxy*, to be experiments by mice carried out on humans. Mice are merely the physical manifestation in our galaxy of hyperintelligent pan-dimensional beings who built the earth to answer *the* fundamental question of life, the universe, and everything (or rather to work out what that question is). Experimental psychologists take one step further back from this problem and ask, do mice think at all? Even if mice said that they were actually hyperintelligent pan-dimensional beings, would the psychologists believe them? Probably not; at the very least, they would need to prove it, experimentally that is. It's very hard not to believe, when your dog gives you a big wag of his tail, and, if you're really lucky, some slobber on your hand, that the animal is not pleased to see you. We routinely impute such mental activity to animals, without, if we think hard about it, much justification. It's equally likely in your dog's case that tail wagging and hand licking are learnt responses that increase the chances of getting what the animal wants (food, a walk, etc.) and have nothing to do with an emotional state. This sort of problem doesn't really crop up in human behavioral genetics. People point out the difficulties of diagnosing schizophrenia, but even Thomas Szasz (who thinks psychiatric diagnoses are entirely arbitrary man-made categories) wouldn't go so far as to say that patients have no mind (Szasz, 1974).

Animal research brings its own problems (not least of which are death threats from the Animal Liberation Front), which you might think outweigh the opportunities it provides for investigating gene function. But in forcing us to think about mental states and psychological processes, the analysis of animal behavior illuminates in a rigorous way what we mean by genetic effects on behavior. Think of it this way: it often happens in medicine that work on a disease tells us about normal function. So investigating why certain families with abnormally high levels of fat in their blood also have high rates of heart disease led to an understanding of how the body processes fat and the role of different forms of cholesterol (high- and low-density lipoproteins—healthwise, the good and the bad types of cholesterol). Psychiatry is

no exception: finding the biological basis of depression through genetic analysis could tell us something of general significance about mood in everyone, not just those needing psychiatric help. The difference is that the discovery of cholesterol transport could draw upon a theory of metabolism: the process by which one organic compound is turned into another by the use of the biological catalysts (enzymes) as governed by the laws of thermodynamics. In contrast, we don't have a similarly well-established theory of mood to make sense of the genetic analysis. Instead, we have to make do with the neurobiology and psychology we have to hand. It's as if we have to do two things at once: use genetics to make discoveries about the biology of behavior, while using the biology of behavior to understand what our discoveries mean.

What makes for a good explanation?

In fact, the problems are not just ones of empirical knowledge, of the results we obtain, and how we place them within the canon of accepted facts. It's a truism that there is no such thing as theory-free data, but theories themselves have to emerge from a particular viewpoint, a set of assumptions, or, in short, a philosophy about how the world works. When, in the last part of the book, we consider how genes contribute to the production of behavior, we have to determine to what extent we can reduce the biological basis of behavior to a more fundamental level. Reductive explanations are attractive and very powerful. They explain complex phenomena very successfully. An increase in the mean kinetic energy of water molecules is a reductive explanation of why, when we heat up a pot of water, bubbles form on the side, steam rises from the top, and finally the pot becomes a seething cauldron. Physics is full of simple laws that explain much of our world in this way, like $F = ma$ (force equals mass times acceleration, which we owe to Isaac Newton) and $E = mc^2$ (energy equals mass times the square of the speed of light, which we owe to Albert Einstein).

Do similar explanations work for behavior? We know that genes encode information about an organism: the entire set of proteins that it can make and many aspects of its developmental trajectory, from egg to adult and all the intervening steps. Its metabolic pathways that fuel the process and the machinery for the immense physical transformations involved— all are determined by the linear structure of DNA. In some instances, you can even observe developmental order reflected in the physical order of genes along a chromosome. Many aspects of the problem of how an organism develops are hence reduced to the problem of how genes are turned on and off in a coordinated fashion. Is the same true for behavior? Can the problem of how a nervous system, with all its connections between neurons, branching dendrites, cellular architecture, and anatomical organization into a brain, gives rise to behavior be reduced to a problem of which genes specify which neural components? Even more challenging, can we reduce the nature of our mental experiences—part of what you might call the 'internal' aspects of our own behavior—our emotions, perceptions, wishes, and fears down to the simple level of genes and their associated biology? Our views on these questions will make more sense to you after you have journeyed with us through the whole

book. There is a tremendous amount that we do not know and a lot we are still learning. But we think we now know enough to see the broad shape of how genes really impact on behavior. We hope to explain that still incompletely formed vision to you.

Summary

1. Genetics plays a major role in present-day life sciences and behavioral research.

2. The methods and findings in behavioral and psychiatric genetics are important to understand because many of the findings have not held up.

3. Animal studies can provide models to test for functions of genes identified in human genetic studies.

4. The issue of what is an adequate explanation for how genes influence behavior calls into question the adequacy of reductionism.

References

Egeland, J.A., Gerhard, D.S., Pauls, D.L., Sussex, J.N., Kidd, K.K., Allen, C.R., Hostetter, A.M., and Housman, D.E. (1987). Bipolar affective disorders linked to DNA markers on chromosome 11. *Nature* **325**:783–787.

Hamer, D.H., Hu, S., Magnuson, V.L., Hu, N., and Pattatucci, A.M. (1993). A linkage between DNA markers on the X chromosome and male sexual orientation. *Science* **261**:321–327.

Szasz, T. (1974). *The Myth of Mental Illness*. Harper Collins, New York.

2 Schizophrenia

All in the family?

[On studies with families and what they tell us about the inheritance of schizophrenia]

Q. Are you feeling ill?

A. You see as soon as the skull is smashed and one still has flowers with difficulty, so it will not leak out constantly. I have a sort of silver bullet which held me by my leg, that one cannot jump in, where one wants, and that ends beautifully like the stars. Former service, then she puts it on her head and will soon be respectable, I say, O, God, but one must have eyes.

Emil Kraepelin. Textbook of Psychiatry, 7th edn (1904).

Schizophrenia is the most debilitating of adult psychiatric disorders. Onset is typically in early adulthood. Only a small minority of affected individuals truly recover. For most, their ability to live a full life—to have a meaningful job, to sustain lasting love relationships—is substantially impaired. Schizophrenia strikes around one out of every 150 individuals. In the 1950s prior to the deinstitutionalization movement that emptied many of our large public psychiatric hospitals, this one disorder—schizophrenia—accounted for more than half of all the hospital beds in the USA.

Schizophrenia is the psychiatric disorder that comes closest to epitomizing what we understand as madness. Delusions, hallucinations, and thought disorder (as illustrated in the quote above) are all characteristic symptoms. In addition to the biomedical view of schizophrenia—as a poor-prognosis neuropsychiatric disorder—schizophrenics have also

Figure 2.1 Emil Kraepelin (1856–1926).

been described as the shamans of our culture, in touch with the magical and divine nature of our world. However, in non-literate hunter–gatherer societies, they are far from being high-status shamans who contact a spirit world. Instead, there too they are stigmatized low-status individuals living on the periphery of the village, tolerated but not valued—rather like the unwashed homeless man muttering to himself that many of us see on the street corners of our major cities.

More intriguing is the possible relationship between schizophrenia and creativity. This has been remarkably hard to pin down empirically one way or the other. Anecdotally, the number of highly creative unconventional individuals who have schizophrenic relatives has been noted. For example, in the 20th century, Albert Einstein, James Joyce, and James Watson—all known for their quirky genius—had children with schizophrenia. Joyce's ill daughter was named Lucia. The Republic of Ireland—to which our story now turns—designated July 26 as 'Lucia Day' to promote schizophrenia awareness. Figure 2.2 shows two pictures of artist Louis Wan's cat. The first was painted earlier in his life, while the second was painted as he slid into a schizophrenic psychosis. The later picture conveys a rather frightening hint of what the world might begin to look like for those who suffer from schizophrenia.

Does schizophrenia run in families?

Awareness of the disease in Ireland has already spawned one of the most informative studies to date of the genetics of schizophrenia. The Irish public health agencies had been

Figure 2.2 The 19th- and 20th-century artist, Louis Wain, who was fascinated by cats, painted these pictures over a period of time in which he developed schizophrenia.

keeping detailed case registries: records of all individuals showing up at hospitals, clinics, or doctors' offices for any kind of psychiatric treatment. These registries helped us to find large families that would be likely to have a number of brothers, sisters, and other relatives (the more family members recorded, the better the chance of demonstrating a genetic link). Beyond this, Ireland has the advantage of a relatively homogeneous population; immigration to Ireland was a rare event prior to the last few years. With all of these attractions, and because of the long and complicated relationship between England and Ireland, in 1987 the US National Institutes of Health, rather than an agency in the UK, launched a study of the genetics of schizophrenia in the west of Ireland.

The idea that schizophrenia ran in families was far from new. The first modern describer of this disorder—Emil Kraepelin (Figure 2.1), writing towards the end of the 19th century—noted the apparent increased risk of schizophrenia in close relatives of his affected patients. This impression was validated by more systematic and increasingly sophisticated studies over the course of the 20th century. We report one such study here.

The Roscommon Family Study

Key paper

Kendler, K.S., McGuire, M., Gruenberg, A.M., O'Hare, A., Spellman, M., and Walsh, D. (1993). The Roscommon Family Study. I. Methods, diagnosis of probands, and risk of schizophrenia in relatives. *Arch Gen Psychiatry* **50**:527–540.

A detailed account of the methods and initial results of the Roscommon Family Study.

Working with a number of Irish researchers, one of us (K.S.K.) came to know well (at times,

perhaps, too well) the bed and breakfast houses and psychiatric hospitals of the Western part of the Republic of Ireland. During a five-and-a-half-year period, we first tried to track down all individuals in the county of Roscommon born after 1 January 1930 who had been treated for schizophrenia. There were a total of 285 such individuals. (The location of county Roscommon in Ireland is seen in Figure 2.3.) At the same time, we identified another 100 individuals who had been hospitalized with depression and other severe mood disorders. Finally, we identified an additional 150 people, selected at random from the voter registration roles, for comparison as our control group. These individuals are called 'probands', meaning the people through which a family of interest is contacted.

The first steps in the study were to follow up and try to interview probands. We succeeded in 88% of the cases where they were alive and

Figure 2.3 The location of county Roscommon in Ireland, shown on the map in blue.

Figure 2.4 Picture of rural Ireland, typical of the areas covered by the Roscommon Family Study and the Irish Study of High-Density Schizophrenia Families.
Source: © Michael Walsh/istockphoto.

traceable. When we found them, we conducted a structured psychiatric assessment that included detailed questions about the kinds of emotional and psychiatric problems they may have experienced in their lives. We also searched for hospital records and these were systematically reviewed and abstracted.

The next step was to identify, locate, and attempt to interview all of the first-degree relatives of the controls, those with mood disorder and those with schizophrenia—that is their parents, full siblings, and offspring. By the time we were done, we had used up a lot of index cards (laptops did not exist when we started this work), identifying a total of 2,043 relatives who were still alive and hadn't fled to somewhere inaccessible (like Australia).

Next, we tried to interview these relatives; most were still in Ireland, but many were abroad, in Liverpool, Birmingham, London, and other parts of England. And, as before, we interviewed everyone we could find, 1,753 in all, speaking to them mostly at home, but occasionally in parked cars, pubs, libraries, or even standing in fields. Our interviewing team were 'blinded', meaning that they did not know (and asked the respondent not to tell them) whether they were interviewing a relative of a control, or a mood disorder or schizophrenic patient. Similarly, when senior psychiatrists (including K.S.K.) reviewed the interviews and abstracts of hospital records if they had been hospitalized, they were similarly blind. (This approach helps protect research from the creep of subjective bias. Like most people, scientists can make the mistake of seeing the world as they want to, rather than as it really is. Blinding the interview process makes it much less likely that we impose our biases on our results.)

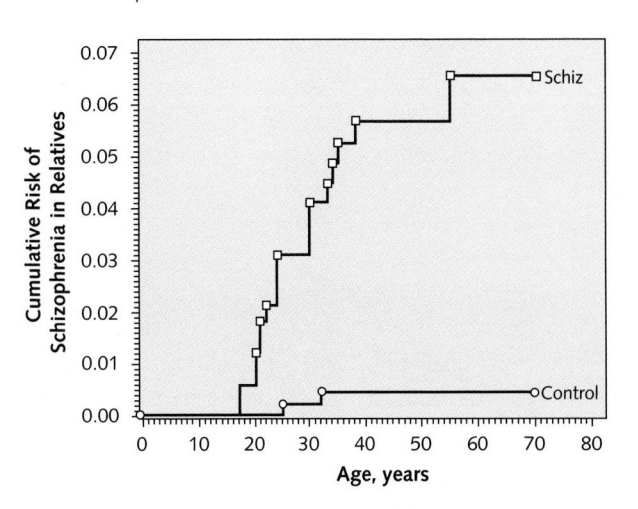

Figure 2.5 Graph showing cumulative risk for schizophrenia in first degree relatives of schizophrenic (schiz) and control probands as a function of age. From Kendler *et al.*, 1993.

At the end of all this interviewing—it took our team over 5 years and about 18 person years of work—we had enough data to answer definitively the question of whether first-degree relatives of an individual diagnosed with schizophrenia are more likely to be schizophrenic than someone picked at random from the same population. Our key result is shown in Figure 2.5 as a life table. The figure shows the cumulative risk for schizophrenia on the y-axis and age on the x-axis. The difference in risk for schizophrenia in the relatives of our schizophrenic versus our matched control probands was striking.

We found that if you are in the immediate family of someone with schizophrenia, the chances are 13 times higher that you too will develop schizophrenia compared with being related to a randomly chosen individual from the electoral role. The odds are not actually all that high in absolute terms, 65 out of 1,000 compared with five out of 1,000, but given the nature of this disease for those affected by it and their families, any number of cases is a tragedy. Either

way, a family history is a better predictor of future disease than any other factor. Other studies came to a similar conclusion: at least ten other family studies of schizophrenia conducted since 1980, using similar methods, all showed that close relatives of individuals with schizophrenia have approximately ten times the risk of suffering from the illness themselves.

Key paper

Kendler, K.S. and Diehl, S.R. (1993). The genetics of schizophrenia: a current, genetic–epidemiologic perspective. *Schizophr Bull* 19:261–285.

A good review of the modern family studies of schizophrenia.

Roscommon is a predominantly rural region consisting of small villages connected by winding narrow lanes. One summer evening during one of many home visits, an elderly grandmother took me (K.S.K.) aside after the interview had ended. '*Now doctor,*' she asked, '*what is this you've been doing, driving all about the place, asking all these questions of my relatives?*' I explained to her that we were studying mental illness and trying to understand if it ran in families, and to do so we needed to study all kinds of families. '*Do you mean to tell me,*' she said, with a slight sense of indignation, '*that you are spending all this time just to see if being daft runs in families? Why everybody knows that! Take the O'Donnells for example. They are mad as can be and it goes back generations!*' She proceeded to give me a detailed genealogy of the O'Donnell family and the characteristics of each member, describing how, when she was a little girl, the grandfather had taken off in the family tractor down to the main town shouting and carrying on, talking about God and the Devil and who knows what else, and ended up in the local mental hospital (St Pat's, as it was known). She told me about his children and grandchildren many of whom had had psychiatric difficulties. Then she told me about the McGuires with a similar level of detail. That was enough for her. She went back into the house shaking her head and laughing gently to herself. '*What will these crazy Americans think of next? You'd think they have all the time and money in God's creation.*' I felt a bit foolish. After all, was it really necessary to go to all this trouble to demonstrate what so many people take for granted, that madness does indeed run in families?

Traditional assumptions about heredity, mental illness, and behavior

In an earlier era, no doctor would have had any doubts about the certainty of the inheritance of mental illness. Medical training in the early 19th century included a heavy dose of hereditarianism—the belief that disease was transmitted from parent to offspring. This perspective included the notion that an adult's behavior would affect a child's hereditary endowment. For instance, it was considered important to know whether a child was born before or after its mother had 'gone mad'. If before, then the child was considered to be at greater risk of eventual insanity (Rosenberg, 1976). There was no research to back up these beliefs—they were the accepted, and obvious, wisdom.

After the discovery of the principles of inheritance in the late 19th and early 20th century, it was immediately assumed that there were hereditary factors (genes) for each human

disease and trait. One of the main proponents of this view, Charles Davenport, sent out staffers to knock on doors all over central Long Island, New York, to interview families in pursuit of evidence for a gene that determined 'nomadism'. In a 1915 monograph with the title 'Nomadism, or the wandering impulse, with special reference to heredity' (Davenport, 1915), he reported 100 family histories showing the '*distribution of the nomadic tendency*'. In contrast to the Roscommon study described above, Davenport's methods were not what we would consider rigorous. His diagnostic criteria were vague and subjective, and he had personally interviewed only a very small proportion of his sample. To give you a flavor of his clinical methods, here are a few of the 'remarks' we see about members of his first 25 pedigrees: '*Mother has 2 sisters of good repute. Mother's father was a Western desperado who married a good woman,*' '*A bear-hunter of note,*' '*A stage-driver,*' and '*At one time an itinerant tinkerer.*' One the basis of these descriptions, Davenport concluded that nomadism is a sex-linked recessive trait such that '*Sons are nomadic only when their mothers belong to nomadic stock. Daughters are nomadic only when the mother belongs to such stock and the father is actually nomadic. When both parents are nomadic expectation is that all children will be*' (p. 26).

We might see this and similar work of this era as simply a product of its time. After all, the science of statistics was just in the process of being invented and the social sciences of psychology and sociology were still very young and survey methods were primitive. Few alternative explanations were available and all traits were assumed to be hereditary (Cravens, 1978). However, this work has a more ominous side to it in that results from this and other studies, especially of idiocy or feeble-mindness, were used by the US Congress in subsequent decades to restrict immigration into the USA.

What exactly is schizophrenia?

Is schizophrenia any more precisely defined than the 'wandering impulse'? Has our work really progressed very far from the days of Davenport? Most psychiatrists have at one time or another faced this question at social or family gatherings: What do you mean by madness (or more specifically schizophrenia)? The questioners might themselves offer definitions: madness is an extremity of passion ('*the very ecstasy of love*'), a consequence of unkindness ('*Your old kind father, whose frank heart gave all, oh, that way madness lies, let me shun that, no more of that*') or simply the assumption of socially deviant beliefs—not an illness at all.

Up until the early 1970s, definitions of mental illness, including schizophrenia, consisted largely of clinical theories articulated by German psychiatrists formulated in the late 19th and early 20th centuries. During the 1960s, psychiatry in general, and psychiatric diagnoses specifically, were under attack by the 'antipsychiatry' movement—associated with such names as Szasz, Laing, and Foucault. Psychiatric diagnoses at that time were not that reliable (but neither were diagnoses in most of the rest of medicine). Diagnostic manuals contained vague descriptions of psychiatric disorders, open to varying interpretations. The situation wasn't helped by several high-profile court cases featuring 'expert' psychiatric testimonies that completely disagreed with each other.

But the problems were not intractable and the field of psychiatry responded. A first critical step was the realization that much of the difficulty resulted from differences in training and in concepts about the nature of the illness. This insight arose from efforts to understand why admission rates for schizophrenia were

higher in the USA than in the UK. In the 1960s, the US–UK Diagnostic Project compared 250 patients admitted to the Brooklyn State Hospital and a comparable number to Netherne Hospital, south of London. In order to assure uniform criteria, they developed a structured interviewing procedure. When this standardized form of assessment was used, they found that there was no significant difference in the way key diagnostic symptoms and signs were rated on either side of the Atlantic (Cooper *et al.*, 1972). (Physicians make a distinction between a *symptom*, which is something a patient tells you about, and a *sign*, which is something that a doctor observes about a patient.) What *did* differ was the way those symptoms and signs were assembled into a diagnosis.

The solution to this problem, which had two major components, arose over a decade on both sides of the Atlantic. The first was the development of clear operationalized diagnostic criteria for psychiatric illness, first proposed in a famous article published by John Feighner and colleagues in 1972 (Feighner *et al.*, 1972). Instead of vague diagnostic descriptions, psychiatric diagnostic manuals came to contain rather clearly specified individual criteria. Secondly, structured psychiatric interviews were developed, first in England by John Wing (Wing *et al.*, 1967) and later by a number of psychiatrists and epidemiologists in North America. Instead of the typical free-flowing interview, these were heavily scripted, so that no matter who was giving the interview, the same questions would be asked.

One of the first major studies that utilized the first generation of structured psychiatric interviews was called the International Pilot Study of Schizophrenia. Researchers in nine centers worldwide, including hospitals in Africa, India, South America, and Russia, interviewed patients clinically diagnosed with schizophrenia

(WHO, 1973). The goal was to address this simple but important question—were the main features of schizophrenia similar in patients from varying world cultures? The answer was pretty clear: yes. The most consistent and salient features of schizophrenia were seen at all of the centers: delusions of control, thought insertion, thought withdrawal, thought broadcasting, and third-person auditory hallucinations.

Psychiatric interviews have now been standardized to the point that it is possible to run them on a computer. (If you are interested, download an example from http://www.hcp.med. harvard.edu/wmhcidi/instruments_download. php.) You can get a feel for the way the interview works from these questions, taken from the start of one of the most recently developed instruments—the CIDI (which stands for Composite International Diagnostic Interview):

1. Now I want to ask you about some ideas you might have had about other people. Have you ever believed people were spying on you?
NO (SKIP TO 2)
YES
   A. How did you know that was happening?
   IS EXAMPLE IMPLAUSIBLE?

2. Was there ever a time when you believed people were following you?
NO (SKIP TO B)
YES
   A. How did you know people were following you?
   IS EXAMPLE IMPLAUSIBLE?
   B. Have you thought that people you saw talking to each other were talking about you or laughing at you?
   NO (SKIP TO 3)
   YES
   C. What made you think it was you they were discussing or laughing at?
   IS EXAMPLE IMPLAUSIBLE?

3. Have you ever believed you could actually hear what another person was thinking, even though he or she was not speaking?
NO (SKIP TO 4)
YES
   A. How was it possible for you to hear what a person thought if that person didn't say anything?

4. Have you ever been convinced that you were under the control of some power or force, so that your actions and thoughts were not your own?

Schizophrenia, then, can be reliably diagnosed by the presence, and absence, of a number of well-characterized psychological and behavioral phenomena. These include hallucinations (typically hearing voices), delusions (very distorted and unrealistic beliefs), and thought disorder—well illustrated by the opening quote of this chapter. The reliability of diagnoses was carefully assessed in the Roscommon Family Study. Two well-trained psychiatrists (one of them K.S.K.) reviewed 69 cases weighted towards those with symptoms. They each used 12 different diagnostic categories and agreed 83% of the time. While few studies have quite this high level of reliability, many have shown that using modern methods, schizophrenia and other forms of severe psychiatric illness can be assessed at least as reliably as many other medical conditions. For example, 933 physicians, when asked to match a set of taped heart sounds to 15 possible diagnoses, agreed in less than 80% of cases (Butterworth and Reppert, 1960). We should, however, recognize that being able to make a consistent diagnosis may not reflect anything about the underlying disorder. What if different underlying causes can produce the same set of symptoms? This takes us back to the Irish woman's question: why ask if madness runs in families?

Adoption, heredity, and environment

In human families, relatives can be similar because they share environments or because they share genes, or both. Relatives share all kinds of environments. They live in the same neighborhoods, often attend religious services together, eat a similar diet, are all exposed to the same level of harmony or conflict in the home, and might all live close to an industrial plant that pumps out pollution into the air or water.

All of these reasons and more could explain the resemblance among members of the same family. If we could find cases where genetically related individuals are exposed to different environments, we might be able to sort out the relative importance of genetic and environmental factors in the origins of a disease such as schizophrenia. Studying what happens to adopted children provides one way to separate genes from environment, although as we shall see the approach has its limitations. For more details about adoption studies, see Box 2.1.

Infants who have been adopted at birth have two kinds of relatives: the adoptive relatives with whom they share the environment in which they grow up, and biological relatives who gave them their genes. The two adoption strategies

BOX 2.1 Adoption studies

Adoption studies are one of the two main 'experiments of nature' that can be used in human populations to separate out the effects of nature and nurture. Twin studies are the other. The design requires subjects to have been adopted at an early age by individuals who are genetically unrelated to them. The power of the design arises from the fact that adopted individuals share genetic but not environmental factors with their biological relatives and share environmental but not genetic factors with their adoptive relatives.

Two different adoption designs have been most commonly used. The first begins with ill mothers who have given children up for adoption and a matched group of well mothers who similarly have given children up for adoption. The risk of illness is then compared in these two groups. If genetic factors influence the transmission of the disease within families, then the adopted-away offspring of the ill mother should have a higher rate of illness than the adopted-away offspring of the control mother. The second design begins with ill adoptees and requires an evaluation of their biological and their adoptive relatives. If genetic factors are responsible for the familial nature of the disorder, then the biological relatives of the ill adoptees will have higher rates of illness than the biological relatives of the control adoptees. If the disorder runs in families for environmental reasons, then the adoptive relatives of the ill adoptees will have higher rates of illness than the adoptive relatives of the control adoptees. The second design is superior because it allows for independent tests of 'nature' (genetics) and 'nurture' (environment).

outlined in Box 2.1 have both been applied to schizophrenia. The first and simplest method begins by identifying mothers with schizophrenia who have given up their children at an early age for adoption. A control group of women without schizophrenic illness are identified who have also given up their children for adoption. In adulthood, these adoptees are then tracked down and psychiatrically assessed. If the risk for schizophrenia runs in families for genetic reasons, then the rate of schizophrenia should be substantially higher in the adopted-away offspring of the schizophrenic mothers than in the adopted-away offspring of the control mothers. If, however, the risk for schizophrenia is familial because of the effect of shared environment, then the risk rates of schizophrenia in the adopted-away children of schizophrenic mothers should not be substantially increased.

An adoption study in Oregon

While still completing his psychiatric training at Oregon State Hospital in the 1960s, Leonard Heston noted that pregnant mothers with schizophrenia were typically urged to give their children up for adoption, usually never to see them again. Reviewing records of births from 1915 to 1945, Heston identified 58 adoptees from schizophrenic mothers who, within 3 days of birth, were placed in either adoptive or foundling homes and had little or no further contact with their mother or with her biological relatives. He then found a matched set of control adoptees from the same agencies whose biological mothers and fathers had no record of psychiatric hospitalization.

Key paper

Heston, L.L. (1966). Psychiatric disorders in foster home reared children of schizophrenic mothers. *Br J Psychiatry* **112**:819–825.

Heston's epic adoption study that had such a prominent impact on thinking about the nature of schizophrenia.

Heston made exhaustive efforts to track down all of the adoptees, just as we had had to do in order to find people for our study in Ireland. Fourteen adoptees had died in infancy or childhood, and there was no information at all about a further five. This left 47 high-risk and 50 control adoptees whom he interviewed personally. Reasonably good records from a variety of sources were available for the other adoptees.

All of the information about each adoptee was organized into a dossier, omitting all information about the mental health of the biological mother, and evaluated by two psychiatrists as well as by Heston. A fourth psychiatrist was brought in to resolve diagnostic disagreements. The results are summarized in Figure 2.6. Five of the 97 subjects were diagnosed as having schizophrenia. All five were adopted-away offspring of schizophrenic mothers; none came from the control adoptees. In fact, the rate of schizophrenia in the adopted-away offspring of schizophrenic mothers (10.6%) was indistinguishable from the rates of illness seen in prior studies of children who were born of and reared by schizophrenic parents. Although the number of subjects was small, these results had a dramatic effect on the field at their time of publication because of the compelling evidence that schizophrenia ran in families for genetic reasons.

The Danish studies

The second kind of adoption design used in schizophrenia begin with adoptees who themselves developed schizophrenia rather than biological mothers. Seymour Kety and Fini Schulsinger, in a very influential series of studies, utilized this design. They began

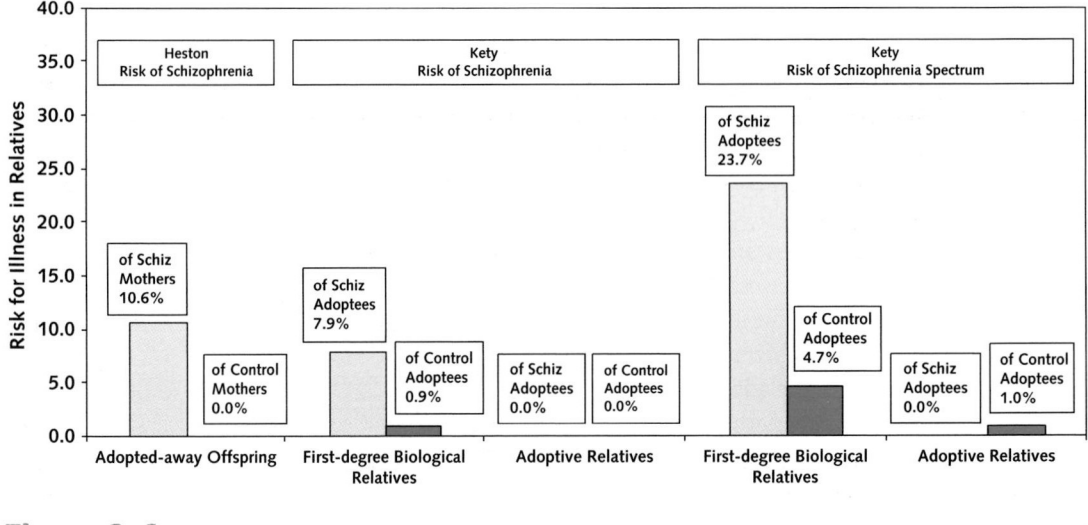

Figure 2.6 Results of adoption studies of schizophrenia conducted by Heston (1966) and Kety (1987). Schiz, schizophrenic.

by contacting the Department of Justice in Denmark, which records every legal adoption. They identified almost 6,000 adoptees born in the Greater Copenhagen area between 1924 and 1947. To identify those who had gone on to develop schizophrenia, they searched through the National Psychiatric Registry, which documents every psychiatric hospitalization in Denmark. (This is not a bad place to start, as we know from a number of studies that almost every individual affected with schizophrenia is psychiatrically hospitalized at some point in their life.) In this 'Copenhagen sample', the investigators identified 34 adoptees who were hospitalized for schizophrenia, 34 control adoptees and all of the biological and adoptive relatives. Over a decade later, they did something rarely accomplished in human studies: they replicated the entire project, searching the adoption records for cases that occurred elsewhere in Denmark (called the 'provincial sample'). From a total of 8,944 adoptees, they identified 41 adoptees later hospitalized for broadly defined schizophrenia, and a matched set of control adoptees.

Key paper

Kety, S.S. (1987). The significance of genetic factors in the etiology of schizophrenia: results from the national study of adoptees in Denmark. *J Psychiatr Res* **21**:423–429.

One of a series of reports from the justly famous Danish adoption study of schizophrenia.

When all of the findings were collated, analyzed, and re-analyzed using modern diagnostic criteria, one of us (K.S.K.) along with a close colleague (Alan Gruenberg) found that the rate of schizophrenia in the first-degree biological relatives of the schizophrenic adoptees was 7.9% versus 0.9% in the control adoptees (Figure 2.6). So sharing genes but not environment with a schizophrenic individual produced a nearly tenfold increased risk for schizophrenia. Among the adoptive relatives, no cases of strictly defined schizophrenia were diagnosed in either the schizophrenic or the control groups. So sharing rearing environment but not genes with an individual who has schizophrenia produced no increase in risk of schizophrenic illness.

Key paper

Kendler, K.S., Gruenberg, A.M., and Kinney, D.K. (1994). Independent diagnoses of adoptees and relatives as defined by DSM-III in the provincial and national samples of the Danish Adoption Study of Schizophrenia. *Arch Gen Psychiatry* **51**:456–468.

This study describes the results of the diagnostic re-analysis using more modern diagnostic criteria of the famous Danish Adoption Studies of Schizophrenia.

In reviewing hundreds of these detailed interviews, we could not help but be impressed by the persistence and skill of the interviewers in this study. In the Copenhagen sample, nearly all of the interviews were done by one Danish psychiatrist, Bjorn Jacobsen. Jacobsen was extremely successful at getting withdrawn and reluctant individuals to participate in the interviews, through a combination of persistence and tact. The nature of the illness means that affected individuals frequently live at the margins of society, in the poorer more disadvantaged areas, and can be extremely difficult to engage in anything, let alone research projects. Jacobsen had visited one individual relative in the Copenhagen sample over ten times, at all times of the day. He would knock on the door and no one would answer, despite evidence from sounds inside the apartment that someone was home. One evening, coming home from the opera relatively late, Dr Jacobsen decided to drive past the apartment of this recalcitrant relative and noticed that the light was on. He pulled his car over and went up and knocked. For the first time, the man opened the door. Jacobsen's notes record that the door opened just a crack and a quite suspicious-looking individual peered out, asking him what he could possibly want at this time of the evening. Through charm and persistence, Dr Jacobsen was able to get himself invited into the apartment and did not finish the extensive interview until the small hours of the morning. This is merely one of many such stories repeated in the course of the project.

The Danish adoption studies have turned out to be crucial in several ways. In addition to explaining why schizophrenia ran in families (showing convincingly that it was due to genes), they also helped to sort out some of the inconsistencies nagging the diagnosis of schizophrenia. The international pilot study of schizophrenia, alluded to previously, had found that no matter where the patients were or who saw them, there was agreement in two-thirds of cases on the diagnosis of schizophrenia. That meant that one-third of the patients had symptoms that left room for doubt. Some of these cases were marginal and unlikely to be diagnosed as schizophrenic outside of two particular centers. The remaining 20%, on the other hand, manifested some aspects of schizophrenia, but not a complete enough set of symptoms to meet a strict definition. This raised the possibility that there might be a number of distinct conditions, with different causes, hidden under the label 'schizophrenia'. Psychiatrists talk about schizophrenia spectrum disorders, a set of conditions that possess some but not all of the features of narrowly defined schizophrenia. Sometimes the symptoms are not so severe, or don't last as long and don't interfere with the patient's lifestyle as obviously as the frank delusions and hallucinations that are characteristic of the full-blown psychosis. One of the most interesting disorders within this spectrum is known as 'schizotypal personality disorder.' For the last 100 years, clinicians have noted that some relatives of individuals with schizophrenia seem to possess, in mild form, some of the key symptoms of schizophrenia. Such individuals tend to be socially odd, suspicious, are often both physically and socially awkward, commonly have unusual ideas (e.g. thinking that people are looking at them or making fun of them in public places), and are prone to unusual patterns of communication.

The Danish adoption studies discovered that almost a quarter of the first-degree biological relatives of schizophrenic adoptees (those with strictly defined disease) could be diagnosed by this broader definition of schizophrenia. By contrast, the rate was less than 5% in the first-degree relatives of the control subjects, 1.0% in the adoptive relatives of the controls, and 0% in the adoptive relatives of the schizophrenic subjects (Figure 2.6). In other words, whatever genetic predisposition increased the susceptibility to schizophrenia, strictly defined, also increased the likelihood of developing other syndromes within the schizophrenia spectrum, particularly schizotypal personality disorder. This led to an important conclusion: the spectrum of symptoms in schizophrenia and the variability of their appearance are all subject to the same underlying hereditary factors.

There is almost a recursive property to this finding: we learn not only about the nature of the gene action, but the gene action also tells us something about the boundaries of the disorder itself. The relationship thus revealed between genes and phenotype has implications for how we go on to interpret the molecular findings described later.

Consistency and pitfalls in adoption studies

Altogether, there have been five major adoption studies of schizophrenia performed in the USA, Denmark, and Finland; all found strong and consistent evidence for substantial genetic effects on the risk for schizophrenia. But even the best adoption studies can have important limitations.

In the ideal adoption study, there should be no correlation between the characteristics of the biological parents who are giving the child up and the adoptive family into which the child is going. This is critical in order to separate the effects of genes and family environment. In reality, however, adoption agencies are sometimes asked to match characteristics of the adoptive family with the biological parents. In the USA, adoption agencies are often affiliated with religious organizations, where Catholic, Protestant, and Jewish babies are given to homes of the same religious background. Adoptive parents sometimes ask for adoptive children with a certain eye color, or from parents with musical or athletic ability, or of a certain height or particular complexion.

Another concern in adoption studies is the possible impact of the intrauterine environment and early (pre-adoption) childhood experiences. Some resemblance between the biological mother and her child might be due to what happens before birth, during the 9 months of pregnancy, when in effect child and mother inhabit the same body. Furthermore, many children are not adopted until *after* they have spent the earliest years of life with their biological parents. If being raised as an infant and toddler by an individual with a severe psychiatric illness contributes to future risk of illness (although the evidence to date does not suggest that this is the case), it could confound adoption studies.

Finally, biological or adoptive parents of adoptees are not generally representative of the population at large. Adoption agencies see it as their task to try to find ideal homes for their adoptees. Because of this, adoptive parents have higher socio-economic status and lower rates of drug, alcohol, and psychiatric problems than are found in the general population. The biological relatives of adoptees are also not really a random sampling either, but the nature of the bias varies with social circumstances and historical period. Immediately after World War II, for example, a large proportion of adoptions in Europe took place as a result of poverty. Most adoptees came from poor rural families that were intact. In general, the rates of psychopathology are not elevated in such biological parents. However, in the late 1990s, the large majority of adoptees were from the children of teenage mothers in urban areas, born out of wedlock. Rates of psychiatric illness, as well as drug and alcohol abuse, were much higher than normal in these parents. In addition, the identity of the father might be impossible to

determine, as the mother was often highly active sexually. In other words, either biological or adoptive parents may be quite unrepresentative of the population, biasing the findings.

Twins

None of the completed adoption studies of schizophrenia was free of some methodological limitations (as indeed are all human genetic studies—which can never approach laboratory sciences in the degree of the control of the experimental variables). To increase our confidence in the validity of these findings, it would be best to try to replicate these adoption results in a completely different kind of human study that could also separate out the effects of genetic and environmental influences. Fortunately, there is one such other method—twin studies.

The first such study was conducted in Britain by one of the founders of genetics and statistics, Francis Galton (Figure 2.7). The title of his 1875 paper, 'The history of twins, as a criterion of the relative powers of nature and nurture' says it all.

Two types of twin

Human twins come in two fundamentally different kinds. One kind of twin, called monozygotic (MZ) or identical, is a result of a single egg being fertilized by a single sperm. In the first 2 weeks of development, the fertilized egg splits apart into two genetically identical organisms that then grow up into two adults who are always of the same sex. We still do not really understand what causes splitting, but it happens at a similar rate (approximately three per 1,000 births) regardless of ethnic background

Figure 2.7 Francis Galton (1822–1911).

or maternal age. The second kind of twin is called dizygotic (DZ) or fraternal, and results from the female producing two eggs instead of one during ovulation. We understand more about the biology of dizygotic twinning. It is, in essence, a misfiring of the female reproductive cycle due to 'overdrive' of the ovaries by hormones secreted from the pituitary gland. Dizygotic twinning is most common in African and least common in Asian populations. The rates are also higher in older women. As the two eggs are nearly always fertilized by separate sperm from the same father, dizygotic twins are, from a genetic perspective, exactly like regular brothers and sisters except that they are fertilized at the same time, born at the same time, and grow up together at the same age in the family.

For all intents and purposes, therefore, monozygotic twins are genetically identical: they share 100% of their genes. Fraternal twins, like regular siblings, on average share 50% of their genes. For traits where the resemblance is due solely to inherited factors, identical twins ought to resemble one another twice as much as fraternal twins (although because of experimental error, this will never be exactly true). On the other hand, if we make the reasonable assumption that the environments of identical and fraternal twins are approximately similar, you would predict that, if the causes of resemblance for a trait are due to environmental factors, the level of similarity between identical and fraternal twins ought to be approximately the same.

Twin studies are based on the idea that resemblance among twins results from two distinct sets of factors: genes and shared environment. We start by working out how similar each twin is to his or her twin sibling. In this case, we are measuring similarity in terms of a diagnosis (schizophrenia), but it

could equally well be height, personality, or intelligence. We record similarity as a correlation, which can range from 0 (meaning that the two traits are completely unrelated to each other) to 1.0 (meaning the two traits are perfectly related to each other). The standard twin study assumes that shared environment contributes equally to the correlation in MZ and DZ pairs. This is not true, however, for genetic factors. As MZ twins are genetically identical while DZ twins share half their genes, the genetic component of the correlation in the MZ twins should be twice the value of that seen in DZ twins.

By comparing the degree of correlation for a trait in MZ and DZ pairs, it is possible to infer the role of genetic versus shared environmental factors. Take religious affiliation, for example—whether people self-identify as Catholic, Jewish, Methodist, Baptist, Muslem, etc. Twins strongly resemble one another in their religion, but the degree of resemblance is virtually the same in MZ and DZ twins. These results suggest, consistent with common sense, that genes have nothing to do with one's religious identity. Resemblance in twins for religious affiliation appears to result from shared environmental experiences.

Contrast this to the pattern seen for height, where the correlation in MZ twin pairs is typically very high (around 0.90) and the correlation for height in DZ twin pairs is moderate (around 0.45). When correlations in MZ twins are approximately twice those seen in DZ twins, we can conclude that twin resemblance is driven primarily by genetic factors. Of course, there are traits that are influenced both by genes and shared environment. In this case, the correlations in MZ twins are greater than those seen in DZ twins, but the difference between them is less than the 2 : 1 ratio expected if only genetic factors are operating.

More details about twin models

One method commonly used to work out the contributions of genetic and environmental effects to phenotypic variation in twins is to use path analysis. The method can be explained with a simple example. Suppose we have two brothers and we have measured their personality, so that we can say that one brother scores 10 points and the other 14 after they have both been asked to fill in a questionnaire. The two measures are P1 and P2 (here P stands for phenotype).

We know that two factors contribute to the similarity of the phenotypes: the genetic variants that both siblings share and the environmental factors that make the brothers similar, which we call the common environment factors. In the path diagram (Figure 2.8), the common environment is denoted by capital C and the genotypes of the brothers are denoted A1 and A2 (where A stands for the additive genetic effect). The genotypes are unknown, but if the brothers are dizygotic twins, sharing half of their genes by descent, we know that the correlation between the genotypes must be about 0.5. If they are monozygotic twins, sharing all of their genes, the correlation is 1.0.

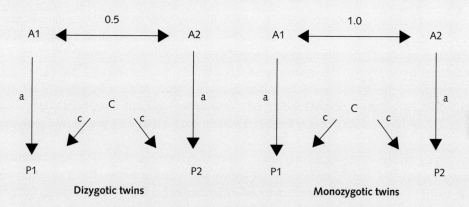

Dizygotic twins   **Monozygotic twins**

Figure 2.8 Path analysis of dizygotic and monozygotic twins.

The lower-case letters in the path diagram, *a* and *c*, alongside the arrows are called path coefficients. By the rules of path analysis the correlation between P1 and P2 (denoted *r*) is given by the sum of the two connecting paths. So for dizygotic twins the correlation (denoted r_{dz}) is:

$$r_{dz} = 0.5(a \times a) + (c \times c)$$

and for monozygotic twins the correlation (denoted r_{mz}) is:

$$r_{mz} = 1.0(a \times a) + (c \times c)$$

or more simply:

$$r_{dz} = 0.5a^2 + c^2$$

and

$$r_{mz} = 1.0a^2 + c^2.$$

To estimate the values of the two terms a^2 and c^2, we use some algebra to give equations for heritability:

$$a^2 = 2(r_{mz} - r_{dz}) \qquad \qquad (1)$$

and for the environmental effect:

$$c^2 = 2r_{dz} - r_{mz} \qquad \qquad (2)$$

The individual specific or non-shared environment (e^2) is $1 - (a^2 + c^2)$ or:

$$e^2 = 1 - r_{mz}. \qquad \qquad (3)$$

In this example, a^2 reflects the role of additive genetic effects and equals the heritability of the trait (sometimes, just to confuse you, heritability is termed h^2). The model, which takes into account genetic, common, and unique environment, is thus often referred to as the ACE model, for the additive genetic (A), common environment (C) and non-shared (or unique) environment (E) components that make twins the same or different.

The equations can be explained in words as follows: the correlation in liability for a disorder or trait between MZ twins is the result of all of the additive effects of genes (because they share all their genes in common) and their shared environment. The correlation in liability between DZ twins is the result of half of the effect of the additive genes (because they share, on average, half of their genes in common) and their shared environment. So, if you want to estimate the heritability of a disorder, take the difference between the MZ and the DZ correlation and double it. If you want to estimate the effect of shared environment, double the DZ correlation and subtract from that the MZ correlation.

If we have estimates of the values of r_{mz} and r_{dz} we can calculate a^2 and c^2. All of these calculations assume that the MZ and DZ correlations are known with equal accuracy. This is never precisely true, so the estimates obtained in this way will differ somewhat from those obtained using one of several statistical software packages.

To illustrate this method, let's take data from a twin study of alcohol abuse (as reported by Temperance Boards in Sweden) that we will describe in detail in Chapter 4. The correlation in liability for alcohol abuse in the male MZ and DZ pairs from that study was estimated at +0.67 and +0.41, respectively. Apply equations (1) to (3) and you should be able to come up with rough estimates for a^2, c^2, and e^2 of 0.52, 0.15 and 0.33, respectively. So, these results suggest that alcohol abuse is strongly affected by genes, but environmental effects of both the shared and individual specific variety are also both important. These rough estimates are quite close to those obtained by much more sophisticated estimation procedures implemented in the Mx software package (Neale *et al.*, 2003): $a^2 = 0.54$, $c^2 = 0.14$ and $e^2 = 0.33$.

These rules are worth repeating:

1. If the correlation in identical (MZ) twins is at least twice as large as in fraternal (DZ) twins, twin resemblance is likely to be due entirely to genetic factors.

2. If the correlations are approximately the same magnitude in both types of twin, twin resemblance is likely to be due to shared environmental effects.

3. If the magnitude of the correlation in DZ twins is between 50 and 100% of that seen in MZ pairs, then it is likely that both genetic and shared environmental effects are operative.

Heritability and twin studies

Just how useful are these rules? Any conclusions about the relative influence of genetics versus environment in studies of this sort rely on the statistical concept of heritability. Because heritability is an often misunderstood and sometimes maligned statistic, we want to spend a bit of time explaining what it is and what it is not.

Most importantly, heritability is based on the concept of variability. Assume that we are studying height in a population of 5,000 individuals and imagine that we could line up all these individuals from the tallest to the shortest. We would see a great deal of variation, with the largest number of people of middling height and a diminution in numbers at the extremes of the very tall and the very short.

We also know that, just as individuals differ in height, they also have differences in their genomes. The extent of DNA variation among humans is still not fully known, but it's definitely there. Heritability is nothing more than *the proportion of variation in height (or whatever phenotype we study) that is due to the genetic differences between individuals in the population.* This is important enough to express in a different way as the following ratio:

$$\text{Heritability} = \frac{\text{genetic variance}}{\text{total variance}}$$

In this formula, total variance in a trait is in turn broken down into genetic and environmental variance. If height had a heritability of 100%, it would mean that all of its variability could be explained by genetic differences between individuals. In fact, the heritability of height is about 90%. A heritability of 0% would indicate that genes contribute nothing at all to the observed differences between individuals. This is close to what is seen when we study religious affiliation in human populations.

The difficulty with heritability is that it is inherently a population-based statistic. In fact, a disease in a single person does not, by definition, have a meaningful heritability. Diseases themselves do not really have heritabilities. Only given diseases in specific populations at specific times have a defined heritability; that is, heritabilities could change between populations or within a population over time if genetic variability changed or if environmental variability changed. To drive this point home, imagine an isolated population, somewhere on the edge of Europe, where, together with the environmental risks for schizophrenia, the population contained ten different genes each of which independently influenced the risk for the disease. Psychiatric geneticists carry out a twin study and determine that the heritability of schizophrenia is 70%. Now it so happens that a virus, passed from birds to humans, like avian flu, arrives and randomly infects part of the population. This fictional infection does not kill, but it substantially increases the risk of developing schizophrenia.

Psychiatric geneticists, keen to add another publication to their curriculum vitae, rush back into the field and reassess the heritability. They find that the figure has now dropped to 50%, because the total variability in risk to schizophrenia has increased. Some people are infected, but not all. The increased variability in risk is due entirely to an environmental variable.

A little later, a group of immigrant laborers arrive, settle, and begin marrying the inhabitants. The immigrants carry a gene that increases susceptibility to schizophrenia, hitherto unknown in the indigenous population. After a few generations, when this gene has begun to spread through the population, and the virus is no longer present, psychiatric geneticists scent another publication. For the third time they assess heritability. This time the estimate has increased, to 80%. New variability to risk of illness has been introduced into the population, but in this case the new risk is genetic in origin.

Controversies over heritability

How useful is heritability as determined by twin studies? The answer is controversial. Let us begin by summarizing the views of the psychologist Leon Kamin, who thinks that twin studies are not worth the paper they are printed on. Here he is in full flood, lambasting practitioners of twin studies of intelligence, aiming his barbs at the psychologists' measure of intelligence, the intelligence quotient or IQ (these and subsequent quotes are all from Kamin, 1974): '*There exist no data which should lead a prudent man to accept the hypothesis that I.Q. test scores are in any degree heritable... The fact that twin correlations are high, and that MZs resemble one another more than DZs, are wholly consistent*

with the expectations of an environmental view.' He also pointed out that potential for bias in sampling that would prejudice the results. '*Suppose that twins tend to become less alike as they grow older, and, suppose as well that this tendency is more marked in poorly educated, "deprived" households.*' If this were true and not taken into account, a significant difference between MZ and DZ twins could be misinterpreted as arising from genetic effects. If twins are not generally representative of the population, the results will also be suspect. And there is more. Errors occur in the determination of zygosity, that is to say, the care with which a given twin pair has been classified as either MZ or DZ. This, Kamin argued, can make a difference if physical similarity (a simple method used to measure zygosity) is related to the trait: '*Misclassified true DZs could conceivably increase the observed I.Q. correlation for MZs, while the misclassified true MZs could be decreasing the correlation for DZs.*'

Kamin reserves the major part of his scorn for the assumption that MZs and DZs grow up in similar environments: '*The various sampling problems, however, pale into relative insignificance compared to a fundamental objection...the essential assumption that relevant environmental differences impinging upon MZ pairs and DZ pairs are equal is, on its face, absurd.*' There then follow a few pages debunking the idea that the environments could ever be thought equal ('*the quaint notion of a constant "within-family environmental variance" acting equally on all categories of twin pairs seems clearly untenable*') with the final conclusion that '*our study of kinship correlations has revealed no evidence sufficient to reject the hypothesis of zero I.Q. heritability.*'

Kamin's diatribe joins a long history of controversy surrounding twin studies of behavior and genetics. Much of the passion comes from the mixing of politics with science that always seems to accompany these studies. From the very beginning, Galton saw genetics as a means of improving the human race through selective breeding. This philosophy gave rise to the eugenics movement, which found one of its most ardent supporters in the American geneticist whom we discussed above: Charles Davenport. His studies of hereditary *'feeble-mindedness'* (in addition to those of the *'wandering impulse'*) were inspired at least in part by his wish to eliminate what he saw as a genetic plague. Through his efforts and those of others, the movement eventually succeeded in reinforcing the prejudices of US public policy makers in several infamous cases. Laws mandating the compulsory sterilization of mental patients were passed in many states, and in 1924 the US Congress reversed its open-door immigration policy with an ethnically restrictive quota system. The ultimate embodiment of eugenics, however, came under the National Socialist (Nazi) program in Germany, starting with the compulsory sterilization of mental patients (modeled after US statutes) and ending with the Final Solution.

Twin studies and schizophrenia

Given Kamin's harsh and strident criticisms, is there any reason to believe the results of twin studies of schizophrenia? In the last 80 years, more than a dozen studies have been conducted that have assessed the presence of schizophrenia in both members of MZ and DZ twin pairs (referred to as the concordance rate). The work cuts across many countries, involves many different investigators, and has used a variety of different methods. Two representative twin studies of schizophrenia are described below.

The first investigation, known as The Maudsley Twin Study, started shortly after World War II when any individual who registered for treatment at the Maudsley Hospital in South London was asked whether or not they were a twin. If they said yes and gave the proper permissions, they were entered into the research project. The most recent update of this study covers the years 1948–1993.

Key paper

Cardno, A.G., Marshall, E.J., Coid, B., Macdonald, A.M., Ribchester, T.R., Davies, N.J., Venturi, P., Jones, L.A., Lewis, S.W., Sham, P.C., Gottesman, I.I., Farmer, A.E., McGuffin, P., Reveley, A.M., and Murray, R.M. (1999). Heritability estimates for psychotic disorders: the Maudsley twin psychosis series. *Arch Gen Psychiatry* **56**:162–168.

The most recent complete analysis of this famous and influential twin study of schizophrenia.

Of the 224 individuals with symptoms of severe mental illness, 106 met the criteria for strictly defined schizophrenia. The correlation in MZ twins for the liability to schizophrenia was quite high (0.81), and a bit more than twice as high as in DZ twins (0.31). By Rule 1 above (p. 25), genetic factors are very likely to be influencing the risk for schizophrenia, and shared environmental factors are probably making very little contribution.

The main strengths of this study were the systematic method used to locate the twins and the relatively high quality of the clinical information available on each individual. The diagnostic evaluations were done with care. However, the twins were obtained from a single facility and one that is a specialist center. How representative of the general population are such results likely to be?

The second study was conducted in Finland by a combined American–Finnish team.

In some ways, its strengths and weaknesses are the mirror image of the Maudsley study: the quality of the diagnosis was variable, but the sample collection credentials are hard to fault. Because of the high quality of medical and social records in Finland, the investigators were able to examine virtually every twin born in Finland from 1940 to 1957—a total of 19,124 individuals. The researchers then matched these records to three registries that contained information about psychiatric illness: the national hospital discharge register, which contains diagnoses assigned during any hospital stay in all of Finland, the Pension Register, and the Free Medicine Register. The latter two contain information provided by physicians to justify eligibility for either a pension, access to state-subsidized medications, or both. We know from other studies that nearly all individuals with schizophrenia in a country like Finland would at some point come into medical care, seek a pension or receive state-subsidized medication, or both, so it is unlikely that many cases of schizophrenic illness in twins would have been missed.

Key paper

Cannon, T.D., Kaprio, J., Lonnqvist, J., Huttunen, M., and Koskenvuo, M. (1998). The genetic epidemiology of schizophrenia in a Finnish twin cohort. A population-based modeling study. *Arch Gen Psychiatry* **55**:67–74.

A detailed report of the results of the excellent Finnish twin study of schizophrenia.

The investigators looked in these three registries from the years 1969–1991 and identified 670 twins who had a diagnosis of schizophrenia in one or more of the databases. Diagnoses were recorded by a variety of different clinicians under a range of circumstances, which means that their quality almost certainly varied widely. Determining which twins were

MZ and which were DZ was also difficult. A mailed questionnaire was sent out to members of the twin registry in 1975, but individuals with schizophrenia are not always cooperative with such research requests. In nearly a quarter of the twin pairs, no information was available about which type of twin they were. Nevertheless, the investigators obtained 508 useable pairs, a much larger sample than studies in the Maudsley twin series, and compared them with all other twins in the registry. This is a better method than that used in the Maudsley study, which had to assume an estimate of the population risk for schizophrenia. The correlation for the liability to schizophrenia in Finnish MZ and DZ pairs was estimated at 0.84 in MZ twins and 0.34 in DZ twins, remarkably close to the figures for the Maudsley series (0.81 and 0.31). Given the wide differences in method, the similarity in the results of these two studies, one from a hospital in South London using personal interviews and the other from the entire country of Finland relying on medical, pension, and pharmacy records, is striking.

While the Maudsley and Finnish studies both had limitations, each had been systematic in their collection of twin individuals with schizophrenia. This has not always been true in other twin studies of schizophrenia.

Recently, one of us (K.S.K.), with colleagues Patrick Sullivan and Michael Neale, combined the results of all of the major studies that met reasonable methodological criteria. Several key findings emerged from these analyses. Firstly, all but one of the 12 studies provided strong evidence that genetic risk factors were of critical importance in schizophrenia. Across all these studies, the heritability of liability to schizophrenia was estimated to be 81%. Secondly, and perhaps most importantly, the results of the methodologically strongest studies did not differ from those of the more problematic ones. Thirdly, familial environmental factors played a modest, but nevertheless detectable, role in causing schizophrenia, accounting for 11% of the variance in liability.

Key paper

Sullivan, P.F., Kendler, K.S., and Neale, M.C. (2003). Schizophrenia as a complex trait: evidence from a meta-analysis of twin studies. *Arch Gen Psychiatry* **60**:1187–1192.

A recent and statistically sophisticated review of the major twin studies of schizophrenia.

Challenging the assumptions

How well will these data withstand the type of assault Kamin mounted against the IQ studies? Ideally, we should be able to address these concerns using data from the twin studies of schizophrenia. However, for the reasons we've discussed, such studies are difficult to carry out, and relatively few exist. However, as the criticism is leveled not so much against genetic analysis of psychosis per se as against the methodology of twin studies in general, we can draw upon a larger and remarkably rich literature on the quantitative genetic basis of individual differences, inferred from twin studies.

The first methodological concern, and one that Kamin raises, is whether the assumption that the environmental exposures of MZ and DZ twins are equally similar is valid. Standard twin analyses assume that the greater resemblance in MZ twins compared with DZ twins results entirely from sharing greater genetic

similarity (the 'equal environment assumption' or EEA for short).

One approach to evaluating the EAA is to examine the physical similarity of the twins. Identical twins, on average, resemble each other more than fraternal twins. Perhaps the world treats people more similarly if they look more similar. Is greater similarity for psychiatric disorders in fact predicted by greater physical similarity? By taking photographs of twins, rating them on the level of physical similarity, and comparing the results with other measures, it is possible to test this hypothesis. With substantial, but not complete uniformity, the answer has been 'No'. For disorders of behavior and personality, looking alike does not appear to make you more alike.

Another more direct way to evaluate the EEA is to ask twins about the similarity of their environmental experiences. Most of these studies have focused on childhood environments. Without doubt, monozygotic twins are more frequently dressed alike as children than are dizygotic twins. Other studies ask whether twins shared the same room at home, had similar playmates, or shared the same classroom when children. Putting all of this together, it is possible to create an index of 'childhood environmental similarity.' Such an index is nearly always greater in monozygotic than in dizygotic pairs, sometimes quite substantially so. The question can then be asked whether 'childhood environmental similarity' can explain the greater similarity in the trait being studied (e.g. schizophrenia). In the vast majority of studies where this has been asked, the answer is no.

Sometimes, twins and their parents are misinformed about their true twin status; that is, some twins who are really MZ think they are DZ and some who are really DZ think they are MZ. This provides an ideal natural experiment to test whether the self-perception of twins about their zygosity, or the expectations of them by their family and social environment, or both, might actually influence the degree of resemblance. This test of the EEA—whether twins who are really MZ but think they are DZ are any less similar than twins who are truly MZ and also think they are MZ—has been applied in several different studies to personality measures, IQ, and risk for psychiatric disorders. In nearly all cases, the results have been consistent: in misidentified twins, self-perception of twin status is not a good predictor of resemblance.

Yet another method used to test the EEA examines what might be termed the 'parental philosophy' toward raising twins. Most parents of twins approach the task with one of two extremes: either by tending to treat the twins as a unit or by treating them as distinct individuals. Not surprisingly, the former approach is more common among parents of MZ twins than parents of DZ twins. Perhaps MZ twins turn out more similarly than DZ twins, in part, because they are more frequently treated as a unit by their parents. One study examined this issue, and the outcome was that twin similarity for common psychiatric and drug-use disorders could not be explained by parental treatment.

The last approach comes from a famous study with the provocative title 'Do parents create, or respond to, differences in twins?' The psychologist Hugh Lytton and his research team examined a detailed set of behavioral interactions between two-and-a-half-year-old male twins and their parents in their natural home environment. They observed 48 different aspects of parent–child interactions in 17 MZ and 29 DZ twin pairs. Parents treated the MZ twins more similarly than the DZ twins in only seven of these behaviors, which included the mother's tendency to use material reward, such as candy, for reinforcing behavior, the degree to which the mother encouraged independent behavior by the child, and the frequency with which the father used reasoning to justify his commands and rules. Although only a fraction of parental behavior was involved, the results might, on the face of it, be thought to represent an obvious violation of the EEA; parents do treat identical twins more similarly than fraternal twins.

Key paper

Lytton, H. (1977). Do parents create, or respond to, differences in twins? *Dev Psychol* **13**:456–459.

A brief but influential and sophisticated evaluation of the equal environment assumption in twin studies.

However, Lytton then asked whether parents treat MZ twins more similarly than DZ because MZ twins really do behave more similarly than DZ or because the parents expect them to behave more similarly. To resolve this question, he was able to observe parental behaviors that were not directly elicited by a child. He divided all parent-initiated behaviors into four broad classes: 'command prohibitions,' 'suggestions' (a milder form of parental control), 'positive actions' (which included parents doing things such as showing pleasure, approving, expressing affection, and playing with the child), and 'neutral actions' (involving emotionally neutral parental behaviors such as talking, approaching, or showing things to their twin sons). He then compared the similarity of parent-initiated actions in these four categories between identical and fraternal twins, separately for mothers and fathers. In only one of the comparisons, mother's suggestions, was there the expected finding of greater similarity in parent-initiated behaviors in identical than in fraternal pairs. In the other seven categories of parental behavior, there was not even a trend for parent-initiated actions to be more similar in identical versus fraternal twins. Lytton made the following observation about his data:

> ...the results...lead to the conclusion that: a) parents do treat MZ twins more alike than DZ twins in some respects, but, b) they do not introduce systematic greater similarity of treatment for MZ twins in actions which they initiate themselves and which are not contingent on the child's immediate preceding behavior... In other words, parents respond to, rather than create, differences between the twins...

This study carries an important potential message: in measuring similarity of treatment or social environments in twin studies, it is important to consider that MZ twins, because of their more similar behavior, can elicit more similar treatment.

So, what can we say about the validity of the EEA assumption for twin studies of psychological and psychiatric traits? Tests have with substantial but not perfect consistency supported its validity. The studies are not faultless and may not, for example, have identified the right kind of environment that truly impacts on twin resemblance (for example, the impact of intrauterine environment). In sum, however, it seems unlikely that most twin studies are seriously biased by violations of the EEA.

There are, as you might imagine, other objections to the twin method. As twins constitute no more than roughly 1.5% of most human populations, what we learn about them may be irrelevant to the rest of us. A large literature addresses the question of the similarity between twins and singletons on a variety of medical, physical, psychological, and psychiatric traits. Twins are at increased risk for a few problems such as low birth weight and pre-natal or peri-natal complications. (This

is because the reproductive system of the human female has largely evolved to have 'womb for one'.) However, the risk of twins for a very broad array of other medical conditions and for psychiatric disorders and symptoms is entirely typical of the general singleton population. Aside from traits directly related to the risks of twin pregnancy, it seems entirely justified to apply the results from twin studies to the general population.

Recall that we noted above that heritability estimates are population specific. How good a job have we done in determining whether the heritability of schizophrenia is broadly consistent across different human populations? To date, twin studies of schizophrenia have been conducted in the USA, England, Japan, Denmark, Norway, Sweden, Finland, and Germany: nearly all studies are from Europe or North America. No large-scale twin (or adoption) studies of schizophrenia have been performed in populations of African descent and very few in Asian populations. When we compare the various findings for the same trait across populations that have been tested, the results have generally been encouraging: consistent findings emerge in the main pattern of results for twin studies of schizophrenia. But major ethnic groups of humans have yet to be studied.

Should we rely on twin and adoption studies?

There are a few important conclusions we can now draw from the foregoing discussion. Firstly, research studies using adoptees and twins are far from flawless. Like most other kinds of science, these studies can be done well or poorly, and the confidence that we should have in the results relates directly to the quality of the methodology employed. Secondly, the main worry about the validity of the twin method is the equal environment assumption. Based on the available empirical studies, this assumption is probably not seriously violated in most twin studies. Other concerns with the twin method—for example that twins are highly atypical—have little evidence in their favor. Like other epidemiologic methods, however, twin and adoption studies are susceptible to unrepresentative sampling. Thirdly, the evidence to date suggests no large differences in results across various countries, although far more studies are needed representing additional human populations.

What can we conclude from research efforts to disentangle the effects of genes and family environment (nature versus nurture) for schizophrenia? Most importantly, the various twin and adoption studies generally agree that genetic risk factors play a major role in the development of schizophrenia. However, we have also seen that there is no such thing as a flawless genetic study when investigating humans. Both twin and adoption studies have many possible methodological problems. Fortunately, the problems in the two kinds of studies are rather different. Therefore, if twin and adoption methods give broadly similar answers, the probability that the results are spurious is low. As one colleague put it, '*Nature would have to be particularly perverse to provide us with a set of different biases that would each produce quite similar findings in twin and adoption studies.*' We do not claim that these methodological issues are entirely resolved, but the consistency of findings across the two different methods strongly suggests that genes are important in schizophrenia.

Another general point is worth making here. One way to divide sciences is into those that observe the world and those that go out and manipulate it—typically in laboratory situations. The first kind of science includes astronomy, geology and human genetics. Laboratory genetics, by contrast, belongs in the second group. We cannot do traditional genetic studies in humans. Human genetics researchers always have to be on their toes, looking for the unsuspected bias—because we cannot control anything in our studies. We can just look at the experiments that nature provides us with.

So if genes are important, how are they important? The foregoing results treat genetic effects, in some ways, like a huge black box. Trying to peer into that black box is the next critical step.

Summary

1. The first question that should always be asked about a disorder by a psychiatric geneticist is whether it runs in families.

2. The key features of a high-quality family study for a psychiatric disorder include representative ill and matched control probands, use of structured interviews, blind assessment of relatives, and blind final diagnosis.

3. As illustrated by the Roscommon Family Study, the first-degree relatives of patients with schizophrenia have an approximately tenfold increased risk of illness.

4. The next logical question that should be asked by a psychiatric geneticist is: why does the disorder run in families? To what degree is this familial aggregation a result of genes or shared family environment?

5. In humans, there are two quasi-experimental approaches to answering this question—adoption studies and twin studies.

6. They are two major adoption designs for psychiatric disorders that begin either with ill biological mothers who put their children up for adoption, or with ill adoptees.

7. We have reviewed one example of each such study, the results of which both support the hypothesis that the risk for schizophrenia is transmitted in families largely or entirely for genetic reasons.

8. Twin studies depend on a comparison of the level of resemblance for a trait or a disorder in monozygotic versus dizygotic twins.

9. The concept of heritability reflects the proportion of phenotypic variance for a particular trait or disorder in a population that results from genetic differences between individuals in that population.

10. The best current evidence from twin studies suggests that the heritability of schizophrenia is high—around 80%.

11. Twin studies have a number of potential methodological limitations, especially the equal environment assumption. The best evidence to date suggests that in most situations, these biases are modest and do not substantially distort results.

12. For schizophrenia, added confidence is gained from the congruent findings about the importance of genetic factors from both adoption and twin studies.

References

Butterworth, J.S. and Reppert, E.H. (1960). Auscultatory findings in myocardial infarction. *Circulation* 22:448–452.

Cooper, J.E., Kendell, R.E., Gurland, B.J., Sharpe, L., Copeland, J.R.M., and Simon, R.J. (1972). *Psychiatric Diagnosis in New York and London: A Comparative Study of Mental Hospital Admissions*. Maudsley Monograph 20. Oxford: Oxford University Press.

Cravens, H. (1978). *The Triumph of Evolution: American Scientists and The Heredity–Environment Controversy, 1900–1941*. Philadelphia: University of Pennsylvania Press.

Davenport, C.B. (1915). *The Feebly Inhibited: Nomadism, or the Wandering Impulse with Special Reference to Heredity: Inheritance of Temperament*. Washington, DC: Carnegie Institution of Washington.

Feighner, J.P., Robins, E., Guze, S.B., Woodruff, R.A. Jr, Winokur, G., and Munoz, R. (1972). Diagnostic criteria for use in psychiatric research. *Arch Gen Psychiatry* 26:57–63.

Kamin, L.J. (1974). *The Science and Politics of IQ*. Potomac, MD: Lawrence Erlbaum Associates.

Neale, M.C., Boker, S.M., Xie, G., and Maes, H.H. (2003). *Mx: Statistical Modeling*. Box 980126, Richmond VA 23298: Department of Psychiatry, Virginia Commonwealth University Medical School.

Rosenberg, C.E. (1976). The bitter fruit: heredity, disease, and social thought. In *No Other Gods: On Science and American Social Thought*, pp. 25–53. Baltimore: Johns Hopkins University Press.

Wing, J.K., Birley, J.L., Cooper, J.E., Graham, P., and Isaacs, A.D. (1967). Reliability of a procedure for measuring and classifying 'present psychiatric state'. *Br J Psychiatry* 113:499–515.

WHO (1973). *Report of the International Pilot Study of Schizophrenia. Volume 1: Results of the Initial Evaluation Phase*. Geneva, Switzerland: World Health Organization.

3 Molecular genetics
Linkage analysis

[Using genetic relationships within families to map genes]

From the black box of aggregate genetic effects, from quantitative analysis of families and twins to the identification of the molecular drivers of behavior, the identification of DNA sequence variants that contribute to disease susceptibility moves us from dilapidated offices full of paper into laboratories full of extremely expensive equipment, operated by people from a very different cultural background, trained in molecular genetics; wet-lab not dry-lab science. Yet, despite the greater resemblance to the world of hard science, molecular approaches to psychiatric genetics have not been uniformly successful; in fact, as we will see in the following chapters, it is a story of false leads and broken promises.

There were so many wrong turns taken, so many high-profile successes that turned out quite simply to be wrong, that some people believed the whole endeavor would never work. We describe some of these disasters, partly because they're fun to read about but also because the failures arise not so much out of the usual run of misadventure and hubris, but from a misunderstanding of what we were looking for in the first place. Attempts to find the causes of psychiatric illness arose from a model that we can now see, with hindsight, was much too simplistic, and probably wrong.

In this chapter and the next, we look at that model, how it arose, how it was applied to behavior, and how much more modest were the results obtained than first expected.

Genes 'for' psychosis?

At the beginning, when molecular biologists first took an interest in psychiatric genetics, although they might not say so, they were looking for genes for psychosis. It's not just that gene-jocks working all night in the lab (when they can play heavy metal without upsetting the Health and Safety Executive) would boast that they were finding the gene for schizophrenia, even if political correctness enforced the rule that there are no genes for psychosis (instead we have to say that genetic variants in a gene contribute to susceptibility to a disease). The paradigm went deeper than that: it had to do with how we know what we know, how sure we are that we have established a finding.

A lot of undergraduates, probably a lot of people, think that life in the laboratory can be, simply put, fun. A combination of intelligence and technology applied to taxing but interesting biological problems leads to ground-breaking discoveries that could cure disease or change our understanding of the universe. Let's be clear here: more than 99% of the work in the laboratory is dull, repetitive, and probably a waste of time. Furthermore, most of the experiments simply don't work. It's very rare for a graduate student actually to discover anything, let alone anything useful or groundbreaking. And here's the thing: if they should be so fortunate (though luck comes second to days, weeks, and then months of tedious but demanding work) as to have made a breakthrough, then the first question they face from the laboratory head is: why is this finding wrong? Not surprisingly, they get a bit upset when they hear this (*I've just spent three miserable years to get this result and you're telling me to find out why it's wrong?*). They face this question in part because other scientists don't want them to be right (that's the competing laboratory, which really hasn't done too well in the last few years, no big papers at all in fact). They face this question in part because it will be deeply embarrassing to publish something that turns out later to be wrong. But most importantly, they face this question because it's only by publishing findings that are robust to any possible criticism that we'll make any progress. That's not, of course, how it always works, but departures from scientific excellence only demonstrate the need for us to be more rigorous, more critical, more prepared to argue with supposedly established fact—a stance that largely defines what science is about.

As we showed in the last chapter, psychiatric geneticists have had a hard time convincing people that their findings were robust. Molecular biologists have had much less of a problem. You know when you wander around a molecular biology laboratory that real science is being done. People wear white coats, doors have signs warning about radioactive contamination, and enormously expensive machines fill entire rooms. The wet lab has nothing to do with the often rather ramshackle offices with bulging filing cabinets out of which family, adoption, and twin studies are run. In the wet lab, we deal with electrophoresis equipment, automated DNA sequencing machines, ranks of PCR machines, microarray facilities. Here we make molecules, not P values. We don't just observe and use statistics, we intervene: we alter the structure of DNA in animals and observe the consequences. If you want to know whether a mutation in a gene causes a disease, then we can make that mutation (in a mouse at least) and find out what happens. This degree of certainty in our science, the immense self-confidence that characterizes molecular biology, this is what psychiatric genetics wanted to acquire. So psychiatric genetics wanted to become something else—to become molecular psychiatry. In its first incarnation, it adopted a methodology that used families to try and find the genes contributing to psychosis. The methodology is called linkage analysis and it required a set of molecular markers.

Just as the discovery of foreign lands required mastery of longitude and latitude, that internal journey, into the molecular origins of disease, needs a cartography of the human genome. The sequencing of our genome, completed in 2005 (although announced in 2003 to coincide with the 50th anniversary of the discovery of the structure of DNA), is the final stage in the quest for that map. In the 1980s, we had no map at all and no one had the least idea of how to sequence a genome. However, using linkage analysis, even a simple map, with just a few markers on each chromosome, is enough to begin the job of disease-gene discovery.

Families + molecular biology = linkage analysis

DNA sequence variants are common. When the same piece of human DNA is sequenced in different people, the base pairs, the string of As, Cs, Gs and Ts that make up the DNA code, will be found to differ at a rate of about 0.1% (or one base in 1,000). As far as we know, the vast majority of these sequence variants have no effect. They are not mutations, in the sense that they don't tamper with a gene's function, and many are very common, so common that half the population has the variant. Moreover, sequence variants differ between populations; the same variants occur at different frequencies in two populations and each population may have its own unique set of variants.

Sequence variants come in different types: some are small deletions or insertions of a few base pairs, some consist of variation in the number of repeats of a sequence motif, others are simply differences in one of the four base pairs (called A, C, G and T). Public databases now contain about 7 million of the latter type, which are called single nucleotide polymorphisms or SNPs (pronounced 'snips') for short (molecular biologists love acronyms).

Key papers

International HapMap Consortium (2005). A haplotype map of the human genome. *Nature* **437**:1299–1320.

International HapMap Consortium (2007). A second generation human haplotype map of over 3.1 million SNPs. *Nature* **449**:851–861.

These two papers describe the haplotype map of the human genome—they introduce the terms used, from the basic to the complex, and the methods for finding sequence variants, and describe

the results of an international effort to characterize sequence variation in the human genome (see Chapter 6 pp. 102–104).

The realization that these apparently useless variants could be put to work to discover the molecular basis of disease occurred in the later 1970s. David Botstein described the origin of the critical insight (Gitschier, 2006). It took place in the middle of a typical academic argument—this one reviewing a genetics training grant in Utah. A student was presenting a plan to map on the human genome a rather common disease—called hemochromatosis—which involves abnormal deposits of iron all over the body but especially in the liver. This effort was focused on a quite special place in the human genome called the HLA region (human leukocyte antigen). This is one of the most variable regions in the genome, the place that makes us all immunologically different from each other. At the HLA region, almost all human beings (except monozygotic twins) have different copies of a series of immune genes. Botstein and his close colleague, Ron Davis, were defending the efforts of this student because the audience, mostly immunologists, did not understand the first thing about the principles of gene mapping. Quoting Botstein:

> So finally I say something like, 'Look there is nothing special about HLA. What's good about HLA is that it has many alleles, and because it has many alleles, you can tell if you have linkage, and if you have many multiallelic markers all over the genome, you can map anything!' And as soon as the words were out of my mouth, I look at Davis, Davis looks at me, and we both understand that of course there are such markers, and we could make a map of the human genome tomorrow.

Botstein's paper (Botstein *et al.*, 1980), outlining the insight that he had that day, showed how the map could be used to find the chromosomal location of mutations that give rise

to a genetic disease. The method required no prior knowledge of the gene involved, indeed no information about the biology at all, just some assumptions as to how the mutation was passed down through the generations, one of the well-understood patterns of Mendelian inheritance that most of us learned about in school biology classes: recessive, dominant, and X-linked.

At the time, the idea was controversial. It was technically challenging: detecting the sequence variants in each person was laborious. The methods available in the 1980s involved gels, blotting paper, toxic reagents, and lots of radioactivity. It was expensive: that radioactivity did not come cheap. And there was no guarantee it would work. But the first success, proving the value of molecular biology to genetic illness, came remarkably quickly.

An early success: Huntington's disease

Huntington's disease is an adult-onset neurological condition. The first symptoms, usually mental disturbances and mild uncontrolled movements, typically emerge at an age when the sufferer has already started his or her own family, in their 40s. The condition worsens

over a number of years, leading finally to a vegetative state in which the patient needs 24-hour care. The inheritance is a classic example of dominance: one copy of the mutation is sufficient to cause a disease as severe as that due to two mutations (one on each chromosome). Look at the pedigree below, drawn in the way that clinical geneticists use to recognize patterns of inheritance. Figure 3.1 shows five generations of an American family who have Huntington's disease.

Squares represent males and circles females. Unaffected individuals are depicted by open and affected individuals by filled-in squares and circles (a line through them means they were dead when the pedigree was drawn up). About half of the offspring at each generation are affected individuals. This is the pattern of dominant inheritance: it fits a model in which a single mutation in one copy of the gene is sufficient to cause disease. Note that the pattern does not prove the presence of a dominant mutation; it just makes other explanations less likely, and it's possible to work out how unlikely.

Look again at the pedigree in the Figure and imagine that you have a single sequence variant, a SNP for example, which can be either A or G (the SNP has therefore two alleles, A and G).

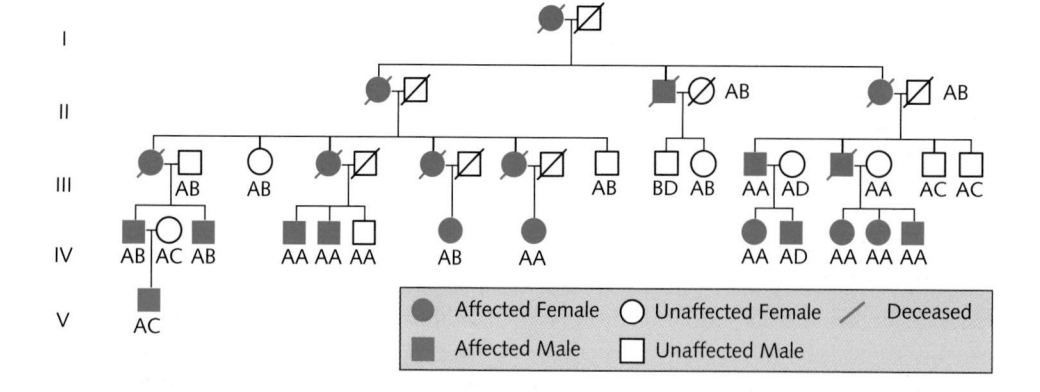

Figure 3.1 Pedigree of an American Huntington's disease family. From Gusella *et al.* (1983).

As each person has a pair of chromosomes, there are only three possible configurations (genotypes) at this particular SNP: AA, AG, and GG. In the first generation, suppose you find that the father (unaffected) has the genotype AA and the mother (affected) is AG. In the next generation, the three affected children are AG. And so on for the subsequent generations—all the affected individuals are AG and the unaffecteds are AA. If you were to find this result, you'd think it unlikely to be due to chance, a probability you can work out by assuming that genotypes and disease status are independent, rather than linked.

When Jim Gusella and David Housman of the Massachusetts Institute of Technology tried the genetic mapping approach in the early 1980s, they imagined it would take years, possibly decades, before they would hit a linkage. Gusella began testing markers in the summer of 1982. The third marker he tried gave weak evidence of linkage and when he tested the marker on a larger cohort of patients the evidence in favor became overwhelming (Gusella *et al.*, 1983). No one at the time imagined that it would be so quick.

To be successful at linkage, one thing you need is a good sample of pedigrees with carefully diagnosed individuals and a well-run lab. But above all, you need luck. Choose at random from two or three hundred markers and cross your fingers. In the 1980s, when linkage mapping was the thing to be doing, this made presenting results at conferences pretty tough; if you gave away what you had looked at, what had not worked, your competition, who would also have been testing each marker, could combine your data with their own and quickly move to the last remaining chromosome. Even worse, should you tell anyone of your success with a marker before it was published, others could quickly reproduce the results, and submit their paper for publication. From that point on, credit for the discovery would be shared

(there are some fairly nasty stories about the behavior of scientists during these 'gene hunts' that circulate to this day).

Finding linkage is not the same as finding the causative mutation. Rather it means that there have been few, or no, occasions on which the chromosome pairs in the pedigree have swapped over, or recombined. During recombination two copies of the same chromosome—one from our mother and the other from our father—swap DNA. This is an event that occurs many times almost randomly throughout the human genome every time an egg or sperm is produced. If we are very unlucky, the mutation we're after could be many millions of base pairs away from the marker. Linkage gets you into a rough area of the human genome—the information the test provides is equivalent to helping you find an individual's whereabouts in the USA by telling you in which state to look. There's a considerable amount of work ahead, as there are often hundreds of genes in a linkage region. Progressing from linkage to mutation is a process called positional cloning (see Appendix, pp. 233–234).

Work on Huntington's disease was the first demonstration that molecular mapping delivered; it was also the condition that set the standards of how difficult disease gene cloning could be. When the gene was finally identified, Peter Goodfellow, a Cambridge geneticist who had identified the gene that determines sex, admitted: '*In the satirical masterpiece Catch-22 by Joseph Heller, Major Major Major's father makes a living by not growing alfalfa. In a moment of uncalled-for unkindness stimulated by alcohol, I once accused a close colleague of making a living by not cloning the HD gene.*' A key to success was the establishment of a collaborative research group, held together primarily by Nancy Wexler, then a psychologist at Columbia University, whose father established a research foundation after

his wife was diagnosed with Huntington's. '*Although everyone had agreed to collaborate, until then they had not realized just what they were in for,*' says Wexler. Tempers flared at a meeting in Boston 1986, with charges of withheld data, unreturned phone calls, and probes lost in the mail. The ostensible problem was that they were all planning to do essentially the same experiment. But the real issues, says Wexler, was simply, how much can I trust you? Were others being honest or were they going off to be the Lone Ranger? At that time, everyone thought it would be easy to find the gene, she says, and part of the tension was the fear that someone in the group would find and clone it before the others even heard about it. '*But it wasn't the case and the difficulty in tracking down the gene has helped pull the group together.*' Hard as it was to identify the Huntington's disease mutation, the identification of disease susceptibility genes in complex traits like schizophrenia was to prove even harder.

When more than one gene may be the culprit, we call it 'complex'

In the decade following the first successful linkage studies of human genetic disease, there were attempts to apply this molecular strategy to disorders where the pattern of inheritance was not so clear cut. When an individual with a disease-predisposing gene variant will always become ill and one without the gene never does, linkage analysis is very robust. You can be confident that you are not being misled into chasing a genetic effect on the wrong part of the chromosome. Think how disastrous that would be for the cloning enterprise: even with

Huntington's disease this was a problem. For a while, they had mapped the disease gene to two different places on chromosome 4.

But it was clear that molecular genetics would have a much broader impact on medicine if it could be applied to diseases such as high blood pressure, diabetes, asthma, and schizophrenia. Most diseases, and most traits, though, don't follow a Mendelian pattern of inheritance, which is the pattern shown in Figure 3.1 for Huntington's disease. There is a family resemblance, but it can't be explained by a single genetic variant passing through the family. So it is not obvious how to apply the linkage paradigm.

One option is to see whether at least some cases of the disease were due to mutations that cause a disease to run through families following one of the classical patterns described by Mendel (e.g. dominant or recessive patterns). That is, these mutations produced quite powerful genetic signals always resulting in illness in gene carriers. Alzheimer's dementia is a common disease, as is breast cancer, but genetic susceptibility varies between families. Clinicians knew that in some families breast cancer struck young and was often accompanied with other cancers, especially of the ovaries. Concentrating on these, quite rare, families, a single gene effect could be seen, mapped, and finally cloned. The same was true for rare forms of Alzheimer's dementia. While the vast majority of cases of Alzheimer's disease have only a modest tendency to run in families and follow no clear Mendelian pattern, in a very few families, Alzheimer's disease is an autosomal dominant condition. Interestingly, in these families, the age of onset of the disease is much younger than is typically seen—often in the 40s or 50s. Investigations in these families have resulted in the discovery of three different genes that cause this rare form of Alzheimer's

disease (Tanzi and Bertram, 2001). These studies have resulted in fundamental advances in our understanding of the causes of breast cancer and of dementia, with consequent improved diagnosis and the possible development of novel therapies.

Linkage analysis of a more subtle behavioral trait: the KE family

Even in the 1980s, when gene hunting first hit the press, some psychiatrists were asking whether molecular approaches would work in their discipline. After all, Huntington's disease has psychiatric complications; admittedly the neurologists claimed it was their illness, but that was just an issue of demarcation (Alzheimer, after all, was a psychiatrist). Alzheimer's disease was just as much a neurological condition as Huntington's, yet patients with Alzheimer's were often looked after by psychiatrists. And one of the other high-profile races, always in the press, was the hunt for the gene for fragile X syndrome, a mental retardation disorder, another condition that belonged to psychiatrists (Fu *et al.*, 1991; Oberle *et al.*, 1991). What other diseases could be tackled this way?

One of the most striking successes was to come with a condition even closer to the psychiatric heartland: language disorder. Families become famous for various reasons, but the nature of the KE family's fame is unique. They suffer from a mutation that affects their speech. Affected family members are almost incomprehensible, but not just because of difficulties in pronunciation (Hurst *et al.*, 1990). There is a defect in the production of correctly formed language. For example, the affected individuals would fail tests such as filling in the missing word: 'This creature is *smaller* than this one, but this creature must be the [*smallest*]' or 'Every day I *wash* my clothes; yesterday I [_____] my clothes;' or fill in the missing non-word: 'This creature is *ponner* than this one, but this one must be the [*ponnest*].' In fact, family members had both verbal and non-verbal cognitive impairments, but what has attracted most attention is the language impairment, because of the evidence that the deficit was due to an abnormality in a single gene.

The pedigree of the KE family is shown in Figure 3.2. There are 15 affected individuals and 16 unaffected (ignoring the unclassifieds) with roughly equal numbers of males and females in both groups. Look at the second generation and you will see that both offspring of the unaffected male (marked '5') are unaffected, while about half of the offspring of the affected individuals are affected. This is the pattern expected of dominant inheritance: it fits a model in which a single mutation in one copy of the gene is sufficient to cause disease. Note that it does not prove the presence of a dominant mutation; it just makes other explanations less likely. On the other hand, if the unaffected individual '5' had an affected child, a simple dominant inheritance would be excluded (although, as with all things biological, there are always exceptions).

Simon Fisher and Tony Monaco, geneticists in Oxford, mapped the gene to a region of chromosome 7 in 1998 (Fisher *et al.*, 1998) and by 2001 confirmed that a mutation in a single gene (called *FOXP2*) gave rise to the speech disorder (Lai *et al.*, 2001). Genetic analysis revealed a complete concordance between inheritance of the mutant gene and presence of the speech disorder; conversely, family members without the mutation are normal, at least with respect to their speech.

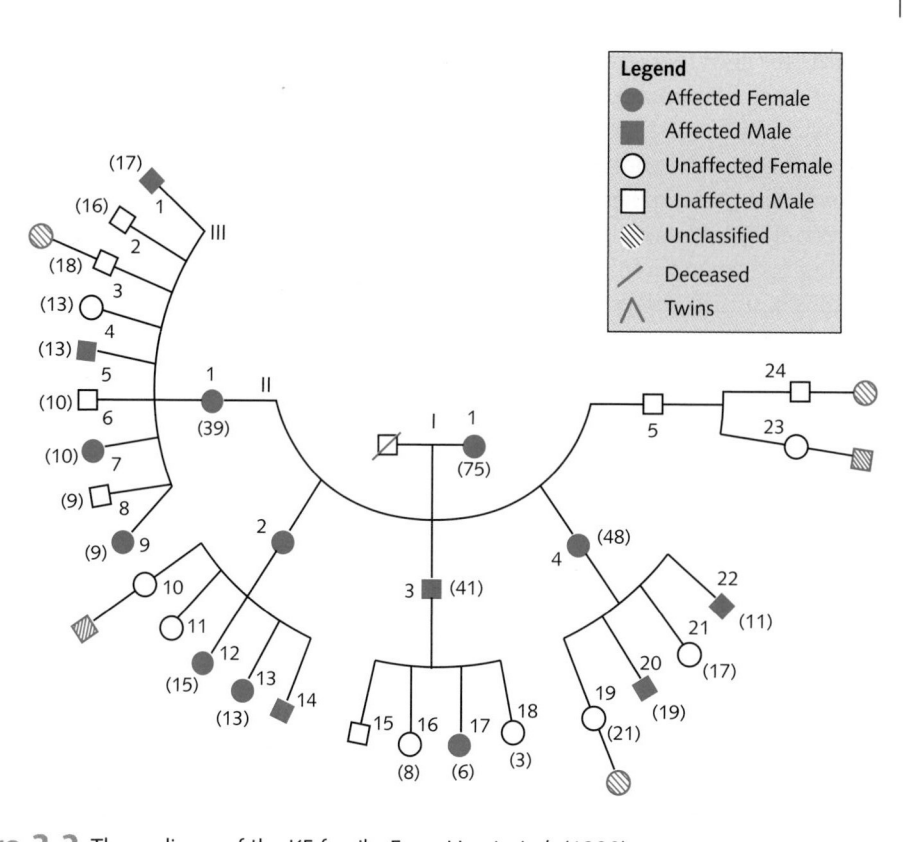

Figure 3.2 The pedigree of the KE family. From Hurst *et al.* (1990).

Faraneh Vargha-Khadem and colleagues at the Institute of Child Health in London have looked closely at the KE family, trying to find out what exactly is wrong (Vargha-Khadem *et al.*, 1995). Is this really a case of a mutation having a specific effect on grammar?

Vargha-Khadem's team has shown that the impairment in the KE family is not restricted to aspects of grammar. The disorder certainly does involve deficits in generating word inflections and derivations, but it affects many aspects of grammar and language ability. Moreover, affected individuals have difficulty controlling complex co-ordinated face and mouth movements (orofacial dyspraxia). This means they have difficulty talking, leading to the conjecture that their speech problems are secondary to a deficit in motor control. In fact

that hypothesis can be rejected, on a number of grounds, of which perhaps the most important is that the affected individuals have trouble with language comprehension as well as production. And brain imaging of affected KE members has shown that there are abnormalities in language-related cortical regions, further evidence that their problems extend beyond uncoordinated motor activity (Vargha-Khadem *et al.*, 2005).

So the genetic effect of the mutation in FOXP2 is not specific. Nevertheless there is an undeniable effect on language from a Mendelian mutation. The KE family doesn't have dyslexia, they have a speech problem, but it is intriguing that genetic analysis of communication disorders has proved so successful while that has not been so for other psychiatric conditions.

The discovery of *FOXP2* certainly advances our understanding of the relationship between genes and behavior, but we're not dealing here with one of the usual conditions that psychiatrists treat. Does success with genetic analysis of a speech disorder imply that finding genes contributing to schizophrenia, manic–depressive psychosis, autism, depression, or anxiety is possible? Or what about the gene that makes you happy, or a psychopath, or makes you gay? Could those genes be identified using the same molecular approaches? Finding more 'KE'-like families would be good, that is finding families in which a single genetic mutation could be held responsible for schizophrenia or indeed any of the common psychiatric illnesses. If psychiatrists could identify families with Mendelian mutations then there was a good chance they would find mutations that give rise to psychiatric disease.

Psychiatry goes molecular

In 1988, a London-based research group headed by Hugh Gurling published in *Nature* evidence for a susceptibility gene for schizophrenia on chromosome 5 (Sherrington *et al.*, 1988). The results were reported in seven large British and Icelandic families containing multiply affected members with schizophrenia. Not surprisingly, the finding created a huge stir both in the scientific community and in the more general public. It appeared as if the genetic puzzle of schizophrenia had been solved. Moreover, in February 1987, a US team had reported that a locus on chromosome 11 was linked to bipolar disorder (manic–depressive psychosis) (Egeland *et al.*, 1987).

A few weeks prior to the publication of the chromosome 5 paper, one of us (K.S.K.) was being visited by a colleague of Hugh Gurling and recalled:

> I had put him up in my home and we were driving into work. Twenty-one years later, I can still clearly recall exactly where on the highway he casually told me about Gurling's discovery. He commented that the data 'looked very strong.' Although typically a very careful driver, I nearly drove the car off the road in my astonishment! Nothing that I knew, or thought I knew, about schizophrenia, was consistent with the finding of a Mendelian gene for this illness. I was in a state of shock for hours.

Information that had been available to the field for decades indicated that although schizophrenia was strongly influenced by genetic factors, it was very unlikely to be due to the effects of one or even a small number of genes. Two sets of data are particularly relevant here. Firstly, the risk of schizophrenia in various classes of relatives (siblings, parents, nieces, nephews, etc.) does not in any way resemble that which would be expected by genes that act in a Mendelian manner. Recall that if one member of a pair of monozygotic twins has schizophrenia, the co-twin has a risk of only about 50%. In all Mendelian disorders, that rate would be 100%. Secondly, and probably more importantly, a number of researchers had attempted to find subsets of families where schizophrenia would look like a Mendelian condition. No such families had ever been convincingly found, despite many efforts, some in quite obscure corners of the world.

The logical way to tell whether the finding was correct or not was to repeat the experiment on a different set of patients. No one was able to replicate the chromosome 5 findings. Furthermore, the team that had originally reported linkage on chromosome 11 for bipolar disorder published, again in *Nature*, a paper entitled 'Re-evaluation of the linkage relationship between chromosome 11p and the gene for bipolar

affective disorder in the Old Order Amish' (Kelsoe *et al.*, 1989). The addition of a few additional families turned a highly significant finding on chromosome 11p into a non-significant result (thereby leading some to believe that working in the field of psychiatric genetics could get you a publication in *Nature* if you were right and another publication in *Nature* when you discovered you were wrong).

In fact, there was already a history of failed linkage findings in bipolar disorder, involving other regions of the genome than the end of chromosome 11. As suggested in 1969, bipolar disorder has been linked to various diseases known to be due to genetic mutations on the X chromosome, such as color blindness and glucose-6-phosphate dehydrogenase deficiency. Miron Baron published a study (in *Nature*) in 1987 (Baron *et al.*, 1987) claiming to have found a susceptibility locus for bipolar illness on the X chromosome and a few years later, in 1993, reported in another high profile paper that there was 'Diminished support for linkage between manic depressive psychosis and X chromosome markers' (Baron *et al.*, 1993).

At first sight these setbacks are reminiscent of the gene-hunting stories: the Huntington's disease locus was placed at two positions on chromosome 4 for example. But there is an important difference. Discarding the idea that common psychiatric illness could arise from a single mutation left a serious problem. How did genes operate in these conditions? Were we dealing with ten, 100, 1,000, or more? How did these mutations work? Were they really mutations at all or just common variants that in some unlucky individuals combined in a particularly malignant manner to produce illness? How would we recognize them at a molecular level? Almost all of the subsequent problems arose because we didn't know the answer to these questions, and so we guessed.

Hunting for schizophrenia genes by linkage analysis

At the time, it didn't seem unreasonable to guess that a few genes might be detectable for a complex disorder like schizophrenia. Perhaps God would be kind to schizophrenia researchers—they certainly needed the help. For example, even if 100 genes contributed to susceptibility to schizophrenia, it would be extremely unlikely that they were all equally important. It was much more likely that they differed in the extent to which they conferred susceptibility. Some might be rather important, others quite small in their impact. Low-hanging fruit that might hold the secrets of the etiology of psychiatric illness have continued to tempt psychiatric geneticists ever since.

We all thought it was possible that a few genes could be found using modifications of the methods used to find the Huntington's disease gene. Even if the chance of success was slim, it was worth trying because the rewards were so great. An expectation of failure had, of course, been the prevailing view when the molecular assault on Huntington's disease began. So a number of groups around the world began to collect samples of the appropriate size and composition, and to use the appropriate analyses, to find the mutations responsible for schizophrenia and other psychiatric illnesses. Here is the story of one such effort.

County Roscommon revisited

The Irish Study of High-Density Schizophrenia Families grew out of the Roscommon family study described in Chapter 2. Between April 1987 and November 1992, teams of investigators, supervised by a group of American collaborators lead by K.S.K. and Irish collaborators led by Dermot Walsh and Tony O'Neill visited a total of 39 separate public psychiatric facilities in Ireland and seven in Northern Ireland. These facilities together provided over 95% of inpatient psychiatric care to the people of Ireland. All of these institutions had community nursing services that provided follow-up care for the chronically mentally ill in their communities. Because staff turnover at these facilities was low (the ongoing joke was that the staff were often as chronic as the patients), the hospital personnel and particularly the community nurses were very knowledgeable about the patients and their families. Ireland was an ideal place to complete such a study because the population is considerably less mobile than that in the USA and relatives in a family often live in close proximity to one another. Family size is relatively large and individuals are typically quite co-operative in medical research. Many of the Irish are amateur genealogists.

The research team would begin by meeting with the hospital staff and explaining the importance of the project. This would be followed by a request for families that contained two or more individuals who might have had some form of psychotic illness. The research team would then obtain and review the available psychiatric records and if that information was insufficient to make a preliminary diagnosis, care-givers or the individuals themselves would be interviewed to obtain further information. Over 1,000 families were screened in this way and 265 were identified who met the criteria for inclusion in the linkage sample. This meant that at least two of the first-, second-, or third-degree relatives met the criteria for schizophrenia, and they and their relatives were cooperative in permitting us to interview them and to obtain blood samples for DNA extraction. It hardly needs saying that the diagnostic assessments

were very time-consuming. Individual senior clinicians including K.S.K. personally reviewed all of the personal interview and hospital abstract information blind to knowledge about other relatives, and extensive series of diagnostic assessments were completed. At the end of the project, the research team, sitting around a table, tried to figure out exactly how many person-years the entire data collection effort had taken. Estimates varied from 45 to 60.

Key papers

Kendler. K.S., O'Neill, F.A., Burke, J., Murphy, B., Duke, F., Straub, R.E., Shinkwin, R., Ni, N.M., MacLean, C.J. and Walsh, D. (1996). Irish study on high-density schizophrenia families: field methods and power to detect linkage. *Am J Med Genet* **67**:179–190.

Straub, R.E., MacLean, C.J., Ma, Y., Webb, B.T., Myakishev, M.V., Harris-Kerr, C., Wormley, B., Sadek, H., Kadambi, B., O'Neill, F.A., Walsh, D., and Kendler, K.S. (2002). Genome-wide scans of three independent sets of 90 Irish multiplex schizophrenia families and follow-up of selected regions in all families provides evidence for multiple susceptibility genes. *Mol Psychiatry* **7**:542–559.

These are the two key references for the Irish Study of High-Density Schizophrenia Families. The first describes, in rather terse scientific prose, the methods and power of this study. The second gives the results of the genome-wide linkage scan, first of the three subsets of families and then of these subsets combined.

Once we had the DNA from the 270 families in Ireland we had to carry out the molecular genetic analysis. This was never an easy operation. Think about the numbers involved: because we needed to genotype the parents, we had to look at about 1,400 people, so that in the end we had well over a quarter of a million results. That's not done by machine; somebody has to check every result, and that is not straightforward. The markers we used, which are still used by many groups around the world, were not SNPs. As we want to find out which alleles have been inherited from each parent, we prefer a marker that has more than two alleles. Such markers are in fact abundant in the human genome; in the early 1990s, a number of groups discovered that short stretches of repetitive DNA, for example the sequence CACACACA, differed in length between people; some have 12 repeats, some ten, some eight, some six, and so on (see Appendix).

We carried out the linkage study in stages, analyzing 90 families at a time. Figure 3.3 shows one group for each of the three graphs (family sets A, B, and C). The y-axis reflects the probability of linkage. This is a logarithmic scale so that a value of 1 reflects a 10 : 1 likelihood of linkage, a value of 2 is 100 : 1, of 3 is 1,000 : 1, etc. However, if we tested 1,000 markers, then we'd expect there to be one marker showing linkage by chance at a level of 1,000 : 1. In this case, we tested about 300 markers, so we'd expect three markers to exceed 2 on the y-axis. The x-axis depicts the human genome laid end-to-end from the very top of chromosome 1 at the far left to the bottom of chromosome X at the far right.

The first result looked really good. There was a group of markers on chromosome 10 that almost reached 3.5. Unfortunately, chromosome 10 showed nothing when we looked at the results from the second set of 90 families, and not much from the third and final set. By contrast, a not very impressive bump on chromosome 6 in the first set of families did occur in the second and indeed also in the third sets. If you look at the left-hand area of the region of chromosome 8 in the three family sets, you will also find a pattern of consistent

but modest linkage peaks, tallest in family set A but clearly detectable in family sets B and C. A slightly less impressive set of findings was obtained on chromosomes 5 and 4. So while we produced satisfying levels of replication for linkage peaks on chromosomes 6, 8, 5, and perhaps 4, our results on chromosome 10 showed relatively robust evidence for linkage in one sample and no evidence at all in another.

While family, twin, and adoption studies of schizophrenia performed by a diversity of investigators in a range of countries have produced quite similar findings about the genetic contribution to the disease, agreement across studies of genetic linkage in schizophrenia is, at best, modest. Table 3.1 provides a summary covering all of the major linkage studies of schizophrenia published over a decade (from 1994 to 2003). The table lists all of the major linkage studies of schizophrenia by year, author, number of markers used, number of families, and, most importantly for our present purpose, those chromosomal regions that produced statistically significant results. Look down the last column. It is hard to see an obvious pattern. You would hope that the same region would be identified by nearly every study. Not so and not even close.

But we cannot rely on simply looking for a pattern in the results. We need an objective assessment of whether the studies agree with each other. One of the critical papers in this area was a joint analysis of 20 linkage studies of schizophrenia. Douglas Levinson and Cathryn Lewis were able to get most investigators with large linkage studies of schizophrenia to put their results in a standardized form so that they could be jointly analyzed. The 20 independent genome scans agreed with one another far more than would be expected by

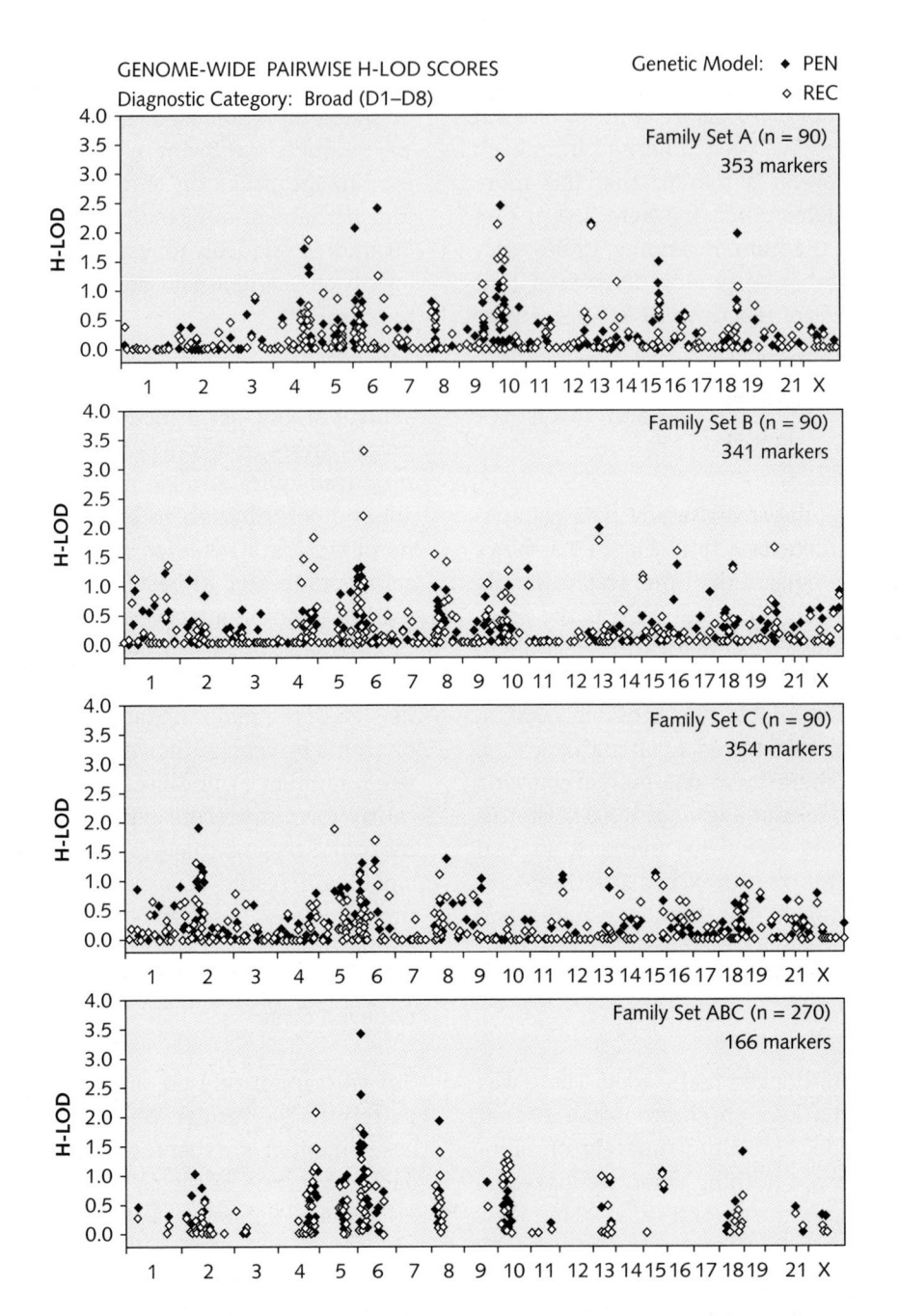

Figure 3.3 Pairwise LOD (logarithm of the odds) scores from three independent subsets of 90 families each (family sets A, B, and C) and the entire 270 families (family set ABC). The *y*-axis reflects the probability of linkage. The *x*-axis depicts the human genome laid end-to-end from the very top of chromosome 1 at the far left to the bottom of chromosome X at the far right. From Straub *et al.* (2002).

Table 3.1 Published genome scans of schizophrenia

Year	First Author	No. of Markers	No. of Families	Positive Regions at $P < 0.01$
1994	Coon	329	9	4p, 22q
1995	Moses	413	5	2pq*, 4q, 9q, 12q, 14q, 20p
1998	Levinson	310	43	2q, 10q
1998	Faraone	459	43	10p*
1998	Kaufman	459	30	None
1998	Coon	406	1	2p*
1998	Blovin	452	54	7q, 8p*, 13q*, 14q, 22q
1999	Williams	229	196	4p, 18q, Xcent
1999	Hovatta	351	20	1q32*, 4q*, 9q
2000	Schwab	463	71	6p*, 10p*
2000	Brzustowkicz	381	22	1q2*, 8p, 3q
2001	Gurling	365	13	1q33*, 5q*, 8p*, 11q*
2001	Staber	356	12	15q*, 22q
2002	Straub	650	270	2pq, 4p, 5q*, 6p*, 8p*, 10p
2002	DeLisi	396	382	2pq, 3q, 10p*, 12q, 22q
2002	DeLisi	404	95	1p, 5q, 14p
2002	Stefansson	950	33	8p*
2002	Devlin	~330	5	5q*, 2p
2003	Fallin	382	29	1p, 6p, 10q*

*$P < 0.001$.

chance. In particular, 12 regions of the genome were found where the positive results found across the various studies were unlikely to occur by chance. While this does not mean that all these regions will yield genes (some could still be false positives), it is likely that at least some of them may do so.

Key papers

Levinson, D.F., Levinson, M.D., Segurado, R., and Lewis, C.M. (2003). Genome scan meta-analysis of schizophrenia and bipolar disorder, part I: methods and power analysis. *Am J Hum Genet* **73**:17–33.

Lewis, C.M., Levinson, D.F., Wise, L.H., DeLisi, L.E., Straub, R.E., Hovatta, I., Williams, N.M., Schwab, S.G., Pulver, A.E. *et al.* (2003). Genome scan meta-analysis of schizophrenia and bipolar disorder, part II: schizophrenia. *Am J Hum Genet* **73**:34–48.

Segurado, R., Detera-Wadleigh, S.D., Levinson, D.F., Lewis, C.M., Gill, M., Nurnberger, J.I. Jr, Craddock, N., DePaulo, J.R., Baron, M. *et al.* (2003). Genome scan meta-analysis of schizophrenia and bipolar disorder, part III: bipolar disorder. *Am J Hum Genet* **73**:49–62.

Ng, M.Y., Levinson, D.F., Faraone, S.V., Suarez, B.K., DeLisi, L.E., Arinami, T., Riley, B., Paunio, T., Pulver, A.E. *et al.* (2009). Meta-analysis of 32 genome-wide linkage studies of schizophrenia. *Mol Psychiatry* **14**:774–785.

The first three papers describe the methods and results of an attempt to summarize the results of linkage scans of schizophrenia and bipolar disorder in 2003, while the fourth provides an update of the analyses of schizophrenia in 2009, which, disconcertingly, found less evidence for linkage peaks for schizophrenia, despite the larger number of studies contained in the analysis.

Chromosomal abnormalities as a cause of schizophrenia

We'll return later to the efforts that have been made to identify the gene, or genes, that contribute to the linkage signal we identified. But before we do so, we'll describe some of the other discoveries that were being made about the molecular basis of schizophrenia. We have chosen two in particular because they illustrate an alternative way of approaching the problem. The clue that the researchers exploited in both cases was something we have not yet talked about: chromosomal anomalies.

It happens that about 1% of Mendelian mutations are due to large alterations in DNA structure, brought about by the deletion, or other large-scale rearrangement, of part of a chromosome (Tommerup, 1993). You can see these changes down a microscope so it is possible to screen for this sort of mutation without recourse to a genome sequencing center. Sometimes a whole chromosome is involved, as in Down syndrome where there is an additional copy of chromosome 21. Sometimes the

changes are more subtle: a small piece is missing. (Small is relative here. The smallest deletion observable down a microscope takes out about 50 genes, on average.)

The majority of these small deletions cause mental retardation, often with other physical anomalies, typically affecting the face, limbs, and heart. One such anomaly, not restricted to a single pedigree, occurs on chromosome 22q and is called velocardiofacial syndrome (VCFS). Affected children (for typically it is diagnosed in childhood) have heart defects, a cleft palate, and unusual facial features. Not all children have all of these features, and sometimes the chromosomal deletion appears to have no effect at all. But occasionally there is another feature. In the mid-1990s, Maria Karayiorgou reported that some VCFS patients have psychosis (Karayiorgou *et al.*, 1995). Unfortunately, the deletion affects a number of genes and the relationship between psychosis and the deletion of part of chromosome 22 is complicated (Karayiorgou and Gogos, 2004).

Sometimes two chromosomes swap material (Figure 3.4). This is normal if the chromosomes are the same, as in the exchanges that go on between pairs of chromosomes during recombination, but it is not normal when the exchange takes place between non-homologous pairs. An exchange of information between chromosomes 1 and 11 will have the unfortunate consequence of disrupting any genes that have the bad luck to lie at the point of exchange, and the even more unfortunate consequence that any offspring of individuals carrying translocated chromosomes may inherit only one of the rearranged pairs. This would mean, for example, having three copies of part of chromosome 11 and only one copy of part of chromosome 1.

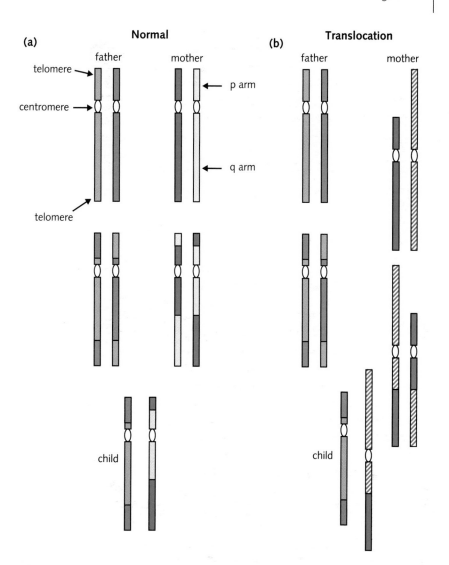

Figure 3.4 Chromosomes have two ends (telomeres), a centre (centromere), and two arms, the shorter of which is the p arm, the longer the q arm. In the sex cells where meiosis occurs, chromosomes find their partners and recombine to generate a mosaic of the paternal and maternal chromosomes, as shown in (a). One of these chromosomes is chosen at random to pass on to the next generation. Sometimes the pairing fails and chromosomes recombine with the wrong partner, as shown in (b), giving rise to a translocation. One of the consequences can be that children receive an unbalanced amount of chromosomal material—too much of one chromosome and not enough of another.

A group of psychiatrists in Edinburgh asked whether chromosomal translocations were associated with schizophrenia. There's a unit in Edinburgh that has specialized for a long time in the detection and description of chromosomal anomalies so there was a registry of confirmed cases for the psychiatrists to go through. They looked at 283 pedigrees and in

1990 reported that they had found psychosis associated with one chromosomal abnormality (a translocation involving chromosomes 1 and 11) (St Clair *et al.*, 1990). This led, by the usual tortuous, grueling route, to the discovery of a gene called *DISC1*, which lies at the chromosomal breakpoint (the acronym stands for disrupted in schizophrenia 1; there is also a *DISC2*, as the translocation affected two genes, but *DISC2* does not get much of a mention) (Semple *et al.*, 2001). David Porteous and his colleagues in Edinburgh reported another patient with psychosis and a translocation on a different chromosome (chromosome 16). Remarkably, the gene (*PDE4*) disrupted at the breakpoint turns out to interact with *DISC1*— the two proteins physically touch each other and that interaction appears to be important for their function (Millar *et al.*, 2005).

Considerable excitement has ensued about the emergence of a new scientific discipline: the cell biology of schizophrenia. But before we celebrate its birth, we'd better check that we aren't nurturing a cuckoo. It doesn't need a huge amount of scientific imagination to think up the experiment of testing whether *DISC1* is an important contributor to schizophrenia by genetic association (see Chapter 5, p. 77). Many groups have tried this, with a mix of positive and negative findings; nothing, in other words, definitive. *DISC1* is no different from other candidate genes in this respect. It's still just a candidate, but it was discovered in this unusual fashion, by looking at people with chromosomal translocations, and we need to revisit that observation. This is what the Edinburgh psychiatrists wrote about their finding in 1990:

> **Psychiatric diagnoses had been recorded for 16 of the 34 members with the translocation compared with only 5 of the 43 without it. The LOD scores (against chance linkage of the translocation with mental illness) were greatest when the mental disorders in the phenotype were restricted to schizophrenia, schizoaffective disorder, recurrent major depression, and adolescent conduct and emotional disorders. Although the mental illness in this family may not be typical of that in the general population, the findings suggest that the q21–22 region of chromosome 11 may be a promising area to examine for genes predisposing to major mental illness.**

There are two important observations here. Firstly, the association between mutation and disorder is not what we expect from a Mendelian effect. It is quite different from the *FOXP2* mutation in the KE pedigree, where every affected member has the mutation and it is not found in the unaffected. Secondly, the psychiatrists argue that the effect is not specific to schizophrenia. They suggest that the genetic abnormality results in a number of different conditions, including emotional disorders.

The chromosomal abnormality story is complicated. It tells us that, yes, there are some cases in which a single genetic insult can produce a psychiatric disease, but it seems that by itself this is not sufficient, nor necessary: in the pedigree with the translocation there are people who have the genetic abnormality and do not have a psychiatric illness and conversely people with psychiatric illness and no translocation. It also tells us that the typical, classical, common-or-garden variety schizophrenia may have a different genetic origin (although we don't know that yet for certain).

Summary

1. Linkage studies make use of common variations in DNA sequence as markers in conjunction with large family genealogies.

2. The genetic mutation causing Huntington's disease, a neurodegenerative disorder, was identified by linkage analysis in a very large extended family, followed by positional cloning.

3. A mutation in a transcription factor gene **FOXP2** gives rise to a language disorder and was identified by linkage analysis and positional cloning.

4. Analysis of schizophrenic families by linkage analysis has proved far less successful.

5. Chromosome abnormalities are also mappable genetic lesions, some of which correlate with schizophrenia, but not in a clear-cut manner.

References

Baron, M., Risch, N., Hamburger, R., Mandel, B., Kushner, S., Newman, M., Drumer, D., and Belmaker, R.H. (1987). Genetic-linkage between X-chromosome markers and bipolar affective-illness. *Nature* **326**:289–292.

Baron, M., Freimer, N.F., Risch, N., Lerer, B., Alexander, J.R., Straub, R.E., Asokan, S., Das, K., Peterson, A. *et al.* (1993). Diminished support for linkage between manic depressive illness and X-chromosome markers in three Israeli pedigrees. *Nat Genet* **3**:49–55.

Botstein, D., White, R.L., Skolnick, M., and Davis, R.W. (1980). Construction of a genetic linkage map in man using restriction fragment length polymorphisms. *Am J Hum Genet* **32**:314–331.

Egeland, J.A., Gerhard, D.S., Pauls, D.L., Sussex, J.N., Kidd, K.K., Allen, C.R., Hostetter, A.M., and Housman, D.E. (1987). Bipolar affective disorders linked to DNA markers on chromosome 11. *Nature* **325**:783–787.

Fisher, S.E., Vargha-Khadem, F., Watkins, K.E., Monaco, A.P., and Pembrey, M.E. (1998). Localization of a gene implicated in a severe speech and language disorder. *Nat Genet* **18**:168–170.

Fu, Y.H., Kuhl, D.P., Pizzuti, A., Pieretti, M., Sutcliffe, J.S., Richards, S., Verkerk, A.J., Holden, J.J., Fenwick, R.G. *et al.* (1991). Variation of the CGG repeat at the fragile X site results in genetic instability: resolution of the Sherman paradox. *Cell* **67**:1047–1058.

Gitschier, J. (2006). Willing to do the math: an interview with David Botstein. *PLoS Genet* **2**:e79.

Gusella, J.F., Wexler, N.S., Conneally, P.M., Naylor, S.L., Anderson, M.A., Tanzi, R.E., Watkins, P.C., Ottina, K., Wallace, M.R. *et al.* (1983). A polymorphic DNA marker genetically linked to Huntington's disease. *Nature* **306**:234–238.

Hurst, J.A., Baraitser, M., Auger, E., Graham, F., and Norell, S. (1990). An extended family with a dominantly inherited speech disorder. *Dev Med Child Neurol* **32**:347–355.

Karayiorgou, M. and Gogos, J.A. (2004). The molecular genetics of the 22q11-associated schizophrenia. *Brain Res Mol Brain Res* **132**:95–104.

Karayiorgou, P., Morris, M.A., Morrow, B., Shprintzen, R.J., Goldberg, R., Borrow, J., Gos, A., Nestadt, G., Wolyniec, P.S. *et al.* (1995). Schizophrenia susceptibility associated with interstitial deletions of chromosome 22q11. *Proc Natl Acad Sci USA* **17**:7612–7616.

Kelsoe, J.R., Ginns, E.I., Egeland, J.A., Gerhard, D.S., Goldstein, A.M., Bale, S.J., Pauls, D.L., Long, R.T., Kidd, K.K. *et al.* (1989). Re-evaluation of the linkage relationship between chromosome 11p loci and the gene for bipolar affective disorder in the Old Order Amish. *Nature* **342**:238–243.

Lai, C.S., Fisher, S.E., Hurst, J.A., Vargha-Khadem, F., and Monaco, A.P. (2001). A forkhead-domain gene is mutated in a severe speech and language disorder. *Nature* **413**:519–523.

Millar, J.K., Pickard, B.S., Mackie, S., James, R., Christie, S., Buchanan, S.R., Malloy, M.P., Chubb, J.E., Huston, E. *et al.* (2005). *DISC1* and *PDE4B* are interacting genetic factors in schizophrenia that regulate cAMP signaling. *Science* **310**:1187–1191.

Oberle, I., Rousseau, F., Heitz, D., Kretz, C., Devys, D., Hanauer, A., Boue, J., Bertheas, M.F., and Mandel, J.L. (1991). Instability of a 550 base pair DNA segment and abnormal methylation in fragile X syndrome. *Science* **252**:1097–1102.

Semple, C.A., Devon, R.S., Le Hellard, S., and Porteous, D.J. (2001). Identification of genes from a schizophrenia-linked translocation breakpoint region. *Genomics* **73**:123–126.

Sherrington, R., Brynjolfsson, J., Petursson, H., Potter, M., Dudleston, K., Barraclough, B., Wasmuth, J., Dobbs, M., and Gurling, H. (1988). Localization of a susceptibility locus for schizophrenia on chromosome 5. *Nature* **336**:164–167.

Straub, R.E., MacLean, C.J., Ma, Y., Webb, B.T., Myakishev, M.V., Harris-Kerr, C., Wormley, B., Sadek, H., Kadambi, B., *et al.* (2002). Genome-wide scans of three independent sets of 90 Irish multiplex schizophrenia families and follow-up of selected regions in all families provides evidence for multiple susceptibility genes. *Mol Psychiatr* **7**(6): 542–559.

St Clair, D., Blackwood, D., Muir, W., Carothers, A., Walker, M., Spowart, G., Gosden, C., and Evans, H.J. (1990). Association within a family of a balanced autosomal translocation with major mental illness. *Lancet* **336**:13–16.

Tanzi, R.E. and Bertram, L. (2001). New frontiers in Alzheimer's disease genetics. *Neuron* **32**:181–184.

Tommerup, N. (1993). Mendelian cytogenetics. Chromosome rearrangements associated with Mendelian disorders. *J Med Genet* **30**:713–727.

Vargha-Khadem, F., Watkins, K., Alcock, K., Fletcher, P., and Passingham, R. (1995). Praxic and nonverbal cognitive deficits in a large family with a genetically transmitted speed and language disorder. *Proc Natl Acad Sci U S A* **92**:930–933.

Vargha-Khadem, F., Gadian, D.G., Copp, A., and Mishkin, M. (2005). *FOXP2* and the neuroanatomy of speech and language. *Nat Rev Neurosci* **6**:131–138.

Other human phenotypes

Genetic influences on alcoholism, depression, and personality

[On the generality of genetic approaches to studying other psychiatric conditions as well as personality traits in general, and the interaction of gender, environment, and development with genetic variation]

Up to this point, our discussion of human psychiatric disorders has focused on schizophrenia, largely because it is provides such excellent examples of the historical and conceptual points we wanted to make. In this chapter, we're going to broaden the reader's perspective. Psychiatric genetics has tackled many disorders and we wouldn't want to leave the reader with a restricted vision of what has been achieved. Furthermore, the disorders and traits discussed in this chapter—alcohol dependence (or more generically alcoholism), personality, and major depression—differ in important ways from schizophrenia, thereby exemplifying some further principles. We also want to address some important questions about how genes impact on risk for psychiatric disorders: how genetic and environmental factors inter-relate, whether genetic risk factors are fairly disorder specific or more non-specific in their impact on different psychiatric disorders, and how genes act over developmental time.

Alcoholism

As an introduction to the human face of alcoholism, this quote from James Joyce's Dubliners describes the sequelae of an evening's heavy drinking by an office worker in Dublin around 1900.

A very sullen faced man stood at the corner of O'Connell Bridge waiting for the Sandymount train to take him home. He was full of smouldering anger and revengefulness. He felt humiliated and disorientated; he did not even feel drunk; and he had only twopence in his pockets. He cursed everything. He had done for himself in the office, pawned his watch, spent all his money and he had not even got drunk. He began to feel thirsty again and he longed to be back again in the hot, reeking public-house. He had lost his reputation as a strong man, having been defeated twice by a mere boy. His heart swelled with fury and when he thought of the woman in the big hat who had bumped against him and said *Pardon!* his fury nearly choked him.

His tram let him down at Shelbourne Road and he steered his great body along in the shadow of the wall of the barracks. He loathed returning to his home. When he went in by the side-door he found the kitchen empty and the kitchen fire nearly out. He bawled upstairs:

—Ada! Ada!

...A little boy came running down the stairs...

—Light the lamp. What do you mean by having the place in darkness? ...The man sat down heavily on one of the chairs while the little boy lit the lamp... When the lamp was lit, he banged his fist on the table and shouted:

—What's for my dinner?

—I'm going ... to cook it Pa, said the little boy.

The man jumped up furiously and pointed to the fire.

—On that fire! You let the fire out! By God, I'll teach you to do that again!

He took a step to the door and seized the walking stick which was standing behind it.

—I'll teach you to let the fire out! he said, rolling up his sleeve in order to give his arm free play.

The little boy cried O Pa! and ran whimpering round the table, but the man followed him and caught him by the coat. The little boy looked about him wildly but seeing no escape fell upon his knees.

—Now you'll not let the fire out the next time! said the man striking him vigorously with the stick. Take that, you little whelp!

Both alcohol and alcohol problems have been a part of human culture for a very, very long time. Both the ancient Egyptians and Mesopotamian civilizations had organized alcohol-brewing industries. Indeed, in ancient Babylonia, one of the world's first legal texts included a law regulating drinking houses. The observation that problems with alcohol run in families also goes a long way back.

In 110 AD, Plutarch, the Roman historian and biographer, famously wrote, 'Ebrii gignunt ebrios' meaning approximately 'one drunkard begets another.'

Alcoholism is a very different disorder from schizophrenia, and sorting out what causes it is even more complicated, partly because of the multifarious nature of the disorder, its mix of physiological and psychological components, and partly because of the importance of cultural factors (drinking patterns vary widely among, for example, Italians, English, Japanese, and Jews), developmental differences, and gender effects. For one thing, alcoholism is much commoner than psychosis. In one large-scale representative study of the US population (Kessler *et al.*, 1994), the lifetime risk for alcohol dependence was 20.2% for males and 8.2% for females. Then there are issues of diagnosis. What sort of disorder are we dealing with here? While you can see how schizophrenia might be the product of a disordered brain, it's not so easy to see what's wrong with an alcoholic. Obviously, the addiction can't happen when there's no alcohol (alcoholism is uncommon in Islamic countries and unheard of in cultures such as the Pennsylvania Dutch Amish, who ban use of any alcohol), so what's the cause? It's at least conceivable that the whole problem arises because some people simply don't have the strength of will to say no when offered a drink. Is addiction just a disorder of will power?

Because its effects are so corrosive, so destructive of relationships, the social consequences of alcoholism are different from those of schizophrenia. It's difficult to study the families of alcoholics, because often they have none. While for many families, having several members with schizophrenia brings the family together and increases family cohesion, alcoholism has just the opposite effect. It tears families apart.

This makes it difficult to study the genetics of alcoholism because it is difficult to obtain the family data. After completing the large-scale study of families with a high density of schizophrenia in Ireland described earlier, one of us (K.S.K.) undertook a similar study of alcoholism. When the study started, it was felt that it would be a comparably easy study to conduct, but it proved to be much harder. Ask a sibling about how to contact his alcoholic brother and we would frequently get responses like:

> I haven't seen him in 15 years. I don't know where he is and I don't want to know. He has ruined his own life and for many years, he just about ruined mine. I am sorry for him but he has brought it on himself. I have just had enough of it. I won't have anything to do with him ever again.

One way to avoid traveling around winding Irish lanes, staying in rural boarding houses with no heat after 8 p.m., is to obtain access to data someone else has already collected. Remarkably, this proved possible for an extraordinary twin sample of alcoholism by taking advantage of the records kept by the Swedish medical system. About the time that prohibition was gathering force in the USA, Sweden took a different approach to the problems of alcohol abuse by developing a system of local Temperance Boards. Physicians, police, and public prosecutors were legally enjoined to report all information on alcohol-related problems to these boards, which then had to investigate each individual case. An individual's record would follow him throughout life. While initially existing only in paper form, the Swedes eventually computerized the records of all of the local Temperance Boards into one large national registry. However, in the early 1970s, at a time when concern in Sweden was particularly high about privacy, the government made a decision to destroy the Temperance Board records.

A twin study of alcoholism in Sweden

Sweden also maintained a twin registry, which has not been destroyed. We've already mentioned that the heritability estimates provided by most twin studies have very broad confidence intervals: even though the mean estimate of heritability for many conditions may look impressive, often the study is not powerful enough to rule out quite different values. So you can imagine the attraction of a national twin registry for people like K.S.K., who have been frustrated by years of working on smaller samples. Here is the story in his voice:

> The Swedish twin registry had accumulated various accretions and appendages over the years; it has been collected by numerous people and worked over by numerous researchers, each with their own interests and own ways of working. I had worked with Nancy Pedersen at the Swedish Twin registry on the heritability of depression in a small subset of the registry, just 486 pairs [Kendler *et al.*, 1993a]. I was interested to see what else might have been collected that was relevant to depression, so I requested a list of the whole data base. It arrived and was quite faint, having passed through several generations of photocopies. Furthermore, it was in Swedish, a language with which I was only faintly familiar. I wasn't expecting much, as I sat in my office, flipping through the multi-paged document. Generally these exercises turn up very little. But as I leafed through, a heading caught my eye. Even without knowledge of Swedish, I knew that *registreringskontor* might mean the Temperance Board registration data. If so, here, in front me, was evidence of the largest twin data set ever collected for the study of alcoholism. This was the early days of email. I wrote to Nancy Pedersen at once.

Two days later, I had an answer. Shortly prior to the formal destruction of the Temperance Board data, somebody had matched it, using the Swedish ID system which uniquely identifies each citizen, to the Swedish Twin registry. For some reason, this was only done on male–male twin pairs. The data had been sitting in a data file unrecognized and unanalyzed for over two decades. We had complete data on alcohol-related problems in over 8,900 twin pairs born from 1902 to 1949. Registration was not a rare thing. Fully 14% of the sample, 2,516 twins to be precise , had presented to medical or legal authorities with alcohol-related problems. What was so remarkable about this data set is that the information in it was extraordinarily unbiased.

Key paper

Kendler, K.S., Prescott, C.A., Neale, M.C., and Pedersen, N.L. (1997). Temperance board registration for alcohol abuse in a national sample of Swedish male twins, born 1902 to 1949. *Arch Gen Psychiatry* **54**:178–184.

This presents the methods and initial findings from this rather remarkable study.

If you had set out to collect data on alcoholism, the more typical approach would be to interview twins or adoptees and ask about their past experiences: how much they drank, how it interfered with their lives, had they had withdrawal symptoms, etc. Inevitably such data (we call it 'self-report') will have its biases: some people won't want to divulge this information, and even if they do, their memory may not be very reliable (particularly if they have been alcohol-dependent). By contrast, the information from the Temperance Board records was contributed by third parties (doctors, police, and so on) at the time that the alcohol-related problems occurred. It's likely that a large majority of individuals with true

alcohol problems had come into contact with the Temperance Board, as alcoholism is typically a rather public phenomenon. While some psychiatric disorders, such as major depression, often go untreated, as the affected individuals live what Thoreau has called '*lives of quiet desperation,*' few who are severely affected by alcoholism escape coming to the attention of legal or medical personnel. Thus, the data were of high quality and were available in large quantity.

We found that the concordance rates for Temperance Board registration were substantially higher (47.9%) in monozygotic than in dizygotic (32.8%) twins. Model-fitting using the kinds of statistical models that we explained in Chapter 2 produced a heritability estimate of 54% for alcohol abuse. The results of this large Swedish study were remarkably consistent with findings from population-based twin studies in the USA and Australia, which involved personal interviews. Nearly all of these studies have found estimates of the heritability of alcoholism in the range of 50–60% (Heath *et al.*, 1997; Kendler *et al.*, 1992a; Pickens *et al.*, 1991; Prescott and Kendler, 1999). Major adoption studies of alcoholism have been performed in Denmark, Sweden and the USA (Cadoret *et al.*, 1980; Cloninger *et al.*, 1985; Goodwin *et al.*, 1973; Sigvardsson *et al.*, 1996). All four studies utilized the same design—look at the risk for alcoholism in the adopted-away offspring of alcoholic parents versus the adopted-away offspring of biological parents without alcoholism. All four found the same broad pattern of results. Adopted-away sons of alcoholic parents were at considerably increased risk for developing alcoholism. The results were a bit less clear for daughters. So, the results are rather consistent—alcoholism is not merely a weakness of will or a personality quirk. It is quite a heritable condition, although somewhat less so than schizophrenia.

Alcohol is also of interest to us because we know a lot about responses to alcohol in model organisms such as worms, mice, and flies. Given that alcohol has been a part of the environment of planet earth since the appearance of micro-organisms (which happened some 2 billion years ago), all animals have had to develop a method of dealing with this two-carbon molecule. Finally, alcohol is interesting because most of us have both tried alcohol ourselves and observed others using it in social situations. If you have not already done so, we suggest that the next time you're in a group of people who are drinking, notice how people differ in their responses to alcohol. Some individuals get intoxicated quite easily with relatively low amounts of alcohol. Others can 'hold their liquor' and consume large amounts with little obvious effect. In consuming the same amount of alcohol, some people get quite 'high' and 'giddy' while others become quiet and morose. People also vary in their sensitivity to the unpleasant side effects of alcohol. Some can drink a great deal with no apparent adverse effects, while others, even after only two glasses of wine in an evening, wake up the next day definitely worse for the experience.

The molecular genetics of alcoholism

One way in which molecular genetic studies of alcoholism differ quite dramatically from those for schizophrenia is that we have good physiological candidate genes for alcohol dependence. For most psychiatric illnesses, we know so little about the underlying biological cause that it is not possible to pick good candidate genes. Not so for alcoholism. Here we have candidates that are every bit as good as insulin is for diabetes or a cholesterol receptor is for heart disease.

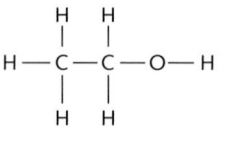

Figure 4.1 The ethanol molecule: two carbon atoms (C) joined to hydrogen (H) and an oxygen molecule (O).

The main difference between alcoholism and schizophrenia can be easily summed up: the ethanol molecule (ethanol is the chemical name for the kind of alcohol humans consume). We know a lot about how ethanol is metabolized in the body and quite a bit about how it acts on the brain. It does not take a physiological genius to figure out that differences in how the ethanol molecule is handled in the body might make a difference to the risk for alcoholism. And indeed, that is the case. So, in contrast to the situation with schizophrenia described above, the physiological candidate gene approach has worked for alcoholism.

The ethanol molecule shown in Figure 4.1, is almost entirely broken down in the human body in two simple steps. As shown in Figure 4.2, the first step involves a group of enzymes called alcohol dehydrogenase, or ADH for short. These enzymes (there are seven known variants) convert alcohol into a compound called acetaldehyde. Acetaldehyde is toxic. Even moderate concentrations induce dysphoria, and higher concentrations consistently produce bad headaches, nausea, and flushing. The second family of enzymes, called acetaldehyde dehydrogenase, or ALDH, converts acetaldehyde into a benign

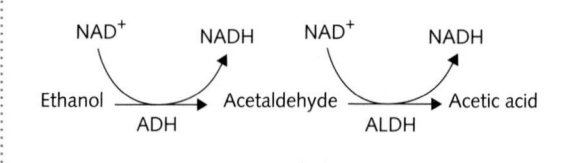

Figure 4.2 The metabolism of ethanol.

molecule, acetic acid, that is easily excreted in urine.

We have quite a bit of evidence that the level of acetaldehyde is critical to the subjective effect we humans have after drinking alcohol. If the level is kept low, few acute side effects are experienced. If the level rises, the drinker often doesn't feel good, and if the level gets quite high, the drinker feels quite ill.

From Figure 4.2, it should be clear that you can get high levels of acetaldehyde in two ways. Either you make it too quickly or break it down too slowly. It turns out that both paths are important for influencing risk for alcoholism, although the latter is more dramatic than the former. In East Asian populations, a substantial proportion of people (43% in one study) have a form of one ALDH gene (ALDH2) that barely works at all. Individuals who possess even one copy of this form (called ALDH2*2) do such a poor job of breaking down acetaldehyde that, even after only one drink of alcohol, the concentration of acetaldehyde rises to high levels. The results are predictable—the individual turns as red as a beet, develops a splitting headache, and feels generally awful. This is sometimes called the 'flushing reaction.' Many studies have shown that individuals with this variant of ALDH are rather unlikely to develop alcoholism. Although it might be considered as yet another example of science proving the obvious, we now know with some confidence that it is hard (but not impossible) to develop alcoholism if drinking substantial amounts of alcohol makes you ill.

So, if you hear that 'science has not yet found a gene that conclusively influences risk for a psychiatric disorder,' remember that ALDH is such a gene. It might not fit your preconception of what such a gene should be like. It is, for example, expressed largely in the liver, not the brain. While some civilizations regarded the liver as an important psychological organ (and Hamlet bemoaned that '*I am pigeon-liver'd and lack gall to make oppression bitter*'), currently we don't attribute much consciousness to our livers.

That is not the end of this story. In both Asian and non-Asian populations, there are genetic variants of two forms of ADH gene (called ADH1B and ADH1C) that differ in the speed with which they convert alcohol to acetaldehyde. Increasing evidence has now suggested that if you have the 'fast' version of one of these enzymes (ADH1B*2 and ADH1C*1), you are somewhat protected against risk for alcoholism. This is because these versions of the enzyme work so quickly that after drinking alcohol you get a rapid little 'bump' in your blood acetaldehyde levels rather than the more gentle rise seen with the more typical slower-working versions of these enzymes. This 'bump' probably makes individuals with the enzyme variant more prone to feel unwell after drinking. Having less fun drinking makes it less likely that an individual will develop drinking problems.

Molecular genetic studies of alcoholism have not been restricted to studies of the alcohol-metabolizing enzymes. We will briefly mention one other set of studies. Although alcohol is remarkably promiscuous in its effects on the brain—producing notable changes in many neurotransmitter systems—it is clear that a number of the important effects of alcohol are mediated through receptors for the neurotransmitter GABA (which stands for gamma amino butyric acid) and more specifically by one class of brain GABA receptors—GABA$_A$ (see p. 80 for an explanation of neurotransmitters). At the last count, there were nine association studies of alcohol dependence and various GABA$_A$ subunits. Remarkably, eight of these studies were positive—the kind of replication rarely seen in candidate gene association studies of psychiatric disorders.

Key paper

Enoch, M.A. (2008). The role of GABA (A) receptors in the development of alcoholism. *Pharmacol Biochem Behav* **90**:95–104.

A good review of the role of GABA$_A$ receptors in alcohol dependence.

Of the many other genetic associations tested with alcoholism, we cannot resist mentioning one that reported that variants in the bitter-taste receptor, hTAS2R16 (Hinrichs *et al.*, 2006), were associated with the risk for alcohol problems. The mechanism seems plausible: those with sensitive bitter-taste receptors find it harder to drink at least certain alcoholic beverages. This might be working for at least one of us (K.S.K.). Despite years of working in Ireland and many evenings spent in a wide range of Irish pubs, many efforts to acquire a taste for Guinness (thereby establishing some aspects of an Irish version of his masculine identity) were repeatedly unsuccessful. '*It is just too bitter. It makes me shudder every time I drink it.*'

Major depression

Like many terms in psychiatry, 'depression' is slippery, having multiple meanings that can easily result in misunderstanding. Depression can mean just a transient sad or gloomy mood that at one time or another occurs to all of us. That is not what psychiatrists mean when they use this term. Rather, they refer to a syndrome that starts with a mood that is persistently low, sad, or 'down in the dumps,' but is also accompanied by a range of other symptoms including altered appetite, disturbed sleep, difficulty with concentration, impaired ability to experience pleasure, persistent guilt, hopelessness, and, in more severe cases, suicidal thoughts or behaviors. To discriminate the psychiatric concept

Figure 4.3 A picture by the famous painter Vincent Van Gogh (who himself suffered from psychiatric illness), which captures some of the sense of acute and severe depression.

of depression from mere run-of-the-mill sad mood, psychiatry has for many years used the term *major* depression, or as we will call it MD. If you want to fluster a psychiatrist whom you might meet in a social situation, ask about *minor* depression. No such diagnosis exists.

MD is disturbingly common. While epidemiologic studies have produced a range of estimates, about one in five women and about one in eight men will, at some point in their life, meet the criteria for this disorder.

What do we know about the genetics of MD? Many studies have shown that depression 'runs in families.' Our best investigations show that the risk for MD in the first-degree relatives of patients with MD is about threefold higher than that seen in the general population

(Sullivan *et al.*, 2000). What is the source of this familial aggregation? Only three adoption studies have examined depression, and each of them has one or more major limitation (such as reliance only on hospital or work leave records or never directly interviewing the relatives or having a quite small sample size). Of these three studies, two produced results suggesting that genetic risk factors were important for the etiology of MD (Sullivan *et al.*, 2000).

Key paper

Sullivan, P.F., Neale, M.C., and Kendler, K.S. (2000). Genetic epidemiology of major depression: review and meta-analysis. *Am J Psychiatry* **157**:1552–1562.

A detailed review of the family, adoption and twin studies of major depression along with relevant meta-analyses.

When a careful meta-analysis of twin studies of MD was completed in 2000, there were six studies that were of sufficient quality to be included. Two important results emerged from this analysis. Firstly, these studies all agreed well with one another. However, these studies were all done in predominantly European populations in Europe, the USA, and Australia. So we do not know whether similar results would be obtained in other ethnic groups. Secondly, across all of the studies, the estimated heritability for MD was 37%. This figure is much lower than the heritability estimates for schizophrenia and alcohol dependence. So we can draw one important conclusion about the genetics of psychiatric disorders: there are significant differences in heritability.

Since this meta-analysis was published, one additional twin study of MD has been completed. This investigation, completed using the Swedish Twin Register directed by our colleague Dr Nancy Pedersen, is remarkable for its very large sample size (Kendler *et al.*,

2006a). Personal interviews were conducted on over 42,000 twins and both members of over 15,000 pairs. Thus, this single study contained considerably more twin pairs than all of the previous twins studies put together. When parameters were constrained to be equal in males and females in this study, the estimated heritability for MD was 38%, reassuringly close to the results from the meta-analysis of the etiology of MD (Sullivan *et al.*, 2000).

Key paper

Kendler, K.S., Gatz, M., Gardner, C., and Pedersen, N. (2006). A Swedish national twin study of lifetime major depression. *Am J Psychiatry* **163**:109–114.

By far the largest twin study yet performed for major depression on a sample with excellent epidemiological properties.

Personality

Typically, psychiatrists are interested in disorders that you *have*. However, they (and their professional cousins, psychologists) are also interested in the kind of person you *are*. This is captured by what we call 'personality', which we take to reflect the stable part of an individual's attitudes, behavioral patterns, and emotional responses. Over the last 30 years, psychologists have come up with a bewildering array of different scales to measure human personality. From this tower of Babel, something approaching a consensus has emerged over the last 15 years. A substantial proportion of the personality researchers now agree that human personality can be rather well described by five factors, which are often and rather melodramatically called (drum roll please): the Big Five.

I see myself as someone who...

1. ...Is talkative

Disagree   1 ○   2 ○   3 ○   4 ○   5 ○   Agree

2. ...Tends to find fault with others

Disagree   1 ○   2 ○   3 ◑   4 ◐   5 ◑   Agree

3. ...Does a thorough job

Disagree   1 ○   2 ○   3 ○   4 ○   5 ○   Agree

4. ...Is depressed, blue

Disagree   1 ○   2 ○   3 ○   4 ○   5 ○   Agree

5. ...Is original, comes up with new ideas

Disagree   1 ◑   2 ○   3 ◑   4 ○   5 ◑   Agree

6. ...Is reserved

Disagree   1 ○   2 ○   3 ○   4 ○   5 ○   Agree

7. ...Is helpful and unselfish with others

Disagree   1 ○   2 ○   3 ○   4 ○   5 ○   Agree

8. ...Can be somewhat careless

Disagree   1 ◑   2 ○   3 ◑   4 ○   5 ◑   Agree

9. ...Is relaxed, handles stress well

Disagree   1 ○   2 ○   3 ○   4 ○   5 ○   Agree

10. ...Is curious about many different things

Disagree   1 ○   2 ○   3 ○   4 ○   5 ○   Agree

11. ...Is full of energy

Disagree   1 ◑   2 ◑   3 ○   4 ○   5 ○   Agree

12. ...Starts quarrels with others

Disagree   1 ○   2 ○   3 ○   4 ○   5 ○   Agree

13. ...Is a reliable worker

Disagree   1 ○   2 ○   3 ○   4 ○   5 ○   Agree

14. ...Can be tense

Disagree   1 ◑   2 ◑   3 ○   4 ○   5 ○   Agree

15. ...Is ingenious, a deep thinker

Disagree   1 ○   2 ○   3 ○   4 ○   5 ○   Agree

Figure 4.4 Questionnaire from the 'Big Five Inventory'.

In good psychological tradition, a wide variety of different scales has been developed, all of which purport to measure these five factors (see http://homepage.psy.utexas.edu/homepage/faculty/gosling/scales_we.htm for examples of the scales).

Key papers

Eysenck, H.J. (1967). *The Biological Basis of Personality*. Springfield, Illinois: Thomas.

Gosling, S.D. (2008). *What Your Stuff Says About You*. London: Profile Books.

Two books on personality, the first from one of the founders of the field, Hans Eysenck, who worked to establish the validity and utility of questionnaire-based assessments of personality. Eysenck was an early exponent of the idea that personality traits index risk for psychiatric disorder (neuroticism for depression, for instance). The second book is a more recent extension of personality assessment—using your belongings to judge your personality.

For illustrative purposes, we will here focus here on the 'Big Five Inventory' (John and Srivastava, 1999). Part of the questionnaire is shown in Figure 4.4.

One advantage of the Big Five system is the acronym available for their five scales—OCEAN. Thinking about it can make you feel warm and cosmic—bathing in the ocean of human diversity. Here is how the acronym works, along with the selection of items sorted into the five dimensions (where a '–' means the item is reverse-coded):

Openness: items 5, 10, and 15

Conscientiousness: items 3, 8(–), and 13

Extroversion: items 1, 6(–), and 11
Agreeableness: items 2(–), 7, and 12(–)
Neuroticism: items 4, 9(–), and 14

A lot of research has been done on human personality. We know that, once over the age of 30, personality is relatively stable over time (sunk in concrete, some might say). The pattern of personality looks similar across a variety of cultures and people's descriptions of their own personality agree well with how other people describe them.

While assessing a lifetime history of a psychiatric or drug-use disorder is a time-consuming and expensive business, personality is far more simply (and cheaply) measured. All you need to do is convince people to fill out the questionnaire, which typically can be sent and returned by mail or now increasingly on the world-wide web. Using such methods, a number of adoption studies and a quite large number of twin studies, some with enormous sample sizes, have examined the heritability of personality. A thorough review of all of these studies published some years ago found that the heritability for all five major dimensions of personality were in the range of 30–45%, with good agreement across studies (Loehlin, 1992). This means that between one-third and one-half of the differences between people in their personality come from differences in their genes.

A recent study examined the sources of individual differences in one of these scales that we will hear more about, neuroticism, in over 45,000 twins and their relatives, making it one of the largest such studies conducted to date (Lake *et al.*, 2000). Reassuringly, this huge study calculated the heritability for neuroticism to be 41% in females and 35% in males, well within the range of results from smaller studies.

Key paper

Lake, R.I., Eaves, L.J., Maes, H., Heath, A.C., and Martin, N.G. (2000). Further evidence against the environmental transmission of individual differences in neuroticism from a collaborative study of 45,850 twins and relatives on two continents. *Behav Genet* 30:223–233.

The largest and a carefully analyzed twin study of the key personality trait of neuroticism.

Neuroticism reflects the propensity of individuals to experience negative or unpleasant emotions such as anxiety, worry, sadness, anger, and irritability. People with low levels of neuroticism are typically easy-going and imperturbable. It really takes a lot to get them distressed. By contrast, individuals with high levels of neuroticism are easily upset and, once upset, take a long time to calm back down.

Genes for what?

Until now, we have examined one psychiatric or substance-use disorder at a time. We have been asking the question: how important are genes in explaining the variability among people in their risk for developing these disorders? An implicit assumption of these analyses is that the diagnostic categories we have been using—schizophrenia, major depression, alcohol dependence—are the right units of analysis. Here, we ask whether that assumption is correct. Do the definitions that psychiatrists apply to different disorders correspond to the structure of the genetic risk factors?

Depression and anxiety

If asked, most of us would be able to distinguish clearly between the subjective states of being anxious/tense/jittery versus sad/gloomy/depressed. However, epidemiological and clinical studies in psychiatry have long indicated that if you meet the criteria for MD, you are far more likely to also have an anxiety disorder than would be expected by chance. (In the world of medicine, this kind of association between diseases is called co-morbidity.)

One of us (K.S.K.) set out in the early 1990s, using over 1,000 female–female twin pairs from the Virginia Twin Study of Psychiatric and Substance Use Disorders, to try to understand how genes contributed to this co-morbidity. Specifically, we studied MD and the most closely related anxiety disorder that goes by the catchy name of 'generalized anxiety disorder'. The term 'generalized' here means that the affected individual experiences relatively prolonged periods of excessive anxiety and worry that are hard to control and cause distress or impairment, and that they have a range of specific symptoms such as feeling restless or on edge, irritability, muscle tension, and sleep problems. The syndrome is clinically quite different from those where anxiety arises only in specific circumstances, such as before public speaking, when confronted with a nasty looking spider, or when being stuffed into a dark closet by a vindictive older sibling.

This first study published in 1992 of MD and generalized anxiety disorder reached a remarkable conclusion: from a genetic perspective, the two syndromes were for all intents and purposes the same disorder (Kendler *et al.*, 1992b). Of the many parameters that can emerge from statistical genetic models, the genetic correlation (r_g to the aficionado) is one of the most useful. The genetic correlation between two disorders reflects the degree to which these disorders are influenced by the same genetic risk factors. In this first study, the genetic correlation between MD and generalized anxiety

disorder was estimated at +1.00. Correlations can't get any higher than that.

This seemed at first a rather implausible result. Yes, these two disorders might share some risk factors, but to be perfectly correlated...? So, we repeated the study in 1996 with a follow-up of the same twin sample. We got the same results—a genetic correlation of +1.00 (Kendler, 1996). Maybe there was something unusual about female twins from Virginia—although we had no idea what that might be. So we repeated the study in 1,484 male and female twins ascertained from the Swedish Twin Registry (Roy *et al.*, 1995). The estimated genetic correlation between generalized anxiety disorder and MD in the sample was, again, +1.00! We tried one last time—with a far bigger (and more statistically powerful) sample—37,296 twins reflecting an entire national sample from the Swedish Twin Registry. In the women in this sample, estimated genetic correlation between generalized anxiety disorder and MD in the sample was, again, +1.00 (Kendler *et al.*, 2006b). However, at least we found that in males the genetic correlation was less (+0.74)—still quite high, but not unity.

Key paper

Kendler, K.S., Gardner, C.O., Gatz, M., and Pedersen, N.L. (2006). The sources of co-morbidity between major depression and generalized anxiety disorder in a Swedish national twin sample. *Psychol Med* **37**:453–462.

By far the largest study to examine the degree of genetic similarity between major depression and generalized anxiety disorder.

What do these results mean? In humans, our genes appear to put us at low or high risk for a general negative emotional state. However, whether that state tends to be sad, depressive, and gloomy or anxious, worried, and tense is actually a result of our environmental experiences. The preconception that the gene–behavior relationship comes in nice neat packages—one set of genetic risk factors impacting on only one behavioral disorder or trait—is probably not true.

Seven common disorders

Let us expand our playing field. Instead of looking at two disorders at a time, let's look at seven disorders, again in the Virginia twin sample (Kendler *et al.*, 2003). The seven disorders are all relatively common. In addition to the two we have just met—MD and generalized anxiety disorder—we also studied phobias, alcohol dependence, drug abuse or dependence, adult antisocial behavior, and conduct disorder (phobias reflect irrational and disabling fear of a range of objects or situations, while conduct disorder is a nice name for very badly behaved children). Using multivariate statistical genetic techniques, we looked at the pattern of genetic risk factors for these seven disorders and obtained the results seen in Figure 4.5.

Before looking at these results in detail, let's review what we might expect. One possibility would be that the people who designed our psychiatric diagnosis really got it right. There was one specific and unique set of genetic risk factors for every single disorder (or you might see it the other way—that the genes are very respectful of psychiatric categories). Alternatively, it could be that there is no specificity

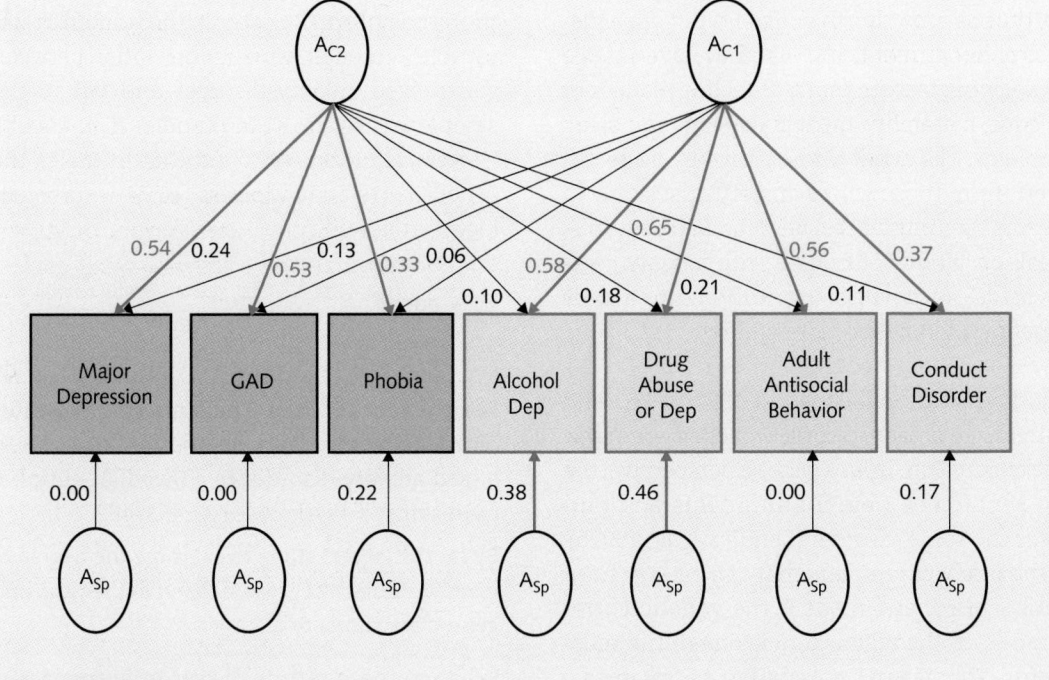

DEP – dependencies
GAD – generalized anxiety disorder

Figure 4.5 Genetic risk factors in common psychiatric and drug use disorders.
Source: Adapted from Kendler *et al.* (2003).

whatsoever with genetic risk factors for these common psychiatric illnesses. That is, there is just one big clump of genes that impact on your 'screwed-upedness.'

So, let's now turn to what we found. Rather than focusing on all of the numbers, you can concentrate on the thick lines in Figure 4.5, which reflect strong statistical effects. Factor A_{C2} at the top left is a set of genetic factors that impact strongly on risk for MD, generalized anxiety disorder, and phobias. We have a name for these kinds of conditions in psychiatry—internalizing disorders. We call them 'internalizing' because they involve people making themselves miserable. Factor A_{C1} at the top right is a set of genetic factors that impact strongly on risk for alcohol dependence, drug abuse or dependence, adult antisocial behavior, and conduct disorder. We also have a name for these kinds of conditions in psychiatry—externalizing disorders. We call them 'externalizing' because they involve people acting out their distress, often in impulsive ways, rather than experiencing it inside.

In addition to these two general factors, there are two sets of disorder-specific genes (A_{sp}) that influence alcohol dependence and drug abuse/dependence. These disorder-specific genes are expected to include the gene for alcohol dehydrogenase (*ADH*), which we discussed above and other similar genes that impact *only* on the risk for alcohol dependence because they specifically affect the metabolism of alcohol.

The truth is probably somewhere in between our two prior hypotheses. Mostly, genetic risk factors—at least for these common disorders—impact on groups of disorders, not on individual diseases. To put that another way—most genes that act on risk for psychiatric illness are not disease specific in their effect. But there is not just one big dimension of genetic

'screwed-upedness.' Rather, there are at least two dimensions (and there would certainly be more if our model included other psychiatric disorders such as schizophrenia, bipolar illness, autism, or anorexia nervosa).

MD and personality

In our quest to understand the specificity versus non-specificity of genes with respect to psychiatric disorders, we have now explored two examples. Before we leave this area, let's briefly examine a related question. What is the relationship between genes that impact on our personality and those that predispose to a common psychiatric disorder: MD? The idea of a depressive (or melancholic) temperament goes back to Greek times. Most of us know people who, by nature, seem gloomy, worried, and prone to depression. What does the data say about this intriguing question?

Trying to keep up with the times, one of us (K.S.K.) has helped to establish a web site where interested twins and other individuals can sign up and fill out a range of questions (if you are interested in participating, have a look at http://www.outofservice.com/twins/). The questions include the Big Five Inventory we described above and questions that do quite a good job of assessing the lifetime history of MD. Using the same kinds of statistical techniques outlined above applied to the twins who visited this web site, we obtained genetic correlations between MD and each of the Big Five dimensions. Here is what the data looked like:

Openness: +0.17
Conscientiousness: −0.36
Extroversion: −0.06
Agreeableness: −0.18
Neuroticism: +0.43

From a genetic perspective, three of the personality dimensions (O, E, and A) have little to do with the risk for MD. Confirming the results of prior studies in the Virginia and Swedish samples (Kendler *et al.*, 1993b, 2006c), the genes that predispose to high levels of neuroticism are moderately correlated with those that predispose you to develop MD. More surprising was the inverse genetic relationship between conscientiousness and risk for MD. Readers who are consistently careful, reliable, and good at planning might take some solace in this result—you may have a bit of genetic protection against developing depression.

Genes and sex

Although we don't wish to disappoint the reader who is hoping for a bit of excitement in the middle of a long and boring chapter, this short section will describe the impact of sex on genes rather than genes on sex. Or, to be more precise, we will explore the ways in which sex moderates the impact of genes on behavioral phenotypes.

To introduce us to this topic, let's start with a simple example of what geneticists call 'sex-limited genetic effects' where genes influence a phenotype in one sex but are 'silent' in the other. A woman might carry one of a variety of demonstrated risk genes for prostate cancer and pass on that risk to her sons, but those genes will have no phenotypic effect on her, as she lacks a prostate gland.

A subtler but related concept is 'sex-modified genetic effects.' Here, the impact of genetic risk factors is altered but not eliminated by the sex of the body in which they exist. The degree of modification can be estimated by the genetic correlation (r_g). In this instance, the genetic correlation means the degree of resemblance of genetic risk factors for a given phenotype in men and women. A value of +1.00 means that the exact same genes do the exact same thing in the two sexes. A value of 0.00 would mean there was absolutely no relationship between the genes that influenced that particular trait in men and the genes that impacted on that same trait in women. We have good evidence for such effects in MD.

Two large-scale twin studies have estimated the genetic correlation for MD in men and women and have come up with two quite similar estimates of +0.55 (Kendler *et al.*, 2001) and +0.63 (Kendler *et al.*, 2006b). With some confidence, we can conclude that, while related, the genetic risk factors for MD are not entirely the same in men and women. One plausible (but unconfirmed) scenario might help illustrate this phenomenon. Women are at increased risk for developing MD after giving birth. This vulnerability for what is called post-partum depression runs in families and is probably influenced by a set of genetic risk factors at least partly independent from the more 'run-of-the-mill' depression. Males might carry the genes that put them at risk for post-partum depression, but they will never get a chance to manifest them because they never give birth, thereby avoiding the profound psychological and biological changes that occur around that time. The prediction, born out by early molecular studies of MD, is that, when the individual genetic variants are found that predispose to MD, some will differ substantially in their impact in men versus women. MD is not the only psychiatric disorder showing genetic correlations between the sexes of less than 1. The same thing has been found for alcohol dependence (and is in this case backed up by rodent studies) (Prescott *et al.*, 1999). From a biological and psychological perspective, males and females are different enough that we cannot always assume that genetic effects on behavior will be the same in the two sexes.

Genes and the environment

Up until now, we have rather ignored the effects of the environment. This is not so surprising because we, the authors, are geneticists. However, in this section, we aim to convince you that the impact of genetic risk factors on psychiatric disorders is often so closely intertwined with environmental factors that studying genes in isolation is often asking for trouble.

We need to describe two quite different but sometimes confused ways in which genes and the environment can inter-relate in contributing to the risk of illness. The first mechanism is termed *gene–environment interaction* (or, as we prefer to call it, *genetic control of sensitivity to the environment*) and the second is *gene–environment correlation* (or, as we prefer to say, *genetic control of exposure to the environment*).

Gene–environment interaction

The common sense model of how genes and the environment combine to contribute to risk for a disease is that they add together; that is, an individual's total risk for a given illness, such as MD or alcoholism, is simply the sum of the risk provided by his genes and the risk created by his various life experiences. This additive model is portrayed in Figure 4.6. The figure depicts the liability of developing a given illness for three hypothetical individuals with low, intermediate, and high genetic liability when exposed to varying levels of environmental risk. Most importantly, the slopes of the lines of total liability are the same for each individual; that is, as individuals move from a low-risk ('protective') to a high-risk ('predisposing') environment,

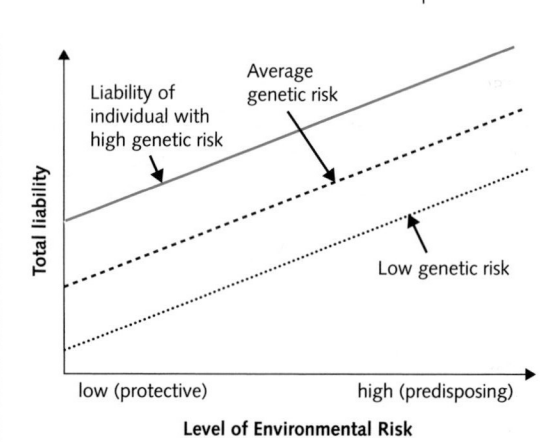

Figure 4.6 Schematic of the additive model for the combination of genetic and environmental risk. Source: Kendler and Prescott (2006).

their liabilities increase by the same amount, regardless of their level of genetic risk.

Contrast this additive model with the one depicted in Figure 4.7. Here, as in the additive model, the liability to illness increases from lower to higher genetic risk individuals and with increasing levels of environmental risk. However, the slopes of the lines are now different in individuals with different levels of genetic risk. Individuals with high genetic risk

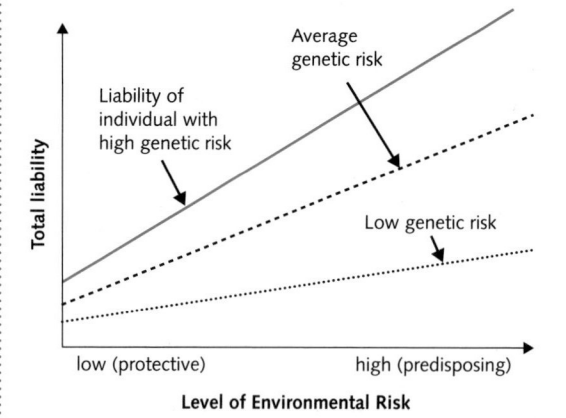

Figure 4.7 Schematic of genetic control of sensitivity to the environment (gene–environment interaction). Source: Kendler and Prescott (2006).

have the steepest slope and those with low genetic risk the flattest slope. In other words, the increase in liability that occurs in moving from a protective to a predisposing environment is itself related to genetic risk.

This is worth restating. In the model depicted in Figure 4.7, genetic risk contributes to disease liability in two different ways: firstly, it impacts on overall liability to illness; secondly, it alters the individual's sensitivity to the pathogenic effects of the environment. The observation that individuals have important differences in their level of stress responsivity is summarized by Burton in his classic text *The Anatomy of Melancholy*, written in 1621:

> **...according as the humour itself is intended or remitted in men [and] their...rational soul is better able to make resistance; so are they more or less affected [by adversity]. For that which is but a flea-biting to one, causeth insufferable torment to another; and which one by his singular moderation and well-imposed carriage can happily overcome, a second is no whit able to sustain, but upon every small occasion of misconceived abuse, injury, grief, disgrace [and] loss...yields so far to passion, that...his digestion hindered, his sleep gone, his spirits obscured, and his heart heavy...he himself [is] overcome with melancholy.**

Burton (1932).

Of the many examples of gene–environment interactions in psychiatry, we will limit ourselves here to examining two. Examining 367 adoptees studied in Iowa, an attempt was made to predict the risk for adolescent antisocial behavior in adolescents from their genetic risk (indexed by a history of antisocial or alcoholic behavior in the biological parents), their environmental risk (indexed by an adverse adoptive home environment), and the interaction of these pachs (Cadoret et al., 1983). What was found is shown in Figure 4.8. In line with the results predicted Figure 4.7, in those who had an 'absent' genetic risk factor, adding a high-risk environment produced a minimal increase in antisocial behavior. However, in those who had a high level of genetic vulnerability (genetic factor 'present'), adding a high-risk environment produced a very large increase in antisocial behaviors. With respect to the development of antisocial behavior, those at high genetic risk were more sensitive to the pathogenic effects of an adverse adoptive home environment.

Our second example involves MD. In addition to the clear evidence of genetic risk factors for MD reviewed above, adverse stressful life events have been shown to consistently and strongly increase the risk for MD. In the Virginia twin study, we asked whether these two risk factors added together or interacted (Kendler et al., 1995). We focused only on the most severe kinds of stressful life events, which in this study included death of a close relative, assault, serious marital problems, and divorce or romantic break-up. The results are shown in Figure 4.9.

Genetic risk was assessed as a function of the history of major depression in their co-twin and zygosity (mono- versus dizygotic). As predicted from the interactive model, the impact of a severe stressful life event on the risk for depression was more striking in those at highest genetic risk than in those at lowest genetic risk. In this example, genetic risk factors altered an individual's sensitivity to the depressogenic effects of these very stressful life events.

Gene–environment correlation

Genes, it would appear, can often moderate the pathogenic effects of adverse environmental

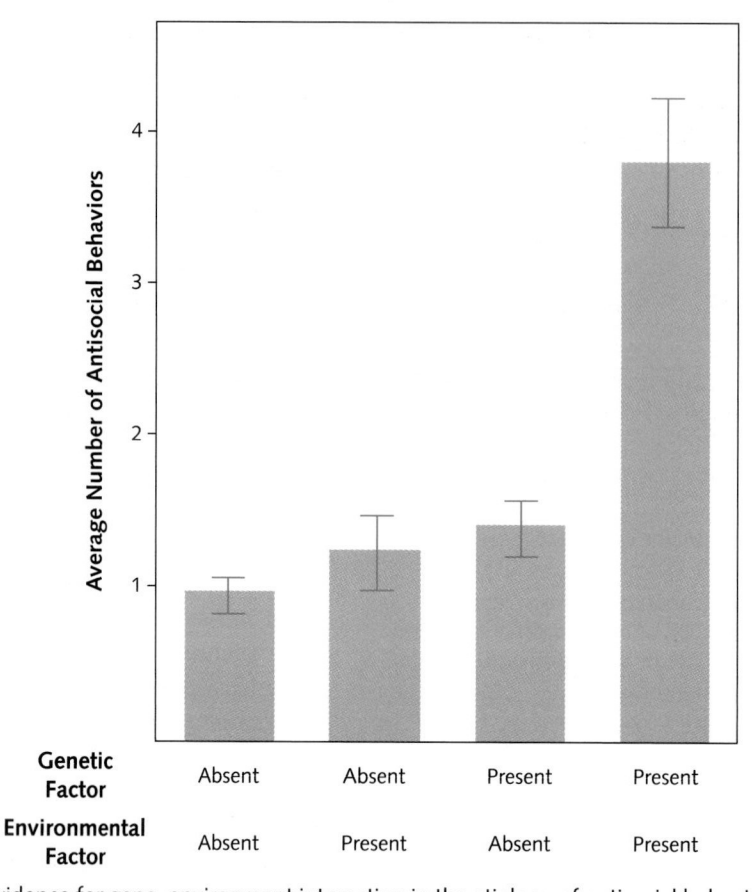

Figure 4.8 Evidence for gene–environment interaction in the etiology of antisocial behavior. Using an adoption sample, this study examined the relationship between the number of rated antisocial behaviors and the presence or absence of genetic and environmental risk factors.
Source: Cadoret *et al.* (1983).

experiences. In this section, we seek to demonstrate something at least as remarkable—genetic effects on our exposure to adverse environmental experiences. It sounds paradoxical. How can environmental experiences be genetically influenced? But, once you get over the surprise of the concept, it is in fact quite commonsensical.

A good way to introduce you to this concept is to quote at length from the summary of an article published in 1949 entitled, 'The accident-prone automobile driver' (Tillmann and Hobbs, 1949):

In this study the existence of accident-prone drivers has been demonstrated in the records of accidents from a bus company extending over a period of 6 years. The frequency of appearance of the same individual in the high accident group in multiple years has been noted. It has been shown that because of their high accident rate their importance in contributing to accidents far exceeds their numbers ... A group of high and low accident drivers ... have been interviewed and the differences in their personality and background have been noted. It has been demonstrated that the high accident

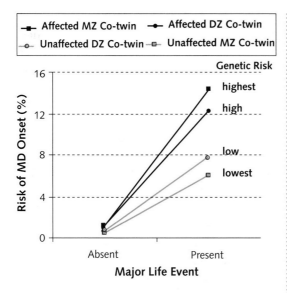

Figure 4.9 Risk of onset of major depression in a month as a function of inferred genetic risk and the presence or absence of a major stressful life event during that month.
Source: Kendler *et al.* (1995).

taxi driver most frequently comes from a home marked by parental divorce and instability... In adulthood, his occupation record is marked by frequent short-term employment and his connections with any firm are frequently terminated by the employer.

If our 'environmental risk factor' is traffic accidents, they will not be randomly distributed throughout the population. Furthermore, the rates of such accidents will result in part from personality traits that we know are heritable. So it is not so absurd to think that genes can influence aspects of our environment.

Indeed, a number of researchers have examined whether stressful life events are heritable. The answer has consistently been 'yes but only modestly.' Some of the bad things that happen to us in life are truly just bad luck. But for some of these bad things (and more than we would likely want to admit), we have played some

role in their occurrence. When we divided life events into those whose occurrence we could probably influence (such as inter-personal difficulties or legal problems) from fateful events such as medical illnesses or the death of relatives that were probably independent of anything we might do, we found much stronger evidence for genetic effects in the former than in the latter (Kendler *et al.*, 1999).

Our genes can influence our chances of exposure to at least some stressful life event experiences. Another important aspect of our environment is captured by the concept of social support. Social support can be defined as the degree of caring and emotional and physical sustenance an individual obtains from his or her social environment. Interest in the nature of human social relationships and their impact on health has a long tradition in the field of mental health and in the disciplines of sociology, social psychology, and public health. A large body of research has shown that the quality of social relationships predicts general health and mortality, psychiatric symptoms, and emotional adjustment to stress.

You can probably guess what is coming next. A series of twin studies have shown that social support is heritable—quite heritable, in fact. In one study where we measured social support twice over a 5-year interval, we found that the heritability of the stable part of social support was over 50% (Kendler, 1997). Our genetically influenced temperament has a lot to do with whether we are or are not typically exposed to large and caring social networks.

A third example of genetic control over exposure to the environment examines the concept of peer deviance. Peer deviance is important because it is a very strong predictor of future drug use and antisocial behavior. Thinking back to your teenage years, you can probably

remember some well-behaved teenagers who did their homework regularly, did not smoke or drink, and never got into trouble at school. You were also probably exposed to others who rarely did their school assignments, got started quite early with smoking and drinking to drunkenness, and enjoyed flaunting authority. In assessing peer deviance, we might ask you how much your friends were like the first or the second group of teenagers.

What influences the deviance of the peers that teenagers like to associate with? Part of it is the family and neighborhood you grew up in—what genetic epidemiologists would call 'shared environment.' But a longitudinal study of male twins in the Virginia twin study showed that, as twins got older, the genetic influences on peer deviance got stronger and stronger. We summarized these results as follows: '*As male twins mature and create their own social worlds, genetic factors play an increasingly important role in their choice of peers*' (Kendler *et al.*, 2007).

Although we have not dealt much with molecular genetics in this chapter, one recent research result published in *Nature* in 2008 so clearly illustrates the concept of 'genetic control of exposure to the environment' that we could not resist including it here. We quote from the abstract (Thorgeirsson *et al.*, 2008):

> **Here we identify a common variant in the nicotinic acetylcholine receptor gene cluster on chromosome 15q24 with an effect on smoking quantity, ND [nicotine dependence] and the risk of two smoking-related diseases in populations of European descent.**

One of these two 'smoking-related diseases' is carcinoma of the lung. What is going on here? Nicotine is the addictive substance in cigarette smoke. As found in a range of other studies, variants in certain brain nicotine receptors are

associated with risk for nicotine dependence, perhaps by increasing the pleasurable effects of nicotine or reducing its unpleasant side effects. If you have this genetic variant, you are more likely to go out into the environment, repeatedly purchase little paper-wrapped sticks of tobacco, light them, and inhale deeply into your lungs a mixture of smoke and hydrocarbons that, with repeated exposure, substantially increases your risk for lung cancer. So in some sense this nicotinic receptor gene is a cancer gene, but not at all in the usual sense. It causes cancer by increasing your probability of going out into the environment and exposing yourself to a quite carcinogenic environment—repeated inhalations of cigarette smoke.

By now we should have convinced you of the plausibility of the claim that genetic effects on our exposure to adverse environmental experiences are widespread for humans. One important consequence of these results (as well as the prior findings about gene–environment interaction) is a blurring of the boundaries between genes and environment (or nature and nurture). It won't be possible to understand the action of genes on human behavioral disorders and traits without a consideration of the environment.

Genes and development

All of our prior analyses of the impact of genetic risk factors have assumed that genes are static in their effects. In this final section of this long chapter, we hope to show you that, at least for some traits over some time periods in human development, this is a bad assumption to make. We inherit one set of genes from each of our parents, and aside from the occasional somatic mutation, those genes are with us until we die. But that does not mean that the effects of genes remain the same throughout our lives.

One of the most dramatic events in human development is the onset of menstruation in females. This has been studied extensively in humans and is strongly influenced by genetic factors. The last pair of monozygotic twins that K.S.K interviewed reported starting menstruating on the same day when they were 12 years old. The timing of many other features of human development—the onset of baldness in men, the graying of our hair or even the paunch in our bellies—is strongly influenced by our genes. So genes can be developmentally dynamic.

We will illustrate this with a single example taken from a longitudinal study of 2,490 Swedish twins under the direction of Dr Paul Lichtenstein (Lichtenstein *et al.*, 2007). In this study, symptoms of anxiety and depression were assessed by questionnaires filled out both by the twins and their parents at ages 8–9, 13–14, 16–17, and 19–20. The study covered a period of tremendous physical, intellectual, and emotional change—from mid-childhood through puberty and adolescence to young adulthood. In our analyses, we were able to take into account reports on the symptom levels of the twins both from themselves and their parents, and we could examine the continuity and discontinuity of the genetic and environmental influences. Focusing solely on genetic effects, these are most easily presented graphically and are shown in Figure 4.10.

In reading this figure, let's start with section A, which reflects the genetic risk factors for anxiety and depression that are active at age 8–9. What happens to those genetic effects over time? They attenuate dramatically between the

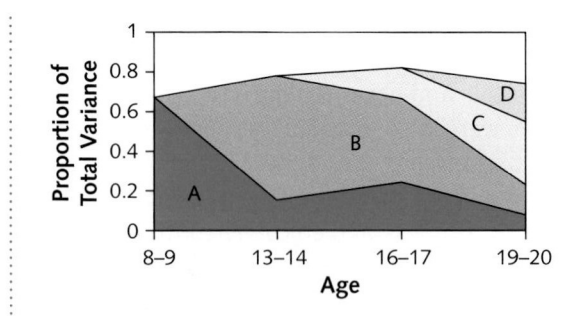

Figure 4.10 Genetic influences on symptoms of anxiety and depression from ages 8–9 to 19–20. See text for more details.
Source: Kendler *et al.* (2008).

ages of 8 and 9, and then sputter along, having a modest effect through to age 19–20. What this is telling us is that genetic influences on anxiety and depression that occur in childhood decline quite rapidly in their impact after puberty.

Section B of the figure reflects genetic effects on anxiety and depression that start at age 13–14, pretty soon after puberty for most of the sample. Compared with the genes that start prepubertally (section A), these effects attenuate much less over time. Although this is already rather complex, it is not the end of the story. There are small spurts of genetic innovation, as new genetic effects 'come on line' during development at age 16–17 (section C) and even age 19–20 (section D).

The bottom line in this short story is that, with respect to a quite common and important human trait, levels of symptoms of anxiety and depression, genetic effects are strikingly dynamic over time from childhood to young adulthood. We have evidence for genetic innovation (new genes coming on line) and genetic attenuation (genetic factors that decline in phenotypic impact with development). In thinking about genes and their impact on behavior, the time and stage of development matter.

Summary

1. Alcoholism is a particularly complex disorder, the risk of which is influenced by cultural, religious, psychological, and biological factors.

2. Both adoption and twin studies support a strong genetic contribution to the risk for alcoholism, with heritability estimates of around 50%.

3. Progress has been made in molecular genetic studies of alcoholism. We know that differences in alcohol-metabolizing genes, and in particular neurotransmitter receptors that interact with the alcohol molecule, can impact on the risk for alcoholism.

4. Major depression is one of the most common psychiatric disorders. The results of twin studies have been relatively consistent in suggesting a moderate degree of genetic influence on this disorder, with heritability estimates of 35–40%.

5. The leading current theory of human personality is known as the 'Big Five' and comprises Openness, Conscientiousness, Extroversion, Agreeableness and Neuroticism. All personality dimensions appear to be modestly influenced by genetic factors, with heritability estimates of 30–45%.

6. Genes often disrespect diagnostic boundaries between psychiatric disorders. Genetic risk factors for major depression and generalized anxiety disorder are very closely related. When a range of common psychiatric disorders is examined, genetic risk factors appear to predispose broadly to either internalizing disorders (characterized by anxiety and depression) or externalizing disorders (characterized by acting out behaviors and/or substance abuse).

7. Genetic factors that influence personality may also alter the risk for psychiatric disorders. For example, genes that predispose to high levels of the personality trait of neuroticism impact substantially on the risk for major depression.

8. From a biological and psychological perspective, males and females are different enough that the impact of genetic factors on behavior may not be the same in the two sexes. This is called a 'sex-modified genetic effect' and occurs in several psychiatric disorders including major depression and alcoholism.

9. Genes and environment often do not simply add together in their impact on risk for psychiatric disorders. Sometimes genes can moderate the sensitivity of individuals to the effects of environmental adversity. This is called gene–environment interaction. Genes can also influence an individual's selection of low- or high-risk environments. This is called gene–environment correlation.

10. Genes often act dynamically over time in their effect on psychiatric and psychological traits. For example, the genes that influence levels of anxiety and depression appear to change substantially pre- and post-puberty.

References

Burton, R. (1932). *The Anatomy of Melancholy*, Vol. 1. New York: E.P. Dutton and Co.

Cadoret, R.J., Cain, C.A., and Grove, W.M. (1980). Development of alcoholism in adoptees raised apart from alcoholic biologic relatives. *Arch Gen Psychiatry* **37**:561–563.

Cadoret, R.J., Cain, C.A., and Crowe, R.R. (1983). Evidence for gene–environment interaction in the development of adolescent antisocial behavior. *Behav Genet* **13**:301–310.

Cloninger, C.R., Bohman, M., Sigvardsson, S., and von Knorring, A.L. (1985). Psychopathology in adopted-out children of alcoholics: the Stockholm adoption study. In *Recent Developments in Alcoholism*, Vol. 3, pp. 37–51. Edited by M. Galanter. New York: Plenum Press.

Goodwin, D.W., Schulsinger, F., Hermansen, L., Guze, S.B., and Winokur, G. (1973). Alcohol problems in adoptees raised apart from alcoholic biological parents. *Arch Gen Psychiatry* **28**:238–243.

Heath, A.C., Bucholz, K.K., Madden, P.A., Dinwiddie, S.H., Slutske, W.S., Bierut, L.J., Statham, D.J., Dunne, M.P., Whitfield, J.B., and Martin, N.G. (1997). Genetic and environmental contributions to alcohol dependence risk in a national twin sample: consistency of findings in women and men. *Psychol Med* **27**:1381–1396.

Hinrichs, A.L., Wang, J.C., Bufe, B., Kwon, J.M., Budde, J., Allen, R., Bertelsen, S., Evans, W., Dick, D., *et al.* (2006). Functional variant in a bitter-taste receptor (hTAS2R16) influences risk of alcohol dependence. *Am J Hum Genet* **78**:103–111.

John, O.P. and Srivastava, S. (1999). The Big-Five trait taxonomy: history, measurement, and theoretical perspectives. In *Handbook of Personality: Theory and Research*, 2nd edn, pp. 102–139. Edited by L.A. Pervin and O.P. John. New York: Guilford Press.

Kendler, K.S. (1996). Major depression and generalised anxiety disorder. Same genes, (partly) different environments—revisited. *Br J Psychiatry Suppl.* 68–75.

Kendler, K.S. (1997). Social support: a genetic–epidemiologic analysis. *Am J Psychiatry* **154**:1398–1404.

Kendler, K.S. and Prescott, C.A. (2006). *Genes, Environment, and Psychopathology: Understanding the Causes of Psychiatric and Substance Use Disorders*. New York: Guilford Press.

Kendler, K.S., Heath, A.C., Neale, M.C., Kessler, R.C., and Eaves, L.J. (1992a). A population-based twin study of alcoholism in women. *J Am Med Assoc* **268**:1877–1882.

Kendler, K.S., Neale, M.C., Kessler, R.C., Heath, A.C., and Eaves, L.J. (1992b). Major depression and generalized anxiety disorder. Same genes, (partly) different environments? *Arch Gen Psychiatry* **49**:716–722.

Kendler, K.S., Pedersen, N., Johnson, L., Neale, M.C., and Mathe, A.A. (1993a). A pilot Swedish twin study of affective illness, including hospital- and population-ascertained subsamples. *Arch Gen Psychiatry* **50**:699–700.

Kendler, K.S., Neale, M.C., Kessler, R.C., Heath, A.C., and Eaves, L.J. (1993b). A longitudinal twin study of personality and major depression in women. *Arch Gen Psychiatry* **50**:853–862.

Kendler, K.S., Kessler, R.C., Walters, E.E., MacLean, C., Neale, M.C., Heath, A.C., and Eaves, L.J. (1995). Stressful life events, genetic liability, and onset of an episode of major depression in women. *Am J Psychiatry* **152**:833–842.

Kendler, K.S., Karkowski, L.M., and Prescott, C.A. (1999). The assessment of dependence in the study of stressful life events: validation using a twin design. *Psychol Med* **29**:1455–1460.

Kendler, K.S., Gardner, C.O., Neale, M.C., and Prescott, C.A. (2001). Genetic risk factors for major depression in men and women: similar or different heritabilities and same or partly distinct genes? *Psychol Med* **31**:605–616.

Kendler, K.S., Prescott, C.A., Myers, J., and Neale, M.C. (2003). The structure of genetic and environmental risk factors for common psychiatric and substance use disorders in men and women. *Arch Gen Psychiatry* **60**:929–937.

Kendler, K.S., Gardner, C.O., Gatz, M., and Pedersen, N.L. (2006a). The sources of co-morbidity between major depression and generalized anxiety disorder in a Swedish national twin sample. *Psychol Med* **37**:453–462.

Kendler, K.S., Gatz, M., Gardner, C., and Pedersen, N. (2006b). A Swedish national twin study of lifetime major depression. *Am J Psychiatry* **163**:109–114.

Kendler, K.S., Gatz, M., Gardner, C., and Pedersen, N.L. (2006c). Personality and major depression: a Swedish longitudinal, population-based twin study. *Arch Gen Psychiatry* **63**:1113–1120.

Kendler, K.S., Jacobson, K.C., Gardner, C.O., Gillespie, N.A., Aggen, S.H., and Prescott, C.A. (2007). Creating a social world: a developmental study of peer deviance. *Arch Gen Psychiatry* **64**:958–965.

Kendler, K.S., Gardner, C.O., and Lichtenstein, P. (2008). A developmental twin study of symptoms of anxiety and depression: evidence for genetic innovation and attenuation. *Psychol Med* **38**:1567–1575.

Kessler, R.C., McGonagle, K.A., Zhao, S., Nelson, C.B., Hughes, M., Eshleman, S., Wittchen, H.U., and Kendler, K.S. (1994). Lifetime and 12-month prevalence of DSM-III-R psychiatric disorders in the United States. Results from the National Comorbidity Survey. *Arch Gen Psychiatry* **51**:8–19.

Lake, R.I., Eaves, L.J., Maes, H.H., Heath, A.C., and Martin, N.G. (2000). Further evidence against the environmental transmission of individual differences in neuroticism from a collaborative study of 45,850 twins and relatives on two continents. *Behav Genet* **30**:223–233.

Lichtenstein, P., Tuvblad, C., Larsson, H., and Carlstrom, E. (2007). The Swedish Twin study of CHild and Adolescent Development: the TCHAD-study. *Twin Res Hum Genet* **10**:67–73.

Loehlin, J.C. (1992). *Genes and Environment in Personality Development*. Newbury Park, CA: Sage Publications.

Pickens, R.W., Svikis, D.S., McGue, M., Lykken, D.T., Heston, L.L., and Clayton, P.J. (1991). Heterogeneity in the inheritance of alcoholism. A study of male and female twins. *Arch Gen Psychiatry* **48**:19–28.

Prescott, C.A. and Kendler, K.S. (1999). Genetic and environmental contributions to alcohol abuse and dependence in a population-based sample of male twins. *Am J Psychiatry* **156**:34–40.

Prescott, C.A., Aggen, S.H., and Kendler, K.S. (1999). Sex differences in the sources of genetic liability to alcohol abuse and dependence in a population-based sample of U.S. twins. *Alcohol Clin Exp Res* **23**:1136–1144.

Roy, M.A., Neale, M.C., Pedersen, N.L., Mathe, A.A., and Kendler, K.S. (1995). A twin study of generalized anxiety disorder and major depression. *Psychol Med* **25**:1037–1049.

Sigvardsson, S., Bohman, M., and Cloninger, C.R. (1996). Replication of the Stockholm Adoption Study of alcoholism. Confirmatory cross-fostering analysis. *Arch Gen Psychiatry* **53**:681–687.

Sullivan, P.F., Neale, M.C., and Kendler, K.S. (2000). Genetic epidemiology of major depression: review and meta-analysis. *Am J Psychiatry* **157**:1552–1562.

Thorgeirsson, T.E., Geller, F., Sulem, P., Rafnar, T., Wiste, A., Magnusson, K.P., Manolescu, A., Thorleifsson, G., Stefansson, H. *et al.* (2008). A variant associated with nicotine dependence, lung cancer and peripheral arterial disease. *Nature* **452**:638–642.

Tillmann, W. and Hobbs, G. (1949). The accident-prone automobile driver. *Am J Psychiatry* **106**:321–331.

5 Genetic association analysis and candidate genes

[On the use of specific 'candidate' genes to measure association with a trait, some faltering efforts, and some strategies for improving reliability]

Academic life contains many torments. One is public speaking when you have to cram months of work that you still only partly understand into 15 minutes with an audience half asleep from the combined effects of lunch and three prior grueling hours of such talks by others. Then there is the agony of receiving the funding decision on a grant application, a grant that took weeks of anxiety-filled effort to complete and a decision that will impact on whether your post-docs and lab technicians will have a pay check or not. We should not forget the agony of having to attend strategy review meetings organized by funding agencies whose pointlessness you cannot comment on as the agency pays for your science. However, as bad as all these torments are, a thing you do not wish even on your competitors (well, at least not all of them) is to have to review psychiatric genetic association studies.

What makes them so dreary? Why is it after reviewing dozens of them over years, one looks with dread at seeing another invitation from a well-respected journal in your inbox? Reviewing these papers should be a simple decision: have the investigators shown that the DNA sequence variant they have studied is commoner in the group with the disorder than in the unaffected controls; that is, is it correct to conclude that possessing this sequence variant increases the chances of becoming psychotic, violent, depressed, autistic, or whatever disease they have studied? But it is not simple, and understanding why this is so takes us closer to many of the issues that surround the deeper question of how genes influence behavior.

The attraction of genetic association studies is their power to indicate cause. A functional DNA sequence change—a mutation that alters a protein—that changes a site at which the RNA molecule is cleaved or alters a promoter so as to discourage the start of RNA transcription will have been present since birth. Finding that everyone with the same change has a disease, and that no one without the disease has the variant, comes very close to proving a causal relation—the sort of finding all scientists strive for and dream about. This is true because of a simple principle: the genome that we are saving to make the next generation, the DNA in our eggs or sperm, is inviolable. The environment can't change it.

This means that, in claiming that a particular genetic variant is associated with schizophrenia, we do not worry that schizophrenia could cause the DNA to mutate. Genetic association studies are quite unlike studies that look for associations between sugar intake and hyperactivity, marital conflict and depression, watching violent films and committing crimes, studies where it is difficult, often impossible, to establish what is causing what.

The difficulty in interpreting genetic association studies lies not in confusing association with cause, but with assuming from the genetic data that 'gene X really is associated with schizophrenia'. There are hidden traps, a problem of unacknowledged assumptions that surface later to confound any simple interpretation of the findings. We need to explain how this could happen and we begin by contrasting the two ways psychiatric geneticists have used to find susceptibility genes: linkage and association.

Linkage versus association: 'candidate' genes

As we outlined in Chapter 3, linkage analysis has the major virtue of interrogating the entire genome all at once. In doing a genome-wide linkage study—when you place some 300 evenly spaced markers over all the chromosomes—you have a chance of detecting a signal from any gene, anywhere in the genome. A gene of large effect (meaning one that confers a more than fourfold risk of developing a disorder) has no place to hide from a well-designed linkage study. You don't need to know anything about that gene, where it is, or what it does. Because we are so ignorant about the causes of psychiatric disorders, linkage analysis is an attractive method.

However, linkage analysis has two important drawbacks. Firstly, it has low power. It is only good at detecting relatively large genetic signals—gene regions that contain variants that quite substantially alter the risk for a disorder. Secondly, even when you find positive results, linkage signals are very broad, typically smeared over tens of millions of base pairs, a region large enough to contain hundreds, if not thousands, of genes.

Association analysis has the opposite combination of strengths and weaknesses. Firstly, signals detected by association are much more focused, typically stretching over tens of thousands rather than tens of millions of DNA base pairs. Secondly, association analysis can detect genes with modest effects on disease risk. The main drawback to association is that, until recently, it could not screen the genome, as linkage can. Instead, you could use a few (typically less than 20) markers in what is called a 'candidate' gene. You gather affected individuals—your cases—and a group of matched unaffected individuals—your controls—and see whether the frequency of the marker variants differs between the two groups.

Firstly, a sequence polymorphism is needed, preferably in the coding region of a candidate gene (shown at the top of Figure 5.1). In this example, the polymorphism has two alleles (a and g), which form three genotypes (the two homozygotes, aa and gg, and the heterozygote, ag). Secondly, you need a couple of hundred patients with a psychiatric illness (such as schizophrenia) and the same number of controls (unaffected people who are the same in every way to the cases (same age, sex, and so on)). Thirdly, cases and controls must be genotyped and classified as aa, ag or, gg, as shown in the lower right of the figure. Finally, a statistical test is needed to determine whether the two columns of figures are significantly different (in this case they are) or not.

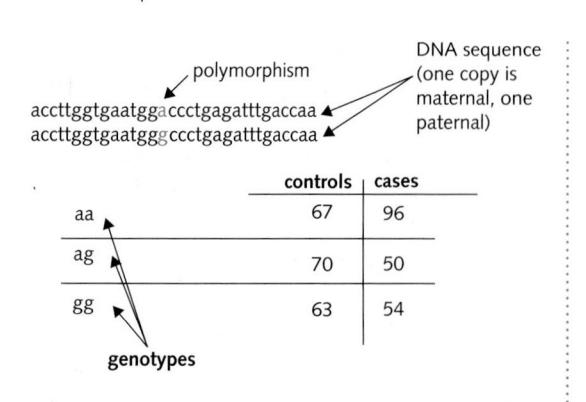

Figure 5.1 Ingredients of a genetic association test.

The candidate gene approach itself comes in two flavors. In the more common approach, the gene is picked because you think it might have something to do with the physiology of the illness. Thus, these genes are called 'physiological candidate' genes. In the second approach, genes are picked because of where they lie in the genome; in particular because they are under linkage peaks. Such genes are called 'positional candidates'.

Physiological candidate genes at first seemed appealing, and there were high hopes that their analysis would lead to major breakthroughs in the genetics of schizophrenia. There was, however, one deep problem with this method: you had to be able to pick good candidate genes, genes that had a plausible chance of being involved in the physiology of the disorder. To pick good physiological candidate genes, you needed to know something about what caused the disorder, which of course we did not when it came to schizophrenia. Just to be clear about what we mean here—two examples of good physiological candidate genes would be the insulin gene if you were studying diabetes or a gene for a cholesterol receptor if you were studying heart disease. While there is no guarantee that variants in these genes would influence risk for the disease, at least you know that the

products of these genes are directly involved in the disease process.

Now, one of the great appeals of applying genetic approaches to psychiatric illness was the chance it offered to understand a disorder's origins, its etiology, without recourse to prior knowledge. The old-fashioned top-down approaches had not worked—boiling down urine, blood, or cerebrospinal fluid (the fluid in which your brain and spinal cord float) to look for key biological differences between the psychiatrically well and ill had not worked. Molecular geneticists arrived and said, 'We will solve your problem from the bottom-up. We know from all those good family, twin, and adoption studies that genes must play a role in the etiology of psychiatric illness. Just build us some good labs and give us lots of grant money and we will find those genes that will lead us to the cause.' But when it came to genetic association studies, to get genes they needed to know the cause of the illness—which is what we hired them to find out in the first place.

The fact that the choice of candidate genes might be ad hoc, a question of the scientist's particular interests and prejudices, should not matter if the way of validating their involvement in the disease is robust. And, on the face of it, the validation is straight forward. We ask whether the frequency of a sequence variant in the candidate gene is higher in those with the disease than those without. The question can be answered by well-established tests, tests used in all areas of science, the sort of tests that tell us whether drugs are effective or not, or what risk factors contribute to heart disease and cancer. Entire university departments are staffed with people who do this sort of thing: they are called statisticians. Surely when I carry out or review a genetic association study, if I don't understand how the statistical test works, all I need do is ring up the Department of Statistics and get a statistician to help. Admittedly statisticians may not be fun to talk to ('What's the difference between a statistician and an accountant? The statistician looks at the other person's shoe'), but statistics is a well-established discipline with a lot of quantitative methodology, lots of equations, and computers; in short pretty reliable stuff.

Late on a Friday evening, you get a request from the *Journal of Uninteresting Studies* to review their latest submission, entitled 'Evidence that *DUP25* contributes to the risk of developing anxiety'. It's the first time this prestigious magazine has asked for your views, and it's good for your career to develop a close, friendly relationship with the editors (for after all, you hope soon to submit your own paper, entitled 'Evidence that *DUP30* contributes to the risk of developing anxiety'). How are you going to decide whether the results are right or not?

Fleeting candidates: DUP25

In 2001, *Cell* published a paper about a chromosomal duplication, something you can see down a microscope, that was associated with anxiety (Gratacos *et al.*, 2001). *Cell* has a thoroughbred pedigree as a high-profile, well-respected science journal. The authors, a group from Barcelona, wrote: '*We have identified an interstitial duplication of human chromosome 15q24–26 (named DUP25) which is significantly associated with panic/agoraphobia/social phobia/ joint laxity in families and with panic disorder in nonfamilial cases.*' Figure 5.2 shows a picture from the paper showing what they found.

The dots are two DNA probes labeled with different-colored fluorescent dyes and hybridized

to a patient's chromosomes (a pair of chromosome 15 homologs). You can see that there appear to be four, not two, pale dots. This indicates that the DNA homologous to the labeled probe is duplicated (*DUP25*). '*Ninety percent of patients diagnosed with one or several anxiety disorders had the duplication. Remarkably, all patients with panic disorder with or without agoraphobia and all patients with social phobia carried DUP25.*' An impressive finding, and even if '*20% of patients with DUP25 did not have any anxiety phenotypes*', it was still enough to get the paper through the review process and out into the world. Was the result true?

One way to find out is to replicate: is *DUP25* also more prevalent in the anxious patients in your clinical sample, just as it is in that of the authors' sample? When other groups tried this, the answer was straightforward: no *DUP25* occurred in either cases or controls. So was anxiety in Barcelona due, in part, to a rare sequence variant found only in Catalonia? No, not that either, for when some geneticists in the UK (Tabiner *et al.*, 2003) tested the Spanish samples that had been used in the original study they reported:

> There was no evidence of a duplication of signals in distal 15q that would be indicative of DUP25 in any of the 16 patient samples or in any of the 40 control samples... It is difficult to think of any logical scientific or technical explanation for the differences between the two laboratories in scoring the positive control cultures. However, we were unable to detect any DUP25-positive cells, either in the positive control samples from CEPH or in our patient or control samples. Furthermore, we have never had a report of such a duplication in any of the thousands of diagnostic samples that have been scored on high-resolution chromosomes in our laboratory.

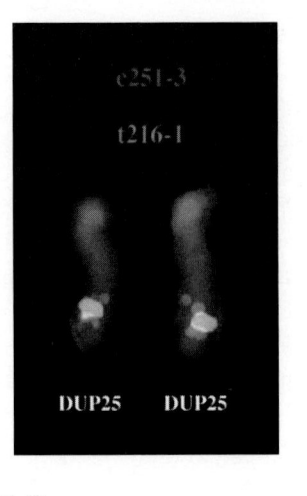

Figure 5.2 Duplication of *DUP25* on chromosome 15.
Source: Gratacos *et al.* (2001).

Coquettish candidates: COMT

DUP25 is unusual in a number of ways: it was not a candidate gene, it could not be replicated, and it probably didn't exist in the first place—it was a technical artifact. So in the end, making a decision as to its importance was easy: it's not important. The more typical situation is more complicated. For example, in genetic association studies of schizophrenia, authors pick a candidate gene implicated from one of the etiologic theories of the psychiatric disease, itself based on a large and forbidding neuroscience literature.

The history of neuroscience can briefly be summarized as progressing from the discovery that a specific type of cell (the neuron) is the functional unit of the brain (the alternative view was that there was a continuous connecting membrane arranged like a set of wires) to the discovery of specialized connections between cells (the synapse) and the chemicals that carried information from one side of the synapse to the other (neurotransmitters) (see Chapter 10 for a description of neurons and neurotransmitters).

Neurotransmitters have always fascinated psychiatrists. Many of the drugs used to treat psychiatric and neurological illnesses act by mimicking, blocking, prolonging the life of, or otherwise interfering with neurotransmitters. Many illicit psychoactive drugs act in the same way: the fact that you can make yourself excited, calm, happy, paranoid, depressed, transcendental, or traumatized by interfering with neurotransmitter function has spurred psychiatrists to investigate whether abnormalities of neurotransmitter function are a cause of psychiatric disease.

The neurotransmitter dopamine has been a magnet for the attention of psychosis researchers in large part because, with stunning consistency, drugs that treat the symptoms of schizophrenia block one particular class of dopamine receptors in the brain. Furthermore, their potency in treating symptoms and blocking the receptor are uncannily correlated. These two sets of observations—which are widely accepted—form the basis of the dopamine hypothesis of schizophrenia—far and away the most influential theory from its first proposal in the 1970s to today. This theory posits that, in schizophrenics, the dopamine system is somehow and somewhere hyperactive.

Dopamine itself is not encoded by a gene: the body makes it from raw ingredients using a series of enzymes that are encoded by genes. Once released, the chemical can be degraded enzymatically or by re-uptake into neurons via a transporter in the cell membrane (Figure 5.3).

Theoretically, alterations in any of these steps could lead to functional hyperactivity: excess production, excess release, excess stimulation,

Why did we persist with linkage studies for so long? Partly from the hope that just one family might be found, a pedigree that might yield one mutation in a gene that would completely open up the biology of these opaque illnesses. Partly, it has to be admitted, hope was justified by the success of the mouse studies we describe in Chapter 7: mapping of complex phenotypes performed in crosses between inbred strains of rodents. Many of the human linkage studies of complex phenotypes undertaken in the 1990s were powered on the basis that the genetic architecture in humans would reflect that observed in rodents: namely that the distribution of effect sizes would be approximately exponential, with a few loci explaining perhaps 10% of the phenotypic variation and lots of genes with increasingly smaller effects. But the main reason we continued to use family-based methods was the lack of anything better.

Predicting success: study power

One simple and unavoidable interpretation of the relative failure of linkage mapping was that the method was underpowered, a point made, among others, by Neil Risch and Kathleen Merikangas in 1996 as follows: '*The modest nature of the gene effects for these disorders likely explains the contradictory and inconclusive claims about their identification*' (Risch and Merikangas, 1996). From which follows the obvious question: 'How large does a gene effect need to be in order to be detectable by linkage analysis?' Risch and Merikangas answered this question as follows. Firstly, they defined the gene effect as the increase in risk of developing illness that a genotype confers, or in short the genotype relative risk

(GRR is the acronym). A GRR of 2 means that, if you have the genotype that confers susceptibility, your risk of becoming ill is twice that of someone who does not have the genotype. From working out how many families would be needed to detect different GRR values, they concluded that '*linkage analysis for loci conferring GRR of about 2 or less will never allow identification because the number of families required (more than ~2500) is not practically achievable.*' In fact more than 10,000 families are needed, and, for smaller effects we're talking millions of mothers, fathers, sons, and daughters. Entire nations would have to give up their family history, their disease status, and a small ocean of blood if geneticists were to find the genes that make people ill.

Key paper

Risch, N. and Merikangas, K. (1996). The future of genetic studies of complex human diseases. *Science* **273**:1516–1517.

A key paper that argued for the use of association studies and led to the development of GWAS.

There is another strategy, which we introduced in Chapter 5: genetic association, where we compare the frequencies of genotypes in those with and without disease. It's a good approach for finding small genetic effects, but it has a major drawback: the method needs a candidate gene, a gene the investigator feels confident is likely to be involved. This might work for metabolic disorders where a wealth of biochemistry could point to likely candidates (in fact, as the diabetologists later learnt to their dismay, this information didn't help), but for psychiatric disorders, where there were almost no good clues, there were no candidates. Furthermore, genetic association required not only a candidate gene, but also a candidate polymorphism to test: someone would have had to sequence the gene to identify the variants.

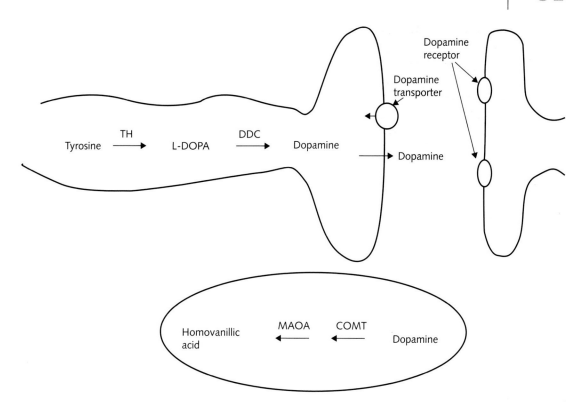

Figure 5.3 Metabolism of dopamine. Dopamine is manufactured from the amino acid tyrosine through the action of two enzymes, tyrosine hydroxylase (TH) and DOPA decarboxylase (DDC), shown here acting within a neuron. Dopamine is released from the neuron and can then act on dopamine receptors, and can then be taken back into the neuron via a dopamine transporter or into another cell type where it is degraded by the action of two enzymes, catechol-*O*-methyl-transferase (COMT) and monoamine oxidase (MAO—there are two variants known as MAOA and MAOB).

excess receptor number, or reduced removal. Despite the accumulated biochemical and neuroanatomical knowledge about dopamine, after 30 years of research no one had been able to prove whether the dopamine hypothesis is true or false.

Genetic association studies, it was widely hoped, would settle this issue once and for all. Dopamine is degraded in several ways, but one of the most important is by an enzyme called catechol-O-methyltransferase or COMT for short (Figure 5.3). As you might gather from the name, it sticks a methyl group (one carbon and three hydrogens) onto the dopamine

molecule. Unlike dopamine, COMT is a protein encoded by a gene and that gene contains a sequence variant that alters the activity of the enzyme: one form is less efficient at breaking down dopamine. Consequently, a test of the dopamine hypothesis is that individuals with the inefficient COMT gene variant will be at greater risk of developing schizophrenia. This is because more dopamine will hang around longer in the synapse in a person with the inefficient form of COMT. Therefore, the question can be put this way: is the inefficient COMT variant more common in schizophrenics than in controls? If it is, then here is evidence in favor of the dopamine hypothesis.

The experiment is straightforward: I determine the frequency of the *COMT* gene variant in 100 cases and 100 controls, which might be 23% in schizophrenics and 30% in controls. I assume that in reality there is no difference in the frequency of the genetic variant between patients and controls, so any difference I do see is due to chance. I then work out the probability that the observed difference is due to chance. This is usually done mathematically, but an easier way to see what's going on (and a method we also use) is to simulate the experiment many times on a computer, on the assumption that there is indeed no real difference. By using a random number generator, I have access to infinitely large populations of cases and controls (of the sick and the well), in which the frequency of the *COMT* variant is the same. I repeatedly select 100 individuals at random from each population and calculate the frequency of the variant in the two samples. I might find that a difference as big, or bigger, than the one I found in my real experiment occurs in a fifth of the simulated experiments. This means the result of the real experiment could easily have occurred by chance alone. Conventionally, when the probability drops to less than 1 in 20 (a 5% chance), I conclude that my results cast doubt on my first assumption, namely that there is no difference in the frequency between the two groups.

In 1996, genetic association was used in exactly this way. '*This study investigated this [COMT] polymorphism in 78 unrelated schizophrenic patients and 78 comparison subjects matched for age and ethnicity. The frequency of the polymorphism [the key variant] was 0.51 in the schizophrenic patients and 0.53 in the comparison subjects, and no significant allelic or genotypic associations were observed*' (Daniels *et al.*, 1996). That should do it. No association. The dopamine hypothesis has failed the test.

But by 2003, there were 18 further publications that reported the results of the same kind of study; by 2006, the number had grown to 44. Nevertheless, 11 years after the first study, we still have no systematic evidence that the presence of an inefficient form of the COMT protein at synapses increases the risk for schizophrenia. A careful meta-analysis was performed by one of us (J.F.) and concluded that when including only the better-designed studies, no evidence was found for any association between the *COMT* gene and schizophrenia (Munafò *et al.*, 2005). (See Box 5.1 for a description of meta-analyses.) Why, you might ask, did scientists keep testing this hypothesis?

One important reason why studies of *COMT* kept coming is that a few of the individual studies did produce significant results. The problem here is that if you do enough statistical tests, a few of them will turn out to be positive by chance alone. Think about rolling three dice. It is, by chance, quite unlikely to roll all 'ones' (if you have true dice it should occur once out of every 6^3 times or once in 216 rolls). But if you sit there for a while and roll the dice enough times, you are guaranteed, if you are patient enough, to get three ones.

Gauging probabilities and biases

When we use genetic association to find genes involved in psychiatric illness, the answer we get back is usually a P value, or some similar statistic, whose interpretation is not simple. The result of the genetic association test, in a rather counter-intuitive fashion, is defined by the likelihood that it is wrong. The P value that is conventionally used is 0.05, 1 in 20, or 5%, a figure that has a sacrosanct place in medical research, not always well deserved. It is particularly inappropriate for association studies of complex diseases and we can explain why.

Let's assume, as a first approximation, that we have 20,000 human genes of which 20 are involved in the etiology of schizophrenia. If I pick a gene at random (which is almost what we are doing when we study physiological candidate genes because we have so little idea of which genes are actually involved), that gene has 20/20,000 or a 1/1,000 chances of being a real schizophrenia susceptibility gene. Imagine I am a successful scientist with a grant to study, by genetic association, 1,000 of these genes using the case–control design. Applying the 5% P value, we would expect that around 50 out of our 1,000 genes will be 'significant' by chance alone—random results that we call by the inappropriately benign phrase 'false positives.' (These are anything but benign because other research groups will often spend months of time and thousands of dollars trying to replicate such results.) Of the 1,000 genes, one is likely to be a true positive. So, to a rough first approximation, our well-funded project would be expected to produce 51 significant results from our 1,000 genes tested of which 50 (roughly 98%) are false.

Clearly, we need to use much more stringent P values (that is, much lower than 5%) to give us a more reasonable proportion of true positive findings. In one of the deeper ironies of the field of psychiatric genetics, this problem was much better worked out for linkage studies. Due to the influence of one statistical geneticist—Newton Morton—it was very early imprinted on the field that an LOD ($\log_{10}$ of odds) score of 3.0 (which depending on some technical issues equals a P value of between 0.001 and 0.0001) was needed to declare significant linkage. This is about right in that most linkage studies would involve something like 300 different tests. With stunning inconsistency, association studies, when they began to appear in the literature, utilized a P value of 0.05, even though the multiple testing problem was far greater

than in linkage studies. This fateful decision allowed many scientists to publish 'significant' association results and was therefore very beneficial to their Curriculum Vitae. But it was certainly not so helpful to the science.

A second reason why people kept testing the *COMT* gene and schizophrenia returns us to the realm of the sociology of science. Put simply, it made such a good story, it just had to be true. In defending a truly powerful theory, this position is not as illogical as it sounds. Astronomers in the 19th century noted abnormalities in the orbit of Uranus that could not be explained by the principles of Newtonian theories. As a result of these findings, they could have concluded that there was something wrong with Newton's theories but they didn't; the theory had been so good in other ways, leading them to suspect that there might be some way of reconciling the findings with Newtonian mechanics. So they kept looking for other explanations, assuming the theory was right. Their perseverance was rewarded when they discovered the new planet of Neptune whose gravitational influences explained the abnormalities in Uranus's orbit.

To put it politely, the dopamine hypothesis of schizophrenia is not in the same league as Newton—not even close. But scientists have strong affiliations to their theories, not unlike many people's affiliation to their political parties. *COMT* was not the only dopamine gene repeatedly tested in schizophrenia. For example, there have been multiple case–control association studies of the dopamine transporter gene (the product of which 'sucks up' dopamine back into the pre-synaptic cell), and dozens and dozens of studies of the dopamine receptors of which there are five, each with their own gene. The results have not all been negative. Indeed, the gene for one type of dopamine receptor—called *DRD2*—has a variant that alters an amino acid in the protein. In 2008, a meta-analysis suggested that this variant did modestly influence the risk for schizophrenia (Allen *et al.*, 2008).

The COMT gene story demonstrates a pattern that is repeated with other genetic association studies: a physiological candidate gene is picked based on quite weak evidence of disease involvement. Lots of studies are done using liberal statistical criteria for significance. Some positive studies emerge that then generate more attempts to replicate them. Meta-analyses then begin to accumulate, typically showing that the combined effect is either small or non-existent. This pattern is common enough to warrant a couple more examples, which also demonstrate some of the pitfalls of interpretation and the difficulties in assessing the robustness of the evidence.

Groundswell candidates: DRD2

Dopamine is also blamed for alcoholism. There is good evidence that part of the pleasurable effect obtained when one drinks alcohol is mediated by dopamine. Not surprisingly attempts have been made to nail the problem of alcoholism to variation in dopamine receptors. In 1990, Kenneth Blum at San Antonio and Ernest Noble at UCLA wrote in the *Journal of the American Medical Association* (Blum *et al.*, 1990):

> We report the first allelic association of the dopamine D2 receptor gene in alcoholism... In the present samples, the presence of A1 allele of the dopamine D2 receptor gene correctly classified 77% of alcoholics, and its absence classified 72% of nonalcoholics.

> The polymorphic pattern of this receptor gene suggests that a gene that confers susceptibility to at least one form of alcoholism is located on the q22–q23 region of chromosome 11.

In other words, Blum and Noble had found a genetic variant that predicted susceptibility to alcoholism, which was big news indeed.

Four years later, the story deserved a commentary in *Science*—two major failures to confirm their findings out of three studies didn't look good for the Blum and Noble work. But the bad news wasn't over. In 1992, a study from a group at Washington University in St Louis initially appeared to support the A1 connection—but Washington University psychiatrist Robert Cloninger says that when the group expanded the sample it found, to his 'chagrin', that the association between the D2 receptor and alcoholism 'faded out.' In all, the article concluded that '*attempts to replicate the finding have been largely unsuccessful.*' Joel Gelernter had complained, '*It is now four years since the paper came out and we still don't have a mutation or anything that could explain the effects that this A1 allele is supposed to convey.*'

Blum and Noble didn't take this lying down. They wrote to *Science*, criticizing the article for sending 'the wrong message' and creating '*embarrassment for scientists who are pioneering at the forefront of research in the genetics of addictive–compulsive disorder.*' In their view, '*We are witnessing the birth of a new paradigm in our understanding of the genetic basis of addictive–compulsive behaviors, and from the total evidence available it should be clear that the DRD2 gene will continue to play an important role in these behaviors*' (Blum and Noble, 1994). Blum and Noble argued against Cloninger's negative result as follows: '*Careful scrutiny of their follow up paper revealed that the sample of alcoholics in the second study was heterogeneous, including both severe and less severe alcoholics. The inclusion of less severe alcoholics diluted the sample.'* In other words, the genetic effect will vary depending on whether it is measured in those with mild or severe alcohol dependence.

Back in 1993, an analysis of all of the available studies of the A1 allele of the *DRD2* gene concluded: *'The findings to date can best be explained by more conservative interpretations than a confirmed physiologically important allelic association between DRD2 alleles and alcoholism'* (Gelernter *et al.*, 1993). By 2007, over 40 studies of the *DRD2* gene and alcoholism had been published. Again, part of the reason for the continuing interest is the inherent attraction of the idea, its biological plausibility.

Another reason, still sociological, is that scientific journals afford more importance to positive than negative results. This is usually difficult to observe, as a lot of studies are needed to detect its effect, but sufficient were available in the *DRD2* alcoholism literature for us to be certain of its existence (Munafò *et al.*, 2007). Figure 5.4 shows the effect size of each study (y-axis) against the year of publication (x-axis). The correlation is clear and highly significant: studies with the largest effects were published first, while negative studies only appeared later.

As with the *COMT* story, there are also biological reasons for the continuing interest in *DRD2*. Firstly, it might be that the effect was just too small too detect. We can estimate just how small by putting together data from all of the published samples: combined analyses of all *DRD2* studies indicated that, if the effect was there, it accounted for as little as 0.2% of the variation in alcoholism. This is so small that no single study had enough subjects to detect the effect reliably. Small effect size could explain the inconsistent results.

Secondly, conflicting results might arise because samples had been taken from different populations that happened to differ at the *DRD2* locus for reasons other than alcoholism. A key assumption of genetic association is that the two groups—cases and controls—are equivalent in all respects other than the disease being tested. Consider what would be found if that assumption was relaxed.

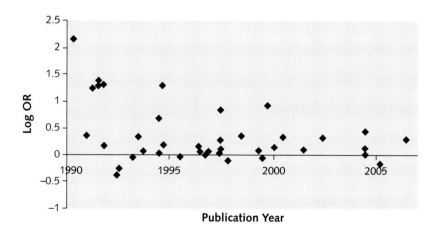

Figure 5.4 Effect size of each study on *DRD2* and alcoholism against the year of publication (OR, odds ratio). Source: Munafo *et al.* (2007).

The frequencies of alleles at many genes differ among ethnic groups, so that an association study comparing alcoholics of one ethnicity with non-alcoholics of another would identify a large number of significant differences, none related to alcoholism. For example, if you carried out a study of the genetic basis of religion and compared gene frequencies in groups who practice Buddhism and those who do not, you would be very likely to find many significant differences, solely due to the fact that Buddhism is commoner in East Asians than it is in Europeans, and there are many genetic differences between East Asians and Europeans. Even a slight degree of mismatching in the ethnicity of the cases and controls could introduce bias into the results.

This problem of genetic admixture is often blamed for the reporting of spurious associations, although, to be fair, it's not that easy to find confirmed examples. In fact, a joint analysis of *DRD2* studies in different ethnic populations gives the same answer as analyzing the studies separately (again the large number of *DRD2* papers makes this possible) (Munafò *et al.*, 2007), indicating that ethnic heterogeneity is probably not an issue in this case, nor indeed in the vast majority of other disorders that have been studied by genetic association.

Prozac party candidates: 5-HTT

In 1996, Peter Lesch, from the University of Wurzburg in Germany, in collaboration with a group at the National Institute of Mental Health (NIMH) in Bethesda, published, in *Science*, the results of a genetic association study between a personality trait and a polymorphism in the serotonin (or 5-hydroxytryptamine, 5-HT) transporter gene (5-HTT) (Lesch *et al.*, 1996).

In the same way that the dopamine theory has dominated neurobiological theories of the cause of schizophrenia, 'something wrong with serotonin' has been a standard theory of the origin of depression for some time, again despite the lack of conclusive evidence. Serotonin, like dopamine, is a neurotransmitter in the brain, released by neurons and degraded or re-used by re-uptake via a transporter in the cell membrane, the serotonin transporter. There's evidence that the amount of serotonin available to neurons correlates with mood: low levels correlate with the occurrence and the lethality of suicide attempts and can be used to predict future suicide attempts. Prozac and other drugs that block the re-uptake of serotonin (serotonin reuptake inhibitors or SSRIs) are effective antidepressants and anxiolytics, presumably because of the increased availability of serotonin at the synapse. Finding any evidence that genetic variants in the serotonin system are associated with mood disorders could, according to NIMH Director Tom Insel, in 2005, '*lead to a genetic test for vulnerability to depression and a way to predict which patients might respond best to serotonin-selective antidepressants.*' So when Lesch found a polymorphism at the start of the serotonin transporter gene that increased the amount of functional transporter (Figure 5.5), you can see how the idea must have struck home: people with the polymorphism will have more transporter—therefore they will take up more serotonin, there will be less available serotonin, and they will be depressed.

In fact, he found the complete opposite. He measured the association between the polymorphism and a personality trait called neuroticism, which is genetically related to anxiety and depression (that is, a large proportion of the

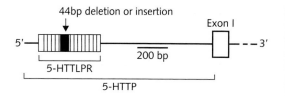

44bp deletion or insertion

Exon I

5′

200 bp

5-HTTLPR

5-HTTP

Figure 5.5 Serotonin is also known as 5-hydroxytryptamine (5-HT), so the promoter is denoted as 5-HTTP. On the left is the region of the gene called the promoter, where transcription starts, containing a repeated sequence motif (shown as a box with bars and marked 5-HTTLPR—the serotonin-transporter-linked polymorphic region). Subsequent work has shown that there is considerable sequence diversity in the promoter, in addition to the length polymorphism.
Source: Lesch *et al.* (1996).

genetic variants that contribute to variation in neuroticism also contribute to susceptibility to anxiety and depression) (see Chapter 4, p. 64). As personality traits are, by definition, stable and enduring characteristics and relatively easy to measure, they could be a better phenotype for genetic studies than mood itself, which is transient and difficult to assess.

Lesch found differences in the DNA sequence at the start of the serotonin transporter gene, differences that altered the amount of gene product. There were two alleles, which he called *s* (for short) and *l* (for long) at the transporter (later work has established that the situation is considerably more complicated and that there are multiple alleles). Individuals with an *s* allele were more neurotic and more prone to anxiety and depression than individuals with an *l* allele. That ought to mean that the *s* allele increases the amount of transporter. However, '*the basal activity of the* l *variant was more than twice that of the* s *form of the serotonin transporter gene promoter.*' Lesch argued his way out of this unexpected finding on the following grounds:

'The therapeutic effects of the SSRIs have primarily been demonstrated in neuropsychiatric patients, who may have some primary serotonin or other neurotransmitter dysfunction that is ameliorated by the SSRIs, whereas our findings are in a sample of the general population.' In other words, serotonin behaves differently in patients than it does in you or me.

The subsequent decade has seen literally hundreds of papers investigating the role of the transporter gene in psychiatric disorders. As with *DRD2* and schizophrenia, many papers report an association and many papers don't. In an attempt to resolve the issue, in 2002, one of us (J.F.) and a colleague, Marcus Munafò, reviewed the data from 20 papers and concluded that there was no effect (Munafò *et al.*, 2003). We also carried out a large study, enrolling the 2,000 most and least neurotic people in the south west of England, selected from a community sample of more than 88,000 people. We tested whether there was an association with the serotonin transporter polymorphism. There wasn't (Willis-Owen *et al.*, 2005). Surely the story would end there?

It did not. A number of objections to our findings were raised: the assessment of neuroticism we used was different from that in the Lesch study, the study was in a different population, the genetic effects at the tails of the distribution might be different from those in the middle, and the environmental effects might somehow be different. A lot of interest was then being paid to gene–environment interactions: might there be a differential effect in people with the *s* allele who had had a stressful life event? It was not enough to have the genetic predisposition: there had to be an environmental stressor for its effect to be manifest.

5-HTT gene–environment interactions

Richie Poulton and colleagues in New Zealand have for many years been collecting information on the same 1,000 people, contacting them every year and flying them back home if necessary, to find out what has happened to them and assess how they are. The cohort were in their 20s when Poulton, together with Terrie Moffitt at the Institute of Psychiatry in London and her partner Avshalom Caspi, carried out a genetic analysis of the 5-HTT gene. They reported in *Science*: '*The effect of life events on informant reports of depression was stronger among individuals carrying an s allele than among l/l homozygotes. These analyses attest that the 5-HTT gene interacts with life events to predict depression symptoms, an increase in symptoms, depression diagnoses, new-onset diagnoses, suicidality, and an informant's report of depressed behavior*' (Caspi et al., 2003).

Psychiatrists and psychologists around the world have loved this piece of work; it's inventive and interesting and suits our belief that genes act in complicated ways, in combination with the environment, to work their effects. Genetic tests for this gene variant are currently being marketed on the internet (for those who can afford them). There are, naturally, attempts to replicate the result—14 independent studies (by 2009) including the original report (Munafò et al., 2009). But only one reported a statistically significant interaction apparently identical to that observed in the original report. Three studies reported no evidence of a statistically significant interaction, one interpreted their results as offering 'modest support' based on subgroup analyses, and six reported a significant interaction, which was different from that observed in the original report.

Overall, when we reviewed the literature, the positive results for the serotonin-transporter-linked polymorphic region (5-HTTLPR) interactions are still compatible with chance findings (Munafò et al., 2009). Moreover, as the main effect of 5-HTTLPR genotype and the interaction effect between 5-HTTLPR and environment on risk of depression are negligible, given reasonable assumptions regarding likely genetic and environmental effect sizes, the published studies are underpowered. And a significant finding from an underpowered study is a false positive.

Why reviewing association studies induces headaches

We hope by now you understand and maybe even sympathize with our suffering at yet another request to review yet another genetic association study. The studies all begin the same way. Some rather unconvincing story is told trying to relate a physiological candidate gene to schizophrenia, alcoholism, depression, personality disorder, or autism. The methods section describes a sample size of about 200 cases and 200 controls (too small to have power to detect any but the largest of effects). Many markers are tested against a range of diagnostic definitions and, sure enough, a few modest P values emerge, allowing the authors to claim in their conclusion that this gene is associated with disease. Perhaps like a lapsed Catholic forced back to mass, you knew what was coming but the sense of belief was gone.

'*The great tragedy of science—the slaying of a beautiful hypothesis by an ugly fact*' (Thomas Huxley,

1825–1895) has not stopped the seemingly endless production of genetic association studies, nor dampened enthusiastic endorsement of claims to have identified genes contributing to psychiatric disease, as well as to personality, sexual orientation, intelligence, even empathy. It is true that there are cases where things have simply gone wrong (as the DUP25 example shows). And there are statistical problems: the significance threshold (the P value to use to decide whether a result is significant or not) has been set too high so that the result is likely to be a false positive. But these factors are not enough to hold back the tide of publications.

We've emphasized the role that the sociology of science plays, in wedding scientists to received opinion, so that there is entrenched opposition to accepting a negative result (which is anyway more difficult to publish than a positive result). The pattern of the COMT and 5-HTT stories is typical: a physiological candidate gene is picked based on quite weak evidence of disease involvement. Lots of studies are done using liberal statistical criteria for significance. Some positive studies emerge that generate more attempts to replicate. And so on, ad infinitum.

One other reason why negative association studies do not slay the theories that gave birth to them is that the experimental design makes it impossible for a negative result to do so. All a negative result tells you is that the effect could not be detected. It might be there, just too small to see. A common thread running through all of the genetic association studies is that the effects are small, contributing to less than 1% of the variation in the phenotype, or increasing the risk of the disorder by a small amount. This realization has led people to consider whether there might be circumstances in which the effects could be increased.

For example, could we study populations in which the total genetic variation is less, so that the contribution of any one variant is relatively increased? This genetic simplification is possible with model organisms but is difficult to do in humans. Results from studying island populations (in Sardinia, Croatia, and the Shetlands, for instance), where the degree of relatedness between individuals is higher than in other parts of the world, has not radically improved things (Eaves *et al.*, 2000): finding the molecular basis of personality variation, such as neuroticism and other traits, has been no easier, implying the existence of many loci of very small effect, as is the case in more outbred, genetically diverse populations.

'Endophenotypes': getting closer to 5-HTT

Could there be phenotypes related to psychiatric disease or behavior that have a different genetic architecture, composed of genetic loci with larger effect sizes? Working with such phenotypes gives the candidate-gene approach a better chance of success. A number of investigators have pursued this idea, among whom Danny Weinberg at NIMH has made the strongest claims for the success of the approach (Meyer-Lindenberg and Weinberger, 2006). In his words:

> Genes do not encode for psychiatric phenomena (for example, hallucinations and panic attacks), and so, almost by definition, the more behavioral the phenotype, the less directly it will be predicted by a genotype. This leads to the strategy of studying underlying quantitative traits that more directly

index biology, analogous to moving from the study of cardiac insufficiency or stroke (complex diseases) to ventricular hypertrophy and cholesterol metabolism. This strategy offers several advantages for behavioral disorders: biological traits are expected to be closer to the genetic substrate, enhancing penetrance; the traits should be observable in genetically at risk but behaviorally unaffected individuals; and, if the traits are sufficiently causally upstream to index a biological process that makes a separable contribution to disease, the genetic architecture should be simplified.

In this context, 'enhancing penetrance' means increasing the effect size. The closer the phenotype is to the site of genetic action, the more direct, the more immediate it is, the larger the effect should be. From this standpoint, working with behavior to find genes is like trying to work out a river's course by standing on its bank and looking back to the mountains from which it descends, standing at such a great distance that the snow peaks appear to be no more than wrinkles on the horizon. Travel up the river closer to the foot hills, so that the mountains are easier to discern, and the route from glacier to river creek emerges.

Figure 5.6 illustrates the concept of the endophenotype. On the left of the figure are the

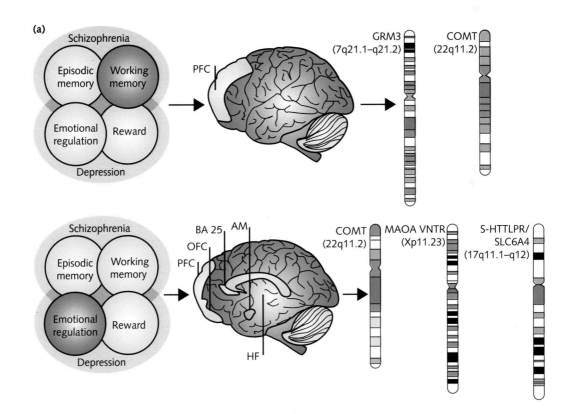

Figure 5.6 Concept of the endophenotype (AM, amygdala; BA, Brodmann's area; HF, hippocampal formation; OFC, orbitofrontal cortex; PFC, prefrontal cortex).
Source: Meyer-Lindenberg and Weinberger (2006).

phenotypes that psychiatrists work with, the diffuse, poorly defined diagnostic entities of schizophrenia and depression. Within these are better but still diffuse psychological constructs such as working memory and emotional regulation. In the middle are the brain regions, the neural circuitry whose activity gives rise to the psychology and psychiatric disease. And on the right are the molecules of DNA from which all of this pathology arises. The closer the researcher is to the DNA, the better the chance of observing its effect. Endophenotypes are measures of brain function that lie between DNA and psychiatric illness.

For example, as shown in Figure 5.6 from Meyer-Lindenberg and Weinberger (2006), cortical dysfunction is genetically analyzed instead of schizophrenia, and emotional regulation instead of depression. Cortical dysfunction is linked to variation in the *COMT* and *GRM3* genes. Emotional regulation is linked to variation in *COMT*, the monoamine oxidase A gene (*MAOA*) and the serotonin transporter polymorphism. Genetic association is said to be easier to find when analyzing these neuronal phenotypes because they are closer to the genetic action.

Do the published data bear this out? It's still not clear. In one influential study, Weinberger and colleagues gave people a task in which they had to match the emotion (angry or afraid) of one of two faces to that of a third (Hariri *et al.*, 2002). People were asked to do this emotional matching test while the activity of brain regions was monitored using magnetic resonance imaging, or MRI. The amygdala, a region known to be involved in emotional processing, was found to be more active in people with an *s* allele (the same allele whose possession Peter Lesch had identified as increasing neuroticism).

The remarkable thing about this study is that the effect was found with just 28 individuals. The genetic effect attributable to the 5-HTT locus explained about 40% of the variation in brain activity. This is almost two orders of magnitude larger than the effects we have been discussing in the genetic association of psychiatric disease, consistent with the idea that intermediate, or endophenotypes, do indeed 'enhance genetic penetrance.' But this is, in design, just another genetic association study, prone to all of the problems that genetic association analyses face, and we should take the same critical stance in assessing its value as we did with the other work. In other words, is it true?

The pattern of results emerging from the genetic analysis of intermediate phenotypes looks very similar to what we saw for case–control studies of psychiatric disease: a high-profile publication reports a large effect size, with a small sample, and is followed by other studies using larger samples that report smaller effects, or non-replication. The difference with the case–control studies we have discussed above is that the number of intermediate phenotypes studies is relatively small. This is because imaging brains is much more expensive (say at least US$400 for each subject) and time consuming than assessing phenotypes by asking people to fill in a questionnaire (costs less than 50 cents and takes about 5 minutes).

By 2007, 14 studies had been published that looked at the relationship between 5-HTT and amygdala activation, far fewer than the hundreds that analyzed the relationship between 5-HTT and personality, but enough to carry out a meta-analysis of the results (Munafò *et al.*, 2008). This showed a significant result, but with a greatly reduced effect size: down to 10%. In fact, Marcus Munafò at Bristol University who carried out the meta-analysis

plotted the downward trend in the estimated effect and predicted that, in 2008, the first study showing an effect in the opposite direction would be published. That prediction was fulfilled, raising the possibility that there may after all be no true effect attributable to the 5-HTT locus, or indicating that the effect is small, just as small as in the classical psychiatric genetic association studies. Similar conclusions have been reached in meta-analyses of other intermediate phenotypes (Flint and Munafò, 2007).

Is there a way out of the quagmire?

What else could be done to improve success rates? One suggestion is to give up candidate genes and find something better, but that means testing all genes, an idea that for technical reasons it has been difficult to realize. In the next chapter, we'll describe how that became possible. Secondly, large sample sizes, much larger than countenanced, could be collected. During the time that the genetic association studies of psychiatric disorders were being carried out, other diseases whose origins were also obscure were subject to the same genetic analysis: cancer, diabetes, hypertension, stroke, arthritis, asthma, and other common illnesses. Researchers in all of these areas were facing the same difficulties. For example, here is David Allison, a statistical geneticist, summarizing progress in obesity genetics (Redden and Allison, 2003):

> Over the past decade, numerous research projects have reported associations between nutritional phenotypes (obesity, type 1 and 2 diabetes mellitus and energy expenditure)

and regions of the human chromosomes. Unfortunately, many of the reported associations have not been replicated in independent research. The nonreplication of these association findings is a concern and has caused some researchers to question the utility of association methodology in genetic studies.

John Ioannidis has been a particularly outspoken critic of genetic association studies. Here he is in an editorial in the *Journal of the National Cancer Institute* lambasting studies of cancer (Ioannidis, 2006):

> In 2005 alone, 194 original research articles were published that probed gene–disease associations for breast cancer; I selected every 10th article (*n* = 19) for perusal. Fifteen of these articles claimed associations overall, in subgroups, or for specific outcomes. The parade of claimed associated genes in this tiny sample is already impressive: HER2, IL10, NCOA3, TGFBR1, TGFB1, ESR2, HFE, IGF-I, ESR1, AR, CHEK2, PAI-1, XRCC1, HSMH2, SULT1A1, and IFNG. If all these claimed associations are real, a 10% sample of the published genetic association research in a single year alone seemingly suffices to explain all that causes breast cancer: the total attributable fraction from this small sample of associations already reaches close to 100%.
>
> Is this an apotheosis of data dredging? Even in my small sample of 19 articles, one comes across an association that is statistically significant only in the sub-sub-subgroup of postmenopausal women who have at least three pregnancies and also have no wild-type allele; a polymorphism with statistically significantly decreased risk for early-stage breast cancer but increased risk for advanced-stage disease; another increasing the risk especially for grade 3 tumors; a marker with 13 variants, of which one shows a statistically significant association versus

all others combined, while hundreds of different groupings are conceivable; polymorphisms that have no statistically significant associations on their own but do in one of their many constructed haplotypes; joint effects of polymorphisms of different genes acting in obvious or not-so-obvious pathways; associations that are not even tested statistically and so forth.

This quote exemplifies the frustration that many of us working on the genetics of common disease, not just psychiatric illness, felt. The job ought to be easy: we knew that the disorders had a heritable component and molecular genetics gave us the power to investigate them at a molecular level. Why could we not find robust results? A few papers were pointing to the importance of sample size. For example, an analysis of over 3,000 people in a study of a gene thought to be involved in type 2 diabetes

(PPARG) gave a clear indication that the investigators had found the correct variant (Altshuler *et al.*, 2000). Studies with similar sample sizes also detected a signal of roughly the same effect size, and combined analyses improved the significance of the result (rather than weakening it as we found in meta-analyses of psychiatric association studies).

Studies that analyzed thousands of cases and controls were extremely rare in psychiatry. It was becoming clear that they were needed. But we also needed a way to interrogate something other than candidate genes. Candidate gene studies in psychiatry were not proving to be productive. Of the 20,000 or so genes in the human genome, about 10,000 are expressed in the brain. How could we test their involvement? The next chapter explains the technological and methodological developments that made it possible.

BOX 5.1 Meta-analysis

Meta-analysis is a quantitative method that combines results from a body of evidence—typically a number of published studies—in order to arrive at a consensus conclusion. The basic elements of meta-analytic techniques can be traced back to Fisher (1925), but Glass introduced the term meta-analysis in 1976 (Glass, 1976). In genetics, the method has been applied to linkage and genetic association studies as a way of determining whether the literature supports claims for a relationship between genetic variants and disease.

The advantage of meta-analysis over simply counting the number of studies that report a positive or negative finding is that it takes into account the power of each study, so that a small study with a highly significant result does not outweigh a much larger, and therefore more powerful, study with a non-significant result.

A meta-analysis produces two key results. First, it tells us if the results from the various studies are statistically homogeneous. That is, can they be seen as replications of one another? If the

answer to this is yes, then a meta-analysis gives an aggregate estimate of the effect under study that is properly averaged over all the studies. This statistic reflects the best possible aggregate estimate of the effect based on all the available information.

A meta-analysis is only as good as its constituent parts, and its success is in part determined by the diligence of the investigators identifying suitable studies and extracting the correct information.

Summary

1. Association analysis, the correlation of variants in specific genes with a trait, offers an alternative to linkage analysis that has greater power and focus, but casts a narrower net and requires knowing enough about the disorder to nominate 'candidate' genes.

2. Results of association studies for behavioral and psychiatric phenotypes have often been inconsistent, difficult to replicate, and influenced by the inevitable preconceptions inherent in choosing candidate genes.

3. 'Endophenotypes' that are considered to be closer to the site of genetic action, such as brain area activation, are a strategy for enhancing effect size in association studies.

4. Larger sample sizes improve the robustness and reliability of results from association studies.

References

Allen, N.C., Bagade, S., McQueen, M.B., Ioannidis, J.P., Kavvoura, F.K., Khoury, M.J., Tanzi, R.E., and Bertram, L. (2008). Systematic meta-analyses and field synopsis of genetic association studies in schizophrenia: the SzGene database. *Nat Genet* **40**:827–834.

Altshuler, D., Hirschhorn, J.N., Klannemark, M., Lindgren, C.M., Vohl, M.C., Nemesh, J., Lane, C.R., Schaffner, S.F., Bolk, S. *et al.* (2000). The common PPARγ Pro12Ala polymorphism is associated with decreased risk of type 2 diabetes. *Nat Genet* **26**:76–80.

Blum, K. and Noble, E.P. (1994). The sobering D2 story. *Science* **265**:1346–1347.

Blum, K., Noble, E. P., Sheridan, P.J., Montgomery, A., Ritchie, T., Jagadeeswaran, P., Nogami, H., Briggs, A.H., and Cohn, J.B. (1990). Allelic association of human dopamine D2 receptor gene in alcoholism. *JAMA* **263**:2055–2060.

Caspi, A., Sugden, K., Moffitt, T.E., Taylor, A., Craig, I.W., Harrington, H., McClay, J., Mill, J., Martin, J. *et al.* (2003). Influence of life stress on depression: moderation by a polymorphism in the 5-HTT gene. *Science* **301**:386–389.

Daniels, J.K., Williams, N.M., Williams, J., Jones, L.A., Cardno, A.G., Murphy, K.C., Spurlock, G., Riley, B., Scambler, P. *et al.* (1996). No evidence for allelic association between schizophrenia and a polymorphism determining high or low catechol O-methyltransferase activity. *Am J Psychiatry* **153**:268–270.

Eaves, I.A., Merriman, T.R., Barber, R.A., Nutland, S., Tuomilehto-Wolf, E., Tuomilehto, J., Cucca, F., and Todd, J.A. (2000). The genetically isolated populations of Finland and Sardinia may not be a panacea for linkage disequilibrium mapping of common disease genes. *Nat Genet* **25**:320–323.

Fisher, R.A. (1925). *Statistical Methods for Research Workers*. Edinburgh: Oliver and Boyd.

Flint, J. and Munafò, M.R. (2007). The endophenotype concept in psychiatric genetics. *Psychol Med* **37**:163–180.

Gelernter, J., Goldman, D., and Risch, N. (1993). The A1 allele at the D2 dopamine receptor gene and alcoholism. A reappraisal. *JAMA* **269**:1673–1677.

Glass, G.V. (1976). Primary, secondary and meta-analysis. *Educat Res* **5**:3–8.

Gratacos, M., Nadal, M., Martin-Santos, R., Pujana, M.A., Gago, J., Peral, B., Armengol, L., Ponsa, I., Miro, R. *et al.* (2001). A polymorphic genomic duplication on human chromosome 15 is a susceptibility factor for panic and phobic disorders. *Cell* **106**:367–379.

Hariri, A.R., Mattay, V.S., Tessitore, A., Kolachana, B., Fera, F., Goldman, D., Egan, M.F., and Weinberger, D.R. (2002). Serotonin transporter genetic variation and the response of the human amygdala. *Science* **297**:400–403.

Ioannidis, J.P. (2006). Common genetic variants for breast cancer: 32 largely refuted candidates and larger prospects. *J Natl Cancer Inst* **98**:1350–1353.

Lesch, K.-P., Bengel, D., Heils, A., Sabol, S.Z., Greenberg, B.D., Petri, S., Benjamin, J., Muller, C.R., Hamer, D.H., and Murphy, D.L. (1996). Association of anxiety related traits with a polymorphism in the serotonin transporter gene regulatory region. *Science* **274**:1527–1530.

Meyer-Lindenberg, A. and Weinberger, D. R. (2006). Intermediate phenotypes and genetic mechanisms of psychiatric disorders. *Nat Rev Neurosci* **7**:818–827.

Munafò, M.R., Clark, T.G., Moore, L.R., Payne, E., Walton, R., and Flint, J. (2003). Genetic polymorphisms and personality in healthy adults: a systematic review and meta-analysis. *Mol Psychiatry* **8**:471–484.

Munafò, M.R., Bowes, L., Clark, T.G., and Flint, J. (2005). Lack of association of the COMT (Val[158/108]Met) gene and schizophrenia: a meta-analysis of case–control studies. *Mol Psychiatry* **10**:765–770.

Munafò, M.R., Matheson, I.J., and Flint, J. (2007). Association of the DRD2 gene Taq1A polymorphism and alcoholism: a meta-analysis of case–control studies and evidence of publication bias. *Mol Psychiatry* **12**:454–461.

Munafò, M.R., Brown, S.M., and Hariri, A.R. (2008). Serotonin transporter (5-HTTLPR) genotype and amygdala activation: a meta-analysis. *Biol Psychiatry* **63**:852–857.

Munafò, M.R., Durrant, C., Lewis, G., and Flint, J. (2009). Gene × environment interactions at the serotonin transporter locus. *Biol Psychiatry* **65**:211–219.

Redden, D.T. and Allison, D.B. (2003). Non-replication in genetic association studies of obesity and diabetes research. *J Nutr* **133**:3323–3326.

Tabiner, M., Youings, S., Dennis, N., Baldwin, D., Buis, C., Mayers, A., Jacobs, P.A., and Crolla, J.A. (2003). Failure to find DUP25 in patients with anxiety disorders, in control individuals, or in previously reported positive control cell lines. *Am J Hum Genet* **72**:535–538.

Willis-Owen, S.A., Turri, M.G., Munafò, M.R., Surtees, P.G., Wainwright, N.W., Brixey, R.D., and Flint, J. (2005). The serotonin transporter length polymorphism, neuroticism, and depression: a comprehensive assessment of association. *Biol Psychiatry* **58**:451–456.

6 Genome-wide association studies

[On the use of whole-genome sequence information and large samples for association mapping and what they have told us about human DNA diversity and the genetic architecture of common, complex disease]

I (J.F.) work in a large genetics centre on the outskirts of Oxford, near to hospitals full of patients with those common diseases like hypertension, asthma, stroke, cancer, and depression that we human geneticists, at the Wellcome Trust Centre for Human Genetics, are expected to pull apart, at a genetic level, so that new diagnostic tests, prognostic information, and, best of all, new therapies can be developed. All of us at the Gene Centre live off research grants that pay our salaries, our staff, our families, and our ever increasingly expensive addiction to genetic analysis. These grants have a common format. They start by stating, or overstating, the importance of the disorder we study (easy for those studying cancer or depression, less easy for those working on systemic lupus erythematosus or restless leg syndrome); they continue by providing an impressive figure for the cost of the disorder to society, in lives lost, expensive and largely ineffective treatments, days off work, resulting in a multi-million dollar sum, ideally billions. The grant application continues, now in a tone of humility, to admit our ignorance, explaining how little we know about the biology of the disorder (very true for psychiatric disorders) and that often

our effective therapies, where they exist, have been discovered by chance (for example antidepressant drugs arose from observation of the effects of anti-tuberculosis therapies). But we have one important insight into the cause of the disease, confirmed by numerous studies, using different, complementary designs: we know the illness has a genetic basis, that genetic variation contributes, in part, to disease susceptibility, or that the heritability has some non-trivial value (let's say 40%—this is generally true for most traits). Finally, the grant explains how a genetic approach will identify the molecular basis of the illness, leading to new insights into the cause of the disease with the promise that new, rationally based, etiologically informed therapies—possibly drugs but other approaches are not ruled out—will emerge, thereby justifying the expense of a few million dollars (remember the cost to society of the illness is billions).

We had been writing grants like this since the early 1990s, each renewal beginning to look increasingly difficult and the language increasingly less promissory, less optimistic. There were even hints that our attempts to find the

molecular basis of the world's ills were never going to succeed, that the hopes placed in the genome projects, the millions spent on medical research, would not lead anywhere. But in 2007, some of the promises we made were at last fulfilled. This chapter explains how new technologies made possible genome-wide association studies (more commonly known by the acronym GWAS), the method that allows us to dissect the genetic basis of complex phenotypes, that is to say, common diseases like stroke, cancer, schizophrenia, and depression.

The success of GWAS was regarded as the scientific breakthrough of the year in 2007, and has turned human genetic analysis of complex traits from a field littered with unreplicated, highly contentious findings to a rapidly expanding area of research where there is now no or little argument about the validity and importance of the finding. Thus, 2007 marked a turning point in human genetics.

How the idea of GWAS came about

By the mid-1990s, the family-based approaches, the sort that we have described in our discussion of schizophrenia, were already showing that the genetic basis of complex traits was much more complicated than our grant applications would have reviewers believe. Breast cancer and Alzheimer's disease have complex genetic origins, more similar to schizophrenia than they are to Huntington's disease, and there were successes using family-based approaches applied to these disorders: a proportion (admittedly small) of cases of breast cancer was attributable to mutations in a gene on chromosome 17 (later identified and imaginatively named

BRCA, until a second gene was found so that we now have BRCA1 and BRCA2); mutations were found that cause early-onset dementia in Alzheimer's disease. These findings encouraged the hope that, with further searching, an appropriate pedigree might be discovered in which mutations giving rise to psychosis could be found.

You can see this in a paper published in *Science* in 2000, in which a group of Canadian researchers claimed to have found a region on chromosome 1 that contributed to susceptibility to schizophrenia (Brzustowicz *et al.*, 2000). The researchers looked for specific families in which multiple relatives were diagnosed with schizophrenia and, critically, in which '*schizophrenic illness appeared to be segregating in a unilineal* [one side of the family only], *autosomal dominant manner.*' And they found what they were looking for ('*the highest LOD score observed was 5.79 (P = 0.0002) under the narrow definition of illness and a recessive mode of inheritance with marker D1S1679, which maps to chromosome 1q22*'). The trouble was, other people did not. Two years later, again in *Science*, a paper from eight groups, looking at the same region, found no evidence of a genetic effect and concluded, '*We cannot determine whether the Canadian finding is a false-positive or a true-positive result whose genetic effect is smaller than reported*' (Levinson *et al.*, 2002).

This story is similar to that for the chromosome 5q linkage reported by Hugh Gurling, to the locus on chromosome 11q that was claimed to contribute to susceptibility to manic depressive psychosis in the Old Order Amish, and to other conflicting, contradictory claims in other illnesses, not just psychiatric disorders. The problem of unreplicated findings in common diseases was widespread: as true for obesity, diabetes, hypertension, stroke, and cancer as it was for schizophrenia, depression, anxiety, and autism.

Suppose we had polymorphisms in all genes and could test them all, regardless of their likely candidacy as the critical gene. Risch and Merikangas (1996), writing before the genome project was completed, assumed that there were 100,000 genes and that five polymorphisms in each would be sufficient (both assumptions turned out to be incorrect, but the argument still holds). This large number of tests poses a problem we have already encountered: the more tests you carry out, the more likely you will be to find a positive result by chance alone. Suppose the positive outcome you are hoping to find is to score six when you roll a die. Roll a single die once and the chance of getting a six is one in six; roll the die 100 times and you'd be extraordinarily unlucky not to get at least one six (0.833 to the 99th power equals 1.4 × 10⁻⁸). The way to deal with this problem is to increase the threshold you accept as significant. In the case of dice-rolling, you would increase the number of sixes—for example when rolling dice 100 times, rather than just a single six you'd have to get more than 50. A simple way to take into account multiple testing is divide the threshold by the number of tests you carry out. So, if for a single test you accept as significant a probability of less than 1 in 20, then for 100 tests you accept a probability of less than 1 in 2000. Testing all of the polymorphisms that Risch and Merikangas suggested would then require you to beat the odds of 1 in 20,000,000. This is a ridiculously small number, but as Risch and Merikangas showed, it can be obtained by genetic association, with some reasonable assumptions about genetic effect size and action: *'The required sample size for the association test, even allowing for the smaller significance level, is vastly less than for linkage, especially for affected sibling pair families when the value of p is small. Even for a GRR of 1.5, the sample sizes are generally less than 1,000, well within*

reason.' As we'll see, less than 1,000 turned out to be optimistic, but the numbers needed are still within reason (Figure 6.1).

Perhaps surprisingly, the main lesson from considering the power of genetic association studies is the need for appropriate technology:

The primary limitation of genome-wide association tests is not a statistical one but a technological one. A large number of genes (up to 100,000) and polymorphisms (preferentially ones that create alterations in derived proteins or their expression) must first be identified, and an extremely large number of such polymorphisms will need to be tested. Although testing such a large number of polymorphisms on several hundred, or even a thousand families, might currently seem implausible in scope, more efficient methods of screening a large number of polymorphisms (for example, sample pooling) may be possible. Furthermore, the number of tests we have used as the basis for our calculations (1,000,000) is likely to be far larger than

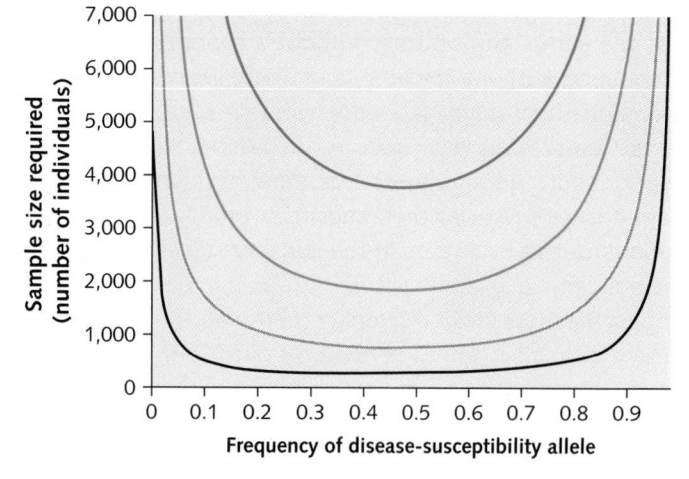

Figure 6.1 Effects of allele frequency on sample-size requirements. The four curves represent results at four odds ratios: black 2.0, gray 1.5, light blue 1.3 and dark blue 1.2. Source: Hirschhorn and Daly (2005).

necessary if one allows for linkage disequilibrium, which could substantially reduce the required number of markers and families needed for initial screening.

Risch and Merikangas (1996).

Cataloging human DNA sequence diversity

At the time that Risch and Merikangas wrote, typing a couple of polymorphisms was onerous (see Appendix). Typing a million was as impossible as sequencing the genome. How many markers were needed, and how were these to be found and then genotyped, emerged as the critical questions, which, if answered, could make possible genetic studies of common disease that had the critical capacity to interrogate the *entire* genome, thereby avoiding the need for prior knowledge about the genes that were involved.

At the end of the century, without a genome sequence, without knowing how many genes, let alone how many sequence variants there were, everything was obscure, all theoretical speculation and plain guesswork, most of which arose from what was then known, or inferred, about human evolution. At the root were ideas about genetic diversity within human populations: the more genetic diversity there was, the more difficult it would be to carry out GWAS because capturing all of that variation would need millions of markers. At about the same time as human genetic linkage studies were first attempted, molecular data emerged that provided empirical evidence about the extent of diversity within, and between, human populations.

Reading human history in our DNA

Was it true, as had been the position for many years, that the amount of genetic diversity within a population was as large as the amount of genetic diversity between populations, a position that rendered implausible a genetic basis for racial differences? Our species—modern *Homo sapiens*—dates back about 250,000 years from origins in Africa. One hypothesis of how humans came to populate the rest of world is that there was a migration out of Africa, between 70,000 and 50,000 years ago. There are various versions of how this might have happened, the dates and the number of migrations varying considerably, but one piece of evidence could not be gainsaid: genetic diversity, from sequence and genotyping data, is greater in Africans than in other populations. This suggested that a small number of people (initial estimates even suggested a handful) had left Africa to populate the rest of the world.

The 'out of Africa' hypothesis has some slightly worrying implications, fully exploited by geneticists wanting to make some money. It means that anyone of European or Asian descent is much more closely related than we might suspect, close enough for the relationship to be still discernible in our DNA. All you have to do is give some spit to the geneticists—or spit on one if you are so inclined—from which they extract DNA, and they will type some markers and tell you who you are related to. Go to the DNA ancestry project website where you will learn:

> Marie Antoinette was the vivacious Queen of France who was, and still is, associated with the extravagant lifestyles of the 18th century monarchy... With a simple swab of your mouth, you can be compared with Marie Antoinette and discover your relation to her.

You will be able to trace your heritage back to times of grandeur, to times of kings and queens and royal balls, and possibly even to Marie Antoinette.

> http://www.dnaancestry-project.com/ydna_intro_famous.php?id=marieantoinette&typ=m

Many people want to know their descendants, and the following story is fairly typical. Tom Robinson, an Associate Professor of Accounting at the University of Miami, decided to try one of the DNA based ancestry projects, Oxford Ancestors (http://www.oxfordancestors.com).

> During 2002, I was doing some work on my family history, trying to develop a family tree. Our family records were not very comprehensive. My uncle had done some research on my maternal side (Mayton) that indicated that this side of the family began in recent history in Virginia, migrated to North Carolina, then Alabama and then Florida over about 7 or so generations.
>
> In April, I received a call from Oxford Ancestors letting me know that they had done additional research (not at my request) based on recent research on the descendants of Genghis Khan.
>
> While Genghis Khan's DNA has not been found, I understand from published research that it has been 'inferred' from living individuals. Subsequently I received a certificate (suitable for framing) that states: '*This is to certify that Thomas R Robinson carries a Y-chromosome which shows him to be of probable direct descent from Genghis Khan, First Emperor of the Mongols.*'

> http://trrobinson.com/2006/06/16/genghis-khan-or-not--that-is-the-question.aspx

The Times newspaper summarized the relationship as follows:

> Mr Robinson, a professor of accountancy at the University of Miami, shares crucial portions of

his DNA with the Mongol ruler. He has little in common with his infamous ancestor. He is not a keen horseman. Though a Republican, his politics are moderate. And while Genghis Khan may have fathered thousands of children, Professor Robinson and his wife, Linda, have no offspring.

> http://www.timesonline.co.uk/tol/news/world/us_and_americas/article669552.ece

Even if you are not more closely related to Marie Antoinette, Genghis Khan and the Romanovs than you suspected, it's still true that, if you are of European or Asian descent, then the genetic differences between you and other Europeans and Asians is less than between Africans and, in general, less than that which differentiates other species. This has important implications for genetic studies of common disease. Soon after Risch and Merikangas' argument in favor of genetic association, Eric Lander laid down ten goals for genomics ('*with the aim of stimulating ferment*'). One goal was the discovery of all common sequence variants within genes (coding variants), because, Lander argued, these variants would be a major contributor to the causes of common disease. His argument ran as follows:

> Human diversity is quite limited in that most genes have only a handful of common variants in their coding regions, with the vast majority of alleles being exceedingly rare. The effective number of alleles...is rather small, often two or three. This limited diversity reflects the fact that modern humans are descended from a relatively small population that underwent exponential explosion in evolutionarily recent time. ...The catalog of common variants will transform the search for susceptibility genes through the use of association studies.
>
> Lander (1996).

Cataloging and testing common variants in coding regions assumes that these variants are causative, enabling a direct association

between the disease and one of the molecular changes that confers susceptibility. Given the arguments in favor of reduced diversity, a complete catalog might consist of a few hundred thousand common variants.

Where in the genome are the SNPs and how many are necessary?

While everyone accepted that not all of the functional variants would be in the coding regions, on the basis of what was then known, it seemed reasonable to think non-coding variants would play only a minor role. Common variants had been found in apolipoprotein E that explained a large fraction of the risk for Alzheimer's disease (Corder *et al.*, 1993), as well as the risk for cardiovascular disease. Other genes, for factor V, angiotensin-converting enzyme, and the chemokine receptor CKR-5, had common variants associated with the risk of thrombosis (blood clots), heart disease, and resistance to human immunodeficiency virus (HIV) infection. Why not expect this pattern to continue? The common disease–common variant hypothesis was attractive and, if true, made common disease amenable to genetic dissection.

But suppose the susceptibility variants did not lie in the genes? An alternative, sometimes called the indirect association strategy, would still detect susceptibility variants, even if they were not themselves cataloged and tested. Suppose that, because markers 1 and 2 are very close on the human genome, every person who has the genotype C/G at marker 1

has the genotype A/T at marker 2; in that case, there is no point in genotyping both markers because we can completely predict one from the other. In an association test, I would not even need to know that there was a marker 2 if I had information from marker 1, as both would give the same result. Of course, from the single result at marker 1, I would not know if the variant I had tested was causative, but the culprit would probably not be far away, genetically speaking. Instead of a complete catalog of variants, a dense set of single-nucleotide polymorphisms (SNPs), distributed across the genome, would capture nearly everything, coding or not (though note that this strategy will not find rare variants; it still assumes that the common disease–common variant hypothesis is true).

Francis Collins, Mark Guyer, and Aravinda Chakravarti argued for the dense SNP map approach in 1997, again based on theoretical speculation about how disease alleles might have arisen and be distributed through the population:

> This strategy is based on the hypothesis that each sequence variant that causes disease must have arisen in a particular individual at some time in the past, so the specific array of polymorphisms (haplotype) in the neighborhood of the altered gene in that individual must be inherited in all of his or her descendants. The presence of a recognizable ancestral haplotype therefore becomes an indicator of the disease-associated polymorphism. The size of this region (in which the genetic markers are said to be in 'linkage disequilibrium') will vary with the age of the variant.
>
> Collins *et al.* (1997).

What this boils down to is that a sufficiently high-density set of SNPs would capture all (or at least most) of the diversity in the genome. The strength of correlation between SNPs is the

major determinant of the number of SNPs that would be needed: if it were low (meaning that most SNPs were independent of their neighbors), then more markers would be required, perhaps millions. If it were high (meaning that most SNPs were highly correlated with their neighbors), then fewer would do the job. On this basis, the policy document concluded, '*Further improvements in the technologies for the discovery and detection of SNPs should be immediately and aggressively pursued. Two goals should be targeted simultaneously: (i) the development of a dense map of at least 100,000 SNPs and (ii) the identification of common cSNPs in as many genes as possible*' (cSNPs is short-hand for sequence variants in coding regions of the genome, the coding SNPs that we mentioned above) (Collins *et al.*, 1997).

In December 1997, a meeting at the National Institutes of Health Genome Research Institute (NIHGRI) decided to collect at least 100,000 SNPs in human DNA donated by 100–500 people in four major population categories: African, Asian, European, and Native American. Costs for the project were put at US$20–30 million over 3 years. That large investment of public money was intended to forestall big academic labs and companies from patenting SNPs. While the meeting participants agreed on the need to do the work, there was considerable debate about where the samples would come from and how to ensure that privacy was safeguarded. As the genetic data would be publicly available, it might be possible to identify donors from their DNA profiles (and determine whether they were descendants of Genghis Khan). These ethical, social, and legal issues have become increasingly important in human genetics and will only become more so as we enter an age when it is cheap enough to obtain complete DNA sequences.

Francis Collins, then head of NIHGRI, emerged as chief architect of the new initiative, which

came to be known as HapMap (haplotype map of the human genome: http://www.hapmap. org). By then it was generally assumed that 100,000 SNPs would do the job, without, it has to be admitted, much supporting quantitative evidence. Even 100,000 SNPs was going to cost a vast amount of money, so when geneticist Leonid Kruglyak argued that 500,000 SNPs were necessary, there was a certain degree of upset in the human genetics community. Based again on what was known about human evolution, Kruglyak's argument was quantitative: he simulated human evolution on a computer. Reflecting best current estimates, '*the general human population was assumed to have constant effective size N until G generations before the present, and to then expand exponentially to its present-day size of 5 billion. The standard assumption was N = 10,000 and G = 5,000 (corresponding to 100,000 years given a 20-year generation time)*' (Kruglyak, 1999).

Kruglyak's basic result is worth quoting, for, despite its technical language, he turned out to be remarkably prescient:

> Consider a common variant (50% frequency) and a nearby marker separated by recombination fraction θ. …Essentially no LD is observed at $\theta = 0.0003$ or greater. This genetic distance on average corresponds to a physical distance of 30kb. A low level of LD ($d^2 = 0.1$, s.d. = 0.1) is observed at $\theta = 0.0001$ (10 Kb). The level of LD increases to $d^2 = 0.4$ (s.d. = 0.2) at $\theta = 0.00003$ (3 Kb), and approaches a maximal level of $d^2 = 0.8$ (s.d. = 0.3) at approximately $\theta = 0.000003$ (300 bp). …These results then suggest that a marker within $\theta = 0.00003$ of every variant is required to avoid a large increase in sample size. This marker density can be achieved with a map of 500,000 SNPs with an average spacing of 6 Kb across the genome. Use of sparser maps would entail considerable loss of power.

Less than 2 years later, the HapMap consortium reported the discovery of more than 1 million SNPs, driven in part by Kruglyak's arguments and made possible by remarkable falls in the cost and methods of genotyping (see Appendix for a description of the molecular methodology involved in this revolution).

Key paper

Frazer, K.A., Ballinger, D.G., Cox, D.R., Hinds, D.A., Stuve, L.L., Gibbs, R.A., Belmont, J.W., Boudreau, A., Hardenbol, P. *et al.* (2007). A second generation human haplotype map of over 3.1 million SNPs. *Nature* **449**:851–886.

This is the latest in the HapMap project publications that describe the characterization of genetic variation in the human genome. See also http://www.hapmap.org.

The first GWAS results

In 2003, as the HapMap data emerged, it was clear that the next question would be whether we could use these dense SNP maps for clinical purpose. Given the expected costs and the possibility that we might not find anything, how could we maximize our chances of success and also cover our backs if nothing turned up? Expensive studies that find nothing generally discourage funding bodies from giving money to those that proposed the study in the first place. So could we design a study in which, if we found nothing, at least we could say, well that means there is nothing there, rather than have to admit that there might be something, but it was not in the genes, not in the population, not in the disease we had studied?

Different diseases, different populations, different genes: all excuses for failure. Could we make a definitive statement about the value of the high-density SNP association study? Such a study was bound to be large, to involve many clinical investigators, to require access to high-throughput genotyping, molecular biologists, computer programmers, and perhaps most importantly statisticians; it would mean working in an inter-disciplinary consortium, on a scale and at a cost common in physics but almost unheard of in biology.

At the time, the Sanger Institute, a large genomics centre outside Cambridge, UK, was generating data for the HapMap project. The Sanger geneticists had focused on chromosome 20 (which at 60 megabases, i.e. 60,000,000 bases, is one of the smallest). By 2004, they had '*all the data from over 30,000 working assays for polymorphic SNPs on chromosome 20, and the map of linkage disequilibrium and common haplotypes in three populations is approaching completion. Chromosome 20 is now ready for piloting the genome-wide approach to association studies.*' Both the Sanger Institute and the Human Genetics Centre in Oxford where I (J.F.) work receive the bulk of our funding from the Wellcome Trust, a private charity based in London that has capital of about US$15 billion. A group of us from the Sanger Institute and from Oxford went down to talk to Mark Walport, the director of the Wellcome Trust, to see whether the Trust would be interested in a pilot project, a test case for a GWAS, in which we would analyze whether any of the SNPs on chromosome 20 was associated with disease. This is how we put the case: '*Up to 35,000 SNPs would be genotyped in a population of 1,000 cases plus 1,000 controls for each of the selected disease phenotypes. A study of this size has the power to detect effects contributing to more than 2% of the total variance of a quantitative phenotype.*' This was going to be expensive: '*The cost of completing analysis of the first 2,000 DNA*

samples is expected to be £5M, with addition of each further sample sets costing £2M (excluding further controls).' Our selling point was the completeness of our analysis: *'We would expect to detect positive associations for follow up in one or more of the sample collections studies. A negative result (no association found in multiple diseases) will also be important information for further evaluation.'*

Over the next year, these ideas matured and the use of a single set of controls emerged (rather than using a set for each disease), as did arguments about which diseases to include, and, most importantly, the cost of genotyping continued to fall. By mid-2004, *'If cost stays to 1.5c per genotype, we can do approaching 85k markers on 10k DNAs.'* Cost reductions meant more markers, which in turn meant the study would not be restricted to looking at just one chromosome. We could test other regions, some of special interest to investigators, such as the region on chromosome 6 that is involved in controlling the immune response (the HLA region), and even testing all coding variants, as Lander had wanted. These SNPs are sometimes referred to as non-synonymous SNPs (nsSNPs) as some cSNPs in the coding region of genes will not alter protein structure because of the degeneracy of the genetic code (these are synonymous SNPs). *'Study will aim to include 35k working nsSNPs; 8k HLA across 8Mb (needs screening and sequencing flank regions); chr 20 (35k), 200 full genes from Fred Hutch study; Encode regions (5Mb).'*

The cost of genotyping fell so dramatically that the projected budget of £8 million bought more and more, to the point that by 2006, a GWAS was affordable. By that stage, the Wellcome Trust Case Control Consortium (WTCCC) had decided on its diseases (seven), on the number of the sample (2,000 cases), and on a common set of 3,000 controls (Wellcome Trust Case Control Consortium, 2007). The results of analyzing 16,179 individuals with 469,557 SNPs were published in June 2007.

Fortunately for all concerned, there were some positive results. (Because so many SNPs were being tested in each subject, prior statistical simulations had suggested that a P value of $<5 \times 10^{-7}$ (i.e. P=0.0000005) would be required to consider a finding as likely to be significant.)

Key paper

Wellcome Trust Case Control Consortium (2007). Genome-wide association study of 14,000 cases of seven common diseases and 3,000 shared controls. *Nature* **447**:661–678.

The paper that convinced the world that GWAS of complex disease worked.

> Case-control comparisons identified 24 independent association signals at $P < 5 \times 10^{-7}$: 1 in bipolar disorder, 1 in coronary artery disease, 9 in Crohn's disease, 3 in rheumatoid arthritis, 7 in type 1 diabetes and 3 in type 2 diabetes. On the basis of prior findings and replication studies thus-far completed, almost all of these signals reflect genuine susceptibility effects… Our yield of novel, highly significant association findings is comparable to, or exceeds, the number of those hitherto-generated by candidate gene or positional cloning efforts. For many of the compelling signals, replication has already been obtained. For others, replication is required to establish a definitive relationship with disease.

Wellcome Trust Case Control Consortium (2007).

These robust findings depended on sample size: had 1,000 cases and 1,000 controls been used (rather than the reality of 2,000 cases and 3,000 controls), just two significant signals would have been detected! The distribution of hits varied markedly across diseases: none were found for hypertension, one for coronary artery disease, but eight for Crohn's disease. The one psychiatric disorder analyzed, bipolar disorder, yielded one signal, but alas that did not stand up to immediate replication.

Are GWAS results valid?

It's a reasonable question. Why believe yet another high-profile paper from a huge consortium? What's so different about the WTCCC results that makes them so convincing? So far we've talked about positive results in terms of exceeding thresholds, and shown that the GWAS analyses identified loci that exceeded a P value threshold of $<5 \times 10^{-7}$, sufficiently low to deal with the multiple testing issues. But the GWAS results can be presented and analyzed in other ways, some of which give interesting insights into the likelihood that the results are correct.

Firstly, the problem of testing hundreds of thousands of markers can be turned into a virtue. If we carry out lots of tests, then, even though there is no genetic effect, some tests will turn up very low P values. Chance variation produces a distribution of P values, some large, some small. If there are a number of true associations, then the results should be enriched for low P values. One simple way to see this is to plot the distribution of observed test statistics against the distribution that occurs by chance. Here, we are not looking for single significant findings—rather we are looking for a broad pattern of results that indicates that something non-random is going on. If the two distributions are the same, the result will be a straight line. If there is an excess of low P values (indicating that there are true findings),

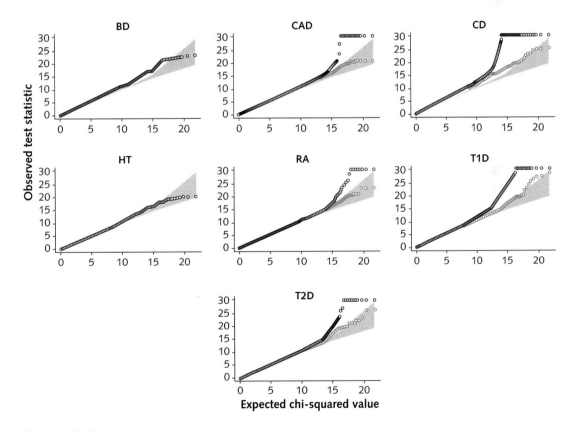

Figure 6.2 Seven diseases mapped by the Wellcome Trust Case Control Consortium (2007) (BD, bipolar disorder; CAD, coronary artery disease; CD, Crohn's disease; HT, hypertension; RA, rheumatoid arthritis; T1D/T2D, type 1/2 diabetes).

then the line will deviate in one direction at the part of the distribution that includes the low P values. Figure 6.2 shows the results for the seven diseases mapped by the WTCCC. The vertical axis is the observed result, so upward deviations from the straight line are evidence for real results. The grey shadow is a confidence interval, so we are looking for the deviation to stray outside the shadow, which it clearly does for five diseases, less obviously for bipolar disorder (BD) and not at all for hypertension (HT). Some of the deviations are very striking (the point at which the deviation becomes horizontal reflects a cut-off—the observed statistic is actually greater than 30). The blue dots represent a re-analysis of the data once the highly significant loci had been removed, just to show that the departures from expectation are due to those loci where there is a strong signal of association. This way of displaying the data is referred to as a quantile–quantile (QQ) plot.

Secondly, the WTCCC insisted on validating their findings. One simple way to do this was to increase the number the controls, which increases the power to detect an effect, assuming that the cases of one disease could act as the controls for a second (it's unlikely that those with type 1 diabetes will be enriched for bipolar disorder). Another more powerful way is to repeat the association in a separate experiment; a series of subsequent reports has, largely, done this.

Thirdly, and perhaps most interestingly, the WTCCC departed from the usual simple reporting of P values by including a Bayesian measure of the correctness of the association. Bayesian statistics needs some explaining and the approach is not even accepted among all statisticians (see Box 6.1). Statisticians, as with the US electorate, are polarized: they are either frequentist or Bayesian.

BOX 6.1 Bayesian methods

Bayesian methods differ from standard statistical methods in the way they treat evidence for and against a hypothesis. Bayesians quantify the degree of belief in favor of the hypothesis before carrying out the test (in Bayesian speak, this is the 'prior probability') and compare that with the degree of belief after evidence has been collected (the 'posterior probability'); on the face of it, a good description of what most people think science is about. In fact, Bayesian approaches to finding the right answer are closer to what most of us do when we weigh up evidence for and against an idea, or the conclusions of a genetic association study. However, Bayesian approaches are more difficult to implement and they are open to the criticism that they depend too much on what we do or do not already know.

The WTCCC statisticians justify their Bayesian analysis as follows: '*After the association data are available, a related but different question is whether a particular positive finding is likely to be a true one. For that calculation, the prior odds must be multiplied by the Bayes factor, the ratio of the probability of the observed data under the assumption that there is a true association to its probability under the null hypothesis*' (Wellcome Trust Case Control Consortium, 2007). The power of the study is included as an important piece of prior information: the more powerful a study is, the more we should be prepared to believe its results. They put this in the following, Bayesian, terminology: '*The posterior odds for a true association are equal to the prior odds multiplied*

by the power of the study divided by the significance threshold… A key point is that interpreting the strength of evidence in an association study depends on the likely number of true associations, and the power to detect them which, in turn, depends on effect sizes and sample size. In a less-well-powered study it would be necessary to adopt more stringent thresholds to control the false-positive rate.'

GWAS results for (some) psychiatric diseases

Up to the end of 2006, a dozen or so loci were widely accepted as susceptibility loci for complex diseases. By the end of 2008, that number was approaching 500. Not all GWAS findings are backed by the seal of Bayesian statistics, but they have all exceeded impressive thresholds and, generally, have been replicated, at least a couple of times. Many diseases have been analyzed: in addition to the WTCCC seven, the list includes several forms of cancer (breast, prostate, skin, and bowel), inflammatory bowel disease, a range of autoimmune diseases where illness arises because an individual's immune system attacks his own body (ankylosing spondylitis, autoimmune thyroiditis, celiac disease, multiple sclerosis, sarcoidosis, systemic lupus erythematosus), and some oddities such as restless leg syndrome. In addition, geneticists have looked at genetic effects on normal variation in height, weight, skin color, and the concentration of compounds in the blood (fats, for example).

What has emerged that we didn't know before? When GWAS was first proposed, one suggestion was to concentrate on the direct method, to test all sequence variants in genes that would have functional consequences: changes that would turn off a gene, or alter its protein product into something strange or even ghastly. Finding non-synonymous variants (remember, these are genetic variants that change proteins) that are associated with the disorder is good because it implicates the gene in which they occur. Knowing which genes are involved helps identify the relevant biology and pinpoint new pathways to illness, thereby potentially leading to new treatments. It is this process that may fulfill the promises made in applications seeking funding for the genetic analysis of disease. One arm of the WTCCC study specifically addressed that question: 14,436 non-synonymous SNPs were tested in 1,000 cases of ankylosing spondylitis, autoimmune thyroid disease, multiple sclerosis, and breast cancer (Burton *et al.*, 2007). Two new loci related to ankylosing spondylitis were found, and two others were identified for autoimmune thyroid disease, although both had been reported previously. Not a big yield. In fact, the general rule is that changes to the protein-coding part of a gene are not common. There are many cases where the association signal comes from what is rather poetically called a 'gene desert'—regions of the human genome with no genes anywhere around. One big problem for the GWAS results is tying results like this back into biology. How could these variants be contributing to disease? Mostly, we do not yet have a clue. That is not the same as saying that these GWAS studies were not successful, or that they have not taught us important lessons about the genetic basis of human disease. They have certainly done that, and perhaps the most important lesson is that each individual effect is so small. Remember the estimates put forward by Neil Risch?

Small as they seemed at the time, they turned out to be overly optimistic.

These studies, as we've said before, don't come cheap. Peter Visscher, a quantitative geneticist based in Brisbane, Australia, reviewed the work on height and pointed out that '*the total number of SNP chips used across these studies was over 63,000, representing a total investment of roughly $30 million.*' That's not to say grant-giving agencies invested US$30 million dollars to indulge geneticists interest in height. In fact '*the genotyping was done by other studies investigating disease, and the researchers cleverly piggy-backed on these studies, taking advantage of the fact that many such studies have included measures on height.*' The enormous number of subjects in the height (and weight) studies means that these are the best powered and therefore should give us the best answers as to what GWAS can find.

Here is the remarkable thing. Twin and family studies have shown with great consistency that height is highly heritable: at least 80% of the variation has a genetic basis. But although 54 SNPs were found, a great advance on what we knew before the advent of GWAS, the total heritability accounted for by all these SNPs is only about 5%! Each variant contributes less than half a percent. Another way of putting this is that if you inherit an allele that increases your height, you'll be about 0.4cm taller as a consequence. And all of the loci are this size; there are no big effects, no exponential distribution with a few large ones and a tail of smaller effects.

The same is true for disease genetics, with a few exceptions. In Figure 6.3, J.F. plotted the odds ratios for 140 loci identified for 20 diseases (odds ratios represent the increase in risk attributable to an allele: they are a close cousin of the genotype risk ratios that we wrote about

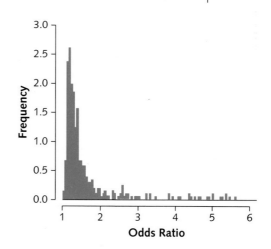

Figure 6.3 The odds ratios for 140 loci identified for 20 diseases.
Source: Hindorff *et al.* (2009)

earlier) (Hindorff *et al.*, 2009). There are in fact a few effects with an odds ratio greater than 5, but the picture is otherwise like that for height: lots of little effects.

While the sample sizes for studying disease are not as enormous as those available for height and weight, they still dwarf those used in the candidate gene studies we discussed earlier. On average 3,500 cases and 6,000 controls were used for each study.

All this is by way of an introduction to the results of the psychiatric genetics studies, of which there are to date few, but this will be changing by the month in 2009 and beyond, so our summary will surely be out of date when you read this.

GWAS have identified a handful of loci with the degree of certainty comparable to that obtained in other diseases and traits. The largest study of schizophrenia included 7,308 cases and 12,834 controls to identify three replicated loci (O'Donovan *et al.*, 2008). In bipolar disorder, 4,387 cases and 6,209 controls were used to identify two loci (Ferreira *et al.*, 2008). None of the loci included genes previously considered to be involved. (In fact, it's not yet clear which genes are involved: ZNF804A appears to be implicated in schizophrenia, and in bipolar disorder, genes called ANK3 (ankyrin G) and CACNA1C (α1C subunit of the L-type voltage-gated calcium channel). In all cases, the odds ratios were small: about 1.2.)

Something unexpected

GWAS studies have been described as 'interrogating the genome', conjuring up images from the basement of a police station with the suspected genome under a spotlight being grilled in turn by a sweaty molecular biologist and a statistician. The initial goal of this cross-examination was to find common genetic variants that contributed to complex diseases. Part way through the questioning, evidence of another sort began to emerge, implicating larger scale variation in the genome (copy number variants or CNVs) as genetic factors contributing to schizophrenia. More recently still (this is written 1 June 2009), the arrival of a new inquisitor may have gotten the suspect—GWAS studies—to yield up yet more important and unanticipated findings (International Schizophrenia Consortium *et al.*, 2009).

Peter Visscher a statistical geneticist in Brisbane, working with Shaun Purcell at Harvard Medical School came up with the following idea for investigating the genetic architecture of schizophrenia; that is, to find out how many loci might be contributing to disease susceptibility. Firstly, screen through all of the genetic markers (SNPs) from a GWAS (call this the discovery sample) and pick those that are statistically independent of one another. Secondly, compare the frequency of

the alleles at those SNPs in cases and controls and rank them with regard to the significance of the differences. Thirdly, pick a threshold for a level of significance and examine all of the SNPs below that threshold in one discovery sample. Fourthly, tabulate all of the alleles that are in excess in the cases versus the controls, and from this tabulation develop a scoring algorithm. Finally, take that scoring algorithm and apply it to a second case–control GWAS sample of the same disorder (call this the test sample). What do you find?

Purcell and his group used males from a large case–control GWAS of schizophrenia as the discovery sample and females from the same study as the test sample. Using a loose threshold that included nearly 50% of all the independent SNPs (~38,000), the scoring algorithm from the males was able to discriminate the affected and control females at a stunning level of statistical significance ($P<10^{-18}$). Two entirely different schizophrenia samples were tested by the same method. Both also yielded very significant findings. What do these results mean?

It is still early days and we expect these results to stimulate much thinking and data analysis and many statistical simulations. If true, then the risk to schizophrenia is influenced by quite a large number of common variants, each with a very small effect on risk. How large is not yet clear, but Purcell's analyses suggest that hundreds and more likely thousands of individual genes contribute to the liability to schizophrenia. How small would their effect be? Given that we know from twin studies the total genetic contribution to schizophrenia (recall heritability estimates of ~0.80), then the effects of these individual genes would be very small indeed—so small that robustly detecting each allele individually might be impossible, requiring samples of hundreds of thousands of cases and controls.

Two implications of these findings are worth pondering. Firstly, the scoring index can be used to look at the relationship between the genetic risk for schizophrenia and other disorders. Applying the scoring algorithm from the schizophrenia discovery sample to two GWAS cohorts with bipolar disorder (two test samples), the authors found substantial association (albeit less significant than with the schizophrenia samples). But, when applied to a range of GWAS of medical disorders, no association was found. So, genetic risk factors for schizophrenia appear to increase risk for bipolar illness, but not common medical conditions. Secondly, all of the samples they studied initially were of European ancestry. When they applied their scoring algorithm to a GWAS sample of individuals with schizophrenia of African–American ancestry, the association was much less significant than that found with European samples, suggesting considerable differences in the genetic substrate of schizophrenia across major ethnic groups. By the time you read this, we are certain this line of research will have moved forward considerably (or maybe have crashed and burned!). But it was just too exciting for us not to try to share with you.

The missing variance: 'dark matter' in the genome

'Could do better' reads the progress report for GWAS. Even if yields for psychiatric disorders achieved the hit rate seen for some conditions (30 loci and counting for inflammatory bowel disease, and diabetes), the indications are that the loci would account for only a tiny fraction of the genetic variance. Some US$30 million was spent analyzing 63,000 people and about 95% of the heritability of height remains unexplained. Results are similar for diseases. Does this mean that there are not enough people on the planet to find the genes?

We should not carp. Finding a single gene involved in a condition as mysterious as schizophrenia should be regarded as a great step forward. Most important, such a discovery can identify biological pathways to illness that can lead to increased understanding and new drug targets. But finding the missing variants, the 'dark matter' of genomic medicine, is more than a question of satisfying our academic interests. The nature of the missing stuff could be different, perhaps radically so, from that already discovered. GWAS are premised on the contribution of common variants to disease: the common disease–common variant hypothesis might not be true. GWAS cannot detect, or rather has a lower power to detect, contributions from rare variants.

We have long known that many different mutations in the same gene can cause single gene disorders such as cystic fibrosis, Huntington's disease, and thalassemias. Literally hundreds of different mutations are known that disrupt the cystic fibrosis gene leading to disease. Some of these are so rare that they are known in only one family. Such 'rare variants' might also be contributing to common disease, and there is now good evidence that they do so.

In 2004, Helen Hobbs and Jonathan Cohen of the University of Texas Southwestern Medical Center in Dallas, USA, sequenced genes known to be involved in the control of cholesterol levels (Cohen *et al.*, 2004). They chose genes in which mutations have been found segregating in families, rare pedigrees whose affected members have cholesterol levels well outside the normal range and who were having heart attacks in their 20s. They then asked whether rare sequence variants might be present in these genes in people whose serum cholesterol lies within the normal range, but at one or other extreme. In their first study, they sequenced two genes in 32 individuals whose cholesterol levels were in the upper and lower 5% of the distribution. Remarkably, they found that '*one of six individuals with HDL-C levels below the fifth percentile in the Dallas Heart Study had a rare mutation in ABCA1 or APOA1.*' So some variants in these genes could produce highly aberrant cholesterol levels that produced disease, but, understandably enough, other variants had milder effects that impacted on cholesterol levels in the 'normal range.'

Richard Lifton at Yale has done the same thing for blood pressure variation, again sequencing genes, this time three (Ji *et al.*, 2008). He used a much larger number of people (1,985 unrelated subjects and 1,140 relatives) taken from the Framingham Heart Study (FHS) a cohort that '*has been followed for up to 35 years with periodic evaluation of cardiovascular risk factors and other traits.*' This is what they found:

> At least 1 in 64 FHS members carries a functional mutation in one of these three genes. This is likely to be an underestimate, given the stringent criteria applied and the expectation that approximately 15% of deleterious mutations lie outside the coding regions. The effects of the carrier state are relatively large, similar in magnitude to those of clinically used antihypertensive agents; these mutations reduced the risk of hypertension at age 60 by nearly 60% and, based on epidemiologic observations in the Framingham cohort, would be predicted to reduce the risk of stroke by 40% and acute coronary syndrome by 15%.

Copy number variants (CNVs): a new kind of variation

Even though focused on only a single gene, sequencing on this scale is extremely expensive. Obviously, it also requires a known gene, which has remained a problem for psychiatric conditions. So how can we assess whether rare variants are important for behavior? Linkage studies will detect rare or common variants segregating in pedigrees, but we have seen the problems that linkage studies face—given that the effects of the gene have to be very large. However, in 2008, a study of autism detected rare variants by using linkage in large inbred pedigrees, where individuals share a common recent ancestor and the same mutation was present in all affected family members (Morrow *et al.*, 2008). The investigators found suitable pedigrees in parts of the world where cousin marriage is preferred, and where large families are the norm. Chris Walsh at Harvard Medical School analyzed 104 families from the Middle East, Turkey, and Pakistan, including 88 pedigrees with cousin marriages. As an index of the increased genetic risk posed by parents being genetically related, consider that marriage between first cousins doubles the prevalence of neurological birth defects. Walsh reported that several single families showed one or two loci with strong support for linkage, and that loci found in one family did not overlap with those found in another.

The autism work found something else as well: evidence that small deletions of chromosomal material were causing the disease. This observation supported one made the previous year by Jonathan Sebat and Mike Wigler at Cold Spring Harbor Laboratory.

Neither Jonathan Sebat nor Mike Wigler are psychiatrists, nor even neurobiologists. Mike Wigler had developed a method that screens the genome for changes in the copy number of DNA and Sebat was working with him to see how those variants might impact on disease. An intact genome comes in two copies, one from each parent, but there are regions, some quite large regions, where the DNA is duplicated, triplicated, or occurs in even higher copy numbers. These regions are often polymorphic, so that some people carry three copies, some carry more, some fewer. And where these regions include genes, there is the possibility that the copy number variants (or CNVs) contribute to phenotypic variation.

By surveying the genome, measuring as it were the CNV load, rather than looking for changes at a specific locus, Sebat found that there were more CNVs in individuals with autism than in controls: 12 out of 118 patients (10%) with sporadic autism, but just two out of 196 controls (1%) (Sebat *et al.*, 2007). They concluded that '*these results suggest that lesions at many different loci can contribute to autism… Lack of recurrence may in fact reflect an underlying reality that autistic behavior can result from many different genetic defects.*'

CNVs are not all unique. Some recur in unrelated individuals. In 2008, a whole-genome analysis of over 800 children with autism identified eight cases with the same small deletion on chromosome 16 (Weiss *et al.*, 2008). The region is one of about 150 predicted to undergo recurrent deletion and duplication. Large stretches of highly similar DNA sequence flanking these regions make them vulnerable to undergoing rearrangement, as if the chromosomal machinery mistakenly matches them up and, imagining there is just one rather than two sequences, cuts out the intervening region. Alternatively, the miscounting means the chromosome ends up with additional copies, and this was observed

at the 16p locus: 11 children with autism had the duplication. This meant that at 16p there is a '*recurrent microdeletion and a reciprocal microduplication that carry substantial susceptibility to autism and appear to account for approximately 1% of cases [of autism]*' (Weiss *et al.*, 2008).

CNVs are also important as a genetic cause of schizophrenia. Sebat found that there is increased CNV load in schizophrenics, reporting that deletions and duplications '*were present in 5% of controls versus 15% of cases and 20% of young-onset cases, both highly significant differences*' (Walsh *et al.*, 2008). Again by using much larger sample sizes, other groups have shown that a small proportion of CNVs are recurrent, as has been known for some time for a deletion on 22q. Deletions on chromosome 15 and chromosome 1 have been found, but they are found in a small fraction of patients, typically 1% or less. Of the 3,500 patients surveyed, the total burden of CNVs is increased 1.15-fold in patients compared with controls: '*On chromosome 15 (28–31 Mb) there were deletions in nine cases and no controls. On chromosome 1 (142.5–145.5 Mb) there were ten deletions in cases and one in controls*' (International Schizophrenia Consortium, 2008).

Key paper

Walsh, T., McClellan, J.M., McCarthy, S.E., Addington, A.M., Pierce, S.B., Cooper, G.M., Nord, A.S., Kusenda, M., Malhotra, D. *et al.* (2008). **Rare structural variants disrupt multiple genes in neurodevelopmental pathways in schizophrenia.** *Science* **320**:539–543.

This study demonstrated that searching for CNVs across the genome could identify genes involved in susceptibility to schizophrenia.

These are small numbers, just an indication of the nature of the genetic dark matter, but potentially a way to access the biology of psychosis. As Sebat points out, '*Genes disrupted by structural variants in our series of cases were significantly overrepresented in pathways important for brain development.*' How to take these genetic observations into functional analysis takes us back into discussion of neurobiology and the role of model organisms.

Summary

1. The small genetic effects that contribute to most behavioral and common disease phenotypes require vary large sample sizes for their robust detection.

2. About 60,000 years ago, humans migrated out of Africa, creating a population bottleneck that reduced our genetic diversity. Consequently, about half a million genetic markers are sufficient to capture a large fraction of the common sequence variants in the human genome.

3. By using high-throughput array-based assays (chips) to genotype millions of markers in thousands of cases and controls, it is possible to find genetic association between disease and common genetic variants anywhere in the genome.

4. Although genome-wide association studies (GWAS) can identify small-effect loci, they still fail to account for much of the phenotypic variance.

5. Additional genetic variation occurs as deletions and duplications of small chromosomal regions, known as copy number variations (CNVs), a few of which have been associated with autism and schizophrenia.

6. GWAS results suggest that hundreds or possibly thousands of genetic variants contribute to the susceptibility to schizophrenia. Some of the genetic loci for schizophrenia appear to overlap with those for bipolar disorder.

References

Brzustowicz, L.M., Hodgkinson, K.A., Chow, E.W., Honer, W.G., and Bassett, A.S. (2000). Location of a major susceptibility locus for familial schizophrenia on chromosome 1q21-q22. *Science* **288**:678–682.

Burton, P.R., Clayton, D.G., Cardon, L.R., Craddock, N., Deloukas, P., Duncanson, A., Kwiatkowski, D.P., McCarthy, M.I., Ouwehand, W.H. *et al.* (2007). Association scan of 14,500 nonsynonymous SNPs in four diseases identifies autoimmunity variants. *Nat Genet* **39**: 1329–1337.

Cohen, J.C., Kiss, R.S., Pertsemlidis, A., Marcel, Y.L., McPherson, R., and Hobbs, H.H. (2004). Multiple rare alleles contribute to low plasma levels of HDL cholesterol. *Science* **305**:869–872.

Collins, F.S., Guyer, M.S., and Chakravarti, A. (1997). Variations on a theme: Cataloging human DNA sequence variation. *Science* **278**:1580–1581.

Corder, E.H., Saunders, A.M., Strittmatter, W.J., Schmechel, D.E., Gaskell, P.C., Small, G.W., Roses, A.D., Haines, J.L., and Pericak-Vance, M.A. (1993). Gene dose of apolipoprotein E type 4 allele and the risk of Alzheimer's disease in late onset families. *Science* **261**:921–923.

Ferreira, M.A., O'Donovan, M.C., Meng, Y.A., Jones, I.R., Ruderfer, D.M., Jones, L., Fan, J., Kirov, G., Perlis, R.H. *et al.* (2008). Collaborative genome-wide association analysis supports a role for *ANK3* and *CACNA1C* in bipolar disorder. *Nat Genet* **40**:1056–1058.

Hindorff, L.A., Sethupathy, P., Junkins, H.A., Ramos, E.M., Mehta, J.P., Collins, F.S., and Manolio, T.A. (2009). Potential etiologic and functional implications of genome-wide association loci for human diseases and traits. *Proc Natl Acad Sci USA.* **106**: 9362–9367.

Hirschhorn, J.N. and Daly, M.J. (2005). Genome-wide association studies for common diseases and complex traits. *Nat Rev Gen* **6**:95–108.

International Schizophrenia Consortium (2008). Rare chromosomal deletions and duplications increase risk of schizophrenia. *Nature* **455**:237–241.

International Schizophrenia Consortium, Purcell, S.M., Wray, N.R., Stone, J.L., Visscher, P.M., O'Donovan, M.C., Sullivan, P.F., and Sklar, P. (2009). Common polygenic variation contributes to risk of schizophrenia and bipolar disorder. *Nature* **460**:748–752.

Ji, W., Foo, J.N., O'Roak, B.J., Zhao, H., Larson, M.G., Simon, D.B., Newton-Cheh, C., State, M.W., Levy, D., and Lifton, R.P. (2008). Rare independent mutations in renal salt handling genes contribute to blood pressure variation. *Nat Genet* **40**:592–599.

Kruglyak, L. (1999). Prospects for whole-genome linkage disequilibrium mapping of common disease genes. *Nat Genet* **22**:139–144.

Lander, E.S. 1996. The new genomics: global views of biology. *Science* **274**:536–539.

Levinson, D.F., Holmans, P.A., Laurent, C., Riley, B., Pulver, A.E., Gejman, P.V., Schwab, S.G., Williams, N.M., Owen, M.J. *et al.* (2002). No major schizophrenia locus detected on chromosome 1q in a large multicenter sample. *Science* **296**:739–741.

Morrow, E.M., Yoo, S.Y., Flavell, S.W., Kim, T.K., Lin, Y., Hill, R.S., Mukaddes, N.M., Balkhy, S.,

Gascon, G. *et al.* (2008). Identifying autism loci and genes by tracing recent shared ancestry. *Science* **321**:218–223.

O'Donovan, M.C., Craddock, N., Norton, N., Williams, H., Peirce, T., Moskvina, V., Nikolov, I., Hamshere, M., Carroll, L. *et al.* (2008). Identification of loci associated with schizophrenia by genome-wide association and follow-up. *Nat Genet* **40**:1053–1055.

Risch, N. and Merikangas, K. (1996). The future of genetic studies of complex human diseases. *Science* **273**:1516–1517.

Sebat, J., Lakshmi, B., Malhotra, D., Troge, J., Lese-Martin, C., Walsh, T., Yamrom, B., Yoon, S., Krasnitz, A. *et al.* (2007). Strong association of de novo copy number mutations with autism. *Science* **316**:445–449.

Walsh, T., McClellan, J.M., McCarthy, S.E., Addington, A.M., Pierce, S.B., Cooper, G.M., Nord, A.S., Kusenda, M., Malhotra, D. *et al.* (2008). Rare structural variants disrupt multiple genes in neurodevelopmental pathways in schizophrenia. *Science* **320**:539–543.

Wellcome Trust Case Control Consortium (2007). Genome-wide association study of 14,000 cases of seven common diseases and 3,000 shared controls. *Nature* **447**:661–678.

Weiss, L.A., Shen, Y., Korn, J.M., Arking, D.E., Miller, D.T., Fossdal, R., Saemundsen, E., Stefansson, H., Ferreira, M.A. *et al.* (2008). Association between microdeletion and microduplication at 16p11.2 and autism. *N Engl J Med* **358**:667–675.

  **Rodents**

[In which we describe how to map genes influencing the behavior of mice]

Consider this simple task. Place a mouse at the end of a T-shaped box and it will run to the junction and then turn either left or right. Suppose it turns left. As soon as it has made its choice, take the animal out, wait a short while and then let it explore the box again. On the second trial, the chances are the mouse will turn right, thereby exploring that part of the apparatus it missed on its first visit. This behavior, called spontaneous alternation, probably results from Darwinian selection for foraging patterns that increase the chances that they will detect at least one food source.

Mice do this task easily. It makes sense to us that they behave in this way. Now try the following. Use an apparatus that has four equal arms that we will call north, south, east, and west. Place a food reward in the west arm and let the animal enter the apparatus from the north arm, blocking the arm to the south so that the animal has to choose either west or east. Allow the animal to eat the food reward if it chooses the correct arm, otherwise remove it from the apparatus. Repeat the process ten times, sometimes starting the animal from the south, sometimes from the north. To get the food reward the mouse has to go west, using any cues from its surroundings to orientate

itself. It's a task of spatial orientation, the sort of skill you need to find your way home and one which you would think most animals that have to forage in the wild would be well-equipped to master. Yet, to learn this task an average laboratory mouse needs 80 attempts every day for at least a week, and even then it chooses the correct direction only 90% of the time.

The difficulty mice have carrying out what we see as a simple task doesn't mean we can't use mice to understand the genetics of behavior, but it might mean that we can only use mice to understand the genetics of mouse behavior—of interest to mice, but possibly not to everyone else. The extent and nature of genetic control over animal behavior could be fundamentally different from genetic influences over human behavior.

One of the reasons for objecting to genetic interpretations of human behavior is that they contradict our common-sense view that we, not our genes, decide what we do. Behavioral flexibility, that characteristic of our own species, is presumably an evolutionary development of more biologically determined behavior found in other organisms. Is it possible that behavior is much more biologically grounded in rodents than in humans?

Behaviorism and fixed action patterns

This problem starts with behaviorism, or at least its incarnation in the work of the psychologist B.F. Skinner, who introduced an experimental apparatus now known as a Skinner box. An animal (usually a rodent) placed into the box has the choice of pressing a bar, which typically results in the appearance of a food pellet. The apparatus is so arranged that only a certain type of bar-pressing (for example five presses in a row, but no more) will release the pellet, so that the animal learns to press the bar in just the right way. Successive slight changes in the conditions under which the response is rewarded shape the response of a rat, or indeed other animals, so that complex behaviors can be produced by a process of successive approximations. This process is known as 'operant conditioning' (Skinner, 1935).

Key paper

Skinner, B.F. (1935). Two types of conditioned reflex and a pseudo type. *J Gen Psychol* **12**, 66–77.

A description of operant behaviorism from one of its most influential proponents.

Operant conditioning

Observations on animal learning using Skinner boxes and other similar paradigms led to some fairly remarkable claims about the origin of behavior. Skinner argued that external factors, consisting of the frequency, arrangement, and withholding of reinforcing stimuli are of overwhelming importance in determining behavior in all organisms: the general principles revealed in laboratory studies could even account for all of the complexities of verbal behavior in humans; the precise prediction of verbal behavior involves the specification of the few external factors he had identified experimentally in lower organisms.

Skinner's enthusiasm for operant conditioning is extreme: once, questioned about the need for brain research, he answered, '*We don't need to know about the brain because we have operant conditioning.*' Clearly such a view leaves little room for genetically influenced behaviors. But not all of Skinner's followers could support his views. In an article entitled 'The misbehavior of organisms,' two orthodox Skinnerians, Keller and Marian Breland, described their attempts '*to determine if animal psychology could stand on its own feet as an engineering discipline*' (Breland and Breland, 1961). Here is how they tried to train a raccoon to pick up a coin and deposit it in a metal box:

> Raccoons condition readily, have good appetites, and this one was quite tame and an eager subject. We anticipated no trouble. Conditioning him to pick up the first coin was simple. We started out by reinforcing him for picking up a single coin. Then the metal container was introduced, with the requirement that he drop the coin into the container. Here we ran into the first bit of difficulty: he seemed to have a great deal of trouble letting go of the coin. He would rub it up against the inside of the container, pull it back out, and clutch it firmly for several seconds. However, he would finally turn it loose and receive his food reinforcement. Then the final contingency: we put him on a ratio of 2, requiring that he pick up both coins and put them in the container. Now the raccoon really had problems (and so did we). Not only could he not let go of the coins, but he spent seconds, even minutes, rubbing them together (in a most miserly fashion), and dipping them into the container. He carried on this behavior to such an extent that the practical application

we had in mind—a display featuring a raccoon putting money in a piggy bank—simply was not feasible.

Key paper

Breland, K. and Breland, M. (1961) The misbehavior of organisms. *Am Psychol* **16**:681–684.

A classic in the history of psychology from two reluctant behavioral psychologists.

'Innateness'

These observations make sense if you assume that the raccoon possesses an innate 'washing behavior', a biologically determined response presumably adapted to aid the animal in getting the flesh out of a crayfish's shell. Training requires the animal to suppress this innate behavior, which it finds difficult. As a general rule, training works best when it manipulates pre-existing innate behavioral patterns. Despite their Skinnerian beliefs, the Brelands had come across what appeared to be biologically determined behaviors that they could not condition.

Further support for the presence of innate behaviors came from ethology, studying animal behavior as it occurs in natural settings (Burkhardt, 2005). When a brooding goose notices an egg outside her nest, the bird rises to extend her neck and bill out over the egg so that she can gently roll it back to the nest. If the egg is removed as the goose begins to extend her neck, she still completes the pattern of rolling the non-existent egg back to the nest. The ethologists Konrad Lorenz and Niko Tinbergen termed this response a fixed action pattern. Tinbergen also discovered that the fixed action pattern of rolling the egg back to the nest could be triggered by anything outside the nest that even marginally resembled an egg (beer cans and baseballs did well).

Key paper

Burkhardt, R.W., Jr (2005). *Patterns of Behavior: Konrad Lorenz, Niko Tinbergen and the Founding of Ethology*. Chicago, IL: Chicago University Press.

A recent introduction to ethology and the work of Lorenz and Tinbergen.

The operant conditioning worldview does without genetics; the fixed action pattern says everything is hard-wired. Neither view accommodates the sort of genetic influences we have been dealing with up to now, where variation in behavior reflects, to a varying degree, differences in genetic constitution. We need to determine whether behavior is heritable in animals.

The heritability of mouse behavior

Recall how we assess heritability in humans, and remember how difficult that can be (finding all those twins, dealing with the assumptions about equal environment and so on). Determining whether there is a genetic effect in mice is much simpler, and quicker, once you have the resource. The resource, in this case as in so much else in mouse genetics, is the inbred animal. In an inbred population, there are no genetic differences among individuals. The chromosomes that every individual receives from their mothers and fathers and all of the chromosomes they pass on to their progeny are the same. Therefore, such populations have no genetic variance at all.

Inbreeding is achieved by encouraging incest. Experimental organisms don't show any restraint about brother–sister (or parent–child) mating and if you organize this for long enough, you end up with completely inbred animals. If you are a worm geneticist, then your favorite organism actually prefers to have sex with itself, so it's really no problem to get rid of all of that genetic heterogeneity that so confuses human geneticists. All you do is the leave the animals alone to eat bacteria (a cheap and easily obtainable foodstuff) for a few generations and they will self-fertilize and end up completely inbred.

Mouse geneticists have to devote more time than worm geneticists to inbreeding their animals; they have to set up brother–sister matings for about 20 generations to create animals that genetically differ only on the sex chromosomes. Once the animals are inbred, they are given some anonymous strain designation (AKR, DBA, and so on, which may mean nothing to you, but means a lot to mouse geneticists). Inbred strains were made as a tool for investigating various aspects of biology: our understanding of immunology has, for example, been critically dependent on having inbred strains that differed in their immune responses, leading to the discovery of regulators of acquired (Snell, 1979), and more recently, innate immunity (Beutler, 2004).

Access to inbred animals substantially simplifies the genetic analysis of behavior. It is this, more than anything else, that stacks the odds in our favor. To show how it works, we'll give as an example the genetics of fearfulness, or anxiety, in the mouse.

Locomotor activity

Rodents prefer living hidden away, in the dark probably because that is the best way for them to avoid predators. When placed in a brightly lit open arena, a strange, new, and potentially dangerous place, typically they freeze, or at least move around much less. The amount of locomotor activity is thus a crude index of the animal's fearfulness or anxiety.

Figure 7.1 shows a measure of locomotor activity in such a brightly lit arena for eight inbred strains. The strain names are on the horizontal axis and the vertical axis shows how much each strain runs about. There are 12 mice in each group and the figure (called a 'box and whisker' plot) represents the distribution of the activity values. The box shows the middle values of the activity score (the black dot is the average), while the whiskers stretch to the greatest and lowest values. You can see there are some outliers (the blue circles) but you can also see that there are big differences between the strains, not all of which are due to the variation in the measure. These differences are due to genetic differences between the strains: as the members of each group are genetically identical, the differences within a group are due to the environment; differences between groups are due to genetic variation.

These data tell us that anxiety (at least as reflected by the level of activity in this environment) is heritable.

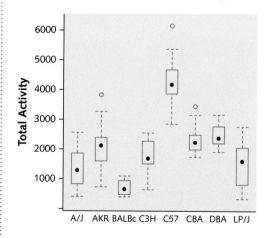

Figure 7.1 A measure of locomotor activity in a brightly lit arena for eight inbred strains of mice.

Inbred strain comparisons are a crude but effective tool in telling us whether genetic differences are important. Think of this as a 'first-pass' experiment to look for genetic effects. Few of the methodological concerns that we dealt with at length in considering human studies are relevant here because we have so much more control over the experiment: there is no selective placement or assortative mating here. We don't have to worry (so much) about our genetic effect being an artifact due to some background environment effect that we cannot control and may not even know about.

Selection

There are other methods that take more time (but they also tell us more), which are again only possible because of the existence of inbred animals. Consider what would happen if you compel the most hyperactive people in each generation (let's say the most active 10%) to marry and breed only with each other, and keep doing that for every generation. Would activity in this population eventually reach a plateau, so that everyone ran about the same? Or would the level of activity continue to climb almost without limit?

Two behavioral geneticists in the USA, John DeFries and John Hegmann, carried out just this experiment using mice (DeFries and Hegmann, 1970). Their measure of activity was the total distance a mouse would travel when placed in an open-field arena (the apparatus in which animals are assumed to be frightened). They started by mating two inbred lines and then selected the most active male and female from each litter for breeding. They also selected the least active male and female, so that they could see the response to selection in both directions. Recall that we are postulating that the most active animals are also the most

relaxed and the low activity mice are the most anxious. DeFries and Hegmann included controls, where pairs of animals were selected at random, irrespective of their activity level, to make sure other aspects of the experiment, apart from selection, had no unexpected effects on behavior.

The results were dramatic. After 30 generations of selection, the mice in the high-activity lines were 30 times as active as those in the low-activity lines (DeFries et al., 1978). Think about the difference in how far you would travel in a car going at 2 versus 60 miles an hour and that will give you a sense of the differences in activity levels (and presumably the associated levels of anxiety) of these two groups of mice.

Key paper

DeFries, J.C., Gervais, M.C., and Thomas, E.A. (1978). Response to 30 generations of selection for open field activity in laboratory mice. *Behav Genet* 8:3–13.

One of the classic selection experiments in behavioral genetics.

Animal and plant breeders have been applying selection for millennia. The size of our wheat plants and tomatoes, the large amount of milk we get from our cows, and the extraordinary diversity of shapes, sizes, and temperaments in domestic dogs all result from selection over many generations. DeFries and Hegmann did the same for anxiety-related behavior in mice.

We can draw a number of conclusions from this single selection experiment. Firstly, it is possible to estimate the heritability: provided there is no non-genetic cause of resemblance between offspring and parents, and no natural selection operating (for instance, the more active animals should be equally fertile and as viable as the inactive animals), then the ratio of response to the selection is equal to the heritability. Heritability estimated in this way is called a realized heritability, and for the experiment described above, it turns out to be about 20%. (For technical reasons, realized heritability will nearly always be lower than the kind of heritability we explored in our twin studies—differences in genetic control of a phenotype in natural populations.)

Secondly, the selection response can also tell us something about how the genetic effects work. If there had been a single genetic variant that substantially increased activity and that accounted for a large proportion of the variation in activity, then applying selection for activity would quickly alter the frequency of that single variant, which would rise rapidly in the group selected for high activity and fall just as quickly in the animals selected for low activity; that is, the selection would quickly reach a floor and a ceiling. However, as Figure 7.2 from DeFries *et al.*'s paper shows, selection resulted in an apparently steady change in both directions (selecting for both high and low activity). We know from these kinds of curves that single genes with large effects on activity are not present in these two inbred lines.

Selection experiments for a range of other behaviors in a variety of organisms tell the same story that we see in humans: behavior is heritable, genetic effects account for less than half the variation in behavior, and the variation in the populations undergoing selection results from many genes.

Heritability estimates for 143 different behavioral traits from a wide variety of organisms, including the fruit fly *Drosophila* and 75 other invertebrate and vertebrate species, show remarkable congruence (Mousseau and Roff, 1987). While there is considerable variation in the heritability of individual traits, the median heritability (a median is the value in a distribution where half the values are smaller and half are greater) was 25%.

Key paper

Mousseau, T.A. and Roff, D.A. (1987). Natural selection and the heritability of fitness components. *Heredity* **59**:181–197.

A catalogue of 1,120 heritability estimates for wild, outbred animal populations.

It is interesting to compare these results with what has been found for the human traits and disorders we have reviewed. The heritability of most mouse behaviors is similar to that seen for human personality and vulnerability to anxiety disorders and depression (Valdar *et al.*, 2006). However, it is hard to find a behavioral trait in mice that is as heritable as schizophrenia, bipolar illness, and autism (where heritability estimates are at least 70% and probably higher).

Mouse geneticists don't usually measure heritability. In fact, in a way, the heritability results are embarrassing. Mouse testing is supposed to be uniform, free from the environmental chaos that is the stuff of human lives and that makes things so difficult for human geneticists. Standard textbooks of genetics, when explaining how heritability is a relative concept, often compare the example of corn grown under uniform, controlled environmental conditions (same soil, same amount of water and sunlight) with corn grown out in the wild, subject to the vagaries of the climate and the field. In the first case, all variation will be due to genetic variation, so the heritability is 100%; in the second, variation is due to both environment and genes, so heritability will be less.

Apply the same argument to the mouse studies and you see the problem: even under the

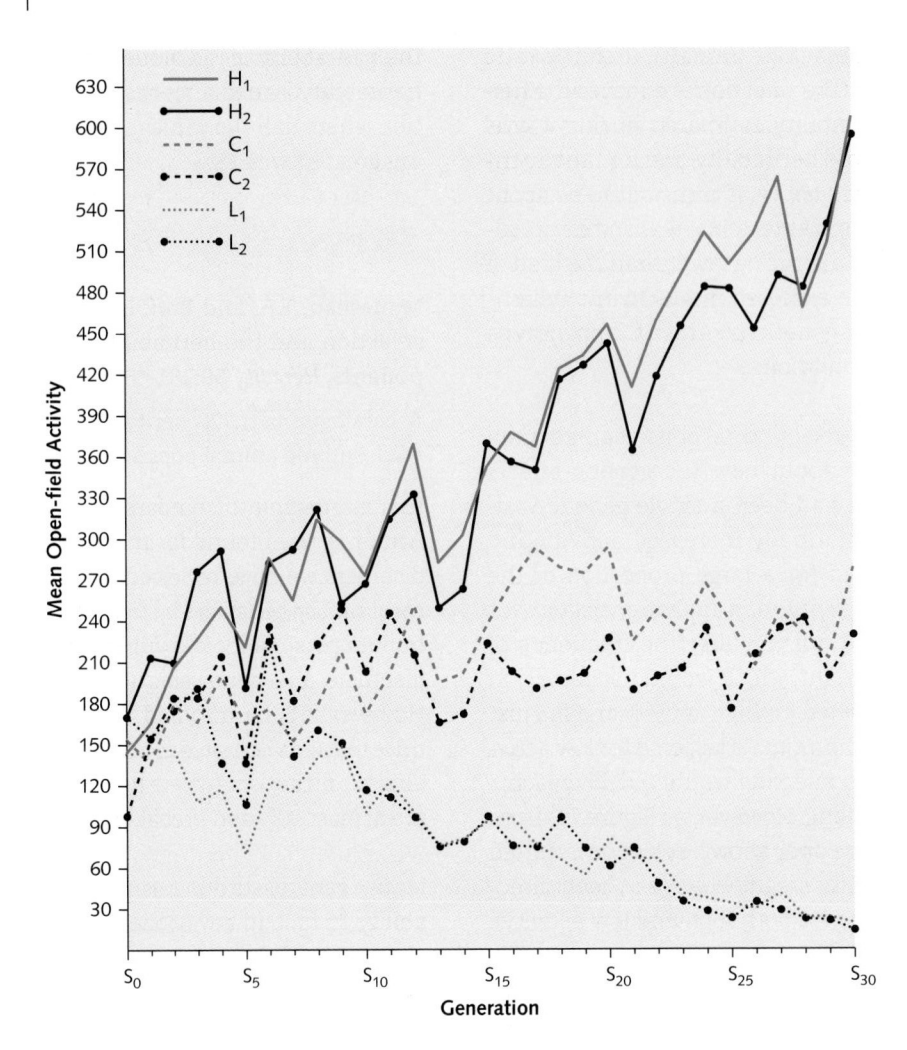

Figure 7.2 Mean open-field activity scores of six lines of mice, two selected for high open-field activity (H₁ and H₂), two selected for low open-field activity (L₁ and L₂) and two randomly mated within line to serve as controls (C₁ and C₂).
Source: DeFries *et al.* (1978).

controlled conditions of laboratory testing, heritability is nowhere near 100%. It's true that there are other sources of variation that we need to take into account, but it is also true that we are not as good as we might like at providing a controlled, uniform, stable environment for testing.

This is not so to say that mouse geneticists aren't interested in whether a trait is heritable or not. They are interested, and they can get that information quickly from looking at the differences between inbred strains, as explained above. It's the quantification of heritability that is less relevant to their intent.

The large number of resources available to mouse geneticists, in the form of inbred strains and their derived crosses, together with the molecular biology tools that make it possible to change the DNA of mice, can be used to finding the molecular basis of genetic differences and to investigate their biology at a level impossible in human genetics. The tools, the way of doing genetics, and to some extent the scientific culture differ between mouse and human geneticists. If the starting point is the same—establish that behavior has a genetic basis—the next step, how they map genetic determinants, is different.

Mapping behavior to a single chromosome

Yeast has never been used for behavioral analysis, but it is great for studying recombination. It's one of the few things yeasts do, apart from making alcohol (good for beer and wine) and carbon dioxide (good for making bread rise). Yeast geneticists exploit their organism's fondness for recombination for their own interests: they add in pieces of DNA, they take them out, they create mutations in any gene, and they even build entirely new chromosomes (yeast artificial chromosomes, or YACs, were one of the tools used for the cloning and sequencing of the human genome). When yeast geneticists write grants to support their work, they have a stock phrase that they use to convince reviewers of the value of their model organism. They write about 'the awesome power of yeast genetics.' Compared with what you can do in mice, it is truly awesome; in the same way, compared with what you can do in humans, mouse genetics is awesome.

Mouse genetics is particularly awesome when it comes to finding where on a chromosome genetic variants influencing behavior are likely to reside

(mapping behavior). To understand why, we have to see how the experiment is done.

Mice have 20 pairs of chromosomes (19 pairs and the two sex chromosomes, the X and Y). One way to find out which of these 20 has gene-influencing behavior is to create mice that have one chromosome from one inbred strain, but all of the others from a second inbred strain (the mice with the appropriate chromosomes are called chromosome substitution strains) (Singer *et al.*, 2004).

If the strains are called A and B, we generate inbred mice that have chromosome 1 from strain A and the remaining 19 from strain B (A.B in Fig. 7.3), mice that have chromosome 2 from strain A (and the remainder from strain B; B.A in Fig. 7.3), and so on until we have a complete set of mice that differ from their parents for each of the 20 chromosomes. It takes a long time to make a mouse with this chromosomal constitution, but it's perfectly possible. It's just a question of highly organized incest.

Once the resource, the set of chromosome substitution strains, is available, mapping to a chromosome is statistically robust, quick, and relatively cheap (the cost of maintaining the animals and the cost of the test). We compare the measure of anxiety (activity in the open-field arena) in strain B mice with mice that have chromosome 1 from strain A (but are otherwise all strain B derived). Any difference will be due to genes on chromosome 1. We repeat the process for the other chromosomes.

As in most cases we measure the trait quantitatively, like height and weight, and because the genetic effect we are seeking is at a locus on the genome, the process is often called quantitative trait locus mapping, or QTL mapping for short. QTL mapping with chromosomal substitution strains actually came onto the market quite

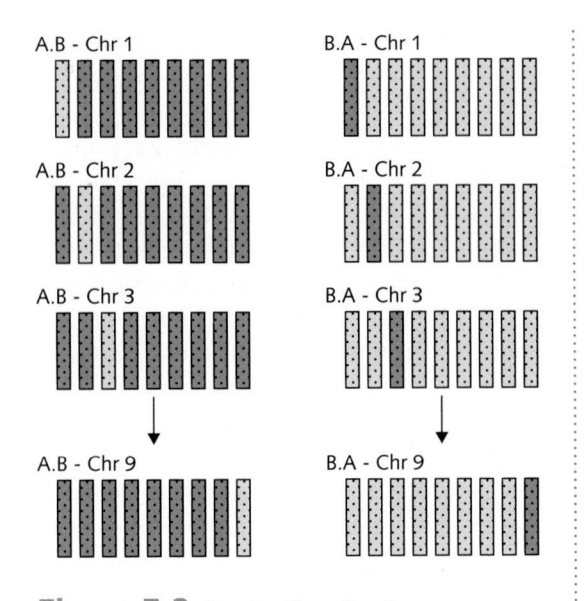

A.B - Chr 1   B.A - Chr 1

A.B - Chr 2   B.A - Chr 2

A.B - Chr 3   B.A - Chr 3

A.B - Chr 9   B.A - Chr 9

Figure 7.3 Construction of a chromosome substitution strain, achieved by recurrent backcrossing to isolate a single chromosome from one strain, with all other chromosomes descended from a second strain.

late, but I have described it first as it provides the simplest way of seeing what is going on.

The drawback is that it does not identify a gene, but a chromosome. If we want genes, we want better mapping resolution, and to do that we have to break up the chromosomes. We rely on recombination and use a method that is in some ways analogous to the family-based linkage method we described for mapping schizophrenia.

Key papers

Pyle, D. (1978). A chromosome substitution analysis of geotactic maze behavior in *Drosophila melanogaster*. *Behav Genet* **8**:53–64.

An example of using chromosome substitutions to map behavior.

Nadeau, J.H., Singer, J.B., Matin, A., and Lander, E.S. (2000). Analysing complex genetic traits with chromosome substitution strains. *Nat Genet* **24**:221–225.

A good review of the methodology involved in mapping with chromosome substitution traits, and a good starting point for understanding mapping.

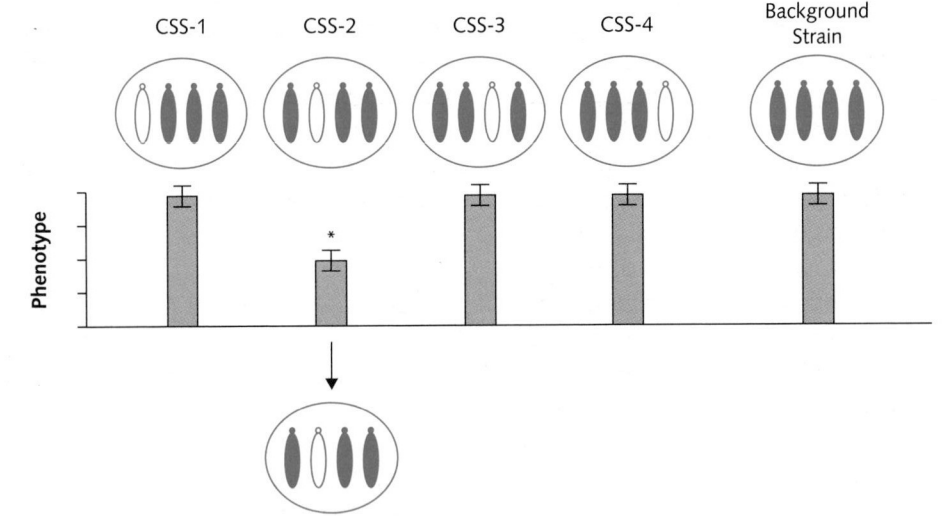

QTL affecting trait on chromosome 2

Figure 7.4 Determining which chromosome has a gene that influences behavior (CSS, chromosome substitution strain; QTL, quantitative trait locus).
Source: Singer *et al.* (2005).

Singer, J.B., Hill, A.E., Burrage, L.C., Olszens, K.R., Song, J., Justice, M., O'Brien, W.E., Conti, D.V., Witte, J.S. *et al.* (2004). Genetic dissection of complex traits with chromosome substitution strains of mice. *Science* **304**:445–448.

The first report of the use of chromosome substitution strains in mice to map multiple phenotypes across the genome.

Mapping behavior to a chromosomal region

Genetic mapping of behavior, or of any quantitative phenotype, such as height or weight, can be carried out by analyzing the offspring of a cross between two inbred strains. The first generation of such a cross (the F_1) will have one chromosome from one inbred strain and one from the other another and so will be genetically identical (no use for mapping), but the second generation (the F_2 intercross) or a backcross (where F_1 animals are bred with the parental strain) will have recombinant chromosomes that are useful for mapping (Figure 7.5).

The basic principal is the same as that used for linkage mapping in schizophrenia. We need to know the parental origin of each piece of chromosome, in this case which piece of chromosome comes from strain A and which piece comes from strain B. As in human studies, molecular markers are used to give the parental origin. It's important to emphasize that the genetic variants used for mapping are not the genetic variants that contribute to variation in anxiety or to any other phenotype. They need not have any function at all. They are simply markers of whether the chromosome is from strain A or strain B (see Appendix pp. 229–230).

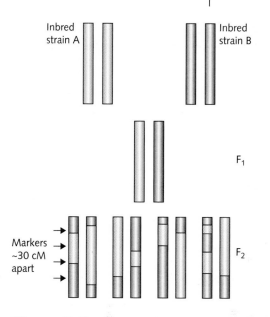

Figure 7.5 Analyzing the offspring of a cross between two inbred strains.

With the molecular information in hand, we can ask whether animals that share a chromosomal segment derived from strain A are more anxious than those with the same segment derived from strain B. Things are a bit more complicated than with the comparison of a single chromosome, as the two groups differ at other regions in the genome, not just at the place we are comparing. But if we test enough mice, those other differences will be randomly distributed between the two groups and their effects will cancel out.

In the early 1990s this method was first used in mice to map the genetic basis of high blood pressure and diabetes. The results of those studies contrasted sharply with the non-replicated and sometimes retracted findings in linkage and association studies for psychiatric disease in humans that we reviewed in Chapters 3 and 5. Just in terms of the P values obtained, the contrast was striking. While human studies struggled to obtain convincing evidence that a locus had been identified, the mouse results were orders of magnitude in excess of the required thresholds. But these were studies of physiological traits. It was not at all clear whether the same would hold for anything to do with behavior.

Key papers

Lander, E.S. and Botstein, D. (1989). Mapping Mendelian factors underlying quantitative traits using RFLP linkage maps. *Genetics* **121**:185–199.

A classic paper that describes how to map quantitative phenotypes in crosses between inbred strains using molecular markers.

Hilbert, P., Lindpaintner, K., Beckmann, J.S., Serikawa, T., Soubrier, F., Dubay, C., Cartwright, P., De Gouyon, B., Julier, C. *et al.* (1991). Chromosomal mapping of two genetic loci associated with blood-pressure regulation in hereditary hypertensive rats. *Nature* **353**:521–529.

Jacob, H., Lindpaintner, K., Lincoln, S., Kusumi, K., Bunker, R., Mao, Y., Ganten, D., Dzau, V., and Lander, E. (1991). Genetic mapping of a gene causing hypertension in the stroke-prone spontaneously hypertensive rat. *Cell* **67**:213–224.

Todd, J.A., Aitman, T.J., Cornall, R.J., Ghosh, S., Hall, J.R., Hearne, C.M., Knight, A.M., Love, J.M., McAleer, M.A. *et al.* (1991). Genetic analysis of autoimmune type 1 diabetes mellitus in mice. *Nature* **351**:542–547.

Three seminal papers that reported that molecular mapping of complex phenotypes in crosses derived from inbred strains could identify genetic loci that contributed to the phenotype.

Anxious mice

At the time that these papers on blood pressure and diabetes were published, I (J.F.) was working in the Institute of Psychiatry, which is carefully situated between two of London's more deprived regions, Peckham and Brixton, so there is rarely a shortage of psychiatrically ill patients. Nevertheless, everyone at the Institute is encouraged to engage in research. I wondered whether mouse behavior could be mapped like mouse hypertension. There was no one then at the Institute with expertise in carrying out genetic experiments in animals, but to my surprise the Head of Psychology (not psychiatry), Jeffrey Gray, took an interest. He introduced me to people who had such expertise, in the Institute for Behavioral Genetics, in Boulder, Colorado. Actually I don't remember much about those introductions. Jeffrey was of the opinion that if you flew over to the States and came back quickly enough you could just ignore the jet lag. That worked fine for him, but it left me nearly comatose for the whole trip. So I don't know how we started working with John DeFries, Al Collins, and David Fulker, but we did.

We worked on anxiety because that was Jeffrey Gray's expertise. He knew how to recognize an anxious mouse. Under stress, mice show many of the same signs as anxious humans. In the brightly lit open-field arena discussed above, their heart rate increases and they stop moving. If stressed further, they defecate and urinate, much as people do in situations of extreme stress, such as under bombardment in war. Drugs that calm anxious people also work on anxious mice; for example benzodiazepines (a class of drug that includes Valium) alter behavior in stressful environments, so that the animal treats the open-field arena as if it were a pleasant Sunday stroll. This indicates that at least some of the machinery involved is probably the same in the two species. On that basis (there is more evidence, explained at length in Gray's work on the neuropsychology of anxiety; Gray 1982, 1987), it seemed reasonable to map anxiety using some behavioral measure, such as activity in a novel, frightening environment.

Key paper

Gray, J.A. (1987). *The Psychology of Fear and Stress*, 2nd edn. Cambridge: Cambridge University Press.

Gray's description of the nature of anxiety and a justification for using many of the animal tests described in this chapter.

I have already shown you John DeFries' experiment in which, by artificial selection as well as by strain comparisons, he worked out the heritability of the novel activity score that he used as an index of being prone to anxiety. His selection experiment had yielded six inbred strains. By brother–sister mating a high-activity line and doing the same for a low-activity line, he had generated a perfect resource for genetic mapping. We could cross a high-activity strain with a low-activity strain and we could map anxiety with the techniques applied to hypertension and diabetes in the mouse.

It wasn't clear to me how many mice we would need. I asked John Todd, a geneticist who had published the paper reporting the first use of mice for mapping susceptibility to diabetes (Todd *et al.*, 1991). Nowadays, you'd expect to get a statistician to work this out for you, making some reasonable (or apparently reasonable) assumptions. John Todd had a much simpler answer: use as many mice as the animal house can produce. This sounded like good advice, particularly as I wasn't going to have to test the mice. I'd never held a mouse before, let alone carried out a behavioral test, so it was unlikely I'd be much help in getting the activity data. I could therefore happily pass on Todd's advice to Collin's team in Boulder, who had agreed to help. They tested 879 mice, about four times as many animals as anyone had tested for a mapping experiment. I soon realized why no one had done so many animals. Someone had

to genotype them all. When we started on this project, I had previously done no genotyping. Three months later, I had carried out about 100,000 PCR amplifications. I used about 100 markers and had results on over 800 animals (see Appendix pp. 227–230).

It takes months to breed the mice, weeks to collect the behavior data, months to carry out the genotyping, and, once you have cleaned up the data, a few minutes to carry out the analysis. The simplest and quickest analysis is to see whether the activity levels vary significantly between the genotypes of each marker. If they do, then the markers are associated with the trait. This analysis can be done on a reasonably good pocket calculator, in a spreadsheet such as Excel, or in one of a variety of statistical packages.

Suppose we have four markers on the chromosome. Each marker has two alleles, that we'll call *a* and *b*. Due to recombination, the grandchildren of strains of A and B can have two copies of *a*, two copies of *b*, or one of each (*ab*) (Figure 7.5). We genotype the mice at the four markers so that for each animal we can say that this animal, at this position on the chromosome, is *aa*, this animal is *ab*, and this animal is *bb*. To make things simpler, we show the results for just the *aa* and *bb* animals at the four markers (Figure 7.6). You can see the differences between the scores reflected in the position of the line in the middle of the box (the average score).

There are many wrinkles in the basic idea, but if you don't see a significant difference between genotypes, then it's extremely unlikely that the more sophisticated analyses are going to turn up anything (not forgetting to take into account the number of tests you have run: in testing 100 markers there's a 1 in 20 chance of obtaining a result of 0.0005, so to be declared significant the result has to be less than that).

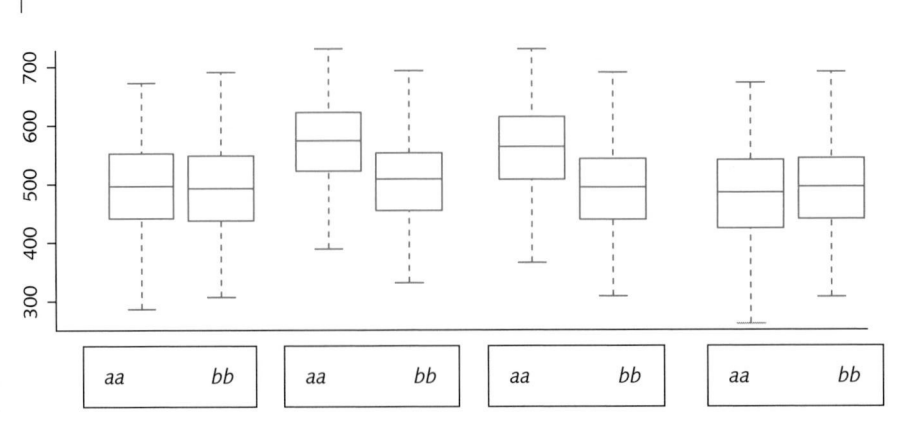

Figure 7.6 Phenotypic variation (*y*-axis) for genotypes (either *aa* or *bb*) at four markers.

Running 100 markers through the test takes a few minutes, half an hour by the time everything has been checked. At the end of that analysis, there were three places on the genome where markers showed significant evidence: on mouse chromosomes 1, 7 and 15.

Key paper

Flint, J., Corley, R., DeFries, J.C., Fulker, D.W., Gray, J.A., Miller, S., and Collins, A.C. (1995). A simple genetic basis for a complex psychological trait in laboratory mice. *Science* **269**:1432–1435.

This describes the first mapping of a behavioral trait in a cross between inbred mice using molecular techniques.

Figure 7.7 shows results with the entire mouse genome laid end to end on the horizontal axis, from the upper tip of chromosome 1 at the left end to the bottom tip of chromosome X at the right end. The significance of the results was remarkable: on chromosome 1, the *P* value was 1 in 1000,000,000,000,000 (15 zeroes). Because the *P* values are so small, they are easier to report as logarithms, typically as negative logarithms to avoid having to write a minus sign. So the chromosome 1 result is 15.

Mice versus humans

There are two obvious differences between these results and those in human studies: the peaks are far more significant, and there is a clear difference between regions containing an effect and those that do not. Furthermore, the result is robust. DeFries had replicated his selection experiment, carrying out two parallel selection studies so that he generated four strains (two high activity and two low activity)(Figure 7.2). We repeated the mapping experiment in the second set of selected animals, again crossing high- and low-activity strains, and obtained almost identical results (Figure 7.8).

Unlike human studies, where results were just about significant, mapping behavior in crosses between inbred strains yields highly significant findings that can, and have, been replicated. Does this mean the genetic basis of behavior is somehow different between the two species?

The short answer is no. The relatively simple genetic architecture that emerges from the studies of inbred strains reflects the simplicity of the experiment. In human studies, every family, every subject, is unique. The genetic

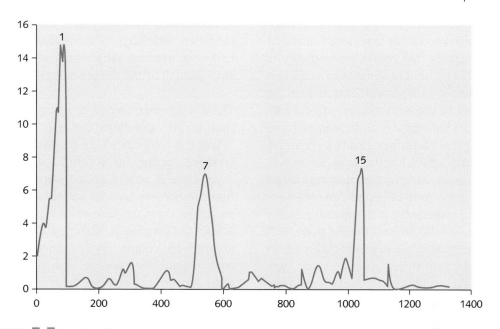

Figure 7.7 Results of genome-wide mapping in the mouse. The y-axis is a measure of the probability that there is a genetic effect and the x-axis is the genetic distance along the mouse genome, from chromosome 1 on the left to the X chromosome on the right. The units for the y-axis are the negative logarithm of the P value (log P), so that 14 represents a P value of 10^{-14}.

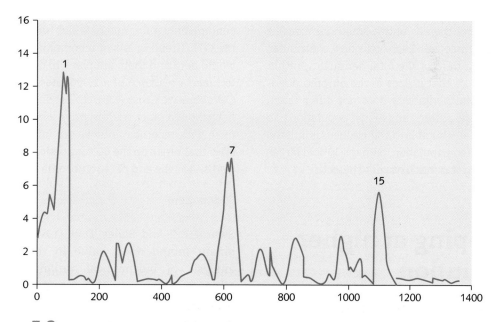

Figure 7.8 A replication of the experiment shown in Figure 7.7.

variants that contribute to schizophrenia susceptibility in one family may not be the same genetic variants that confer susceptibility to another. There could be variants in a different gene, different variants in the same gene, or there could be common variants affecting all families; we have no way of knowing until we try to map the disease genetically. By contrast, every mouse family has the same variants in the same genes, as their chromosomes derive from the same pairs of inbred parental chromosomes. Furthermore, in the inbred cross, the frequencies of the variants are the same (50% in an intercross), while in a fully outbred population, the frequencies of variants will vary: some families will have only one variant in one gene, others will have both variants in another gene, and in others there will be no variation at all.

There is one further reason why the inbred strain experiment simplifies the genetics. Suppose that the total heritability is made up of 100 individual effects in a mouse outbred population. By inbreeding, the vast majority of these effects are lost, so that there is only a small number (for example three) left. Each locus now contributes to about a third of the total heritability, rather than the 1% that it does in the outbred population. Total heritability does not differ much between the outbred and inbred populations, so the effect attributable to a single locus is inflated in the inbred population, perhaps 30-fold larger. This is why it is much easier to detect.

Mapping at higher resolution

Mapping to a chromosomal region is better than mapping to a chromosome, but it is not as good as mapping to a gene. The regions we

identified that were likely to contain the gene (or genes) were large, in some cases covering half a chromosome. What would help us to get close enough to find the genes involved?

There is another way of mapping QTLs, one that in fact pre-dates the use of crosses between inbred strains. By continuing brother–sister mating for about 20 generations beyond the F_2, inbred animals are produced that are homozygous for recombinant chromosomes. Once the position of recombinants across the genome is known, a QTL can be mapped by comparing the phenotypes of each recombinant inbred and determining what genetic material they have in common. This is the same basic idea as mapping in the inbred strain cross. Its advantage is that one set of animals can be used for multiple mapping experiments (no need to set up another cross, just order in the mice) and the set of animals needs to be genotyped just once. The disadvantage is that the mapping resolution is limited: recombinant inbreds will contain a random sampling of recombinants across the genome only a fraction of which will break up the QTL. Creating lots of recombinant inbreds would help and there are plans to do just that, to make a resource of a 1,000 lines, called the Collaborative Cross (Churchill *et al.*, 2004). But how about a quicker alternative where we find mice with recombinants we are interested in, ones that break up the QTL influencing anxiety that sits at the end of chromosome 1?

Key papers

Swank, R.T. and Bailey, D.W. (1973). Recombinant inbred lines: value in the genetic analysis of biochemical variants. *Science* **181**:1249–1252.

A description of recombinant inbred strains and their use in mapping, from one of the creators of the idea.

Churchill, G.A., Airey, D.C., Allayee, H., Angel, J.M., Attie, A.D., Beatty, J., Beavis, W.D., Belknap, J.K., Bennett, B. *et al.* (2004). The Collaborative Cross, a community resource for the genetic analysis of complex traits. *Nat Genet* **36**:1133–1137.

A description of the Collaborative Cross: a set of 1,000 recombinant inbred lines to be used for genetic mapping of complex traits.

This idea raises the question of whether we could find, or make, animals with recombinants where we need them, at the end of chromosome 1 for example, where we have identified the QTL influencing anxiety. Such animals would surely be useful in mapping the QTL at high resolution, and indeed this approach has been tried.

Sufficient patience will usually be rewarded by the creation of animals that do have recombinants in the right place and can break up a QTL region. Using the breeding scheme described in Figure 7.9, mice can be bred whose chromosomes are all from strain A except for a small segment around the locus, which comes from strain B, to generate what is known as a congenic.

By this process, a region can be whittled down to the point where the only cause of genetic variation resides in the small region from strain B. At this point, the heritability attributable to that locus will be 100%. This one small segment now contains the QTL, for example the QTL on chromosome 1 that was identified in the original cross between the inbred strains. In this way, the problem of multiple effects is reduced to that of a single effect, so that the principles of positional cloning can be applied (see Appendix p. 233). In effect, the phenotype has been turned into a Mendelian condition—all genetic effects attributable to a single variant.

Three problems have confounded this hope (Flint and Mackay, 2009; Flint *et al.*, 2005). Firstly, as many people have found to their cost, during the process of reducing the interval, it emerges that there is not one, or even two, but actually multiple genetic effects lying within a single region. So, taking the example of the QTL on chromosome 1, if we applied the approach advocated in Figure 7.9, rather than simply progressing to the point where we had captured the QTL in a small interval, we would find that when we get to N8 or N9 steps, there are two regions not one.

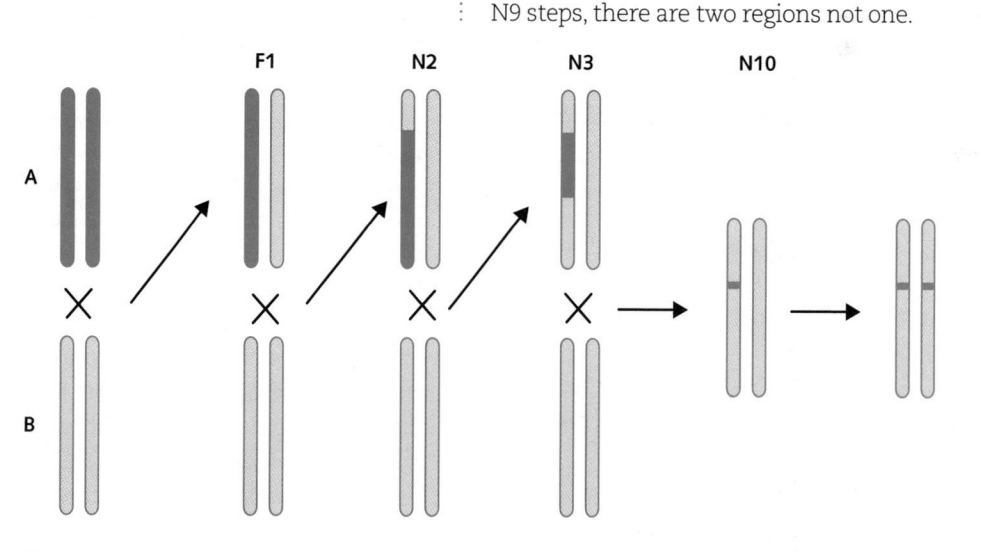

Figure 7.9 How to produce a congenic mouse: breeding scheme to produce mice whose chromosomes are all from strain A except for a small segment around the locus, which comes from strain B.

This might not itself be too big a problem, as presumably we could concentrate just on smaller and smaller regions, ignoring the splinters that otherwise would demand attention. However, we have a second problem: the effect of the single locus depends critically on its context. As the other regions of the genome are homogenized, turned into a uniform genetic background (light blue in the figure), the effect of the single locus we are chasing begins to waver, as if in sympathy with the loss of its partners, and may even disappear altogether. There are even cases where the effect has reversed: what appears to be a genetic effect that increases susceptibility changes into one that decreases susceptibility.

Finally, the third and last problem: no one can find the sequence change that is the cause of all this bother. Adhering to the positional cloning ideology, investigators would sequence all of the genes looking for the mutation, but none would be discovered. Lots of sequence variants are discovered, but none carries a biological mark identifying them as causative. Sequencing the coding regions was expected to identify changes that inactivate the gene or otherwise alter the protein's function, but this has rarely turned out to be true. The Mendelian paradigm, where the sequence changes alter protein function in a predictable fashion, just does not seem to apply.

Key papers

Flint, J., Valdar, W., Shifman, S., and Mott, R. (2005). Strategies for mapping and cloning quantitative trait genes in rodents. *Nat Rev Genet* **6**:271–286.
Flint, J. and Mackay, T.F. (2009). Genetic architecture of quantitative traits in mice, flies, and humans. *Genome Res* **19**:723–733.

Two reviews of the genetic architecture of complex traits in mice and the difficulties presented for identifying the genetic variants responsible for complex traits.

More strains, more recombinations

These difficulties led me (J.F.) to think again about the mapping problem. As in the end mapping resolution depends on recombinants, a population with lots of recombinants is required. Recombinants accrue over time, each generation adding recombinants. So, rather than mapping in a cross from two inbred strains, I mapped behavioral variation using animals descended over 60 generations from eight strains. Due to the use of eight inbred strains, there can now be up to eight alleles at any locus (although in fact we have never seen that many), and the generations of breeding allow the frequencies of genetic variants to fluctuate. Each generation introduces additional recombinations, so the mosaic structure of the chromosomes is much more complex than in the offspring of the inbred cross.

Key paper

Valdar, W., Solberg, L.C., Gauguier, D., Burnett, S., Klenerman, P., Cookson, W.O., Taylor, M.S., Rawlins, J.N., Mott, R., and Flint, J. (2006). Genome-wide genetic association of complex traits in heterogeneous stock mice. *Nat Genet* **38**:879–887.

The use of outbred mice to map multiple phenotypes at high resolution across the genome.

Figure 7.10 shows the results of mapping anxiety on chromosome 1 in a set of outbred mice. It's like using a high-resolution camera: we see much more detail in the picture. The black line shows the results from the inbred cross from one generation of recombination; the blue line depicts the mapping of the same trait after 60 generations. There are clearly many more peaks in the blue line, revealing the presence of multiple genetic effects. This is partly because the

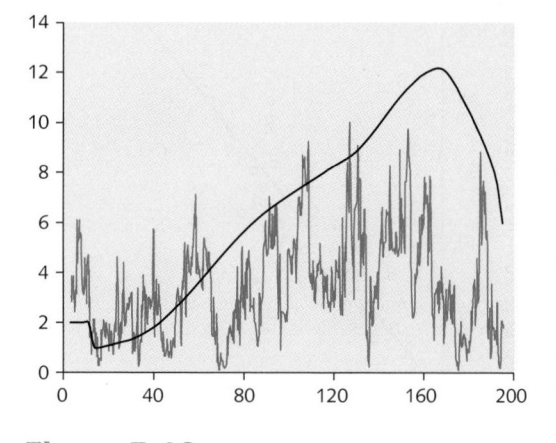

Figure 7.10 Results of mapping anxiety on chromosome 1 in a set of outbred mice. The *y*-axis is log *P* units (see Figure 7.7 legend) and the *x*-axis indicates megabases of DNA across chromosome 1.

outbred animals are descended from not two but eight progenitors; we would expect there to be increased genetic diversity—increased numbers of QTLs compared with an inbred strain cross. Nevertheless, the large number of peaks also represents the fact that the black line is itself the product of other smaller effects, as the work with congenics revealed. The spiky nature of the blue line reflects the high-resolution mapping: we had to use thousands of markers to capture all of this information.

On average, the peaks found in the outbred mice contain about 3 megabases (Mb) of DNA. This is a considerable improvement over the inbred strain cross (with an average resolution of about 20 Mb) but it is not a single gene. However the mapping tells us some important facts about the genetic architecture of behavior.

Firstly, it shows that the genetic architecture of behavior consists of multiple genetic effects, each of which makes a relatively small contribution to the phenotype. Figure 7.11 plots the effect sizes of about 900 QTLs that influence not just behavior but a range of physiological, anatomical, hematological, biochemical, and

immunological traits; everything from how much a mouse weighs to how much hemoglobin its red blood cells contain, the size of its adrenal glands, and its behavior in an open-field arena.

Figure 7.11 is remarkable in showing so little variation among phenotypes. Every trait looks much the same. While there are a few exceptions (the tail of the distribution of effect sizes spreads out on the horizontal axis), the majority of QTLs explain less than 3% of the variation in a phenotype (this is much larger than the average effects found in human outbred populations; the larger figure occurs because of the reduced genetic diversity in the outbred mice; all of the chromosomes derive from just eight progenitors). So the genetic basis of behavior is no different from that of other phenotypes.

Figure 7.12 compares the heritability of each phenotype (on the horizontal axis) with the number of QTLs detected. There is a clear linear relationship: the larger the heritability, the more QTLs are detected. This emphasizes a finding that

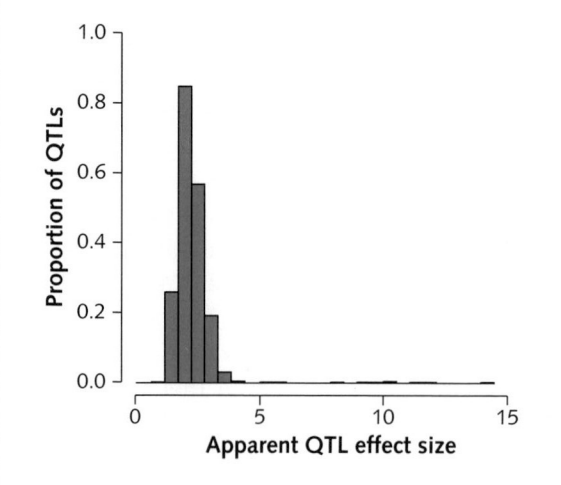

Figure 7.11 Effect sizes of QTLs in the mouse. The *x*-axis is the effect size expressed as a percentage of the variation explained by the QTL. The *y*-axis is the proportion of QTLs found.

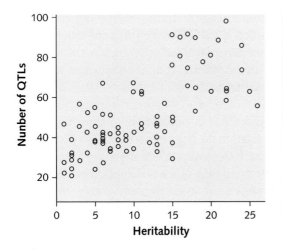

Figure 7.12 Comparing the heritability of each phenotype (on the *x*-axis) with the number of QTLs detected.

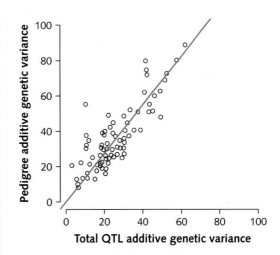

Figure 7.13 The extent to which heritability is accounted for by QTLs. The *x*-axis shows the genetic variance explained for each phenotype by adding up the effects of each QTL. The *y*-axis is an estimate from family data of the total heritability of each phenotype.

may not be intuitively obvious: genetic mapping of a phenotype with a high heritability does not mean that there is an increased chance of discovering a highly significant result. The significance depends on the locus-specific effect, the effect size plotted in the first figure, which as just noted is much the same for all phenotypes. Working with a highly heritable phenotype just means there will be more effects to find (which indirectly does increase your chances of success).

Of course, it could be that these results are deceptive: it is possible that there are many additional genetic effects not detected in the screen. We can (almost) exclude that interpretation, by comparing the heritability assessed from the family data (as quantitative geneticists do when working with human samples) with the sum of the effects from each detected QTL. If every QTL were found, then the two figures would be the same.

Figure 7.13 shows that about three-quarters of the heritability (plotted on the vertical axis) can be explained by summing the effects of identified QTLs (plotted on the horizontal axis).

In other words, the mapping experiment did a good job of finding most of what was there. We are certainly not missing large effects, and while the number of smaller undetected effects remains unknown, we can be reasonably certain that the conclusions we draw from the loci that we do know about will give us a representative picture of the genetic architecture.

Effect of environment

The genetic data also tells us something about how the environment affects behavior. The picture is similar to that described in Chapter 4 where we discussed human studies: there are important interactions between genes and the environment. In fact, on aggregate, the total effect of interactions is at least as important as that of the straight, immediate, unadulterated heritability. We can also see this working at a gene level.

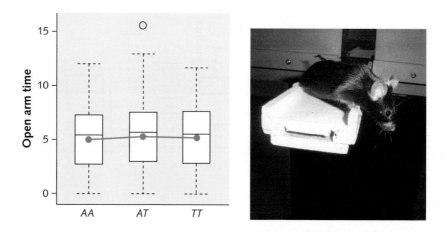

Figure 7.14 A marker that shows no main effect of genotype on behavior, in this case the time spent in the open arms of an elevated plus maze (as illustrated on the right). The phenotypic distributions associated with three genotypes at a single marker are shown on the left.

Figure 7.14 shows a mouse balanced, a little precariously, at the end of short runway, about 1 m above the ground. Usually mice will not come out into such an exposed situation so the extent to which they do so is another measure of lack of anxiety. The apparatus is called an elevated plus maze because the arms are arranged as a cross, with two open and two enclosed arms, and the whole apparatus is elevated. On the left of the figure are the genotypes (AA, AT, and TT) for one marker and the associated effect on the time animals spend in the open arms of the plus maze. There is no significant difference between the three genotypes and on this basis we would say that there is no QTL near the marker contributing to variation in anxiety.

However, there is another way of analyzing the data, taking into account environmental effects. To carry out the test of anxiety, each mouse has to be removed from a cage, placed in the apparatus, and then returned to the cage. That is not automated; someone has to do the work, and as there are more then 2,000 animals, it needs a team of people (if only to alleviate boredom). Over the course of the two-and-a-half years

that the project ran, ten people helped run mice through the elevated plus maze.

We can ask if the person who does the experiment has an effect on the mouse's level of anxiety. The experimenter effect is shown in the next Figure 7.15, where you can see there is variation in the anxiety levels measured for each experimenter. That variation is significant (in fact, highly significant) but the effect is relatively small, accounting for about 5% of the variation.

Now we consider the interaction: does the effect of the experimenter depend on the genotype of the animal? We combine the two figures, plotting the differences in genotype seen for each experimenter (Figure 7.16).

There are quite clearly big differences between experimenters: experimenter 10 elicits a large genetic effect; experimenter 2 none at all. Also the direction of effect differs: at the hands of experimenter 10 and 5, animals with the TT genotype become more anxious, but become less anxious in the hands of experimenter 4. Overall, the interaction effect is large, at least twice as large as the effect of experimenter alone.

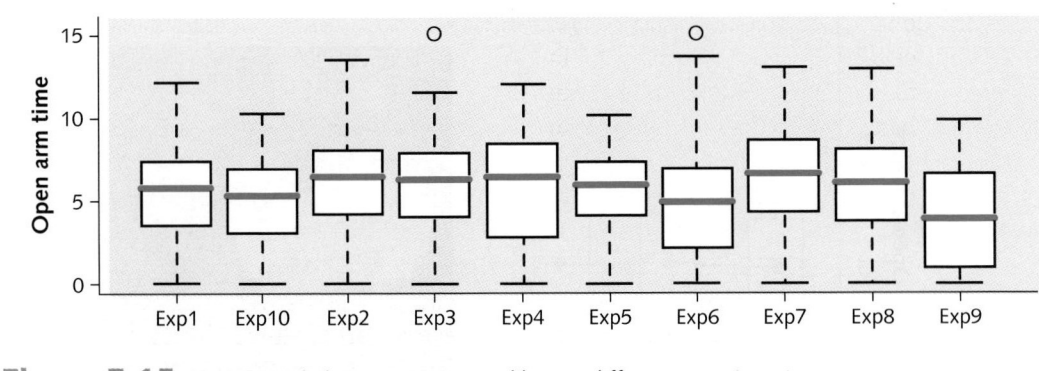

Figure 7.15 Variation in behavior as measured by ten different experimenters.

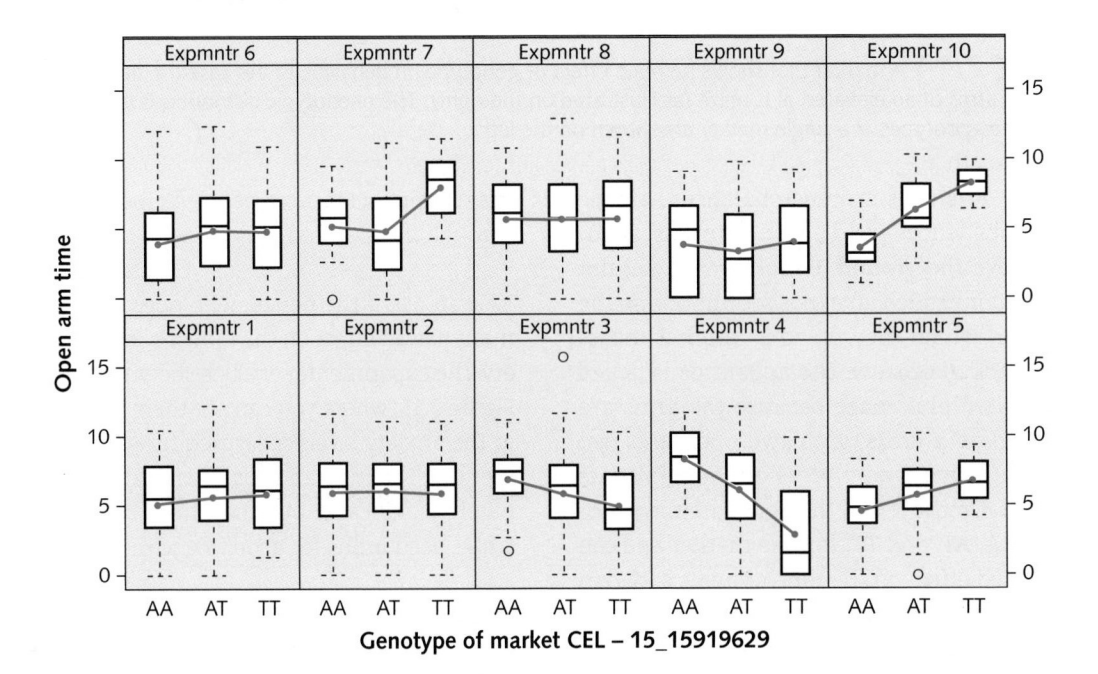

Figure 7.16 The association between genotype and behavior varies between experimenter: an example of the interaction between gene and environment (G × E).

The genetic architecture of mouse behavior

The genetic architecture of behavior in rodents is in many ways very similar to what we have seen emerge from human studies. There are many loci contributing to individual variation in behavior and their effect sizes are consistently small. Exactly how many loci and how small is not clear. The genetic effects operate in a complex fashion, often in interaction with the environment. All of these features have been reported in human studies too, although we should beware of making simple translations from one species to the other.

For example the median effect size of QTLs influencing behavior in rodents is about 3%, but it is much smaller than this in human studies (much less than 1%). This does not reflect a fundamental difference in the genetic architecture of the two species, but rather a difference in the way the effects are estimated. When estimates of effect size are, as here, expressed as the percentage of phenotypic variance attributable to genetic variation at a locus, they vary according to the experimental design.

Suppose we identify a QTL that contributes to 1% of the genetic variation in an outbred population. In a model organism, we could then set up a breeding program to isolate that chromosomal region so that all other genomic regions are inbred. Consequently the locus now contributes to 100% of the genetic variation. Conversely, QTLs identified in simple systems may have smaller relative effects in outbred populations, because the fraction of the total phenotypic variance explained by a QTL with a given effect depends on both allele and genotype frequencies.

There is one other important difference between the rodent and human studies. All of the rodent work takes place with populations where the allele frequencies do not vary much. In an inbred strain intercross, there are just two alleles with frequencies of 0.5. In the most complex design, using animals derived from eight inbred progenitors, the allele frequencies vary much more, but the stock still has a limited number of alleles compared with a fully outbred population. Mouse geneticists, working with animals selected for laboratory life, simplify things so that they work only with common alleles; human geneticists have to work with everything that a combination of environmental constraint, historical accident, and biological necessity can engineer in the genome. Perhaps the remarkable thing is that the picture of genetic architecture emerging from both research fields is so similar (Flint and Mackay, 2009).

At a number of points in this chapter, we have said that mouse geneticists were hoping to find genes, and that there was an expectation that this would be easier than carrying out the same job in humans. That hope has not been realized using the approaches described here, mapping genetic variants that contribute to individual variation. But mouse geneticists can do more than map and clone. They can engineer mutations. This technique has had a profound effect on our understanding of the ways in which genes affect behavior and is the subject of a separate chapter (Chapter 10).

Summary

1. Behaviorism, a dominant school of thought in the mid-20th century, denied any hereditary influences on behavior; ethology countered this with an evolutionary view of 'innateness.'

2. Inbred strains and laboratory selection have provided important sources for studying genetic influences on behavior, such as locomotor activity, and for measuring behavioral heritabilities and estimating genetic complexity.

3. Strain differences may be mapped to individual chromosomes by producing chromosome substitution lines.

4. They may be mapped more accurately by means of recombinant inbred lines, identifying chromosomal regions underlying differences in anxiety.

5. Higher resolution mapping has been facilitated by the use of more strains to produce more recombinations, and by the development of molecular markers for high-density DNA sequence polymorphisms along the chromosomes.

6. There are many loci contributing to individual variation in behavior and their effect sizes are small. Genetic effects operate in a complex fashion, often in interaction with the environment.

7. Laboratory studies in mice reveal a picture similar to humans with respect to small-effect contributions of multiple genes; they differ in the degree of variation, presumably due to the more restricted lineage of laboratory strains.

References

Beutler, B. (2004). Innate immunity: an overview. *Mol Immunol* **40**:845–859.

Breland, K. and Breland, M. (1961). The misbehavior of organisms. *Am Psychol* **16**:681–684.

Burkhardt, J.R. (2005). *Patterns of Behavior: Konrad Lorenz, Niko Tinbergen and the Founding of Ethology*. Chicago, IL: Chicago University Press.

Churchill, G.A., Airey, D.C., Allayee, H., Angel, J.M., Attie, A.D., Beatty, J., Beavis, W.D., Belknap, J.K., Bennett, B. *et al.* (2004). The Collaborative Cross, a community resource for the genetic analysis of complex traits. *Nat Genet* **36**:1133–1137.

DeFries, J.C. and Hegmann, J.P. (1970). Genetic analysis of open-field behavior. In *Contributions to Behavior-Genetic Analysis: the Mouse as a Prototype*, pp. 23–56. Edited by G. Lindzey and D.D. Thiessen. New York: Appleton-Century-Crofts.

DeFries, J.C., Gervais, M.C., and Thomas, E.A. (1978). Response to 30 generations of selection for open field activity in laboratory mice. *Behav Genet* **8**:3–13.

Flint, J. and Mackay, T.F. (2009). Genetic architecture of quantitative traits in mice, flies, and humans. *Genome Res* **19**:723–733.

Flint, J., Valdar, W., Shifman, S., and Mott, R. (2005). Strategies for mapping and cloning quantitative trait genes in rodents. *Nat Rev Genet* **6**:271–286.

Gray, J.A. (1982). *The Neuropsychology of Anxiety: an Enquiry into the Function of the Septo-hippocampal System*. Oxford: Oxford University Press.

Gray, J.A. (1987). *The Psychology of Fear and Stress*. Cambridge: Cambridge University Press.

Mousseau, T.A. and Roff, D.A. (1987). Natural selection and the heritability of fitness components. *Heredity* **59**:181–197.

Singer, J.B., Hill, A.E., Burrage, L.C., Olszens, K.R., Song, J., Justice, M., O'Brien, W.E., Conti, D.V., Witte, J.S. *et al.* (2004). Genetic dissection of complex traits with chromosome substitution strains of mice. *Science* **304**:445–448.

Singer, J.B., Hill, A.E., Nadeau, J.H., and Lander, E.S. (2005). Mapping quantitative trait loci for anxiety in chromosome substitution strains of mice. *Genetics* **169**:855–862.

Skinner, B.F. (1935). Two types of conditioned reflex and a pseudo type. *J Gen Psychol* **12**:66–77.

Singer, J.B., Hill, A.E., Nadeau, J.H., and Lander, E.S. (2005). Mapping quantitative trait loci for anxiety in chromosome substitution strains of mice. *Genetics* **169**:855–862.

Snell, G.D. (1979). Recent advances in histocompatibility immunogenetics. *Adv Genet* **20**:291–355.

Todd, J.A., Aitman, T.J., Cornall, R.J., Ghosh, S., Hall, J.R., Hearne, C.M., Knight, A.M., Love, J.M., McAleer, M.A. *et al.* (1991). Genetic analysis of autoimmune type 1 diabetes mellitus in mice. *Nature* **351**:542–547.

Valdar, W., Solberg, L.C., Gauguier, D., Cookson, W.O., Rawlins, J.N., Mott, R., and Flint, J. (2006). Genetic and environmental effects on complex traits in mice. *Genetics* **174**:959–984.

Many versus one

Genetic variation in flies and worms (and some people)

8

[On what we can learn about natural variation from experimental organisms that is relevant to humans]

How much similarity is there between the genetic influences on behavior in humans compared with 'simpler' organisms? The so-called simpler organisms that have provided us with the most information on this question are the fruit fly *Drosophila melanogaster*, and the nematode *Caenorhabditis elegans*. In this chapter, we will ask what natural variation in behavior looks like in these animals.

Evolving behavior in the laboratory: *Drosophila*

A direct test of the heritability of behavior calls for genetic experiments, and for this purpose nothing beats the fruit fly *D. melanogaster*. At first glance, fruit flies might not appear to be the most suitable animals to work with. They are too tiny (~3mm long) to pick up easily, they don't live very long (a few weeks), and it's not obvious what behaviors they normally carry out. Fortunately, enterprising biologists have been studying their behavior since 1905.

Key paper

Greenspan, R.J. (2008). The origins of behavioral genetics. *Curr Biol* **18**:R192–R198.

A history of early studies in experimental behavior genetics.

It may seem that working with fruit flies is no picnic, but in fact in some ways it resembles a picnic. Fly labs always have anywhere from a few to several hundred stray flies buzzing around at any given time. This was no doubt worse in the early days, when they also kept large bunches of bananas sitting around waiting to be peeled and crushed into the bottom of pint-sized milk bottles and stoppered with cotton. Fly cultures are still transferred by hand, but, for all of our modern technology, we still bang the bottle against a rubber mat to force the flies down from the stopper, where they normally congregate, then dump them into a fresh, clean bottle and jam a clean foam-rubber stopper into the top before they recover enough to fly out. Leaks are nearly unavoidable, and neighboring labs that require sterile conditions for cell culture are chronically grumpy. Fly traps are another ever-present fixture in fly labs—strategically placed bottles with an inch or so of vinegar in the bottom with a funnel placed in the bottle's opening in the desperate hope that a fly will be attracted by the odor of fermented fruit (their first love) and then be trapped inside so they eventually drown. These help, but only a little. Somewhat more effective is using red wine instead of vinegar, but then there is the problem of the lab's graduate students drinking the trap's contents, not to mention the need to document that the lab is a 'drug-free workplace.'

Those early studies of fruit fly behavior were motivated by the idea that so-called 'lower' animals were primarily governed by innate drives or 'tropisms.' This point of view originated with Jacques Loeb, a German-born zoologist who emigrated to the University of Chicago in 1892 to become one of the founders of modern biological research in the USA (Pauly, 1987), and represented the beginning of mechanistic studies of behavior. But it was not until the mid-19th century that researchers took up the challenge of trying to understand how genes might influence these little creatures.

In the late 1950s, Jerry Hirsch undertook such a study, taking fruit flies that he collected from a farm stand on Long Island. He and his students bred them selectively for a behavioral difference: when confronted with the choice of walking up or down in a maze, do they have a preference? This gravitational response ('geotaxis' or to 'go toward gravity') is weak in most flies; they will generally choose randomly. Hirsch constructed a multi-choice maze so that flies would have 15 chances to decide whether

to go up or down, and those consistently choosing to go up would be separated from those consistently choosing to go down.

The original maze was hand-assembled out of rubber tubing and glass 'T' tubes, and it stood several feet tall. Flies were constantly getting stuck part way through. Washing the maze was a major ordeal. All of this merely served as the obligatory apprenticeship that anyone who works with fruit flies must inevitably go through. You have to prove your seriousness before the flies will perform for you.

But Hirsch and his students persevered, collecting flies from the two extremes. They bred the 'Hi' flies with each other and the 'Lo' flies with each other and, after 50 generations of behavioral selection and breeding, they had one strain of flies that consistently showed positive geotaxis (meaning they wanted to go down in the direction of gravity) and another strain of flies that consistently showed negative (up) geotaxis. It was clear that these flies did not need to learn the behavior; they did it first crack out of the starting gate. More importantly, the behavioral differences had 'evolved' over many generations through breeding. In other words, he had enriched for the genetic differences that would alter the behavior, and which were naturally occurring and already present in the starting fly population.

Key paper

Erlenmeyer-Kimling, L.F., Hirsch, J., and Weiss, J.M. (1962). **Studies in experimental behavior genetics.** *J Comp Physiol Psychol* 55:722–731.

Hirsch and his students then went on to show that each chromosome carried genes that contributed to the selected phenotype. Flies only have three major chromosomes and it is relatively easy, using the breeding strategies we described for rodents, to separate individual chromosomes from the Hi or Lo lines. From these experiments and from the statistical analysis of various hybrids between Hi and Lo, they concluded that there were many genes contributing to the behavioral difference.

Each year, Hirsch would teach a genetics lab course at the University of Illinois and the students in the course would reselect the Hi and Lo low lines (Figure 8.1). This went on for 25 more years, with occasional neglect (approximately generation 200) and one year accidentally mixing the strains together but then reselecting them (approximately generation 420). Then, in 1985, after 550 generations, the strains spontaneously stabilized. You can see this at the right end of the graph where the lines start to show much less variability in the mean score. The stabilization meant they could maintain the Hi and Lo phenotypes without further selection. The most likely explanation for this change in the genetic architecture of the behavior is that there was no longer any genetic variation at the loci contributing to geotaxis; that is, all of the relevant genes

had become 'fixed' in the Hi or Lo strains. For example, the flies could have become, like the mice described in Chapter 7, inbred, or at least sufficiently inbred to remove the genetic cause of behavioral variation.

In one of his final studies of these flies, in the late 1980s, Hirsch reported that when he took the strains apart again, isolating individual chromosomes onto a neutral genetic background as before, the contributions of particular chromosomes had changed in comparison to the study carried out 20 years earlier. This showed that further genetic changes had occurred during the long-term maintenance of these strains. Mutations had apparently arisen spontaneously and, because of the continued selection pressure, these mutations had also become 'fixed' in the lines.

Key paper

Ricker, J.P. and Hirsch, J. (1988). Genetic changes occurring over 500 generations in lines of *Drosophila melanogaster* selected divergently for geotaxis. *Behav Genet* **18**, 13–25.

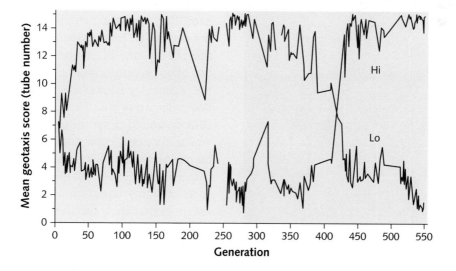

Figure 8.1 Twenty-five years of laboratory selection for geotaxis by Hirsch and his students.
Source: Ricker and Hirsh (1988).

Fifteen years later, after Hirsch had retired, we (R.J.G. and Dan Toma) contacted him to request the fly strains. He had been keeping them in his office all along, and when we tried them out on our spiffy new plexiglass maze (Figure 8.2), they performed like gangbusters.

Finding the genes

Through the 30-year saga of Hirsch's geotactic flies, the nagging question that always lurked behind the scenes was which genes were responsible for the behavioral divergence. Until recently, the techniques for identifying any of them were simply not available. If a naturally occurring difference was primarily due to the

Figure 8.2 Flies from the Hi strain enter the maze and consistently take the 'upward' choice.
Source: Photograph by R.J. Greenspan.

strong effect of one gene, then one could use classical techniques to map that gene to a small region of its chromosome. After that, identifying the gene was a matter of luck, depending on whether any of the genes in that region of the chromosome were known and whether one of them happened to be the culprit. With the advent of gene cloning in the 1980s, genes in the fruit fly could be identified more easily on the basis of their genetic map position (see Appendix, p. 233). None of these approaches could be applied in a situation where many genes of small effect were each combining to produce the phenotype. Such was the case for geotaxis.

One approach to mapping a multigenic trait makes use of DNA markers all along the chromosome to map the location of genes contributing to a trait. This approach works well when the two strains under comparison are well characterized for their DNA sequence differences and when they are homozygous for most of their genes. In other words, it works well on highly inbred strains, such as those in the mouse.

Another approach that also makes use of knowing the animal's entire genome, but does not depend on homozygosity or characterization of sequence differences, was developed in one of our laboratories (R.J.G.) to capitalize on the technology known as DNA microarrays. A DNA microarray is a slide that has tiny spots of DNA deposited or synthesized onto it, each of which has many copies of the DNA sequence for one of the animal's genes. In the case of the fruit fly, this comes to approximately 15,000 spots. Roughly one-third of these sequences are genes that are known for sure because they have been studied to some extent. The remaining ones have been predicted based on reading the genome sequence and applying computer algorithms (and the experience of the person looking at it).

With copies of every fly gene at a known address on the slide, it is possible to measure how active each gene is at any given time in any given tissue. This is the approach that we (Dan Toma, Kevin White, and R.J.G.) took to detect differences between the Hi and Lo geotactic flies—asking which genes are differentially active in the brains of the two strains. The level of a gene's activity is reflected in the relative amount of mRNA for that gene present in a given tissue at a given time, so we isolated mRNA from heads (which consist mostly of brain tissue) in the Hi and Lo strains. We assumed that the flies' behavior ought to be due at least in part to what is going on in their brains.

We then made DNA copies of the RNA using enzymes that are specific for that reaction, and labeled the DNA copies with a fluorescent dye—a red dye for one strain and a green dye for the other. When a mixture of these DNA copies is applied to a microarray slide, the matching sequences find each other so that the green and red gene copies find their appropriate matching spots for that gene on the array. The array has such an enormous excess number of copies for each gene that there are vastly more than enough bound copies to accommodate the labeled copies floating in the DNA soup. If a given gene is five times more active in the Hi strain than in the Lo strain, there will be five times more copies of it in the DNA soup. When all of the labeled copies have found their spot and bound to them, the difference between Hi and Lo for that gene can be read by the relative intensity of green dye versus red dye.

A drawback to this approach is that it does not detect all of the genes whose DNA sequence differs between strains, nor does it look at only those genes. If gene A regulates gene B's level of expression, then we could be detecting an alteration in gene B, even though the cause of that alteration is a difference in the sequence of gene A between strains. On the other hand, if the cascade of gene activities from A to B to C (and so on) are all responsible for the phenotypic difference, then we are one step closer to understanding the mechanisms underlying the behavioral difference.

When we looked at the outcome of such an experiment, lots of genes were different and they spanned every category of gene function—transcription, chemical and electrical signaling, the cytoskeleton, and metabolism. Nearly 250 gene differences were statistically significant, ranging from 2-fold to 18-fold greater in one strain than the other. Given that these strains had been isolated from each other for 50 years by the time we got to them, it was not at all surprising that there should be so many differences. The question was, which ones were relevant to geotaxis. The best way to confirm a gene's role is to test a mutant of that gene in a strain that has never been selected for its geotaxis preference. Where do we find such mutants? We inquire at the huge center in Bloomington, Indiana, that maintains over 23,000 genetically defined strains of fruit flies.

Restricting ourselves to those genes for which there were available mutants helped us narrow down the number of candidates. Sticking to those that are expressed in the brain lowered it further; in fact we were left with four mutants to test. (Nowadays, there would be more available.) Of the four, one gene (*prospero*) was known to be involved in development of the sensory nervous system, two (*cryptochrome* and *pigment-dispersing factor*) were known to be involved in the mechanism of circadian rhythms, and one (*importin-α*) was known to be involved in the general cellular mechanism of importing proteins into the nucleus. All but the last one were expressed at a higher level in the Lo strain, which prefers to go down. The

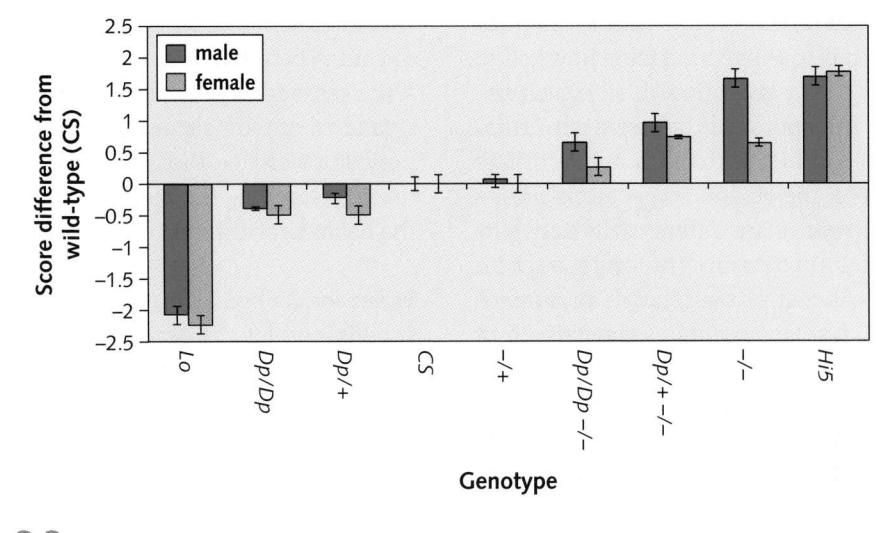

Figure 8.3 Titration of geotaxis behavior with increasing levels of expression of the gene encoding the neuropeptide Pdf (pigment-dispersing factor). Bars indicate behavioral differences compared with the wild-type strain (CS). Lo and Hi are the selected strains, 'Dp' indicates a genetically engineered extra copy of the *pigment-dispersing factor* gene, '+' indicates one normal copy of the gene, and '−' indicates a mutant copy of the gene . Source: Toma *et al.* (2002).

expression of *importin-α*, however, was lower in that strain. The prediction was that the *prospero*, *cryptochrome*, and *pigment-dispersing factor* mutant flies should prefer to go up, whereas the *importin-α* mutant should prefer to do down. All but *prospero* lived up to the prediction: *prospero* mutants failed to meet the prediction and had no effect on geotaxis whatsoever. In the case of *pigment-dispersing factor*, the degree of negative geotaxis was proportional to the amount of gene product produced, as shown using a series of genetic variants that under- and overproduced it (Figure 8.3).

Key paper

Toma, D.P., White, K.P., Hirsch, J., and Greenspan, R.J. (2002). Identification of genes for *Drosophila melanogaster* geotaxis, a complex behavioral trait. *Nat Genet* **31**:349–353.

Genes for geotaxis?

We interpreted these results as saying that three of the genes, *cryptochrome*, *pigment-dispersing factor*, and *importin-α*, were likely to be contributors to the geotaxis phenotype of the selected strains, based on their ability to influence the trait independently. The verdict on *prospero* is equivocal. The result says that it cannot influence geotaxis all by itself. But whether that means it is irrelevant to the phenotype or just that it requires other genes to have an effect cannot be resolved with the data at hand.

The most surprising aspect of these results is that the three effective genes are ones we would never have thought likely to be relevant. Two are involved in the control of circadian rhythms, but apparently are not restricted in their action to that process. Cryptochrome is a light-absorbing protein that is required for entrainment of the fly's circadian rhythm to the rising and setting of the sun (or the incubator lamp, as the case may be). It is expressed in a large set of cells in the brain where it is known to interact with the other components of the circadian clock mechanism. Pigment-dispersing factor is a neuropeptide, a small protein that is secreted by a small set of neurons as a signal that regulates the pattern of daily locomotor activity in the fly. It relays signals from the circadian clock to the rest of the brain to coordinate daily activity. The third effective protein, importin-α, is present in nearly all cells of the fly, where it assists in the essential cellular mechanism of transporting proteins into the nucleus. If the *importin-α* gene is eliminated completely, this is lethal for the fly.

None of these genes would have been expected to produce a specific effect on geotaxis. This is not to say that we know much about how geotaxis works. Unlike humans, where gravity is sensed by the movement of little floating particles in our inner ear, insects apparently sense gravity by the postural pressure of their legs on stretch receptors in their joints and also by the weight of their antenna as sensed by stretch receptors at their base.

These results forced us to rethink our ideas about how genes influence behavior. Perhaps there are no such things as 'genes for geotaxis.' Instead, genes may be versatile and able to participate in many different processes. By this way of thinking, *cryptochrome* and *pigment-dispersing factor* are not circadian rhythm genes, but genes that can affect many functions, two of which are circadian rhythms and geotaxis. As for *importin-α*, the fact that it can exert such a selective effect while being so widely used for other biological functions provides an important insight into the subtle

way gene activities intertwine to affect behavior. It tells us that modest alterations in such widely acting genes, in combination with other similarly altered genes, can produce specific behavioral effects.

Key paper

Greenspan, R.J. (2000). The flexible genome. *Nat Rev Genet* **2**:383–387.

Aggression, or 'Who you calling fruit fly?'

Back when von Frisch and Tinbergen were delving into the innateness of the honeybee dance and the herring gull begging response, their Austrian colleague Konrad Lorenz was speculating on the evolutionary and innate origins of aggressive behavior. He distinguished fighting between species from fighting within species, and only considered the latter to be the socially 'motivated' behavior of aggression. Interspecies attacks usually involve a one-sided meal at the end. Intraspecies aggression, by contrast, serves various social functions including territoriality and access to mates.

Fruit flies, despite their reputation as the carefree hippies of the insect world, do actually show aggression under the appropriate conditions. Male flies will defend a food patch from other encroaching males (see the boxing flies in Figure 8.4), not because they refuse to share their lunch, but rather because that is where they will find females ready to mate. Food patches are attractive to females as the best place to lay their eggs so that the hatching larvae can start eating right away.

Figure 8.4 Male fruit fly combat.
Source: Dierick and Greenspan (2006) courtesy of Nature Publishing Co.

Females presumably favor males who are good at defending their turf. So fruit flies combine territoriality with mate choice, meaning for a male that 'if you get the turf, you can get the girl.'

Aggression is a more sophisticated behavior than the reflex-like geotaxis, involving perceptual, cognitive, and social elements. Is a complex behavior of this sort innate or, more appropriately, does it have genetic components? Fruit fly biologists have long noted that flies caught in the wild and brought into the laboratory are more aggressive than their cousins who have been living the life of luxury in the lab for many generations. These wild-caught flies often lose their aggressive tendencies after several generations in the laboratory, but it has been found that aggressiveness is easily restored in laboratory flies after some generations of selective breeding. Given our prior success with using DNA microarrays to identify genetic differences between selected strains, we (Herman Dierick and R.J.G.) tried the same approach for aggression.

Flies were selected by catching them in the act of fighting in a large (for fruit flies) arena containing many food patches—over 100 males and roughly half as many females. Males engaged in a fight were snatched up gently but quickly into an aspiration tube by a *deus ex machina* (i.e. Herman) and saved for breeding with sibling females at each generation. Two lines were selected in parallel. As a control, two more lines were selected as neutral or unaggressive by removing all fighting males and picking only the remaining, non-fighters for further mating.

After a mere 11 generations of selection, the flies in the 'high-aggression' lines already showed a drastic increase in their tendency to fight and in the intensity of their fighting (Figure 8.5). Even greater increases were seen after 21 generations. Following in our previous tracks, we isolated RNA from the heads of all four strains at generation 21 and compared their levels of gene expression across the whole genome.

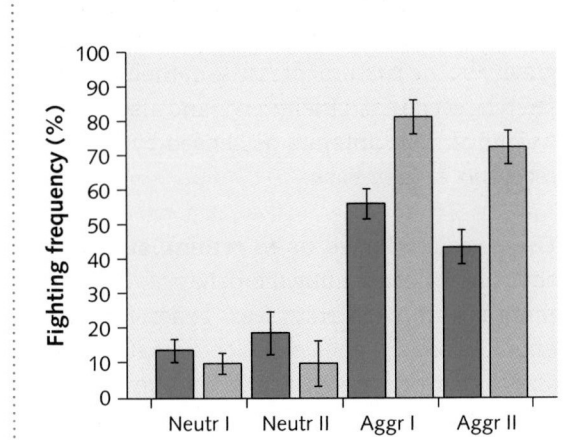

Figure 8.5 Increase in fruit fly aggression after 11 (dark-blue bars) and 21 (light-blue bars) generations of selection. Aggr I and Aggr II were independent lines selected for male aggression. Neutr I and Neutr II were independent lines from which aggressive males were removed.
Source: Dierick and Greenspan (2006).

Key paper

Dierick, H.A. and Greenspan, R.J. (2006). Molecular analysis of flies selected for aggressive behavior. *Nat Genet* **38**:1023–1031.

A study describing a molecular analysis of genetic changes in a population after selection to increase aggression in D. *melanogaster*.

Genes for aggression?

In contrast to the flies who underwent long-term selection for geotaxis, these aggressive strains differed from their controls in only 80 genes, with expression level differences averaging roughly 1.5-fold and a maximum difference of only 2.5-fold. In comparison, 40 of the geotaxis genes had differences exceeding 3-fold up to a maximum of 18-fold. This finding supports the idea that, at early stages of selection (e.g. the experiment with aggressive flies), only those genetic variants that are already present in the population are available for selection. The longer selection proceeds, the greater the likelihood that new variants appear through mutations and are enriched in the strains, or that combinations of variants are put together that act synergistically. The naturally occurring variants routinely present in a population tend to be small in their effect, as these are the kinds of mutation that are easily tolerated by evolution. Long-term selection creates a situation in which mutations with greater effects may have a better chance of surviving and being enriched if they reinforce the selected phenotype and are not unduly harmful.

As in the geotaxis flies, however, the genes that showed up as different included few that might

have been expected based on what is known about the biology of aggression. Serotonin is a neurotransmitter that has been associated with aggression in a variety of species, from lobsters and mice to monkeys and humans. We too have found that when serotonin levels in flies are pumped up, either by feeding them with serotonin precursors or by genetic engineering of their enzymes so that they produce more than normal, the flies become more aggressive. However, to our surprise, none of the genes relating to serotonin function—its enzymes, receptors, or transporters—were altered in the selected aggressive strains.

The classes of genes that differed between aggressive and non-aggressive strains included the same broad range that we saw for geotaxis—from transcription to metabolism. Some were available as mutants and one of these affected aggression when tested independently on a neutral genetic background. It was a gene known as *cytochrome P450 6a20*, one of a large family of genes involved in detoxification and chemical processing. Among the chemicals known to be processed by cytochrome P450s in insects are pheromones—the chemical signals that insects emit to communicate with each other. One possibility is that the flies have become more aggressive because their perception of other flies has changed ('Just because you're paranoid doesn't mean they aren't out to get you.'). This is further reinforced by the finding that an odor-binding protein in the fly's olfactory organ is also one of the genes that differs.

As it turned out, this same *cytochrome P450* gene reared its pugnacious head again in a totally separate study of fly aggression and social experience. When flies are raised in groups, they are less aggressive than when they are raised in solitary confinement. A test of gene expression differences between these isolated and gregarious flies, using the same microarray technology described above, revealed that the self-same *cytochrome P450 6a20* gene was expressed at a lower level in the more aggressive flies, just as in our selection experiment. Further study showed that this gene is indeed active in the part of the fly's antenna that detects odors.

Although our yield of confirmed genes was smaller this time, perhaps due to the luck of the draw, which left us with fewer appropriate mutants to test, the experiment reinforces the same idea that emerged from the geotaxis experiment: behavior can be significantly and specifically altered by genes that are neither dedicated to that behavior, nor restricted in their action. In this instance, the outcome also showed that major behavioral changes can result from minor differences in gene activities.

Key paper

Wang, L., Dankert, H., Perona, P., and Anderson D.J. (2008). A common genetic target for environmental and heritable influences on aggressiveness in *Drosophila*. *Proc Natl Acad Sci USA* **105**:5657–5663.

A study describing a behavioral and molecular analysis of the effects on aggression in *D. melanogaster* in social versus solitary conditions.

Behavior, the single gene, and the mind of a worm

In one sense, all neurons resemble each other; they must be excitable, able to transmit electrical signals and produce and respond to chemical transmitters. They must be equipped with very similar, possibly commonly specified biochemical machinery. Yet, in another sense, they are all very different; cells are located at specific places and are connected to each other in definite ways. How is this complexity represented in the genetic program? Is it the outcome of a global dynamical system with a very large number of interactions? Or are there defined subprograms that different cells can get a hold of and execute for themselves? What controls the temporal sequences that we see in development?

One experimental approach to these problems is to investigate the effects of mutations on nervous systems. In principle, it should be possible to dissect the genetic specification of a nervous system in much the same way as was done for biosynthetic pathways in bacteria or for bacteriophage assembly. However, one surmises that genetical analysis alone would have provided only a very general picture of the organization of those processes. Only when genetics was coupled with methods of analyzing other properties of the mutants, by assays of enzymes or in vitro assembly, did the full power of this approach develop. In the same way, the isolation and genetical characterization of mutants with behavioral alterations must be supported by analysis at a level intermediate between the gene and behavior. Behavior is the result of a complex and ill-understood set of computations performed by nervous systems and it seems essential to decompose the problem into two: one concerned with the question of the genetic specification of nervous systems and the other with the way nervous systems work to produce behavior. Both require that we must have some way of analyzing the structure of a nervous system.

Brenner (1974).

Key paper

Brenner, S. (1974). The genetics of *Caenorhabditis elegans*. *Genetics* **77**:71–94.

When he wrote this in 1974, Sydney Brenner was working at the Laboratory of Molecular Biology (LMB) in Cambridge, sharing an office with Francis Crick, co-discoverer of the structure of DNA. Brenner's background was in biochemistry and molecular biology, a discipline in part created by scientists at the LMB. Like Crick, Brenner's interests were turning to the analysis of behavior, but while Crick wanted to tackle the complexities of the mammalian brain including the problem of consciousness, Brenner wanted a far simpler, tractable experimental system.

Brenner thought the fly was too complicated and that Seymour Benzer's search for single gene mutations would not lead to fundamental insights into the molecular basis of behavior. As *Drosophila* has 100,000 neurons, far more than could conceivably ever be enumerated and put into circuit diagrams, it would be too difficult to explain how the mutations had an effect. '...*I decided that what was needed was an experimental organism which was suitable for genetical study and in which one could determine the complete structure of the nervous system. ... my choice settled on the small nematode* Caenorhabditis elegans' (worm geneticists have to learn early to pronounce correctly the name of their favorite organism. To make life easy, most people refer to it either as *C. elegans* or, with even more simplicity but less accuracy, as 'the worm'). *C. elegans* lives in soil. It grows to about 1.3mm and reaches maturity at about 3.5 days old. It eats bacteria and can be grown quite easily in the laboratory. There are two sexual forms: a self-reproducing hermaphrodite and a much rarer male form, which makes up about 0.1% of a normal worm population. These useful habits make it easy and cheap to look after in the laboratory.

With the worm, the intention was always to do things to completion: to map the position of every neuron, to map all of the connections (or more technically synapses) between neurons (remember that there are many more connections than there are neurons: a typical sensory neuron in *Aplysia*, a sea slug, has about 1,200 synapses); to know the developmental trajectory of each cell, its pathway from egg to adult; and eventually to sequence the entire 100 megabase genome, so that every gene could be identified and every gene assigned a function. All of this took time and the project is still not complete. However, we now know more about the worm than we do about any other multicellular organism on the planet.

The first complete anatomy and developmental history

The first major achievements were maps of the neuronal circuitry and cell lineage. Brenner's group in Cambridge gradually expanded to take on the challenges. Worms were sliced up into sections small enough to visualize nerve cells at the highest possible resolution (using an electron microscope); every connection, every synapse could be, and was, counted. By 1986, an article of 341 pages was published in the *Philosophical Transactions of the Royal Society* that described the worm's nervous system (White *et al.*, 1986). The title of the paper is benign enough ('The structure of the nervous system of the nematode *Caenorhabditis elegans*'), but open up the article and after a few introductory pages you'll see that each page is headed with something slightly more ambitious: it reads 'The mind of a worm.'

Here's their summary of what they found: '*The hermaphrodite nervous system has a total complement of 302 neurons, which are arranged in an essentially invariant structure. Neurons with similar morphologies and connectivities have been grouped into classes; there are 118 such classes. Neurons have simple morphologies with few, if any, branches... Neurons are generally highly locally connected, making synaptic connections with many of their neighbours*' (Figure 8.6).

Hermaphrodite and male worms differ radically in their neuroanatomy: the hermaphrodite has 302 neurons and the male 381, of which 87 are sex specific. However, males are rare (about 0.1% of worms).

In addition to the circuitry, Brenner and his followers worked on the developmental history of every cell, the origin of every neuron in the worm's body. This was achieved by John Sulston, by systematically observing what happened to each cell as the animal developed from egg through to larva to adulthood.

Key papers

Sulston, J.E. (1976). Post-embryonic development in the ventral cord of *Caenorhabditis elegans*. *Philos Trans R Soc Lond B Biol Sci* **275**:287–297.
Sulston, J.E. and Horvitz, H.R. (1977). Post-embryonic cell lineages of the nematode, *Caenorhabditis elegans*. *Dev Biol* **56**:110–156.

The first complete animal genome

Next came the first determination of a complete animal genome. The first step was to make a complete molecular map using methods that could be applied to any multicellular organism. The principle is shown in Figure 8.7 and described in the Appendix (p. 233).

The clones they used are known as cosmids, pieces of worm DNA about 30 kilobases in size that could be grown in *Escherichia coli* bacteria. Eventually the cosmids were sequenced, leading in 1998 to the first, complete DNA sequence of a multicellular organism and providing the technology that enabled the human genome project to complete its goals.

Key paper

C. elegans Sequencing Consortium (1998). Genome sequence of the nematode *C. elegans*: a platform for investigating biology. *Science* **282**:2012–2018.

Human genetics has something else it owes to the worm community: a communal culture. Worm geneticists share data and resources, a culture that John Sulston made sure was adopted by the less selfless human genetics community when the genome sequencing that Sulston and others had developed for the worm was applied to our own species.

Worm geneticists had a wiring diagram, a developmental trajectory, and a complete genome. But if behavior is the goal, just how much can a creature do with 302 neurons? It turns out that a worm can do most of the things that an average teenager can. It can find its own food, drink alcohol (but not as much as flies), and have sex (it prefers to have sex with itself, whereas

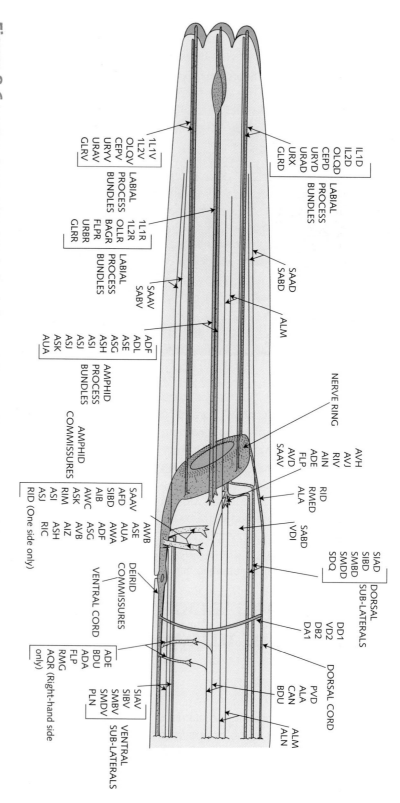

Figure 8.6 Location of neuronal tracts in the head of a nematode worm. Neurons are given arbitrary names consisting of three upper-case letters.

Source: White *et al.* (1986).

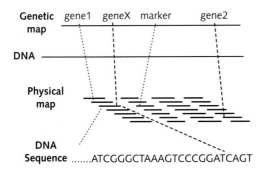

Figure 8.7 The principles of a genome map.
Source: *C. elegans* Sequencing Consortium (1998).

among teenagers this may be common but not by preference, and in the case of the worm at least the females have the excuse that finding a male can be very difficult). Like most teenagers, it likes to live in a dark chaotic world surrounded by decaying objects, specifically a thin film of water between rotting vegetation. It doesn't like being touched and is prepared to travel quite a distance to find food it likes (and to move away from stuff it doesn't). To do all this, it needs to be able to detect traces of chemicals, interpret

what they mean, and act appropriately. A lot of worm neurobiology involves tracing the pathway from outside stimuli (chemical, thermal, pressure, and so on) to internal neuronal circuitry through to a final motor output.

Worm rudiments of social behavior

It has been said that all objects on earth are covered in a thin film of nematode worms. We are not entirely convinced by that idea, but they are certainly common, and variants of the laboratory's favorite species are found practically everywhere. Despite the diversity, wherever they come from, worms can be divided into two categories by observing how they eat: either on their own or together, aggregating into lumps (Figure 8.8), which reflects a worm version of a rugby scrum.

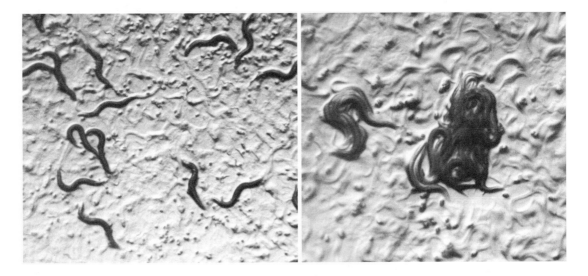

Figure 8.8 Natural variants of the nematode *C. elegans* exhibiting solitary (top) and 'social' or aggregated (bottom) feeding behavior on a lawn of bacteria.
Source: de Bono and Bargmann (1998); courtesy of Cell Press.

Whether or not you believe this is social behavior, it is a behavior. The worms congregate at the edge of a patch of food (this is called 'bordering') and feed together (this is called 'clumping'). Aggregation is under genetic control and a single gene is responsible. This gene has been identified and characterized by Mario de Bono and Cornelia Bargmann. A single base-pair change in this gene, *npr-1* (neuropeptide receptor 1), causes a change in one key amino acid in this protein (a phenylalanine or a valine). All aggregating strains have phenylalanine; all solitary feeders have valine. Think of this as the perfect genetic association study. When worms were genetically engineered to introduce variant forms of the *npr-1* gene, it could turn solitary feeders into social aggregators.

Key paper

de Bono, M. and Bargmann, C.I. (1998). Natural variation in a neuropeptide Y receptor homolog modifies social behavior and food response in C. elegans. *Cell* **94**:679–689.

Aggregation is not the only behavior affected by *npr-1* variants. They also differ in their tendency to wander around for food, to burrow into agar, and to accumulate on the border of a bacterial lawn. When DNA sequences were compared among natural isolates of three other *Caenorhabditis* species as well as *C. elegans*, it turned out that the solitary allele is found only in *C. elegans*, which suggests that it appeared later in the evolution of that lineage and that the 'social allele' is ancestral.

Characterization of the *npr-1* mutants then showed that the gene is involved in the detection of oxygen. Social feeding, it turns out, occurs only when oxygen exceeds the worm's preferred level of between 5 and 12% (Gray *et al.*, 2004). In other words, social feeding is in part a behavioral strategy for responding to high concentrations of oxygen. If this was the entire explanation, the problem of the genetics of social behavior would reduce to a problem of sensory physiology: aggregation (social contact) would be a consequence of worms all seeking the same oxygen concentration (by analogy, explaining social groups in our own species would become a problem of explaining how we detect places where alcohol is given away for free). But we know that oxygen sensation is not the whole explanation, because adding the wild-type DNA of *npr-1* into the neurons that mediate oxygen sensing does not restore wild-type behavior: after genetic rescue, aggregation behavior returns to normal but not the rapid movement of wild-type worms, and the bordering behavior remains atypical.

Cornelia Bargmann, a worm geneticist at the Rockefeller University in New York, found that the behavior could be fully restored in *npr-1* mutants by adding the gene back to a neuron called RMG. Furthermore, specifically killing the RMG neuron (this is possible in *C. elegans* by blasting a laser onto the cell) created the same phenotype as the *npr-1* mutation. RMG is the hub of a network connecting seven classes of neurons, including some oxygen-sensitive neurons (those already implicated in social aggregation). This and other observations led Bargmann to argue, '*The analysis of RMG suggests a hub-and-spoke model for aggregation behavior, in which distributed sensory inputs are coordinated through gap junctions with the RMG hub to produce distinct, distributed synaptic outputs*' (gap junctions are one way in which neurons connect to each other).

The mutation led, through an understanding of the anatomy, to the discovery of a neuronal circuit mediating behavior. Aggregation requires the integration of different sensory information, a task that is performed by the RMG neuron that sits at the hub of a series of neurons. In this model, the neural circuit controls behavior. The role of the protein (the gene

product) might be to close RMG gap junctions, acting to gate the access of sensory neurons to a common neural circuit.

Key papers

Gray, J.M., Karow, D.S., Lu, H., Chang, A.J., Chang, J.S., Ellis, R.E., Marletta, M.A., and Bargmann, C.I. (2004). Oxygen sensation and social feeding mediated by a *C. elegans* guanylate cyclase homologue. *Nature* **430**: 317–322.

Chang, A.J., Chronis, N., Karow, D.S., Marletta, M.A., and Bargmann, C.I. (2006). A distributed chemosensory circuit for oxygen preference in *C. elegans*. *PLoS Biol* **4**:e274.

Macosko, E.Z., Pokala, N., Feinberg, E.H., Chalasani, S.H., Butcher, R.A., Clardy, J., and Bargmann, C.I. (2009). A hub-and-spoke circuit drives pheromone attraction and social behavior in *C. elegans*. *Nature* **458**:1171–1175.

Wanderlust in fly larvae

Like *C. elegans*, fly larvae differ in their feeding habits, and again much of this effect can be genetically traced to a natural variation at a single locus. Food for fly larvae is a mixture of yeast, sugar, and agar, and they forage for food in one of two ways: as 'rovers' or as 'sitters' (Sokolowski, 1980). The sitter strain prefers to remain feeding within a single food patch, while rovers move between food patches and take a straighter path to food than do sitters. (A journalist reporting on this finding when the gene was identified likened it to 'a gene for dining out.') When there is no food to be found, both variants move at about the same speed, so the difference is not because sitters

are intrinsically lazy. Rovers are more common than sitters in nature (70% versus 30%), and selection has been shown to maintain these variants.

Marla Sokolowski in Toronto and her colleagues identified the gene that is responsible for most of this difference: *dg2*, encoding the cGMP-dependent protein kinase PKG. As with the worms, it was possible to change larval behavior by genetically engineering the gene into larvae and thus to show unambiguously that *dg2* is responsible for of the behavioral difference. However, the behavioral change was not entirely due to genetics. After a short period of food deprivation, larval and adult flies with rover alleles could be made to behave as sitters.

Key papers

Sokolowski, M.B. (1980). Foraging strategies of *Drosophila melanogaster*: a chromosomal analysis. *Behav Genet* **10**:291–302.

Osborne, K.A., Robichon, A., Burgess, E., Butland, S., Shaw, R.A., Coulthard, A., Pereira, H.S., Greenspan, R.J., and Sokolowski, M.B. (1997). Natural behavior polymorphism due to a cGMP-dependent protein kinase of *Drosophila*. *Science* **277**:834–836.

Fitzpatrick, M.J., Feder, E., Rowe, L., and Sokolowski, M.B. (2007). Maintaining a behavior polymorphism by frequency-dependent selection on a single gene. *Nature* **447**: 210–212.

The discovery of the rover/sitter difference and the identification of its gene preceded that of *npr-1* in *C. elegans*, so when the worm findings came out, both camps were naturally curious to know whether the behavioral similarities in their wanderlust had a common underlying mechanism. This was

soon shown to be true when the fly version of *npr-1*, known as *neuropeptide-F receptor*, the *C. elegans* version of *dg2*, known as *egl-4*, and the respective neuropeptide-encoding genes in each animal—*npf* in flies and *flp-21* in worms—all turned out to have similar behavioral effects.

Key papers

Rogers, C., Reale, V., Kim, K., Chatwin, H., Li, C., Evans, P., and de Bono, M. (2003). Inhibition of *Caenorhabditis elegans* social feeding by FMRFamide-related peptide activation of NPR-1. *Nat Neurosci* **6**:1178–1185.

Wu, Q., Wen, T., Lee, G., Park, J.H., Cai, H.N., and Shen, P. (2003). Developmental control of foraging and social behavior by the *Drosophila* neuropeptide Y-like system. *Neuron* **39**:147–161.

Laboratory mutants have confirmed a link between PKG and neuropeptide receptors: the neuropeptide receptors initiate a cascade of reactions in the cell that activates PKG. That's not all. In yet another example of gene action crossing species boundaries, the same *PKG* gene is responsible for a major developmental transition in foraging behavior in that most social of insects, honeybees.

Honeybees are probably the most famous social foragers of all time, due in large measure to Karl von Frisch's studies of their dance language. When they are growing up in the hive, females start out as 'nurses,' tending to the feeding and hygienic needs of each larva as it develops in its little hexagonal cubbyhole. When nurses reach a certain age, they graduate to being foragers, capable of venturing outside the hive, exploring for new sources of nectar, and returning to 'tell' their comrades about where to find the goodies and how much is there. A key step in this transition is the developmental activation of their version of the *PKG* gene. If their PKG is inhibited, they will not develop into foragers, and those hive members that precociously develop into foragers (as occurs from time to time) have a precociously active PKG. And if that were not coincidental enough, the homolog of this gene in ants is also involved in the shift to foraging behavior.

Key papers

Ben-Shahar, Y., Robichon, A., Sokolowski, M.B., Robinson, G.E. (2002). Influence of gene action across different time scales on behavior. *Science* **296**:741–744.

Lucas, C. and Sokolowski, M.B. (2009). Molecular basis for changes in behavioral state in ant social behaviors. *Proc Natl Acad Sci USA* **106**: 6351–6356.

Just plain lust in prairie voles

About 3% of all mammalian species are monogamous; basically they bond and remain pretty much faithful to their partner. In some species, this behavior is in part mediated hormonally, oxytocin and vasopressin usually taking the blame or the credit depending on your perspective. The earliest studies linking oxytocin and social behavior demonstrated that oxytocin infused into the brain made rats nurture any pup that ventured into its nest. Oxytocin injected into female sheep makes the ewe accept a foreign lamb, rejecting all others. Oxytocin and vasopressin also have remarkable effects on the love life of a small mammal, the monogamous prairie vole. A single injection of either peptide mimics the effects of mating, instantly bonding the female to the nearest male suitor.

The behavior of prairie voles would make most parents happy: once wed, they remain faithful and bring up their offspring together. The behavior of their cousins, the montane voles, might not be so well received: promiscuous, relatively asocial, and non-paternal (meaning that the males mate but don't hang around to raise their young). But there is a quick fix for this behavioral aberration: it arises (at least in part) from DNA sequence differences in a vasopressin receptor in the brain, as Tom Insel from the National Institutes of Mental Health first reported in 1999. Females of non-monogamous vole species are eternally single mothers, presumably because they lack the relevant receptors. This DNA segment controls the level and pattern of expression of the receptor. Males with the 'long' form tend to be more monogamous than those with the 'short' form. Larry Young, Tom Insel, and their colleagues showed that the polygamous meadow vole could be made monogamous by introducing a prairie vole *V1aR* gene selectively into neurons of its ventral forebrain.

Key papers

Pedersen, C.A. and Prange, A.J., Jr (1979). Induction of maternal behavior in virgin rats after intracerebroventricular administration of oxytocin. *Proc Natl Acad Sci USA* **76**:6661–6665.

Kendrick, K.M., Da Costa, A.P., Broad, K.D., Ohkura, S., Guevara, R., Lévy, F., and Keverne, E.B. (1997). Neural control of maternal behavior and olfactory recognition of offspring. *Brain Res Bull* **44**:383–395.

Lim, M.M., Wang, Z., Olazábal, D.E., Ren, X., Terwilliger, E.F., and Young, L.J. (2004). Enhanced partner preference in a promiscuous species by manipulating the expression of a single gene. *Nature* **429**:754–757.

Young, L.J. and Wang, Z. (2004). The neurobiology of pair bonding. *Nat Neurosci* **7**:1048–1054.

Not surprisingly, oxytocin and vasopressin have attracted a lot of attention. Getting closer to our species, rhesus monkeys raised by humans in a nursery have severely disrupted social behavior and a 50% decrease in brain levels of oxytocin compared with mother-reared monkeys. You can try the effects of oxytocin yourself at http://www.verolabs.com/: '*Liquid Trust Spray—the first oxytocin product, formulated to enhance people's trust in you.*' The spray is said to improve your ability to guess what other people are feeling, by judging their facial expressions. Intranasal oxytocin spray has been found to increase a willingness to accept risks in a social situation and reduces brain activity in response to fear-inducing visual stimuli. What is the evidence that single genetic effects have specific effects on human behavior, comparable at least to the examples we have given for flies, worms and rodents?

Key papers

Winslow, J.T., Noble, P.L., Lyons, C.K., Sterk, S.M., and Insel, T.R. (2003). Rearing effects on cerebrospinal fluid, oxytocin concentration and social buffering in rhesus monkeys. *Neuropsychopharmacol* **28**:910–918.

Kirsch, P., Esslinger, C., Chen, Q., Mier, D., Lis, S., Siddhanti, S., Gruppe, H., Mattay, V.S., Gallhofer, B., and Meyer-Lindenberg, A. (2005). Oxytocin modulates neural circuitry for social cognition and fear in humans. *J Neurosci* **25**: 11489–11493.

Kosfeld, M., Heinrichs, M., Zak, P.J., Fischbacher, U., and Fehr, E. (2005). Oxytocin increases trust in humans. *Nature* **435**:673–676.

Fink, S., Excoffier, L., and Heckel, G. (2006). Mammalian monogamy is not controlled by a single gene. *Proc Natl Acad Sci USA* **103**: 10956–10960.

Domes, G., Heinrichs, M., Michel, A., Berger, C., and Herpertz, S.C. (2007). Oxytocin improves 'mind-reading' in humans. *Biol Psychiatry* **61**: 731–733.

How a gene made me aggressive: 1. Chromosomal abnormalities

Chromosomes don't look like their press picture photos. It's true, they do briefly take on the familiar X-shaped structure when a cell divides, but for the greater part of their lives, they spread out to fill the central structure of the cell, the nucleus, where they wrap their DNA strands around each other in ways still not fully understood and that make it currently impossible for us to recognize them individually. Coaxing sufficient numbers into the condensed, separate structure in which they can be examined and enumerated was achieved in the late 1950s, but remained technically challenging for some time (it still takes considerable skill to make a good chromosome spread: cytogeneticists, the people who do this sort of thing for a living, have a number of slightly obsessional habits—some, for example, check the humidity of the room before they prepare chromosomes). Also chromosomes don't come with a handy barcode appearance that immediately leads to their identification as chromosomes 1, 2, 3, etc. Like every biological feature, they show extensive variation, some of it normal, some of it pathological.

But one relatively easy feature to recognize is the sex chromosomes (the X and Y). The Y chromosome can be recognized because it is the smallest, while the X chromosome is one of the largest. The X chromosome also has the handy feature that in people with two copies (females), one copy is bundled up in protein to form a small knob-like structure that can be seen even in non-dividing cells. The ease of counting X chromosomes led to the finding that, among men in institutions for the 'men-

tally subnormal,' about 1% had an XXY sex chromosome constitution (rather than XY or XX). In the rest of the population, the frequency is much less—about 0.1%.

In the 1960s, Patricia Jacobs, a cytogeneticist working in Edinburgh, noticed that there had been a couple of reports of the presence of additional Y chromosomes in '*institutions for criminal and "hard to manage" males of subnormal intelligence*'; additional Y chromosomes were very rare in '*ordinary mentally sub-normal males.*' Could it be possible that an extra copy of the Y chromosome predisposes its carriers to unusually aggressive behavior? '*We decided, that if this was the case, then we might expect an increased frequency of XYY males among those of a violent nature*' (Jacobs et al., 1965). Jacobs, presumably assisted by some larger male colleagues, took blood samples from '*mentally subnormal male patients with dangerous, violent, or criminal propensities in an institution*' (Carstairs maximum security hospital, outside Edinburgh). Eight out of 197 individuals had an extra Y chromosome. The paper reporting an increased frequency of XYY was published in *Nature* in 1965. By 1973, when the subject was given a substantial review, published in *Science*, there were 35 studies of patients in 'mental–penal' settings. Overall, the frequency of XYY was about 20 times the newborn rate of 0.1%.

Key paper

Jacobs, P.A., Brunton, M., Melville, M.M., Brittain, R.P., and McClemont, W.F. (1965). Aggressive behavior, mental sub-normality and the XYY male. *Nature* **208**:1351–1352.

The nature of this association wasn't clear (Could it be due to some other mediating factor? How specific was this effect?), except to some. Inevitably perhaps, the Y was labeled the 'criminal chromosome.' Apparently not only the press felt this way. A commentary in *Science* in 1974 tells of one geneticist who '*stood up at a small meeting and pushed the XYY stigma to its limits. "We can't be sure XYY actually makes someone a criminal," he said, "but I wouldn't invite an XYY home to dinner."*'

More vocal still was a Science for the People group, established at Harvard. The group objected to a screening program for chromosomal abnormalities in the newborn that was being run out of one of the Harvard teaching hospitals (Boston Hospital for Women). They wanted the program closed down because the XYY findings were a '*dangerous myth*' and the '*the stigma of being XXY or XYY is so great that behavioral problems arise as part of a self-fulfilling prophecy. If you tell parents that their son is going to have problems, they will treat him abnormally and he will, indeed, develop problems.*' By 1975, the pressure on Stanley Walzer, who was running the program, was too much. Lawyers for the Washington-based Children's Defense Fund were questioning him about his work. So he stopped the program. '*This whole thing has been a terrible strain. My family has been threatened. I've been made to feel like a dirty person. And, even after I won with the faculty, it was clear the opposition would go on. In fact, new groups were becoming involved. I was just too emotionally tired to go on.*'

A detailed study of the relationship between XYY and criminality was carried in Denmark, where the availability of records made it possible to screen almost all tall men in Copenhagen (of the same age) for the presence of the chromosome abnormality, thereby avoiding ascertainment bias (Witkin *et al.*, 1976). Among the 4,139 men for whom sex chromosome determinations were made, the investigators found 12 XYY. The penal records appeared to confirm Pat Jacob's findings: 42% of the XYY men had committed criminal offenses compared with 9% of those a normal (XY) karyotype. However, aggression was not

a significant feature: aggressive crimes were not elevated in the XYY group. Furthermore, the excess of crimes could be explained by the lower intelligence of the XYY men and, while the investigators went no further than pointing to intelligence as an important mediating variable, they did suggest that '*people of lower intelligence may be less adept at escaping detection*' (one of the XYY burglars typically broke into houses when the owners were at home).

Few people now study the behavior of XYY men, although there is some evidence that they are antisocial (Gotz *et al.*, 1999). The example shows the importance of considering moderating variables in interpreting genetic effects on behavior, but it does not provide an example of a gene influencing behavior. However, there is another candidate for that, again a gene for aggression.

How a gene made me aggressive: 2. Single genes with large effects

Chromosomal abnormalities typically involve hundreds, if not thousands of genes, which is one reason why there has been relatively little progress in working out why an additional copy of chromosome 21 causes intellectual dysfunction in Down's syndrome, so even if Pat Jacobs had continued her work on the XYY syndrome, it is not certain that much light would have been cast on the biology of aggression. However, there is one striking example, a Dutch family, reported by clinical geneticist Han Brunner in 1993.

Key paper

Brunner, H.G., Nelen, M., Breakefield, X.O., Ropers, H.H., and van Oost, B.A. (1993). Abnormal behavior associated with a point mutation in the structural gene for monoamine oxidase A. *Science* 262:578–580.

Their family pedigree is shown in Figure 8.9. In this diagram squares are males, circles are females. Symbols filled in black are affected individuals and those struck through with a diagonal line were dead when the pedigree was drawn up. You can see immediately that only males are affected. Abnormal behavior was documented for affected males in at least four different sibships living in different parts of the country at different times. Most striking were repeated episodes of aggressive, sometimes violent, behavior occurring in the eight affected males. Aggressive behavior was usually triggered by anger and was often out of proportion to the provocation. Aggressive behavior tended to cluster in periods of 1 to 3 days; the affected males would sleep very little and would experience frequent night terrors. No obvious relationship existed between the abnormal behavior and dietary or other external factors. In one instance, an affected male, aged 23, was convicted of the rape of his sister. He was transferred to an institution for psychopaths, where he was described as quiet and easy to handle. In spite of this, fights occurred with other inmates, and he was repeatedly transferred. At the age of 35 years, while working in the fields, he stabbed one of the wardens in the chest with a pitchfork, after having been told to get on with his work. Another affected male tried to run over his boss with a car at the sheltered workshop where he was employed, after having been told that his work was not up to par. A third affected male would enter his sisters' bedrooms at night, armed with a knife, and force them to undress. At least two affected males in this family are known arsonists. This latter behavior appears to be linked to stressful circumstances, such as the death of a relative. Other abnormal behavior that was recorded in individual cases includes exhibitionism and voyeurism. Several affected males were reported to suddenly grasp or hold female relatives. Teenage females in this family would often avoid being home alone with their affected brother, and some left home because of this problem.

Genetic mapping assigned the mutation to a region of the X chromosome, including two genes that are known to metabolize serotonin—dopamine and norepirephrine. These chemicals exist in the brain as neurotransmitters (molecules that are involved in carrying information between nerve cells). The two genes encode two monoamine oxidase enzymes (MAO for short): MAOA and MAOB. DNA sequencing of the genes identified a mutation in MAOA that truncates the protein, making it ineffective. As men have only one copy of the gene (they have one X chromosome), they had almost no functional enzyme. On the face of it, MAOA mutations were making Dr Brunner's patients aggressive.

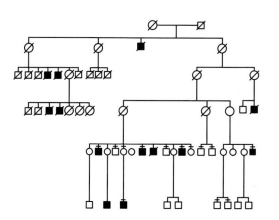

Figure 8.9 Geneology of a Dutch family, showing affected males (black squares).
Source: Brunner *et al.*, 1993; courtesy of AAAS.

There are two reasons why that finding has had relatively little impact. Firstly, the Dutch pedigree is unique. Mutations in MAOA do not contribute to aggression in anyone else (although there is one qualification to this statement that we will come back to later). Secondly, unlike the work in model organisms, we have no context in which to place this finding—no neuronal circuit is identified, no pathway that can be extended and explored in other systems. So while the MAOA family shows that single gene mutations with a large effect on behavior can be found, it has done little to progress our understanding of how genes influence behavior.

With the exception of mutations that affect language and the mutations that give rise to mental retardation, other than the MAOA family, no mutations have been reported that have such a large effect on behavior. This doesn't mean that mutations with behavioral effects do not exist in our species, but it does strongly suggest that the effects are almost always relatively small. However, it's possible that there are mutations that have an intermediate effect, not immediately obvious, but large enough to be found if we compared a group of affected and non-affected individuals, in fact if we carried out a genetic association test. Are there mutations that disrupt a gene's function and have behavioral consequences? There are certainly publications claiming that these genetic abnormalities are out there.

So which is it? Pluribus or unum?

We began by wanting to compare humans to these apparently simpler animals. How did it come out? Are they genetically like humans? Most natural variation in fly behavior certainly appears to be multigenic, as it seems to be in humans. But rare cases of single-gene natural variation in behavior in flies and worms bear an uncanny similarity to each other in the biochemical pathways that are affected, and in the similarity of the behavioral effects they produce.

In all of these examples, human or otherwise, the explanation for what kind of variation can be found must always go back to a consideration of which genes (and which associated biological processes) can tolerate natural variation without causing such undue harm that they will be eliminated from the population by natural selection. It appears that the pathway consisting of the neuropeptide associated with feeding behavior, its receptor, and PKG activated by it can tolerate a fair degree of variation. This variation is apparently, in at least some environments, sufficiently adaptive to the animal that it maintains itself in natural populations.

Feeding behavior is certainly a very basic behavior. It may be so primordial that the pathways and mechanisms for its performance and regulation are so similar in today's fruit flies and nematodes because their ancient common ancestor, who probably lived 500 million years ago, harbored the same mechanism and passed it on to them.

In Chapter 11, we will come back to this central question of 'one or many' in an attempt to summarize how we think genes most commonly contribute to behavior throughout the animal kingdom.

Summary

1. Laboratory selection experiments in fruit flies can produce major behavioral changes, and have a multigenic basis, with longer selection regimes resulting in somewhat larger changes in individual gene expression levels, than short-term selection.

2. *C. elegans* was the first model organism to be studied comprehensively with respect to its anatomy, cell lineage, and genome sequence.

3. A single mutation in a neuropeptide receptor gene, *npr-1*, found both in the laboratory and in the wild, alters the feeding behavior of *C. elegans* from solitary to aggregated or 'social.'

4. A fruit fly gene for cGMP-dependent protein kinase (PKG) also exists as a single-gene behavioral polymorphism in the wild, affecting foraging behavior; it is part of the same signaling system as the worm *npr-1* gene, and also affects analogous behaviors in bees and ants.

5. A single-gene difference in voles may partly account for whether they exhibit monogamous and biparental behavior, and correlates with a DNA sequence difference that affects the expression pattern of their receptor for the neurohormone vasopressin.

6. In humans, a rare single-gene variant with a major effect on impulsive behavior has been seen in an enzyme that regulates the monoamine neurotransmitter monoamine oxidase A (MAOA).

7. While naturally occurring variants in single genes can have large impacts on behavior, this is relatively rare. The vast majority of genetic variation in natural populations that impacts on behavior is contained in genetic variants of small effect.

References

Brunner, H.G., Nelen, M., Breakefield, X.O., Ropers, H.H., and van Oost, B.A. (1993). Abnormal behavior associated with a point mutation in the structural gene for monoamine oxidase A. *Science* **262**:578–580.

de Bono, M. and Bargmann, C.I. (1998). Natural variation in a neuropeptide Y receptor homolog modifies social behavior and food response in *C. elegans*. *Cell* **94**:679–689.

Dierick, H.A. and Greenspan, R.J. (2006). Molecular analysis of flies selected for aggressive behavior. *Nat Genet* **38**:1023–1031.

Gotz, M.J., Johnstone, E.C., and Ratcliffe, S.G. (1999). Criminality and antisocial behavior in unselected men with sex chromosome abnormalities. *Psychol Med* **29**:953–962.

Gray, J.M., Karow, D.S., Lu, H., Chang, A.J., Chang, J.S., Ellis, R.E., Marletta, M.A., and Bargmann, C.I. (2004). Oxygen sensation and social feeding mediated by a *C. elegans* guanylate cyclase homologue. *Nature* **430**:317–322.

Jacobs, P.A., Brunton, M., Melville, M.M., Brittain, R.P., and McClemont, W.F. (1965). Aggressive behavior, mental sub-normality and the XYY male. *Nature* **208**:1351–1352.

Pauly, P.J. (1987). *Controlling Life. Jacques Loeb and the Engineering Ideal in Biology*. New York: Oxford University Press.

Ricker, J.P. and Hirsch, J. (1988). Genetic changes occuring over 500 generations in lines of *Drosophila Melanogaster* selected divergently for geotaxis. *Behav Genet* **18**:13–25.

Sokolowski, M.B. (1980). Foraging strategies of *Drosophila melanogaster*: a chromosomal analysis. *Behav Genet* **10**:291–302.

White, J.G., Southgate, E., Thomson, J.N., and Brenner, S. (1986). The structure of the nervous system of the nematode *Caenorhabditis elegans*. *Philos Trans R Soc Lond B Biol Sci* **314**:1–340.

Witkin, H.A., Mednick, S.A., Schulsinger, F., Bakkestrom, E., Christiansen, K.O., Goodenough, D.R., Hirschhorn, K., Lundsteen, C., Owen, D.R. *et al.* (1976). Criminality in XYY and XXY men. *Science* **193**:547–555.

Model systems

Circadian rhythms

[What we learn about a fly's brain turns out to be useful for learning about our own brain]

The questions we ask about the relationship between genes and behavior are to some extent shaped by the experiments we can imagine, which in turn depends on our experience as scientists, what we have done in the past, what we know works, and what we know doesn't work. Psychiatric geneticists, restricted to working with a model organism whose mating preferences they cannot control or even influence, have struggled with the question of whether most behaviors in natural populations are influenced by many genes or just a few. Mouse geneticists, taking for granted their ability to construct pedigrees of their choosing, also address these questions, but answer them in different ways from their colleagues in the psychiatry department.

Invertebrate geneticists are in a different universe. They can do more to their model organism than interview the first-degree relatives about their drinking habits, or inflict incestuous liaisons. Flies are routinely exposed to the sort of trauma that no ethical committee would ever allow to be inflicted on even a rat. In order to discover single genes that impact on behavior, flies are irradiated and given toxic, highly mutagenic chemicals, all with

the purpose of disrupting their hereditary material. This approach *creates* genetic variation rather than discovering it in nature. It asks a fundamentally different question from that pursued in the last chapter, raising new issues about the relationship between genes and behavior.

In the early 1960s, one of the pioneers of modern genetics, Seymour Benzer (Figure 9.1), inaugurated a new approach to the study of behavior using genetics in the fruit fly *Drosophila melanogaster*. His aim was to 'dissect' behavior into its component genetic parts. In this way, the analysis could go beyond those genes that happen to vary naturally in populations. Benzer's approach represented a distinct departure from traditional 'behavior genetics', which had focused either on the behavioral influences of natural genetic variation, most of which seemed to result from relatively mild differences in multiple genes, or on spontaneous mutations that occasionally appeared in laboratory strains of flies or mice. He was adapting a paradigm from prokaryotic molecular biology—the aggressive search for single genes—by inducing mutations and testing for altered performance in behavioral tests. The single-gene, induced-mutation school

Figure 9.1 Seymour Benzer (1921–2007).
Source: Courtesy of the National Library of Medicine.

took no account of whether a gene would exhibit natural variation. Instead, the interest lay in which genes were essential for the behavior and which neural or biochemical components were selectively altered.

Benzer's interest in genetic influences on the brain was prompted by several events. He had been intrigued with the findings of James McConnell in 1962, a former advertising executive who claimed that RNA isolated from trained flatworms (planaria) could be administered to untrained flatworms and transfer the behavior to them. In McConnell's initial experiments, trained planaria were *fed* to untrained ones, and the behavior was found to be transferred. This finding spawned many experiments in rats and reports in top journals, all of which confirmed McConnell's basic findings, until the bubble burst when it was shown that all of the

results had been unduly influenced by wishful thinking. The excitement at the time, however, is readily understandable, as these findings hinted at a possible molecular mechanism for learning and memory—a true 'neurogenetic code.' Benzer even tried his hand at conditioning planaria, but gave up when he found that an electric shock split the worms in two.

A second influence was reading *The Machinery of the Brain* by Dean Wooldridge. Wooldridge had been Director of Electronics Research at Hughes Aircraft and then one of the founders of the aerospace company TRW. In his 1963 book, Wooldridge laid out a challenge to explain the workings of the brain in terms of physics and chemistry.

The third influence was Benzer's observation that his second daughter differed totally in personality from his first, despite the apparent lack of change in his and his wife's behavior as parents—an observation shared by many subsequent parents including two of the authors of this book (K.S.K. and J.F.).

Key papers

Weiner, J. (1999). *Time, Love, Memory*. New York: Knopf.

A biographical and highly accessible discussion of Seymour Benzer's work on genetics and behavior.

Morange, M. (2006). What history tells us. VI. The transfer of behaviors by macromolecules. *J Biosci* **31**:323–327.

Greenspan, R.J. (2008). Seymour Benzer (1921– 2007). *Curr Biol* **18**:R106–R110.

As we detailed in the last chapter, the fruit fly (*D. melanogaster*) is easy to grow in the laboratory, has a short generation time, and has about 100,000 neurons, which, on a logarithmic scale, is almost exactly halfway between a single neuron and the number of cells in your brain. More importantly, it is *the* classic invertebrate genetic model system that has been intensely studied for a century.

Of the various behaviors that have been studied with fruit fly mutants, none has been more successfully unraveled than the mechanism of circadian rhythms—the process by which the daily timing of activity and sleep are regulated. Although first done in the fruit fly, subsequent identification of genes for circadian rhythms in mice and humans surprised everyone when they turned out to be nearly identical. This is the story we will tell in this chapter.

Mutagenesis

Work in flies had shown that radiation exposure generates mutations, opening up a remarkable opportunity. Hermann Müller (Figure 9.2), who received the 1946 Nobel Prize in Physiology and Medicine for this work, explains the point:

> It was from the first evident that the production of mutations would, as we once stated, provide us with tools of the greatest nicety, wherewith to dissect piece by piece the physiological, embryological, and bio-chemical structure of the organism and to analyze its workings. Already natural mutations ... have shown how the intensive tracing of the effects, and interrelations of effects, of just one or a few mutations, can lead to a deeper understanding of the complex processes whereby the genes operate to produce the organism.

Radiation-induced mutations turned out to be '*a yardstick of what really random changes should be.*' They were found to be of the same

Figure 9.2 Hermann Müller (1890–1967).
Source: Courtesy of the National Library of Medicine.

essential nature as those arising naturally in the laboratory or field. They usually occur in one gene without affecting an identical one nearby. They are distributed similarly in the chromosomes. The effects may be large or small, and there is a similar range of fully lethal to so-called visible gene mutations; that is, the radiation mutations do not give evidence of necessarily being more deleterious. And when one concentrates attention upon given genes, one finds that a whole series of different forms, or 'alleles,' may be produced, of a similar and in many cases sensibly identical nature in the two cases. In fact, every natural mutation, when searched for long enough, can also be produced by radiation (http://nobelprize.org/nobel_prizes/medicine/laureates/1946/muller-lecture.html).

The productive application of mutagenesis had already garnered another Nobel Prize-winning discovery in 1958, for Edward Tatum, Joshua Lederberg, and George Beadle. Their work, which dominates biology today, showed that: (i) all biochemical processes in all organisms are under genetic control; (ii) these overall biochemical processes are resolvable into a series of individual stepwise reactions; (iii) each single reaction is controlled in a primary fashion by a single gene; in other words, in every case a 1 : 1 correspondence of gene and biochemical reaction exists, such that (iv) mutation of a single gene results only in an alteration in the ability of the cell to carry out a single primary chemical reaction.

This model of genetic action, of a single gene controlling a single protein, was worked out using mutants in fungi and bacteria, mutants induced by radiation in the way Müller suggested.

There is no doubt that the model has been productive, that it has resulted in the rigorous demonstration of linear action in many biological processes, but, as has been apparent at a number of points in this book, the model also limits the way we think about genetic action. We also need to clarify one point of disagreement with Müller. While the biological nature of artificially induced mutations may not differ from those that 'arise naturally' in their phenotypic effect, such mutations are often quite different from those seen in natural populations. Man-made mutations can produce dramatic effects that are easy to detect in the laboratory but would not survive for many generations in the wild due to the effects of natural selection. For the moment, though, we need to look in more detail at the origins of an idea that crucially influenced the thinking of many people about the influence of genes on behavior.

The exclusive use of radiation for producing mutations was a short-lived technique. Chemicals that do the same thing were found and are now the tool of choice. A scientist in Edinburgh (J.M. Robson) noted that mustard gas produced effects similar to radiation, leading to a series of experiments that confirmed the mutagenic potential of the compound and similar chemical substances. Two of these, ethylmethane sulfonate (EMS) and ethylnitrosourea (ENU), were later adopted for precisely the purpose Müller suggested: '...to dissect piece by piece the physiological, embryological, and bio-chemical structure of the organism and to analyze its workings.'

Assuming that what is true for biochemical pathways is true for all phenotypes, Benzer thought that mutagenesis could be used to understand the biology of behavior. As he said in 1973: 'The circuit components of behavior, from sensory receptors to the central nervous system to effector muscles, are constructed under direction of the genes. A mutation affecting the structure or function of any of these components may alter behavior. Using classical genetic recombination mapping, the locus of the mutant gene within the one-dimensional chromosomal array can be determined.'

It's worth emphasizing the radical nature of this suggestion, to create in the laboratory fly mutants that had abnormal behavior. What on earth would come out of this? Killer flies maybe, the stuff of science fiction horror and summer movie blockbusters. Flies with superior intelligence, able to hold conversations with their creators and even help them design their experiments? Or maybe just a lot of dead flies.

Consider the alternative view, voiced strongly for example by John Wilcock, a psychologist in Birmingham who had published a long and influential review of gene action on behavior in 1969, 5 years before Benzer's genetics paper quoted above. He dismissed invertebrate behavior as fundamentally uninteresting until 'learning ability is unequivocally demonstrated' and was scathing about the value of single-gene mutations, stating that '...*behavioral differences between mutant and non-mutant animals are in general direct peripheral effects of the mutant gene and are thus devoid of psychological significance. A more fruitful approach to the study of gene action in behavior will involve examination of "polygenes" individually.*'

Key papers

Wilcock, J. (1969). Gene action and behavior. *Psychol Bull* **72**:1–29.

Benzer, S. (1973) Genetic dissection of behavior. *Sc Am* **229**:24–37.

Finding a circadian rhythm mutant

Rhythms dominate our bodies, our physiology, and our behavioral patterns. They determine the regularity with which we get up in the morning and go to bed at night. As day and night, neap and spring tides, seasons and years are enforced upon us all, it seems reasonable to suppose that biological rhythmicity is entrained by environmental cues and to envisage a system that uses diurnal temperature change to increase or decrease the rate of chemical reactions that in turn lead to waking and sleeping.

In fact, organisms have endogenous rhythms. When placed under laboratory conditions of constant darkness and temperature, rhythmic activities persist in plants, insects, and mammals, and they continue to occur once a day with a periodicity that is close to, but not exactly, 24 hours. The period is said to be circadian. Before the days of electric lights, humans were mainly active in the daytime. Mice and rats, on the other hand, are active at night (that is, nocturnal), as anyone who has waited for a subway train late at night knows.

Experiments in birds provide a particularly striking example of the importance of circadian rhythms for behavior. Starlings can be trained to fly to a food reward, thereby allowing investigation into the methods they employ to determine which way to fly. One cue they use is the position of the sun in the sky, a cue that can be replaced in the laboratory by an electric light. Unlike the sun, light bulbs are usually stationary, and birds trained to rely on a light bulb as a direction-giver add 15° every hour to the angle relative to the artificial sun. This means that the starlings must have access to a reliable internal clock. Furthermore, the clock can be reset by shifting the daily cycle of light and darkness to which the bird is exposed (equivalent to giving the birds jet lag). After a 6-hour shift, starlings make a 90° error in the estimate of where the food reward is located; homing pigeons are similarly affected, setting off due east when they should be going north.

Key paper

Hoffmann, K. (1960). Experimental manipulation of the orientational clock in birds. *Cold Spring Harb Symp Quant Biol* **25**:379–387.

Fruit flies are active in the daytime (diurnal) like us. This is easily observable in their movements. At night, they are mostly immobile. They do not lie down or curl up in a corner, but they are actually asleep when immobile, as shown by the fact that it is harder to rouse them when in this state and that if they are forced to be active for prolonged periods during the night, they must recover the lost sleep the next day. The timing of the active/inactive times is not simply due to the lights being on or off. When flies are kept in a regular day/night (light/dark) cycle for several days and then left in constant darkness, they will continue to show the same cycle of active/inactive periods as if the lights were coming on in the morning and going off in

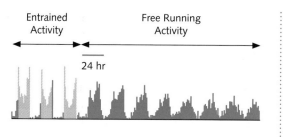

Figure 9.3 Example of circadian locomotor activities in *Drosophila*.
Source: Hyun *et al.* (2005).

the evening (Figure 9.3). Moreover, if the timing of the light/dark cycle is shifted by several hours (e.g. from 8 a.m./8 p.m. to 12 noon/12 midnight), the flies will gradually be entrained to the new daily cycle over several days, just as it takes us several days (1 day per time zone, on average) to adjust to a new time zone when we travel.

The search for circadian rhythm mutants in the fruit fly was one of the first attempts to isolate behavioral mutants in Seymour Benzer's lab at Caltech. Ron Konopka had come to the lab as a graduate student already captivated by the idea of studying circadian rhythms (Figure 9.4). Most of those around him were skeptical. Some thought it would be too difficult to devise a way of screening for alterations in these rhythms. Others thought that such mutations would invariably be lethal; these included Max Delbrück, one of the founders of molecular biology and Benzer's mentor and colleague at Caltech.

Konopka solved the first problem by noting that, when adult flies first emerge from metamorphosis, they prefer to do so around the time when the lights come on in the morning. He realized that if he dumped out the newly emerged flies every morning from each culture vial after the lights had been on for several hours, few flies would emerge during the rest of the day. This gave him a simple screening test for new mutants. If he started many fly cultures, each consisting of a possible new mutant strain,

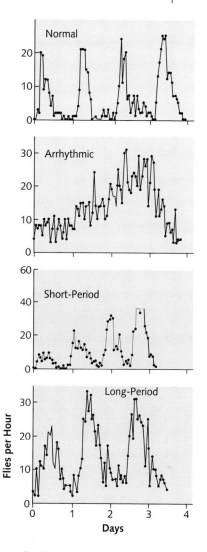

Figure 9.4 Circadian eclosion behavior in normal flies and in three mutants of the *period* gene.
Source: Konopka and Benzer (1971).

he could test them by clearing the flies each morning and looking for those rare cultures in which adults continued to emerge around the clock. To induce new mutants, he fed male flies on sugar water containing a mutagen (the chemical EMS that produces mutations) and then mated them, taking their offspring to start individual cultures that might harbor such mutations. To ensure that all of the flies in these cultures would have the same mutant chromosome,

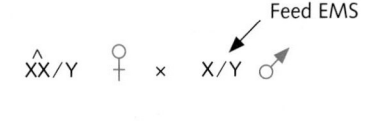
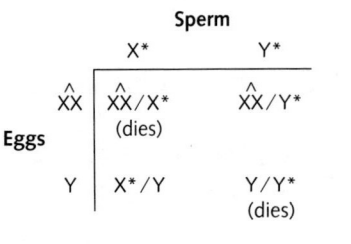
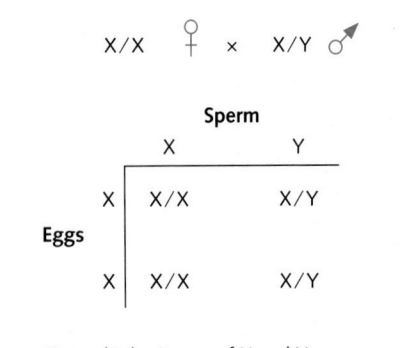

Normal inheritance of X and Y
chromosomes

X*, Y* = chromosomes exposed to EMS

The use of attached-X chromosomes (X^X) in *Drosophila* to facilitate the search for X-linked mutations. Sperm previously exposed to EMS fertilize eggs containing either the attached-X chromosome or the Y chromosome. The treated X chromosomes from the males show up as the hemizygous Xs of the sons, revealing phenotypically recessive mutations.

Figure 9.5 'Attached-X' strategy for mutant screens in *Drosophila* (EMS, ethylmethane sulfonate).

he used a genetic trick available in fruit flies that permits the male's X chromosome to be transmitted directly to male offspring and not to females (as usually occurs). The trick involves mating them to females carrying what is known as an 'attached-X' chromosome (Figure 9.5), in which both of the female's X chromosomes are attached to the same centromere and thus go together into the egg. When that egg is fertilized by an X-bearing sperm from the male, the zygote dies. When it is fertilized by a Y-bearing sperm, it forms a normal female, as the Y chromosome does not determine sex in flies.

Konopka solved the second problem by isolating circadian rhythm mutants that were, indeed, alive. After screening through some 2,000 cultures of mutagenized flies, he found three lines in which adult flies had abnormal times of emergence. Actually, he found the first one after screening only 200 lines. While this may seem like a lot, it is a pittance when stacked up against most others' experience of trying to isolate behavioral mutants, where it is

not uncommon to go through more than 1,000 before finding anything.

To confirm that these were true circadian rhythm mutants, he grew the flies in constant darkness to test their internal clocks, and found that they continued to show abnormal patterns of emergence (see Figure 9.4). In a completely independent test for a different kind of rhythm, he also tested them for their locomotor activity at different times of day and night.

He placed adults in a 12-hour light/12-hour dark cycle to entrain them and then left them in constant darkness while monitoring their movements. Nowadays, there is a commercially available device for doing this (Figure 9.6), but back then he used the lab's spectrophotometer, a piece of equipment designed to detect light absorption and used for measurement of protein concentration and other molecules. Konopka simply put some flies in the little glass vessel, known as a cuvette, normally used for the liquid to be measured,

The three mutants all differed from the normal 24-hour periodicity. One showed a 'long-day' period of 28 hours, another showed a 'short-day' period of 19 hours, and the third was arrhythmic, showing no discernible periodicity (Figure 9.7). The mutants were already abnormal on another measure of periodicity: the time of day that adult flies emerged from metamorphosis. Under normal light/dark conditions, wild-type adult *Drosophila* emerge in the morning. When tested for

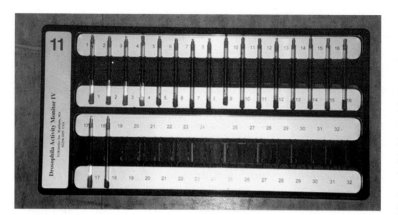

Figure 9.6 Activity monitoring system for circadian rhythms in *Drosophila*.
Source: R.J. Greenspan.

and placed it into the machine. He then ran the chart recorder slowly over the course of the day and night to record any interruptions of the light beam due to the flies jumping up and down. Normal flies are active during the day and in constant darkness during the time that would be the day. If one calculates the periodicity of their activity cycle (represented by the Greek letter τ—pronounced 'tau'), it comes out to very nearly a 24-hour period of activity/inactivity.

adult emergence in constant darkness, the mutants showed the same short, long, and arrhythmic periodicities as they did for adult locomotor activity (Figure 9.4). This finding indicated that the mutants were likely to be affecting the fundamental clock mechanism itself, rather than some secondary or downstream consequence of the clock.

But this was not the only piece of evidence for the fundamental nature of the mutants'

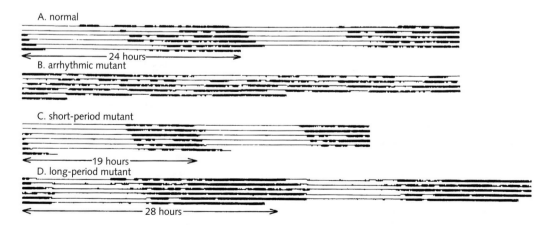

Figure 9.7 Circadian locomotor behavior in normal flies and mutants of the *period* gene.
Source: Konopka and Benzer (1971).

effects. Even more convincing was the fact that, using the methods of linkage analysis (described for humans in Chapter 3), it could be shown that all three mutations mapped to the same place on the fly's X chromosome. Additional genetic tests were performed to see whether they were mutations of the same gene, such as producing female flies in which one X chromosome carried one of the rhythm mutations and the other X carried another of them. In these complementation tests, all three mutations behaved as expected for alleles of the same locus—that is, they reflected different aberrant copies of the same gene. With that, the *period* gene was christened and the genetic analysis of circadian rhythms was launched.

Key paper

Konopka, R.J. and Benzer, S. (1971). Clock mutants of *Drosophila melanogaster*. *Proc Natl Acad Sci USA* **68**:2112–2116.

Molecular clockworks

The world of biological research changed dramatically with the arrival of gene cloning, and this had an immediate impact on the study of circadian rhythms. The *period* gene of *Drosophila* was among the first genes to be cloned using a strategy that was initially only possible in the fruit fly—positional cloning (see Appendix, p. 233). Even if nothing was known about what kind of protein was involved, or where or when it was produced, one could clone the gene simply by knowing exactly where it is on the chromosome and isolating a series of overlapping pieces of DNA that covered that region of chromosome. This approach is also referred to as 'chromosome walking'

because one needs only one starting piece of DNA from somewhere nearby to 'walk' along the chromosome by isolating successive overlapping pieces. The tools of *Drosophila* genetics make it possible to narrow down a gene's location using strains carrying rearranged chromosomes, i.e. chromosomes that have been broken by X-rays and reattached incorrectly. The breakpoints of these rearrangements provide a physical marker for a chromosome region that is visible in the microscope and a molecular marker for that region because it changes the DNA sequence.

Using this strategy, Michael Rosbash and Jeffrey Hall at Brandeis University isolated a piece of DNA containing (i.e. they 'cloned') the *period* gene. Michael Young at Rockefeller University accomplished the same goal in parallel. The definitive proof that this really was the gene came from showing that the isolated piece of DNA could be reintroduced back into a fertilized *Drosophila* egg coming from the arrhythmic mutant strain and rescue its defective circadian rhythm; that is, restore it back to normal.

Having the gene in hand, however, is not the same thing as understanding what makes the clock tick. Looking at the sequence of amino acids encoded by the gene did not provide any immediate answers, nor did seeing where in the brain the mRNA for *period* was actively transcribed. More interesting was the fact that the period protein is localized to the nucleus. These are all pieces of the puzzle, but are not enough. The breakthrough came when they looked at the levels of the *period* gene's products through the course of a 24-hour day. Critically, they found that both the protein and mRNA cycle over the 24-hour period (Figures 9.8 and 9.9).

Not only that, but the short-day mutant's mRNA cycled earlier and the long-day mutant's mRNA cycled later in the day. This all

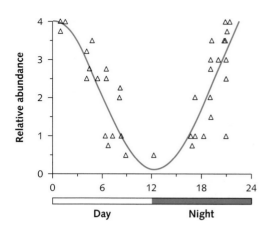

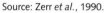

Figure 9.8 Cycling of period protein in the fly brain.
Source: Zerr *et al.*, 1990.

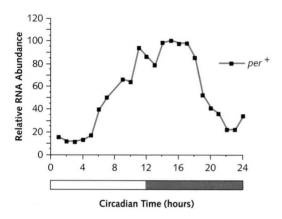

Figure 9.9 Cycling of *period* mRNA (*per⁺*) in the fly brain.
Source: Hardin *et al.* (1990).

occurred in a light/dark cycle. In constant darkness, the wild-type mRNA continued to cycle with a 24-hour cycle, the short-day mRNA with a short-day cycle, and the long-day mRNA with a long-day cycle. Protein levels from the wild type followed suit. In addition to matching the behavioral period in a light/dark cycle and in constant darkness, the wild-type protein and mRNA also showed a gradual shift when the cycle was advanced or retreated, as in jet lag. In the mutants, the short-day protein cycled on a

shorter time period, the long-day mutant made very little protein and had a very dampened oscillation, and the arrhythmic mutant made no detectable protein.

All of this seemed reasonable and consistent, but there was an anomaly. The peak of period protein comes 8 hours after the peak of its mRNA. This is much longer than is normally required for the process of producing protein from mRNA (i.e. translation), and was critical later on for clarifying the entire circadian mechanism.

The real breakthrough came when Rosbash, Hall, and their post-doc Paul Hardin, looked at the levels of period mRNA in the arrhythmic *period* mutant: it remained at a constant level (Figure 9.10). As this mutant had already shown the genetic characteristics of a null (i.e. knockout) mutation, the result gave the key clue to the rhythm mechanism—in the mutant that makes no protein, the mRNA is transcribed but does not cycle. When this is put together with the fact that there is an 8-hour delay between transcription and translation, and then a further delay between translation and entry back

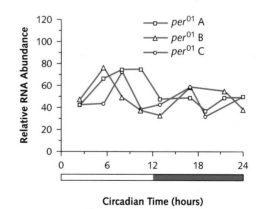

Figure 9.10 Little or no cycling of *period* mRNA in three sets of brains from flies with the *per⁰* (knockout) mutation.
Source: Hardin *et al.* (1990).

into the nucleus, it suggested a novel interpretation: the period protein feeds back to repress its own transcription over a time course that spans 24 hours (Figure 9.11). The next several years' work would bear this out, making these studies on period protein and mRNA cycling the first major breakthrough not only in circadian rhythms, but in the molecular understanding of any behavioral mechanism. The universality of the mechanism also began to surface at this time, when something analogous was found for the circadian clock in the fungus *Neurospora*. But the feedback cycling of the *period* gene product, while compelling, was still incomplete.

More clock genes

No gene is an island, as amply shown by our many examples in earlier chapters of the interactions among many genes to produce a phenotype. To find more of the key players in the clock mechanism, mutant-hunting strategies similar to Konopka's were set in motion. The first to yield was an arrhythmic mutant found in flies in Michael Young's lab at Rockefeller University, called *timeless*. The *timeless* mRNA cycles on a 24-hour period and its transcriptional profile is flat in both the arrhythmic *period* and the *timeless* mutants. In fact, *timeless* is *period*'s döppelganger. Both are transcribed cyclically, both protein products cycle and are translated with a delay, both are localized to the nucleus, and when either one is mutant, the cycling of both of them grinds to a halt. In other words, it was a stroke of luck that this gene came up as the next one after *period*. As it turns out, the protein products of the two genes actually bind to each other to repress their own transcription.

At this point, another phylum enters the fray with the isolation by Joe Takahashi of the first

clock mutant in the mouse, imaginatively named 'Clock.' When it was cloned, the gene was found to encode a transcription factor (a protein that regulates the transcription of other genes). Clock is a member of a family of proteins that are related to each other by having a similar amino acid sequence for a segment of the protein (a 'domain') that binds other proteins with similar domains and also binds to DNA. This is known as a basic helix–loop–helix (bHLH), a less-than-poetic description of the configuration of amino acids in that segment. The second feature of this family of proteins is that they possess an additional protein-binding domain known as PAS, named with the initials of the first three proteins to have been found with it (Per: period circadian protein; Arnt: Ah receptor nuclear translocator protein; and Sim: single-minded protein).

Key papers

Vitaterna, M.H., King, D.P., Chang, A.M., Kornhauser, J.M., Lowrey, P.L., McDonald, J.D., Dove, W.F., Pinto, L.H., Turek, F.W., and Takahashi, J.S. (1994). Mutagenesis and mapping of a mouse gene, *Clock*, essential for circardian behavior. *Science* **264**:719–725.

Antoch, M.P., Song, E.J., Chang, A.M., Vitaterna, M.H., Zhao, Y.L., Wilsbacher, L.D., Sangoram, A.M., King, D.P., Pinto, L.H., and Takahashi, J.S. (1997). Functional identification of the mouse circadian *Clock* gene by transgenic BAC rescue. *Cell* **89**:655–667.

King, D.P., Zhao, Y., Sangoram, A.M., Wilsbacher, L.D., Tanaka, M., Antoch, M.P., Steeves, T.D., Vitaterna, M.H., Kornhauser, J.M. *et al.* (1997). Positional cloning of the mouse circadian *Clock* gene. *Cell* **89**:641–653.

Three papers that changed mouse genetics: in 1994 the use of mutagenesis to find a circadian mutant in the mouse, and 3 years later, two papers describing the cloning of the *Clock* gene.

The lucky streak continued. The next two mutants to be identified in the fly were the actual targets of the *period/timeless* complex—the transcriptional complex to which they bind to shut down their own transcription. These were the genes *cycle* and the fly version of *Clock*. Both were found in a Konopka-like screen for mutants with altered daily locomotor rhythms. The *Clock* gene was so named because it was homologous to the recently identified mouse circadian rhythm mutant. Both *Clock* and *cycle* encode transcription factors of the bHLH/PAS family. They associate with each other and also with the protein products of *period* and *timeless* in one big, happy complex that forms the basis for feedback repression of *period* and *timeless* transcription; that is, *Clock* and *cycle* drive transcription of *period* and *timeless* when no period and timeless proteins are around, but are blocked from doing so in their presence.

The last links in the core mechanism came from further modifications of the original Konopka screen, and all three of the mutants so isolated were in genes encoding protein kinases. These enzymes mark or modify other proteins by adding a phosphate group, which in turn affects their susceptibility to being degraded. As the whole cycling mechanism depends on the timely disappearance of the period and timeless proteins, the tuning of their degradation is important. In contrast to the *period* and *timeless* genes, which can be knocked out without killing the animal, these kinases are more widespread (pleiotropic) in their effects and are lethal when knocked out. To keep flies alive so that they can actually have circadian rhythms, the mutations were screened in heterozygotes or in special strains that selectively produce an excess of the gene product only in the subset of key circadian cells in the brain.

The two kinases that were found as heterozygotes were named *Doubletime* and *Andante*.

Doubletime mutations came in all varieties—long period, short period, and arrhythmic. *Andante* mutants, on the other hand, have narrower effects and only produce a long-period defect. Both kinases are well conserved in virtually all multicellular organisms and are known as casein kinase I (*Doubletime*) and II (*Andante*). Both act on the period protein. The third kinase gene, *shaggy*, was originally isolated in a screen for mutants affecting the earliest stages of embryonic development. It is named for the appearance of the mutant embryos that lack epidermal cells, thus giving the embryo a 'shaggy' look as cells peel off from the outside. It too is widely conserved in many phyla; it is otherwise known as glycogen synthase 3 and is part of a signal transduction pathway. The screen for *shaggy*'s role in rhythmic behavior of adult flies was done by cleverly restricting an overabundance of the kinase to the relevant circadian cells by genetic engineering so that only the cells that make timeless protein would make too much shaggy.

By engineering flies so that *shaggy* is expressed only in a small portion of the whole brain, the animals could survive the abnormal enzyme content. At the same time, it revealed the role of the gene by shortening the period. When there is too little enzyme, the period lengthens. The shaggy kinase acts on the timeless protein.

When all of these pieces are put together, the following picture emerges of a core clock mechanism (Figure 9.11). One mutant was identified that connected the core clock to the external light stimulus that entrains the fly to the day/night rhythm. This gene, *cryptochrome*, is another highly conserved gene, found in all organisms, where it most often serves as a light receptor protein. When flies make too much cryptochrome, they are supersensitive to light entrainment; that is, their biological clock

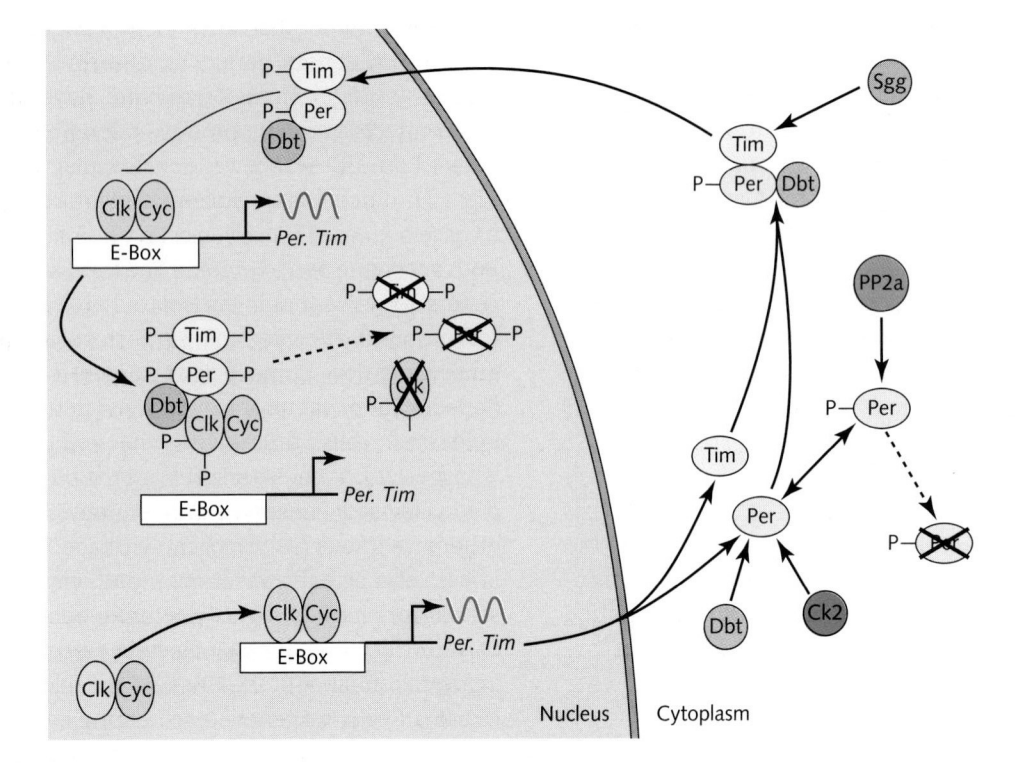

Figure 9.11 The molecular basis of the circadian clock.
Source: Hardin (2005).

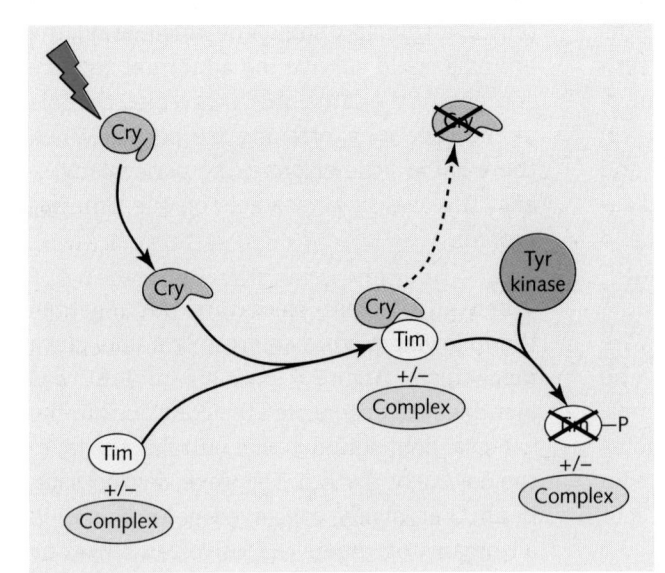

Figure 9.12 Role of cryptochrome in light entrainment in *Drosophila*.
Source: Hardin (2005).

entrains to low-light intensities that are ineffective in normal flies.

When flies are mutant for cryptochrome, they will entrain normally if their visual system is intact, but if they are blind *and* mutant for cryptochrome, then they fail to entrain. On the other hand, blind flies with a normal *cryptochrome* gene entrain normally. This says that flies can use either their visual system or their *cryptochrome* gene to entrain, but they need at least one to be working (Figure 9.12).

The tie-in to the clock comes from the ability of the cryptochrome protein to bind to the timeless protein. More specifically, when cryptochrome absorbs light, it changes conformation, allowing it to bind to timeless. Complexing with cryptochrome makes timeless ripe for degradation. When timeless protein levels fall off, the clock is reset. In this way, the fly's clock keeps up with the advance of sunrise following the winter solstice and the retreat of sunrise following the summer solstice. And as if to reinforce the fly's sensitivity to changes in the time of daybreak, the levels of cryptochrome protein accumulate in the dark and decline in the light so that it is ready when morning comes.

The picture of a mechanism that these findings provide is detailed to an extent that is rare indeed for any aspect of behavior. Imagine everyone's surprise when a nearly identical mechanism was found in our mammalian cousin, the mouse.

Key papers

Zerr, D.M., Hall, J.C., Rosbash, M., and Siwicki, K.K. (1990) Circadian fluctuations of period protein immunoreactivity in the CNS and the visual system of *Drosophila*. *J Neurosci* **10**:2749–2762.

Hardin, P.E., Hall, J.C., and Rosbash, M. (1992). Circadian oscillations in period gene mRNA levels are transcriptionally regulated. *Proc Natl Acad Sci USA* **89**:11711–11715.

Bell-Pedersen, D., Cassone, V.M., Earnest, D.J., Golden, S.S., Hardin, P.E., Thomas, T.L., and Zoran, M.J. (2005). Circadian rhythms from multiple oscillators: lessons from diverse organisms. *Nat Rev Genet* **26**:544–556.

The mouse's clock

As mentioned earlier, the *Clock* gene was first found in the mouse, by screening hundreds of mutagenized mice, in the same way that Konopka had had to screen hundreds of mutagenized flies to find *period* mutants. However, finding mammalian periodicity genes became easier with the cloning of a set of fly rhythm genes. At that point, molecular techniques could be used to identify homologs in the mouse. The proteins are sufficiently similar for the gene in one species to be used as a way of finding the gene in another. In the simplest approach, the DNA from one species can be used to hybridize to the DNA of the other (see Appendix for a description of hybridization). This method avoids the need for a lengthy positional cloning adventure.

As it turns out, mice have three different *period* genes and two *cryptochrome* genes, one *timeless* gene, and one *cycle* homolog (*Bmal*). They also have the same set of kinases present in flies, in some cases in multiple forms. The functional roles of these genes have been tested by engineering knockout mutations—produced by gene replacement in the germ line—and by biochemical tests for protein interactions.

The remarkable finding is that the mouse's clock is so similar to the fly's (Figure 9.13). There are some differences: *cryptochrome* substitutes for *timeless* in the transcriptional feedback loop, and the mouse has multiple forms for many of the genes. Maybe this can be explained by the fact that the mammalian skull blocks all light (this would make it unnecessary for the clock neurons to have a light receptor protein such as cryptochrome, thus allowing them to re-adapt to a different function). But whatever the reason, the similarities are remarkable and more than justify Benzer's intuition that the little fruit fly could teach us about the genes' underlying behavior. Much more has been conserved through evolution than anyone had suspected.

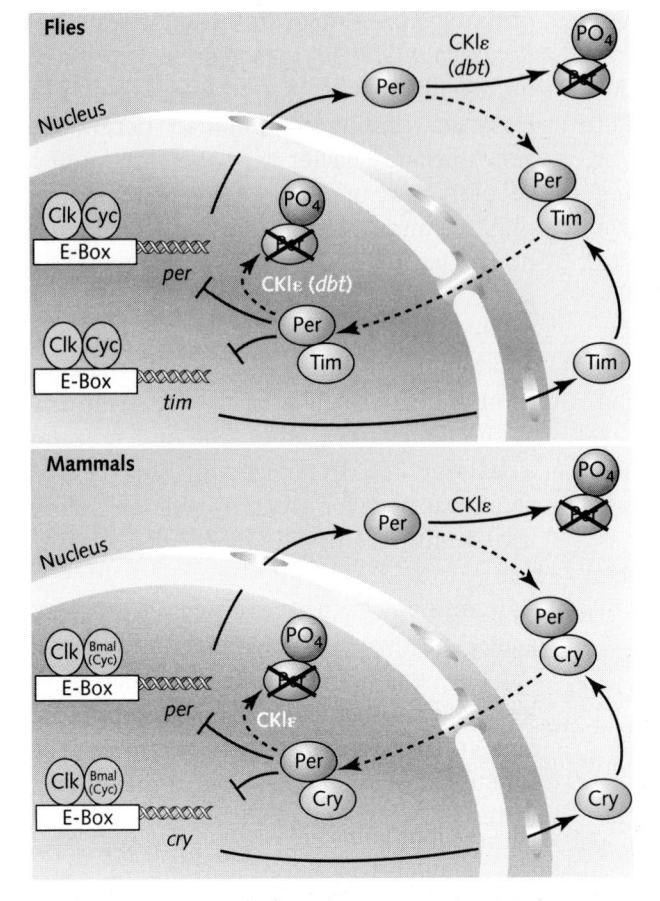

Figure 9.13 Homology between molecular clocks in *Drosophila* and mice.
Source: Young (1998).

Variation in the *period* gene

The mutants described in this chapter differ markedly from the genetic variants discussed in the earlier chapters of this book. They are induced mutations and they were identified by screening for large effects on the rhythm phenotype. Do these rhythm genes show variation in the wild? If so, are they like the natural variants we have discussed previously? Two of the circadian rhythms genes have been examined in this manner—*period* and *timeless*—and they have been found not only to vary in gene sequence but also in functional properties. Moreover, they show geographical distributions that may be giving us a glimpse of how evolution works with natural gene variants to shape genetic and phenotypic changes.

The DNA sequence of the *period* gene varies considerably in populations of *D. melanogaster*. One portion of the gene that shows particular variation is a repetitive stretch of the pair of amino acids threonine and glycine (Figure 9.14). When populations from various geographical locations are sampled, the distribution of these allelic variants follows a north–south pattern based on climate (Figure 9.15). This 'latitudinal cline,' as such distributions are known, suggests that there has been selection for the preponderance of certain alleles in colder climates and of other alleles in warmer climates.

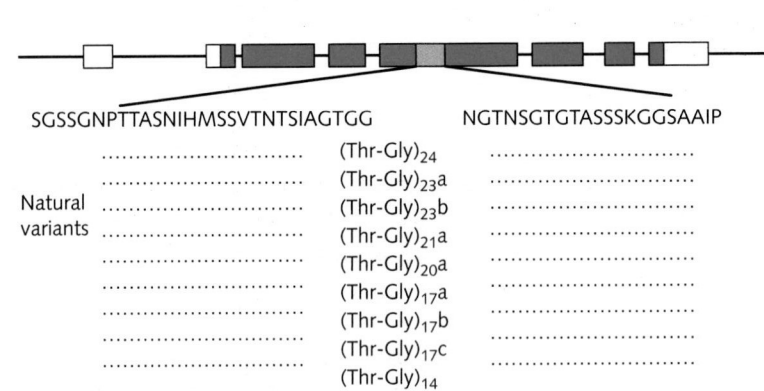

SGSSGNPTTASNIHMSSVTNTSIAGTGG   NGTNSGTGTASSSKGGSAAIP

	$(Thr\text{-}Gly)_{24}$	
	$(Thr\text{-}Gly)_{23}a$	
Natural	$(Thr\text{-}Gly)_{23}b$	
variants	$(Thr\text{-}Gly)_{21}a$	
	$(Thr\text{-}Gly)_{20}a$	
	$(Thr\text{-}Gly)_{17}a$	
	$(Thr\text{-}Gly)_{17}b$	
	$(Thr\text{-}Gly)_{17}c$	
	$(Thr\text{-}Gly)_{14}$	

Figure 9.14 Variation in *period* gene sequences from wild caught flies. Letters indicate variants with additional sequence differences outside the Thr-Gly repeats.
Source: Costa *et al.* (1991).

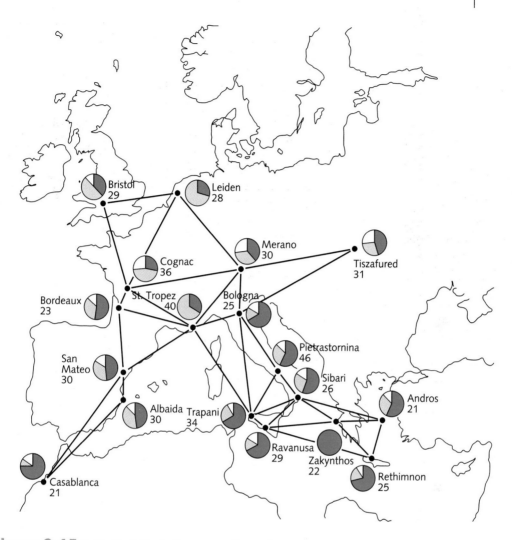

Figure 9.15 Latitudinal cline in frequency of *period* gene natural variants.
Source: Costa *et al.* (1992).

Selection is not easy to prove in any situation, but one kind of corroborating evidence is a functional difference between the genotypes in the different climatic regions. As temperature is the principal factor in this latitudinal cline, an obvious candidate is the clock's ability to compensate for temperature fluctuations. Such fluctuations would be more severe in northern climates than in southern. Fruit flies, like all invertebrates, do not regulate their body temperature. One of the stranger features of their circadian clock is its ability to keep accurate time over a wide range of temperatures, flying in the face of the usual temperature dependence of most chemical reactions.

The latitudinal *period* variants do, in fact, show different abilities to compensate for temperature shifts (Figure 9.16). When the predominant northern climate allele and the predominant southern climate allele are each genetically engineered into the standard laboratory

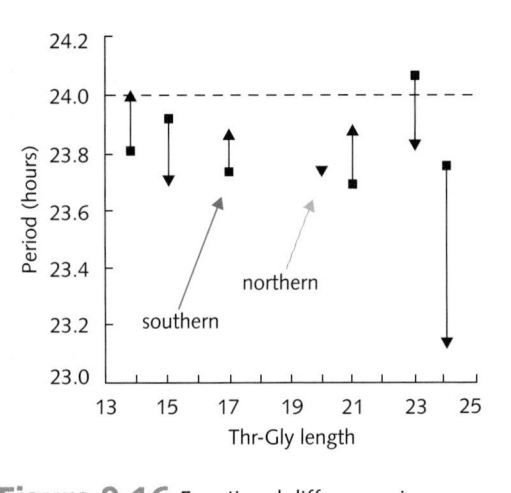

Figure 9.16 Functional differences in temperature compensation among natural *period* variants.
Source: Sawyer *et al.* (1997).

strain of flies, so that the only difference is in that gene, the northern allele shows almost perfect temperature compensation, whereas the southern allele shifts its period by nearly 15 minutes. Without knowing quite how this works, there is certainly the suggestion of an adaptive advantage of the northern allele. Perhaps there is a reciprocal adaptive advantage of the southern allele to its environment that still eludes us. The subtlety of these variants is underscored by the fact that they do *not* impact on basal 24-hour rhythms but only on the temperature constancy of the rhythms; that is, these are mild variants, more like those we have seen in humans in previous chapters than the induced mutants isolated by Benzer and his disciples. The natural variants tinker around the edges of clock function, rather than

hitting it with a sledge hammer as the induced mutants do.

Key papers

Costa, R., Peixoto, A.A., Barbujani, G., and Kyriacou, C.P. (1992). A latitudinal cline in a *Drosophila* clock gene. *Proc Biol Sci* **250**:43–49.

Sawyer, L.A., Hennessy, J.M., Peixoto, A.A., Rosato, E., Parkinson, H., Costa, R., and Kyriacou, C.P. (1997). Natural variation in a *Drosophila* clock gene and temperature compensation. *Science* **278**:2117–2120.

Variation in the timeless gene

Is this apparent adaptive advantage for *period* variants a fluke? A similar investigation of *timeless* sequences from widely distributed populations also revealed a latitudinal cline from the Mediterranean to northern Europe. In the *timeless* case, the variation is in the start site for translation of the mRNA (Figure 9.17).

One variant makes a single, long form and the other has added a new translational start site (marked by ATG, the DNA sequence that signals the start of a protein) so that it can make both a short form as well as the regular long form of the protein. Given the role of *timeless* in clock resetting, the candidate process to look at in this case would be light sensitivity for entrainment. Sure enough, the northern *timeless* variant (the shorter one) is more sensitive to light than the longer variant, as might be expected for the dimmer light found in more northern climates. Once again, the correlation suggests selection and adaptive advantage.

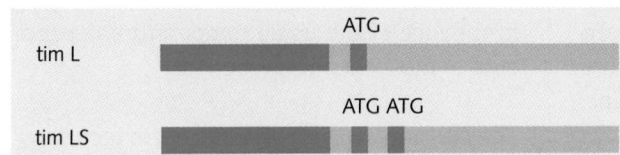

Figure 9.17 Differences in translation start sites in natural variants of the *timeless* gene.
Source: Courtesy of C.P. Kyriacou.

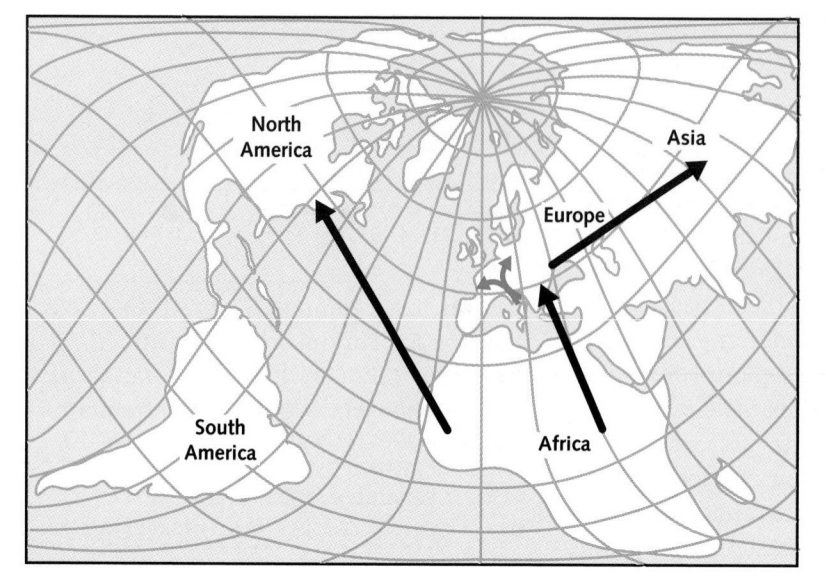

Figure 9.18 Probable migration of *Drosophila* species out of Africa.
Source: Courtesy of C.P. Kyriacou.

Why do we think that *Drosophila* originated in Africa? For the same reason we think that humans did—from comparing DNA sequences of many genes and surveying how much they vary across different parts of the world. For both flies and humans, there is much more variation in Africa than elsewhere, and the non-African variants are generally a subset of those found in Africa.

In contrast to the temperature response of *period* variants, however, there is some idea of how this might be accomplished. For one thing, the short form of the timeless protein is more easily degraded by light than the long timeless protein. Timeless must interact with cryptochrome for light to trigger clock resetting. So it stands to reason that these *timeless* variants might have different tendencies to bind to cryptochrome. In fact, a light-dependent difference in binding affinity does exist for the protein products of these *timeless* variants—the shorter form binds more tightly.

When the sequences of these variant genes from different geographical regions were compared more closely, an even more intriguing suggestion about their evolution emerged. It appears that the shorter variant arose in southern Italy. This is inferred from knowing that *Drosophila* arose originally in sub-Saharan Africa and spread northward, and then finding that the short variant is not found south of the Mediterranean (Figure 9.18).

DNA sequence comparisons can also be used to estimate the amount of time that has passed from when two versions of a gene diverged. Based on this kind of analysis, the two *timeless* genes give an approximate date of 7,000–11,000 years ago for the origin of the new variant. And it may still be in the process of spreading northward.

Once again, a natural variant of a clock gene produces a subtle functional difference of possible adaptive significance, without altering the core clock mechanism. This fits well with the idea that the natural variants that persist in the wild do not cause major defects.

Human clock genes and unquiet sleep

If we consider the natural variants in the fruit fly, and also the high degree of molecular conservation of this mechanism in mammals (us included), then we should not be surprised

to learn that there are human rhythm gene polymorphisms that have effects on human behavior.

Certain sleep syndromes have been found that have been associated with variants in human homologs of the *period* gene. One of the multiple human homologs of *Drosophila period*, *human period 3* (*hPer3*), has been associated with delayed sleep phase syndrome, in which individuals cannot get to sleep until very late at night. A study of Finnish patients with this syndrome revealed a length polymorphism in the *hPer3* gene, such that the long allele favored morning preference and the short allele evening preference; that is, different variants produced different settings of the clock.

Another hereditary sleep disorder, familial advanced sleep phase syndrome (FASPS), is a dominant variant in which affected individuals are 'morning larks' with a 4-hour advance of their sleep, temperature, and melatonin rhythms; that is, they go to sleep early and get up early. The *hPer2* gene in affected individuals has a single difference in an amino acid—substitution of glycine for serine in the part of the protein that is phosphorylated by the human homolog of the *Doubletime* gene, casein kinase I epsilon (*CKIε*). This substitution makes the hPer2 protein harder to phosphorylate and thus affects clock timing. Thus, a variant in human sleep behavior may be attributable to a missense (i.e. amino acid substitution) mutation in a clock component, hPer2, which alters the circadian period. Consistent with this finding, a completely separate case of FASPS in a family was identified as a mutation in the *CKIε* gene itself (Figure 9.19).

These variants are not true disorders of sleep, but rather of the circadian timing of sleep. They are thus consistent with the role of the clock in organizing the circadian pattern of many behaviors, including sleep. And they

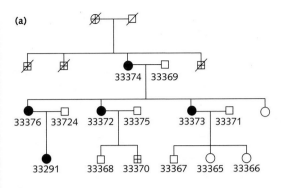

(b)

```
hCK18   GEEVAIKLECVKTKHPQLHIESKIYKMMQ
mCK18   GEEVAIKLECVKTKHPQLHIESKIYKMMQ
hCK18   GEEVAIKLECVKTKHPQLHIESKFYKMMQ
mCK18   GEEVAIKLECVKTKHPQLHIESKFYKMMQ
Dbt     GEEVAIKLECIRTKHPQLHIESKFYKMMQ
        * * * * * * * * * * : : * * * * * * * * * * * : * * * * *
```

Figure 9.19 Geneology (a) in human familial advanced sleep phase syndrome (FASPS) and (b) sequence conservation in the *CKIε* gene among humans, mice, and flies (black, affected; white, unaffected).
Source: Toh *et al.* (2001).

are relatively mild—affected individuals have a functioning clock, but it runs fast or slow.

Lessons from fly rhythms

The foregoing narrative has provided us with a picture of the core clock mechanism at a detailed molecular level that, in turn, has explained how clocks work in humans and has allowed the identification of several human variants affecting circadian rhythms. The natural variants in rhythm genes match our previous descriptions of natural genetic variants in the strength of their effect. What may seem at odds with earlier discussions, however, is the extent to which some of the rhythm genes seem to be dedicated to rhythms. We had previously argued that a gene's effect on behavior is usually one of many roles played by that gene.

Are rhythms an exception? Or are we not seeing the whole picture?

It certainly helps that a fly can survive quite well even if it has no endogenous ability to generate a circadian rhythm. If this were not true, the Benzerian strategy would have been far less successful. On the other hand, many of the genes *are* widespread in their action. All of the kinases result in lethality when knocked out. *Clock* and *cycle* have not been knocked out completely in flies, so we do not know whether such mutations are lethal. The quintessential dedicated genes, *period* and *timeless*, are not entirely rhythm-oriented. This realization comes from studies of cocaine sensitization in fruit flies (that's right, some of our colleagues push cocaine on fruit flies).

Mutants in *period*, *Clock*, *cycle*, and *Doubletime* have all lost the sensitization response to repeated exposure to cocaine. This response does not show any circadian regulation in flies either, so it seems that these genes are regulating the induction of an enzyme necessary for sensitization, independently of the clock.

Is the success of this mutant-hunting approach due to some special feature of circadian rhythms? Mutant hunters would take issue with this because of the many other instances in which the strategy has worked well, but there may be a kernel of truth in it. One factor that smiled upon circadian rhythms is the exceedingly low variance of the behavior itself. Circadian period is one of the most tightly controlled behavioral parameters ever found. As a consequence, the ability to see genetically based differences above background variation—the signal-to-noise ratio—is much better than any other behavior that has been studied.

That said, it does not mean that every single fly shows a beautiful circadian rhythm. Rather, it means that among those flies in the population that do show a good rhythm (most of them), the variance is quite low. There are always clunkers, however, who won't go along with the program. So nature's unstoppable tendency to generate variation shows itself in that way.

Benzer's insight

When Benzer began his explorations of genes and behavior in the fruit fly, traditional neurobiologists told him he was crazy to think that genetics would have anything to contribute to understanding the brain. The circadian rhythm story is the most dramatic, but by no means the only, refutation of the naysayers. The added, completely unexpected, bonus is that not only do we understand more about the fruit fly's brain but also about our own. The extent to which all animals share so many of their genes has been one of the major revelations of genome sequencing, and the circadian clock is one of the many molecular mechanisms that is highly conserved throughout evolution.

Summary

1. The induction of new genetic variants by mutagenesis, originally with radiation and subsequently with chemicals, opened up a new avenue to analyze biological mechanisms, vastly expanding the range and severity of variants that could be obtained.

2. In behavioral analysis, one of the first uses of this approach was in the study of circadian rhythms in the fruit fly *Drosophila*. The first circadian rhythm mutants were all alleles of the *period* gene, producing short-day, long-day, and arrhythmic phenotypes.

3. Molecular cloning of *period* revealed that its mRNA cycles over a 24-hour period in normal flies, its protein is translated with

a delay, and it is then transported back into the nucleus. In arrhythmic mutants, it is transcribed continually, suggesting that it represses its own transcription.

4. Additional clock mutants—*timeless*, *cycle*, *Clock*, *Doubletime*, and *shaggy*—filled out a picture of a transcriptional feedback loop in which the protein products of the *period* and *timeless* genes repress their own transcription by complexing with the Clock and cycle proteins.

5. Entrainment to the light/dark cycle is mediated by the *cryptochrome* gene, whose product absorbs light, complexes with the timeless protein, and facilitates its degradation.

6. An almost identical mechanism is found in mammals, except that there are multiple versions of each gene and *cryptochrome* takes the place of *timeless*. Similar mechanisms also exist in fungi and bacteria, suggesting that the mechanism is exceedingly ancient.

7. Natural variants of the *period* and *timeless* genes in *Drosophila* have been found that show differential geographical distribution suggestive of their playing a role in adaptation to climatic conditions. The *period* variants show a differential ability to maintain constant timekeeping, despite changes in temperature, and the *timeless* variants show a differential ability to associate with cryptochrome and are thus more sensitive to entrainment in dim light.

8. The natural variants all produce a sound core mechanism, with alterations to subtle aspects of clock function.

References

Costa, R., Peixoto, A.A., Thackeray, J.R., Dalgleish, R., and Kyriacou, C.P. (1991). Length polymorphism in the threonine–glycine-encoding repeat region of the *period* gene in *Drosophila*. *J Mol Evol* **32**:238–246.

Costa, R., Peixoto, A.A., Barbujani, G., and Kyriacou, C.P. (1992). A latitudinal cline in a *Drosophila* clock gene. *Proc Biol Sci* **250**:43–49.

Hardin, P.E. (2005). The circadian timekeeping system of *Drosophila*. *Curr Biol* **15**:R714–R722.

Hardin, P.E., Hall, J.C., and Rosbash, M. (1990). Feedback of the *Drosophila* period gene product on circadian cycling of its messenger RNA levels. *Nature* **343**:536–540.

Hyun, S., Lee, Y., Hong, S.T., Bang, S., Paik, D., Kang, J., Shin, J., Lee, J., Jeon, K. *et al.* (2005). *Drosophila* GPCR Han is a receptor for the circadian clock neuropeptide PDF. *Neuron* **48**:267–278.

Konopka, R.J. and Benzer, S. (1971). Clock mutants of *Drosophila melanogaster*. *Proc Natl Acad Sci USA* **68**:2112–2116.

Sawyer, L.A., Hennessy, J.M., Peixoto, A.A., Rosato, E., Parkinson, H., Costa, R., and Kyriacou, C.P. (1997). Natural variation in a *Drosophila* clock gene and temperature compensation. *Science* **278**:2117–2120.

Toh, K.L., Jones, C.R., He, Y., Eide, E.J., Hinz, W.A., Virshup, D.M., Ptacek, L.J., and Fu, Y.H. (2001). An hPer2 phosphorylation site mutation in familial advanced sleep phase syndrome. *Science* **291**:1040–1043.

Young, M.W. (1998). The molecular control of circadian behavioral rhythms and their entrainment in *Drosophila*. *Annu Rev Biochem* **67**:135–152.

Zerr, D.M., Hall, J.C., Rosbash, M., and Siwicki, K.K. (1990). Circadian fluctuations of period protein immunoreactivity in the CNS and the visual system of *Drosophila*. *J Neurosci* **10**:2749–2762.

Model systems and the elements of behavior

Neural mechanisms of learning and memory

[In which we move from genetics to neurobiology and see commonalities in the way snails, flies, and mice remember]

Heritability testing, gene–environment correlations and interactions, genetic mapping by linkage and association, then genome sequences, catalogues of every gene, every genetic variant, genomic technology that consumes a budget large enough to run a small country, the weight of 21st-century molecular genetics is enough to win an argument that genes produce behavior. But of course they don't. Genes, in fact, merely serve as a library that each cell draws upon when it needs to make proteins. Behavior comes out of the ensemble of cellular activities, and the cells that usually matter most are those in the nervous system. Genetic variations that affect behavior often do so by modifying the activity of neurons, and such modifications result from altering the timing, placement, amount, or effectiveness of a gene's product. The relevant neurons, in turn, take part in the brain's complex circuitry. So we need to look at circuits to understand how behavior is produced out of genetic variation.

This is easier said than done, especially for brains as complex as those in humans, mice, and even fruit flies, with 100 billion, 100 million,

and 100,000 neurons, respectively. Circuit 'breaking,' as it is affectionately known in the business, is more easily accomplished in marine crustaceans and molluscs, which tend to have relatively simple nervous systems with large, recognizable neurons. These creatures are not what we would call geniuses, with the possible exception of the octopus, but they do behave. They have to, in order to get by in this world. Some of these behaviors are pretty simple, but then if we can't understand simple behaviors, how can we hope to explain complex ones?

Marine invertebrates: using a sea snail to learn about memory

Why anyone would expect a sea snail to teach us about learning and memory is pretty mysterious. It's not as if this invertebrate is famous for its powers of remembrance. People don't quote its infallible powers of recall. In fact, most people wouldn't recognize one. Furthermore, even assuming a giant marine invertebrate can remember where you left your car keys, is it really likely that something so simple is going tell us anything about something as complex as the mammalian brain? Our own cognitive abilities so dwarf those of invertebrates it looks a sure bet we have a type of neuronal organization qualitatively different from that found in invertebrates. Who on earth ever thought this animal would be a useful model organism?

Eric Kandel did. Eric Kandel, born in Austria before Hitler annexed it, still remembers Kristallnacht as if it were yesterday:

> Of all the cities under Nazi control, the destructiveness in Vienna on Kristallnacht was particularly wanton. Jews were taunted and brutally beaten, expelled from their businesses, and temporarily evicted from their homes so that both could be looted by their neighbors. My father was rounded up by the police together with hundreds of other Jewish men... My early experiences in Vienna almost certainly contributed to my curiosity about the contradictions and complexities of human behavior. How are we to understand the sudden release of such great viciousness in so many people? How could a highly educated and cultured society, a society that at one historical moment nourished the music of Haydn, Mozart, and Beethoven, in the next historical moment sink into barbarism?

The reason Kandel chose the sea snail (*Aplysia*) is the same reason that drove Benzer to use mutagenesis in the fly: a chance to reduce the problem of behavior to its bare essentials. Kandel took note of the breakthroughs

in understanding how nerve cells work by studying squid giant axons, the nerve–muscle synapse of the frog, and the eye of the horseshoe crab, *Limulus*.

Despite discouragement from many of his senior colleagues, Kandel persisted in trying to find an invertebrate that would help:

> I believed that any insight into the modification of behavior by experience, no matter how simple the animal or the task, would prove to be highly informative. After an extensive search that included crayfish, lobster, flies, and the nematode worm *Ascaris*, I settled on *Aplysia*, the giant marine snail. *Aplysia* offered three major technical advantages: (1) its nervous system has a small number of cells, (2) the cells are unusually large, and, as I realized with time, (3) many of the cells are invariant and identifiable as unique individuals.

Note that having a good memory doesn't figure in the list, and note also that *Aplysia* is not a genetic model organism. Kandel was not considering a genetic assault on the problem. That was to come later.

Key paper

Kandel, E.R. (2001). The molecular biology of memory storage: a dialogue between genes and synapses. *Science* 294:1030–1038.

An introduction to the neurobiology of *Aplysia* and similar discoveries made in other organisms.

Aplysia does learn things, although admittedly not a lot. When a wave comes crashing in, it learns to close its gill opening. The neuronal circuitry is simple—a set of sensory neurons capable of detecting water on the gill connects to a set of motor neurons capable of driving muscles that withdraw the gill (Figure 10.1(a)). Gill shutting is a defensive reaction that occurs

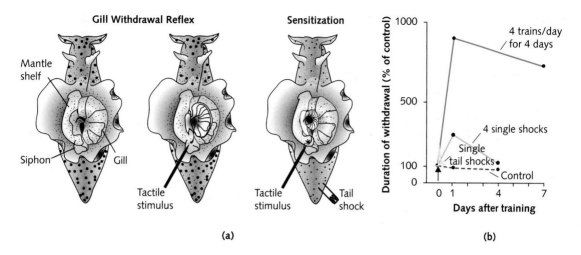

Figure 10.1 A dorsal view of *Aplysia* showing the gill, the animal's respiratory organ.
Source: Kandel (2001).

in response to any mechanical stimulus. If the gill is repeatedly stimulated, *Aplysia* becomes more blasé and gradually responds less and less. On the other hand, if something alarming happens, such as a bite or a blow to some other part of its body or an electric shock, the snail becomes hypersensitive to any kind of gill stimulation. A single shock gives rise to a memory lasting only a few minutes, but four or five spaced shocks gives rise to a memory that lasts several days (Figure 10.1(b)). Thus, as in *Drosophila*, and in our own species, there is both short- and long-term memory.

Kandel and his colleagues were able to define the neural circuitry involved in this response. *Aplysia* has about 20,000 neurons, a fifth the number found in the fly. The cells are organized into ten anatomical units called ganglia, each containing about 2,000 cells. The gill reflex has 24 mechanoreceptor sensory neurons that pass information from the skin directly to six motor cells that cause the gill to withdraw. In addition, there is an indirect path from this sensory input to motor output via interneurons. The pathway turned out to be invariant: in each

animal, the same neurons made the same connections. This turned out to be true for other behaviors as well (e.g. locomotion, feeding, and the other exciting activities of sea snails). Precise wiring raises a problem for learning—how can a flexible behavior be hard-wired?

The answer lies in understanding what happens in the connections between neurons, in the way neurons pass information between each other. Possibly the most influential theory in neurobiology, the ionic hypothesis (proposed by Alan Hodgkin, Andrew Huxley, and Bernhard Katz), explains information flow through neurons as a change in electrical potential. The first step in understanding the neuronal basis for this behavior is to ask what the nerve cells are doing.

Electrical impulses are the language of the nervous system. These tiny signals can be measured directly in single neurons of *Aplysia* by means of microelectrodes, hollow glass needles pulled to a fine tip (~10 µm) that are inserted into the neuron without killing it. The microelectrode contains a salt solution and fine wire that connects to an amplifier. With another wire lead in the fluid surrounding the neuron, the miniscule difference in electrical potential between the inside of the cell and the outside can be accurately measured.

The cell's membrane, full of lipids, provides the insulating barrier for this 'membrane potential,' which amounts to about −70 millivolts (mV). The negative sign on the membrane potential is due to active pumps in the membrane that extrude positively charged sodium and calcium ions, and to the preponderance of negatively charged proteins inside the cell. Most importantly, this membrane potential changes when the nerve cell conducts an impulse.

Figure 10.2 shows that, when the gill is touched, specialized endings in the mechanosensory neurons generate an electrical signal that travels quickly down the length of the cell from the skin to the abdominal ganglion. To the microelectrode, the passing of this impulse looks like a spike as the membrane potential rapidly rises to +30 mV and then falls back down again. A microelectrode in one of the motor neurons shows their response to it several milliseconds

later, and the muscle contraction follows a few milliseconds after that. Within each cell, these spikes (also called action potentials) are always roughly the same size. What varies is the number of them, which is proportional to the strength of the original stimulus to the gill.

Action potentials don't occur randomly, however; they have to be set off. At the sensory end, the membrane at the far end of the sensory neuron in the skin is sensitive to deformation so that when the skin is touched, an electrical potential (called an 'epsp' for 'excitatory postsynaptic potential') is generated locally at the site of the synapse where the sensory neuron contacts the motor neuron. If large enough, this epsp then triggers an action potential. In the motor neuron, the triggering event can be seen in the microelectrode recordings. Just prior to the rapid spike, there is a smaller and more prolonged potential change (Figure 10.3). Moreover, the size and duration of this slower potential varies with the strength of the original stimulus—the more the gill is stimulated, the more spikes are sent down the sensory neurons, and the larger the initial response in the motor neuron. This response, in turn, sets off the action potentials in the motor neurons.

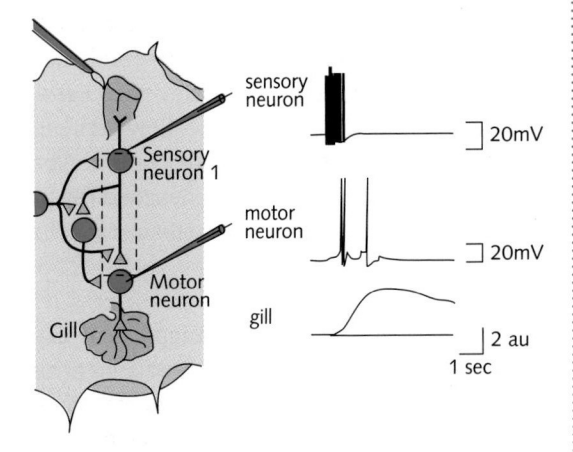

Figure 10.2 Action potentials in gill withdrawal (au, arbitrary units).
Source: Kandel (1976).

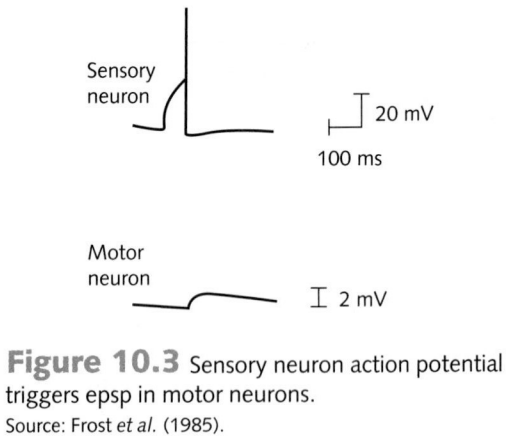

Figure 10.3 Sensory neuron action potential triggers epsp in motor neurons.
Source: Frost *et al.* (1985).

Action potentials move along neurons, but, generally speaking, they don't jump directly from one nerve cell to the next neuron in the chain. The synapse intervenes. Communication between neurons occurs at synapses and uses the same depolarization mechanism. However, this time it is not an electrical signal. Instead, there is a set of small molecules, known as neurotransmitters (for instance glutamate, serotonin, dopamine, and GABA) that are released from the end of the axon, diffuse over to the nearest part of another neuron (often called a dendrite), and bind to receptors. The effect is to open ion channels that initiate new electrical signals, which can then propagate a new action potential.

Key papers

Albright, T.D., Jessell, T.M., Kandel, E.R., and Posner, M.I. (2000). Neural science: a century of progress and the mysteries that remain. *Neuron* **25** (Suppl.):S1–S55.

A historical overview of neuroscience.

Greenspan, R.J. (2007). *An Introduction to Nervous Systems.* New York: Cold Spring Harbor Laboratory Press.

As the title says, this is an introduction to nervous systems and we strongly recommend that you buy it.

Like Skinner, but for different reasons, Kandel wanted to do away with the brain. Could the learning processes so carefully characterized by behavioral psychologists in the first part of the 20th century—habituation, sensitization, classical and operant conditioning—be modeled with a neuronal circuit taken out of the whole organism? Natural sensory stimuli, the wave falling on the animal's skin, would be replaced by an artificial electrical or chemical stimulus. The response, gill withdrawal, would be replaced by a recording electrode to detect the action potential from the motor neuron that, in the normal course of things, would have been making its way to a muscle.

The idea was that neuronal pathways would be stimulated in an *in vitro* system, where nerve impulses would be under the control of the experimenter and the effects on other nerves could be monitored. Would synapses change systematically in response to different patterns of stimulation, and, if so, would the synaptic changes in any way parallel changes in the behavior of intact animals?

By substituting puffs of serotonin for tail shocks, it was possible to model a neural circuit in a dish of cultured neurons. While four or five spaced shocks give rise to a memory in the intact animal that lasts several days, five spaced puffs of serotonin have the same effect in a culture dish full of neurons, making it possible to investigate the molecular basis of long-term memory. Serotonin acts via a group of enzymes (called kinases) that exert their effect on events in the cell by phosphorylating other proteins. Serotonin binds to receptors on the neuron's surface. These receptors in turn activate an enzyme (adenylyl cyclase) to produce a diffusible chemical signal (cyclic AMP), and cAMP binds to a protein kinase called PKA. PKA then phosphorylates yet another enzyme, mitogen-activated protein kinase (MAP kinase), and together the two of them act on a protein called CREB-1 (cAMP response element-binding protein), which is a regulator of gene activity in the nucleus. When CREB is phosphorylated, it enters the cell's nucleus and begins a process of altering which genes are active in that cell. In other words, it changes the proteins that the cell makes, which produces lasting changes to the cell's synapses (including growing new ones) and, as a result, a long-term form of sensitization. It is the formation of these new synapses that underlies long-term memory.

A typical sensory neuron has about 1,200 synapses; following sensitization, the number more than doubles.

Fruit flies remember things using the same cellular machinery discovered in sea snails

Soon after his circadian rhythm work, Benzer initiated a project to isolate new mutants that disrupted learning and memory in the fly, the genetic approach again at the forefront of attempts to understand the biology of behavior. Mutagenesis is a voyage into the unknown, promising to deliver something completely novel. But this promise needs to be tempered with the problem of understanding what is found at the end of the journey. The strength of the method is its power to find the completely unexpected. But discovery comes at a price. When we have the answer, the mutation in the gene, we almost certainly won't know what that answer means. This is why we need to work with a model organism that can be used to do more than genetics. One of the surprises of the fly work was that the same genetic mechanisms appeared to operate in different species, so that what we learned from fruit fly genetics could be interpreted in the context of sea snail neurobiology.

Fruit flies can be trained to remember, to learn to tell the difference between smells or between things they see. If an odor (or image) is accompanied by an electric shock or a heat lamp, flies quickly learn to avoid it; the memory of this association will last for a day at most. What does it take to get them to remember it for longer? Regular conscientious practice (just like your piano teacher may have told you). In other words, as any student knows, cramming for an exam (i.e. all of the training at once), can get you through the next day, but it doesn't stick. Studying at regular intervals, on the other hand, produces a much longer-lasting memory. Fruit flies are no different. If multiple training trials are delivered all at once, memory still only lasts for a day. But if the training trials are interrupted with 15-minute rest intervals, then the flies will remember it for up to a week. This is a substantial portion of a fruit fly's lifespan – mid-life crisis has already set in by their second week of adulthood.

What does a fruit fly need to learn and remember in its brief, itinerant, polygamous life? Given the fact that the training regimens described above are never 100% effective, and that the flies must have the daylights shocked out of them to get above a 70% learning score, you might be tempted to say, 'Not much.' But it turns out that memory mechanisms are constantly used in the short term for tasks as simple as making a choice between two odors, or two food sources, or two females (if you are a male fly looking for a mate). The very act of making a discrimination requires the fly to remember one stimulus so that it can be compared with another.

Beyond the very short term, male flies also remember if they are soundly rejected by a female. This typically occurs if the male tries to court a female who has recently mated. (Courtship itself consists of a series of advances that males must make toward females, including tapping them, following them, extending one wing to 'sing' a courtship song, licking their genitals, and mounting them, if the female permits.) If the female has mated and is unreceptive, she kicks the male repeatedly, buzzes her wings at him, and emits a pheromone that dampens his enthusiasm considerably. He will then not bother her again for hours afterward, and is so crestfallen that he doesn't look elsewhere.

Mutagenizing flies, by chemically inducing single base-pair changes in their DNA (point mutations) is easy to do, but has two drawbacks. Large numbers of animals have to be screened for the behavior of interest and then the altered gene has to be cloned. It took roughly 5,000 lines of mutagenized flies, bred and behaviorally tested over several years, before Benzer, his colleagues, and various others were able to identify five mutants (Waddell and Quinn, 2001). Their criteria for learning-deficient mutants were: (i) during testing, the flies had to fail selectively to avoid the shock-associated odorant; and (ii) this failure could not be due to sensory or motor defects. In their first mutant screen, approximately 500 mutagenized X-chromosome lines were tested. About 20 lines met the first criterion; of these, only one also satisfied the second. The strain was made homozygous and was (for obvious reasons) named *dunce*.

dunce mutants forget more quickly than normal flies in the 30-minute period following conditioning; that is, they have defective short-term memory. This sieve-like memory is not confined merely to those two odors or to electric-shock-induced learning: it generalizes. *dunce* mutants rapidly forget odor cues associated with a food reward as well as with shock, they can't learn to discriminate visual patterns when heat is associated instead of an electric shock, and male *dunce* flies even fail to remember when a female has dumped them. In fact, by every conceivable criterion, *dunce* is

a behavioral mutant due to an abnormality of its central nervous system.

By the turn of the century, nine *Drosophila* learning and memory mutants had been identified: *dunce, rutabaga, radish, amnesiac, latheo, linotte, nalyot, volado* and *leonardo* (Waddell and Quinn, 2001). By 2007, the number had risen to more than 80 (Keene and Waddell, 2007). Who thought up those names? The answer is: whoever isolated the mutants. The choice is sometimes meaningful and sometimes less so. *dunce* and *amnesiac* are self-explanatory. *rutabaga, radish* and *turnip* were so named for being 'as dumb as a vegetable.' Latheo is the name of the 'river of forgetting' in Greek mythology that one must cross before entering Hades. *linotte* comes from the French expression 'tête de linotte,' which is comparable to 'bird brain.' Nalyot was one of Pavlov's dogs. Volado is Chilean slang for absent-minded, and *leonardo* is so named because it is a gene that is versatile (i.e. 'Renaissance') in its functions. Mutagenesis appears to have worked, giving reagents that potentially allow us to answer how genes influence behavior. What are these genes?

Molecular techniques make it possible to find out what these genes are, but, as we have stressed, the techniques are by no means easy. Gene cloning of point mutations in any organism, even when you have the complete genome sequence to hand, is an arduous affair, full of pitfalls. When *radish* was first cloned, it was said to be a mutation in a phospholipase gene. Then, in 2006, it was said to be in another gene, one with no name other than the identifier from the fly genome database: *CG15720* (Folkers *et al.*, 2006). Here's a quote from an article by one of the fly learning researchers that reviewed the evidence of genetic effects on learning and memory in the fruit fly *Drosophila*:

It also is worth noting that the nature of the molecular lesion associated with the *amnesiac* mutation remains unknown despite a report by Feany and Quinn to have found a point mutation in the *amnesiac* transcript [i.e. mRNA]. Moore *et al.* failed to detect any point mutation in *amnesiac* and claimed, rather, that the DNA sequence obtained from *amnesiac+* flies (i.e., the normal control strain) of Feany and Quinn was in error, thereby producing an incorrect coding sequence of the *amnesiac+* gene and an apparent point mutation in *amnesiac*. To date, this critical error in Feany and Quinn has not been clarified or corrected by the authors.

Margulies et al. (2005).

Oh well, *c'est la guerre.*

The first two genes identified from screens for learning and memory defects uncovered two components of a cAMP cascade: *dunce* encodes a cAMP phosphodiesterase and *rutabaga* encodes a type I Ca^{2+}/calmodulin-stimulated adenylyl cyclase (Figure 10.4). These are two components of the same cascade that serotonin acts on in the gill-withdrawal reflex. Furthermore, CREB turns out to be just as important in flies as it is in sea snails: flies with deficiencies of CREB also have poor memory (Yin *et al.*, 1994). The cAMP pathway acts in mammals as well as invertebrates; mutations in CREB, for example, alter memory in mice (Bourtchuladze *et al.*, 1994) and there is a human mental retardation syndrome due to mutations in CREB-binding protein (CBP) gene (Petrij *et al.*, 1995).

There are a couple of odd things here. The first is that memory mechanisms are conserved between species. Is this really saying that my memories are laid down in the same way as a fly or a snail? We have to be precise about the level at which homology occurs: is it at the level of the gene, the transcript, the protein, the cell, the neural network, or the entire physiological process? At this stage, the best answer we can give appears to be that the homology occurs because neurons throughout the animal kingdom have common structural features. In a sense, what these experiments tell us about is how neurons work, rather than how brains function.

The secondly, slightly uncomfortable, observation is the need for the genetics experiments. Why bother with all that complicated mutagenesis, screening, and molecular cloning if the answer was there already from the *Aplysia* work? Of course, we'd have to test the prediction that the same genes were involved, but that is a much easier experiment than cloning induced mutants. One of the recurring lessons from gene cloning experiments is the need to have a physiological context, a mechanism, in which to interpret the finding (see Figure 10.4).

That said, one must take care not to ignore all of the other genes that mutagenesis in the fly has identified. The cAMP story is now only a small fragment of a much larger and still developing story. These other interesting genes include those for α-integrin, fasciclin II neural cell adhesion molecules and mRNA transport and translation control molecules encoded by the *pumilio* (another of Pavlov's dogs), *oskar* (named after the main character of Gunter Grass's *Tin Drum,* because when it is mutant in embryos, it produces a shortened body), and *eIF-5C* genes (Dubnau *et al.,* 2003). Undoubtedly, these, and the other 80 or so that have been identified but not fully characterized could tell us much more about the molecular process of memory. The problem of course remains as to how we set about understanding what those genes do. Perhaps another model organism would help here, one that permits a systematic analysis of genes, neurons, circuitry, and behavior.

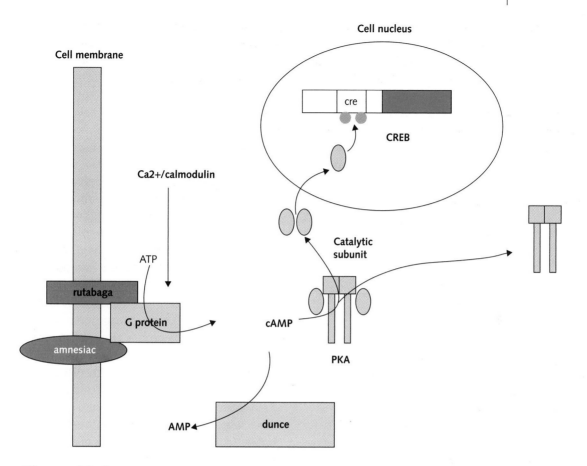

Figure 10.4 The cAMP signaling pathway involved in learning and memory in *Drosophila*. G-protein-coupled activation or Ca^{2+}/calmodulin stimulation leads to phosphorylation of CREB and activation of cAMP response element (cre)-linked genes in the cell nucleus. cAMP-dependent protein kinase A (PKA) mediates this signal. The *rutabaga* mutation affects cAMP signaling by disrupting a Ca^{2+}/calmodulin-dependent adenylate cyclase; the *amnesiac* mutation disrupts a protein that stimulates the cyclase; the *dunce* mutation affects the phosphodiesterase responsible for cAMP degradation.

The origins of genetic engineering as a tool for mammalian neurobiology

In 1999, newspaper reports announced the arrival of the Doogie mouse, the world's first genetically engineered super-intelligent animal (Tang *et al.*, 1999):

> Scientists have boosted the intelligence of mice by adding a gene to the rodents' brains, and it should be possible to do the same in humans one day. Researchers at US universities found that adding copies of a specific gene to the mice significantly raised their ability to find their way through mazes, learn

from objects and sounds and retain their new-found knowledge. They said the discovery could accelerate the development of medicines for human disorders such as memory loss in old age and Alzheimer's disease. But it could also sharpen an ethical debate about creating so-called 'designer children' with enhanced intelligence. The smarter mice have been nicknamed Doogie after a child prodigy character in the US television series 'Doogie Howser, MD'.

Agence France Presse, 2 September 1999.

Princeton University neurobiologist Joe Tsien, working with teams at Massachusetts Insitute of Technology and Washington University in St Louis, was quoted in the magazine as saying: *'They're learning things much better and remembering longer. They're smarter.'*

As it turned out, however, the mice may have learned faster, but they also forgot faster. The hype is typical of the impact of genetic engineering on mammalian neurobiology.

Synaptic plasticity: a cellular model of how memory works

Synapses are an obvious place to regulate the flow of information, a place where 'behavioral integration' could occur, in a phrase coined by Charles Scott Sherrington, one of the great forerunners of neuroscience. But without evidence that synapses actually regulate the flow of information in the nervous system, this idea remained speculative. Some neuroscientists, including Sherrington's contemporary, Karl Spencer Lashley, dismissed the idea entirely, saying '...*there is no direct evidence for*

any function of the anatomical synapse: there is no evidence that synapses vary in resistance, or that, if they do, the resistance is altered by the passage of the nerve impulse' (Lashley, 1930). Other neuroscientists argued that understanding what happened at synapses was the key to understanding behavior. Donald Hebb provided one of the first, and still one of the most influential, accounts of how synapses were involved in learning and memory. He proposed that the information flow between neurons depended on to the amount of traffic (Hebb, 1949). Axons have many inputs, the dendrites, but only one output, the axon. With so many inputs, there are lots of opportunities for the neuron to fire off an action potential. But the neuron does not respond to every incoming message through its dendritic synapses. Hebb's suggestion was that the neuron will pay more attention to those synapses that are relatively more active. This is a cellular form of memory and the 'Hebb rule' has become a basic algorithm for learning. *'Let us assume then that the persistence or repetition of a reverberatory activity (or "trace") tends to induce lasting cellular changes that add to its stability.'* Hebb then states what has become widely known as 'Hebb's postulate': *'When an axon of cell A is near enough to excite a cell B and repeatedly or persistently takes part in firing it, some growth process or metabolic change takes place in one or both cells such that A's efficiency, as one of the cells firing B, is increased'* (Hebb, 1949, p. 62).

In many ways, Hebb's idea (which has been summed up as 'cells that fire together wire together') was not novel; others had proposed that synaptic plasticity was a cellular correlate of behavioral modification. But Hebb wrote a whole book on the subject (a fairly unusual thing for a scientist to do, as rarely do their attention spans last longer than a three-page journal article). Writing a book also made it possible to deal systematically with the problems faced by his theory. So, for instance, a major objection to his postulate was the existence of generalization. If we learn to discriminate a square from a circle or a cross, then we will automatically generalize that learning process, without further training: we recognize squares formed from dots or continuous lines, bigger or smaller than the original stimulus. Generalization without further training, which is true for rodents and for invertebrates, cannot be explained by strengthening of connections at a fixed and specific set of synapses.

Hebb could not ignore generalization, even though his neurophysiological postulate talks about plastic changes taking place at specific synapses resulting in more efficient conduction of impulses. His answer was to propose the existence of an *'irregular three-dimensional net'* that *'would be infinitely more complex than anything one could show with a diagram.'* These 'cell assemblies' consisted of strengthened associations between neurons across structurally modifiable synapses. Later, neuropsychologists would refer to similar assemblies as neural nets, but at the time there was no evidence for modifiable synapses, for the existence of synaptic plasticity, let alone one diffuse three-dimensional net.

Long-term potentiation: a cellular correlate of memory

The first evidence that synaptic plasticity existed in the brain came in the late 1960s and 1970s from both invertebrates, like *Aplysia*, and vertebrates, like frogs and rats. One such case that has become a primary focus of research is long-term potentiation (LTP). The first full description of LTP by Tim Bliss and Terje Lømo in 1973 reported that electrical stimulation to one neuronal pathway in the base of the rat brain (the perforant pathway in the hippocampus to be specific) caused a sustained increase in efficiency of synaptic transmission, consistent with a Hebbian form of synaptic plasticity. LTP is an artificial phenomenon: under normal circumstances, brains don't have electrical currents applied directly to their perforant pathways. However, the persistent changes in synaptic strength they elicited were immediately recognized as a potential model for learning and memory. How did it work?

A critical discovery was the involvement of specific neurotransmitter receptors in the induction of LTP. Graham Collingridge describes how this discovery was made. He had decided to explore the effect of glutamate, the major excitatory neurotransmitter in the brain, on LTP. Ionotropic glutamate receptors are channels in the cell membrane that open when glutamate binds to them, allowing ions of potassium, sodium, or calcium to travel through a central pore in the receptor, which makes a channel through the cell membrane. As it was known that the effects of glutamate are mediated by a number of different receptors, the question was which subtype (if any) might be involved.

There was no *a priori* reason to suspect one type of glutamate receptor over another with respect to a specific role in synaptic plasticity. I therefore decided to investigate the subtypes in a random order... The next agonist I tested was what I thought was N-methyl-DL-aspartate [NMDA], which had little effect in the CA1 region of the hippocampus. I felt unhappy with this result since my previous experiments in the substantia nigra had shown that NMDA was an extremely potent excitant of these neurons. Although this could obviously be due to a regional difference in sensitivity, I was sufficiently concerned to want to test *bona fide* NMDA, which at the time was not commercially available. On a visit to Bristol I raised my concern with Jeff Watkins who let me have samples, not only of NMDA but also two of his latest glutamate antagonists, (D, L)-2-amino-5-phosphonopentanoate (AP5) and DGG. On my return to Vancouver in the spring of 1981 I applied NMDA by ionophoresis to CA1 dendrites and observed dramatic effects.

Collingridge (2003).

NMDA and the drug that blocks its action, the antagonist AP5, were to be major players in the subsequent history of work on memory. While AP5 had no effect on synaptic transmission and no effect on LTP once it had been established, it blocked the induction of LTP in a reversible manner. Furthermore, using the same method, applying drugs that act on the receptors and drugs that block their action, Collingridge found that another, non-NDMA, glutamate receptor mediated synaptic transmission. This

subtype is called the AMPA receptor. When it was discovered that magnesium ions block the NMDA receptor, and that this blockade is voltage dependent (so that depolarization will shift the magnesium out of the NMDA receptor), the idea emerged that the NMDA receptor was a coincidence detector. It works as follows (Figure 10.5): glutamate is released into the synaptic cleft (the gap between the two cells at a synapse) and arrives at AMPA receptors, which depolarize the membrane. Before depolarization, magnesium blocks the NMDA receptor from opening. Depolarization unblocks the magnesium and the NMDA receptor now opens in response to glutamate, allowing calcium to enter the cell, thereby making it much more responsive to subsequent stimuli, just the kind of change required for synaptic plasticity, the Hebbian basis of learning and memory.

The NMDA receptor story raises a set of questions about the molecular mechanisms of plasticity: how does calcium entry result in LTP? Is there a sensor at the mouth of the NMDAR

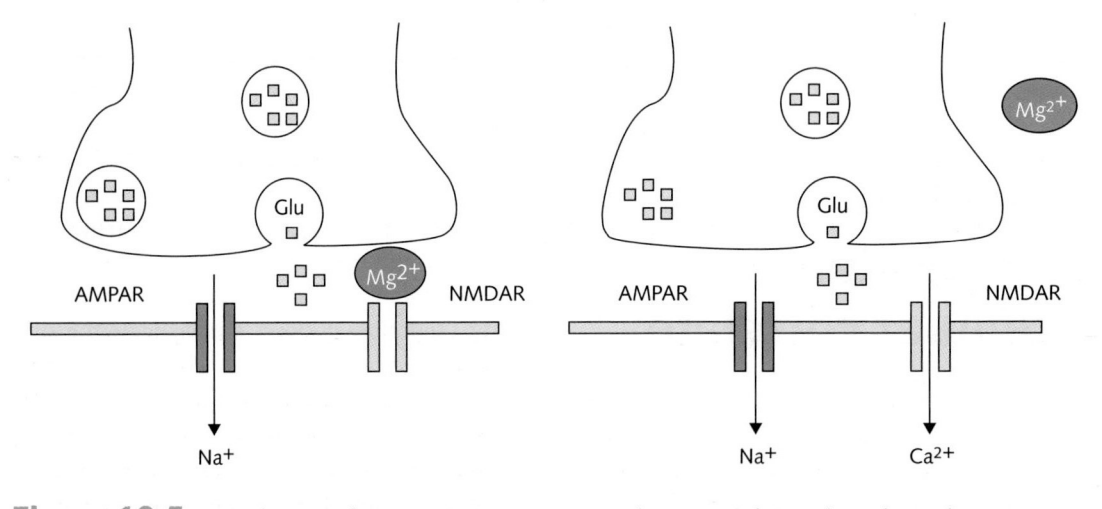

Figure 10.5 A simple view of potentiation at a synapse. Glutamate (Glu) is released into the synaptic cleft and depolarizes the post-synaptic membrane through its action on AMPA receptors (AMPAR). Before depolarization, magnesium ions (Mg^{2+}) block the NMDA receptors (NMDAR). After depolarization, the magnesium block is released and calcium (Ca^{2+}) can now enter the cell.

channel that triggers LTP or does Ca²⁺ have to diffuse further into the cell? What is that sensor? What intracellular signaling pathways does it activate and which are necessary for triggering LTP? These questions, and others like them, could be answered by gene targeting, but their importance to us is the light they cast on understanding the biology of behavior, or more specifically of memory.

Different forms of memory in the mammalian hippocampus

I (J.F.) have considerable sympathy for Karl Lashley. He died in 1958 with a reputation as one of the foremost psychologists of his day, despite a total lack of formal training in psychology (his first research was on very small creatures practically devoid of nervous systems, *Hydra* and *Paramecium*, at a time when it was acceptable to call them lower organisms). Lashley is famous for championing the view that all neural functions are distributed widely throughout the brain: '*...cerebral organization can be described only in terms of relative masses and spatial arrangements of gross parts, of equilibrium among the parts, of directness and steepness of gradients, and of the sensitization of final common paths to patterns of excitation*' (Lashley, 1930).

Fifty years after Lashley's death every self-respecting psychology department practices the modern-day equivalent of phrenology, using functional magnetic resonance imaging to identify which parts of the brain are activated when we see, listen, talk, or think, or which parts of our brain are activated when we are sad, happy, angry, or disgusted; and every psychologist has learnt of the existence of long-term potentiation as a model of synaptic plasticity. What would Lashley have thought of the attempts to put these two beliefs together, to produce a theory that long-term potentiation in specific regions of the brain is responsible for our ability to remember?

Here is the core hypothesis, as the psychologist Richard Morris states it: '*Activity-dependent synaptic plasticity is induced at appropriate synapses during memory formation, and is both necessary and sufficient for the information storage underlying the type of memory mediated by the brain area in which that plasticity is observed*' (Morris et al., 2003).

As Morris goes on to argue, the problem with this hypothesis is that it lacks specificity. Synaptic plasticity has many forms, but, perhaps more importantly, memory is not a unitary phenomenon. For instance, there is a distinction between the unconscious memory for perceptual and motor skills (called implicit or procedural memory) and conscious memory of things, places, and past events (termed explicit or declarative memory). This distinction has good anatomical justification, as became evident with the publication in 1957 of a case report of a man, referred to as H.M., with permanent damage to a region of the brain called the hippocampus.

There's a hotel, a little further up the road from where I'm staying as I write this, called The Hippocampus. The hotel sign shows a badly weathered painting of a sea horse. I've never seen any resemblance between the convoluted bilateral brain structure, either in rodents or humans, and a sea horse, but apparently somebody did. And now probably more psychologists study the hippocampus than any other brain region, so many in fact that there is a journal devoted to presenting their findings, a journal called, appropriately, *Hippocampus*. Consequently, the hippocampus is one brain region whose functions are relatively well understood.

H.M. showed that without a hippocampus you could still talk and think normally and could still learn new motor tasks (intact implicit memory), but you could not learn new facts. Furthermore, while H.M. could remember distant events—his childhood for example—he could not remember events recently before (or since) the onset of amnesia. All these observations suggested that the hippocampus was involved in processing declarative memory, or at least two components of declarative memory: the ability to memorize facts (semantic memory) and the ability to memorize personal experiences (episodic memory), that is to say the memories of what happened to me and when (the distinction between semantic and episodic memory is the difference between knowing that the hippocampus is part of the brain, and knowing when you learnt that bit of information).

Claims that the hippocampus was essential for declarative memory were surprising, because at that time there was no evidence that animals with lesions to the hippocampus suffered amnesia, or that they could not remember new tasks. Psychologists then working in the phrenological tradition investigated brain function by destroying parts of the brain and searching for behavioral abnormalities. This was work Lashley knew well, and it showed that animals with damage to the hippocampus had difficulty suppressing responses that were no longer appropriate. For instance, among the lever-pressing tasks that psychologists liked to teach rats was one that required the animal to delay the rate of lever pressing to obtain a reward (for example leave an interval of at least 5 seconds between lever presses to get the food). Rats with damage to the hippocampus always found this task difficult, and the greater the damage to the hippocampus, the worse the deficit. Thus, until about 1970, the prevailing hypothesis of hippocampal function from animal work was that the hippocampus mediated behavioral inhibition.

John O'Keefe and John Dostrovsky fundamentally changed that view. In 1971, they found that the pyramidal cells of the hippocampus, the same cells later to be stimulated electrically in the discovery of LTP, encode where a rat is: the firing pattern of pyramidal neurons is an internal spatial map (O'Keefe and Dostrovsky, 1971). Within minutes of placing a rat in a new environment, it develops a stable internal representation of the space, such that a pyramidal cell's firing pattern depends on the animal's location: for example, after the rat is placed in a box, specific hippocampal cells will fire when the rat is in the northwest corner, others when it is in the southeast corner and so on. Pyramidal place fields remain stable for weeks if the environment is constant, consistent with the idea that the cells contribute to a particular spatial memory.

If one role of the hippocampus is to make and remember maps, and if the only contender for the cellular basis of memory, LTP, is found in the hippocampus, a critical experiment is to determine whether the two are causally related. Richard Morris developed a spatial memory task, now forever known as the Morris water maze, which could be used to investigate the relationship between memory and LTP. Rats were used for this work and rats are good swimmers, although they are not fond of water. As I can personally testify from trying to wash a pet rat in a sink, rats swim fast and make desperate attempts to climb out when they are put in water.

The Morris water maze isn't a maze at all, at least not the sort of maze I think of, one with large walls, usually made of a dense dark green shrub, forming passages that lead off into blind alleys or back to where you started from, the whole thing designed to confuse and disorientate you so that you lose all idea of where you are and, if the maze is good, stops you from leaving it. Richard Morris' water maze is a large circular pool, about five feet in diameter, containing what looks like milk (the water is made opaque so the animal can't see what's hidden under the surface). The sides are vertical and tall enough to stop the animal jumping or climbing out. The only refuge is one small region of the pool where the water is very shallow, and there is a small platform that the rat can stand on. Using water to hide the platform means the rat can't use smell to identify it. When a rat is put in the pool, it swims around until by chance (it cannot see the platform) it reaches relative safety. Replace the rat in the pool and the animal finds the platform a little quicker as it now has some idea of the hidden location. Keep training the rat in this way and it will eventually learn where the platform is, swimming quickly towards it. By starting the rat randomly at different points in the pool (south, east, north, or west) and providing fixed visual cues (shapes such as stars and squares stuck onto the poolside) as spatial reference points, it's possible to ensure that the only way the rat can solve the maze is by remembering the platform's spatial position, so that the animal might be saying to itself that the platform is to the left of the star and to the right of the square, just as we would use a map to triangulate on a position.

The psychologists' way of asking the rat if it knows the platform's location is to remove the platform, which is of course invisible, and then put the rat into the pool. The rat with intact spatial memory will swim to where it thinks the platform is located and persist in swimming over the missing platform (you can imagine what it must be thinking). A rat that doesn't remember, or hasn't learnt the task, may swim over the missing platform, but won't waste time swimming in pointless circles around one region.

Richard Morris used AP5, the same drug that Graham Collingridge had used to block NMDA receptors, to turn off LTP in the hippocampus. Infusing AP5 into the brain impaired spatial learning in the water maze. Using two versions of the maze, one with a hidden platform below water and one with a visible platform, Morris showed that drugged animals failed to learn the location of the hidden platform only, indicating that NMDA receptor inactivation specifically inhibited spatial learning. This selectivity of effect on learning the task implies a direct action on remembrance.

Morris's paper was one important piece of evidence for a relationship between LTP and spatial memory. However, as Morris points out, these experiments do not prove the assumption that AP5 causes its effects on learning and memory by blocking hippocampal synaptic plasticity. '*The logical difficulty is as follows: blockade of LTP by AP5 is a dependent consequence of the drug treatment. The impairment of learning is also a dependent consequence. However it is fallacious to presume that that one dependent consequence is necessarily the cause of the other*' (Morris et al., 2003). In other words, more direct tests are needed to establish the relationship between NMDA receptors, LTP, and learning and memory. This is what the genetic experiments, described next, set out to do.

Key papers

O'Keefe, J. and Dostrovsky, J. (1971). The hippocampus as a spatial map. Preliminary evidence from unit activity in the freely-moving rat. *Brain Res* **34**:171–175.

O'Keefe, J. and Nadel, L. (1978). *The Hippocampus as a Cognitive Map*. Oxford: Clarendon Press.

Morris, R.G., Anderson, E., Lynch, G.S., and Baudry, M. (1986). Selective impairment of learning and blockade of long-term potentiation by an N-methyl-D-aspartate receptor antagonist, AP5. *Nature* **319**:774–776.

Knocking out memory in the mouse

It was not immediately obvious, at least not to me (J.F.), why the first genes to be targeted in neurobiology were kinases. Why not go for the receptors, the AMPA and NMDA receptors that we know to be important? I asked Seth Grant, one of the first people to do this work, to explain. One reason was practical: knockouts for some kinases had already been made, by cancer biologists, and the genes for others had been identified. As Grant put it, there were good cancer reagents. By contrast, knocking out the receptors meant cloning the DNA to make the targeting construct, and then targeting the embryonic stem cells and so on (see Appendix pp. 235–240 on how to make a knockout).

One reason why NMDA receptors weren't the first genes to be targeted was because they weren't cloned until 1991 and the full complexity of their structure was not appreciated at the time. As it turned out, deleting all NMDA receptors was lethal because they are used in the midbrain to control breathing. As cancer biologists had shown that knocking out kinase genes did not kill mice, and that the mutants

were useful reagents for understanding cancer, they were a promising starting point. The question was whether cancer reagents would be useful for neurobiology.

But why would anyone expect kinases to be involved in long-term potentiation? Kinases are proteins that add phosphates to proteins; phosphatases remove phosphates from proteins. Nobel laureate Paul Greengard had shown how critical phosphorylation reactions were for neurotransmitter function. He had shown that slow signaling pathways modulate fast synaptic transmission in two major ways: '*a) by regulating the state of phosphorylation of synapsins and other key proteins present in the pre-synaptic terminal, thus modulating the efficacy of neurotransmitter release (the amount of neurotransmitter released from the nerve terminal in response to an action potential), and b) by regulating the state of phosphorylation of neurotransmitter receptors present in the post-synaptic cell, thus modulating the responsivity of these receptors to the released neurotransmitter (responsivity referring to the magnitude of the electrophysiological response to a molecule of neurotransmitter)*' (Greengard, 2001).

The reversibility of the kinase/phosphatase reaction had been a contender as a key component of memory for some time, because of the possibility that it could act in a switch-like manner (Lisman, 1985). One kinase had already been proposed to take on this role: calcium/calmodulin protein kinase II (CamKII). CamKII is present in great abundance in neurons (up to 2% of total protein), which is unusual for a regulatory protein, typically present in very small amounts. As its name suggests, the kinase activity of CamKII depends on the levels of calcium in a cell bound to a protein called calmodulin. When calcium/calmodulin binds to CamKII it turns on the kinase, but this dependence on its activator can be bypassed: active CamKII can add phosphate to itself, and when it does so it remains active in the absence of calcium/calmodulin. It can only be turned off by the action of a phosphatase. This is the switch-like property that caught people's attention and suggested that CamKII might be a memory molecule. And NMDA receptors let calcium into the cell. Calcium had to act somewhere to change the cell's responsivity and CamKII was a good starting point.

Seth Grant, believing that kinases had to be important in transforming the signal from the NMDA receptor into LTP, set out to look at mice with deleted kinases. Working with Eric Kandel and Tom O'Dell, he began to examine the knockouts and found that one mutant, for *fyn* kinase, did indeed show a learning abnormality. At the same time, Alcino Silva, working with Susumu Tonegawa at the Massachusetts Institute of Technology, used gene targeting to show that CamKII was required for the induction of LTP. Both Silva and Grant also showed that the knockout animals were deficient in spatial memory, using the Morris water maze.

Key papers

Grant, S.G.N., O'Dell, T.J., Karl, K.A., Stein, P.L., Soriano, P., and Kandel, E.R. (1992). Impaired long-term potentiation, spatial learning and hippocampal development in *fyn* mutant mice. *Science* **258**:1903–1910.

Silva, A.J., Paylor, R., Wehner, J.M., and Tonegawa, S. (1992). Impaired spatial learning in a calcium–calmodulin kinase II mutant mice. *Science* **257**:206–211.

Two key papers that introduced molecular biology to psychologists.

Seth Grant has stressed to me that his paper reported results not on one knockout but on four (a reasonable thing to stress given the amount of work that involved). The other thing he stressed is less obvious: the knockouts did learn to find the hidden platform in the water maze. At first sight, this is at odds with the summary I've given above, but there are a couple of things to explain here. Firstly, the 129 strain of mouse tends to develop tumors (a propensity for which it was developed in the first place) and it may have structural brain abnormalities (which might confound behavioral testing), so typically researchers cross the mutant animal with a more congenial strain (C57BL/6). The offspring of the cross are no longer on a pure strain background, and there will be lots of genetic variants now segregating that affect all aspects of the animals' physiology and behavior. Some may, and in this case did, influence the effect of the mutation, reducing its impact and in fact restoring the animals' spatial learning ability. The importance and relevance of such background genetic effects were to provoke considerable discussion in later years. Seth Grant's report is one of the first to document them, as he found that the behavioral abnormality was only observed when the mutations were placed on the pure 129 strain. The second point is that the worst behavioral consequence of the mutation was seen when the knockout had to learn a new hidden position for the platform in the water maze (sometimes called a reversal learning task): for example, train the animal to find a platform hidden in the south-east corner of the pool and then try to train it to find a platform hidden in the north-west corner. This suggests the mutants are sensitive to a change in contingency. The importance of this observation, and the use of mutants to sort out what was going on, will become clearer in due course.

Mutant mysteries

Why did he do this experiment? It's always seemed completely counter-intuitive why anyone should think of it in the first place. None the less, the experimental psychologist David Bannerman carried out what is known as a two-pool experiment. After training a rat to find a fixed-position platform or a varying-position platform in one room, he put the animal into another room and trained it again. Pre-trained animals were not affected by AP5 (the drug that abolishes NMDA receptor function). Why does pre-training make a difference?

Gene-targeting experiments added to the mystery. After the glutamate receptors had been cloned, the knockouts could be created. NMDA receptor knockouts initially proved useless because the homozygous mutant is lethal—not surprising given the receptor's critical function in the midbrain. But by the mid-1990s, a way around this impediment was found. Using a recombinase (an enzyme that cuts DNA), it is possibly to delete a gene in the adult animal, just in the hippocampus. Joe Tsien in Tonegawa's laboratory did this for the NMDA receptor, knocking out one component of the receptor in one region of the hippocampus and replicated the AP5 results: no LTP and no spatial learning in the water maze (Tsien *et al.*, 1996). However, another mutant, restricted to a different hippocampal region, performed normally in the water maze (Nakazawa *et al.*, 2002), but was severely impaired in the reversal learning version of the water maze (where the animal has to relearn different platform locations in the same apparatus).

An even bigger challenge to the new orthodox interpretation of the molecular biology of memory arose with analysis of a different glutamate receptor mutant. A knockout of the AMPA receptor yielded one of those rare, completely unexpected results that turn out to be remarkably informative. AMPA receptors have four subunits (called GluR1 to GluR4, but also called GluR-A to GluR-D, so expect to be confused if you start reading the original literature on this subject). The adult hippocampus contains receptors made up of GluR2 bound to either GluR1 or GluR3. Knocking out GluR1 is not lethal, but it does abolish LTP in the hippocampus. The mutation should also, according to the hypothesis that LTP is a cellular correlate of memory, prevent an animal from learning to find the hidden platform in the water maze. It doesn't. Mutants learn just as well as their brothers and sisters with intact GluR1 genes (Zamanillo *et al.*, 1999).

A solution emerged with a re-analysis of the GlurR1 mutant on a new task (Reisel *et al.*, 2002). Place the animal at the bottom of an apparatus shaped like a capital T and allow it to run forward to the junction. As we discussed in Chapter 7, the rodent has to make a choice, left or right arm. Once it has chosen, start it over from the beginning again and score which arm it goes into. The average mouse (or rat) will choose a different arm, presumably because it knows there is no point in visiting the same arm twice (no food to find there). For the short time between the first and second task, the animal has to remember which arm it chose first. This type of memory, working memory (or to be more correct spatial working memory because it turns out there are different sorts of working memory) is severely impaired in the GluR1 knockout. This result says that you don't need working memory to learn the usual water maze task; not surprisingly, the knockouts deficient in working memory are impaired on the reversal learning tasks (as these are taxing their ability to remember where they've been a few minutes ago).

Finding and interpreting such specificity of genetic action is a remarkable achievement. It illustrates how behavioral and genetic analyses can work together to find out how genes influence behavior. Only with carefully designed psychological paradigms can we tease apart the effects of individual genes on our behaviors of interest. But I think it is worth returning to a remark by Paul Greengard to remind ourselves how difficult this cooperation between different scientific fields usually is.

> At the time we started this work, neuroscience was not a clearly defined field. There were two types of people studying the brain. There were biophysicists, working in physiology departments, who believed that everything significant about the brain could be explained in terms of electrical signaling. And there were biochemists working in biochemistry departments who would happily throw a brain into a homogenizer, with as much abandon as they would a liver, and look for enzymes or lipids. But these biochemists were rarely interested in brain function. And so these two groups rarely spoke to each other, which is just as well because when they did they didn't have nice things to say.

Nowadays there are molecular biologists, who redesign the genomes of mice and speak a newly minted language, which only they understand, and behavioral neuroscientists who test mice in paddling pools and use the vocabulary of learning theory (which personally I think is equally impenetrable). The two groups do speak to each other but, it has to be said, not much.

Summary

1. *Aplysia*, a sea snail, is a model organism used to dissect the cellular and molecular basis of memory. The animal can be used to study forms of short- and long-term memory.

2. Memory in *Aplysia* is in part mediated by a cAMP signaling pathway in which serotonin receptors activate an enzyme (adenylyl cyclase) to produce a diffusible chemical signal (cyclic AMP). One consequence is the activation of CREB-1 (cAMP response element-binding protein), a regulator of gene activity in the nucleus.

3. Fruit flies have long- and short-term memory, also mediated by a cAMP signaling pathway. Key players in the pathway have been found by using mutagenesis.

4. The cAMP signaling pathway is also involved in mammalian learning and memory.

5. Synaptic plasticity is a form of cellular memory in which neurons learn to pay more attention to those synapses that are relatively more active.

6. Long-term potentiation (LTP), a form of synaptic plasticity, is believed to be a cellular correlate of spatial memory. LTP is an artificial phenomenon, evoked by electrical stimulation to one neuronal pathway in the base of the mammalian hippocampus. LTP is the sustained increase in efficiency of synaptic transmission, consequent upon stimulation.

7. Glutamate, an excitatory neurotransmitter, activates AMPA and NMDA receptors in the hippocampus. The NMDA receptor acts as a coincidence detector and is involved in LTP.

8. Evidence from drug effects and mutants indicates that NMDA receptor inactivation inhibits spatial learning.

9. Mutations in the AMPA receptor disrupt LTP but not spatial learning in the Morris water maze. However, the genetic lesion severely impairs spatial working memory. This is a rare example of specificity of genetic action on behavior.

References

Bannerman, D.M., Good, M.A., Butcher, S.P., Ramsay, M., and Morris, R.G. (1995). Distinct components of spatial learning revealed by prior training and NMDA receptor blockade. *Nature* **378**:182–186.

Bourtchuladze, R., Frenguelli, B., Blendy, J., Cioffi, D., Schutz, G., and Silva, A.J. (1994). Deficient long-term memory in mice with a targeted mutation of the cAMP-responsive element-binding protein. *Cell* **79**:59–68.

Collingridge, G.L. (2003). The induction of N-methyl-D-aspartate receptor-dependent long-term potentiation. *Philos Trans R Soc Lond B Biol Sci* **358**:635–641.

Dubnau, J., Chiang, A.S., Grady, L., Barditch, J., Gossweiler, S., McNeil, J., Smith, P., Buldoc, F., Scott, R. *et al.* (2003). The *staufen/pumilio* pathway is involved in *Drosophila* long-term memory. *Curr Biol* **13**:286–296.

Folkers, E., Waddell, S., and Quinn, W.G. (2006). The *Drosophila radish* gene encodes a protein required for anesthesia-resistant memory. *Proc Natl Acad Sci U S A* **103**:17496–17500.

Frost, W.N., Castellucci, V.F., Hawkins, R.D., and Kandel, E.R. (1985). Monosynaptic connections made by the sensory neurons of the gill- and siphon-withdrawal reflex in *Aplysia* participate in the storage of long-term memory for sensitization. *Proc Natl Acad Sci U S A* **82**:8266–8269.

Greengard, P. (2001). The neurobiology of slow synaptic transmission. *Science* **294**:1024–1030.

Hebb, D.O. (1949). *The Organization of Behavior*. New York: Wiley.

Kandel, E.R. (1976). *Cellular Basis of Behavior: an Introduction to Behavioral Neurobiology*. San Fransisco: W.H. Freeman and Co.

Keene, A.C. and Waddell, S. (2007). *Drosophila* olfactory memory: single genes to complex neural circuits. *Nat Rev Neurosci* **8**:341–354.

Lashley, K. (1930). Basic neural mechanisms in behavior. *Psychol Rev* **37**:1–24.

Lisman, J.E. (1985). A mechanism for memory storage insensitive to molecular turnover: a bistable autophosphorylating kinase. *Proc Natl Acad Sci U S A* **82**:3055–3057.

Margulies, C., Tully, T., and Dubnau, J. (2005). Deconstructing memory in *Drosophila*. *Curr Biol* **15**:R700–R713.

Morris, R.G., Moser, E.I., Riedel, G., Martin, S.J., Sandin, J., Day, M., and O'Carroll, C. (2003). Elements of a neurobiological theory of the hippocampus: the role of activity-dependent synaptic plasticity in memory. *Philos Trans R Soc Lond B Biol Sci* **358**:773–786.

Nakazawa, K., Quirk, M.C., Chitwood, R.A., Watanabe, M., Yeckel, M.F., Sun, L.D., Kato, A., Carr, C.A., Johnston, D. *et al.* (2002). Requirement for hippocampal CA3 NMDA receptors in associative memory recall. *Science* **297**:211–218.

O'Keefe, J. and Dostrovsky, J. (1971). The hippocampus as a spatial map. Preliminary evidence from unit activity in the freely-moving rat. *Brain Res* **34**:171–175.

Petrij, F., Giles, H.R., Dauwerse, H.G., Saris, J.J., Hennekam, R.C.M., Masuno, M., Tommerup, N., van Ommen, G.B., Goodman, R.H. *et al.* (1995). Rubinstein–Taybi syndrome caused by mutations in the transcriptional co-activator CNP. *Nature* **376**:348–351.

Reisel, D., Bannerman, D.M., Schmitt, W.B., Deacon, R.M., Flint, J., Borchardt, T., Seeburg, P.H., and Rawlins, J.N. (2002). Spatial memory dissociations in mice lacking GluR1. *Nat Neurosci* **5**:868–873.

Tang, Y.P., Shimizu, E., Dube, G.R., Rampon, C., Kerchner, G.A., Zhuo, M., Liu, G., and Tsien, J.Z. (1999). Genetic enhancement of learning and memory in mice. *Nature* **401**:63–69.

Tsien, J.Z., Chen, D.F., Gerber, D., Tom, C., Mercer, E.H., Anderson, D.J., Mayford, M., Kandel, E.R., and Tonegawa, S. (1996). Subregion- and cell type-restricted gene knockout in mouse brain. *Cell* **87**:1317–1326.

Waddell, S. and Quinn, W.G. (2001). Neurobiology. Learning how a fruit fly forgets. *Science* **293**:1271–1272.

Yin, J.C., Wallach, J.S., Del Vecchio, M., Wilder, E.L., Zhou, H., Quinn, W.G., and Tully, T. (1994). Induction of a dominant negative CREB transgene specifically blocks long-term memory in *Drosophila*. *Cell* **79**:49–58.

Zamanillo, D., Sprengel, R., Hvalby, O., Jensen, V., Burnashev, N., Rozov, A., Kaiser, K.M., Koster, H.J., Borchardt, T. *et al.* (1999). Importance of AMPA receptors for hippocampal synaptic plasticity but not for spatial learning. *Science* **284**:1805–1811.

11 How genes influence behavior

[In which we try to answer the question of how genes influence behavior]

The work of the behavioral geneticist

Soon after publishing a paper in *Nature Genetics* which described the use of a dynamic programming algorithm to map genetic effects by reconstructing outbred mouse haplotypes as if they were a mosaic of known progenitors, together with the use of quantitative complementation to confirm the involvement of a gene, called *Rgs2*, at a quantitative trait locus (QTL) influencing anxiety (open-field activity) in the mouse, one of us received the following incomprehensible letter:

Fokefiloss for Neurofils (ed) Ken Al Sifr 580
19 nov 2004.
Quaint Train Locos
Wellcome to *Rgs2* 'that modulates anxiety in mice'! Its Ten Authors at Oxford have resurrected the >40-year-old behavioral work of Victor Denenberg *et al.*, with the Other Laboratory Rodent's Emotionality, as measured by their activity & shit-rate in the standard brightlight Open-Field ... the original probers of Rat and Other Animal Emotionality soon found phenotypic & environmental variables to modulate 'anxieties and emotionalities': Mothering & weaning, parental & sibling contact, inbred & outbred strains & mosaics, not least the amount & kind of casual & experimental handling by human caretakers. They might well have been 'arguably human' about those infamous 'genetic–environmental interactions'. Is there any evidence to the contrary for our wellcome mice >40 years on? If so, our Exptl. Psychomice apud Oxon chose to ignore it in the interest of their HAPPY Hap Maps and contiguous colors.

This isn't the only example of a member of the public writing to me. Not all of them write in such an interesting style. Some write letters that are more sober, supplicatory rather than heckling in tone. They often use headed notepaper, which, at least in the UK, often has H.M.P. written in large capital letters, a banner headline for 'Her Majesty's Prison.' Prisoners write because they want a letter from me, headed 'Oxford University,' stating that, in my view, the behavior that put them in prison was in part (or better wholly) attributable to their genes.

This line of reasoning has been tested in court a number of times (Bernet *et al.*, 2007). In 1994, Stephen Mobley was convicted of murder,

armed robbery, aggravated assault, and possession of a firearm and was sentenced to death. His trial occurred soon after the publication of Han Brunner's *Science* paper attributing aggression to a deficiency of MAOA (described in Chapter 4) and Mobley filed a motion seeking funds to hire expert witnesses to assess his potential deficiency in MAOA. The court rejected Mobley's motion and, on 1 March 2005, he was executed by lethal injection by the state of Georgia. This has not put others off trying. In Ohio, Dion Wayne Sanders claimed that he was *'incapable of acting with the degree of culpability which the charges of Aggravated Murder involved.'* The court found that *'whether an accused acted out of a sense or attitude of rage is not relevant to prove that he acted or did not act "purposefully" and "with prior calculation and design."*... *It could not demonstrate that when he shotgunned his grandparents Sanders lacked the specific intent to kill them. It only demonstrates that he was enraged when he did.'* Nevertheless, unlike Mobley, in Sanders' case, the jury returned verdicts of life without parole rather than the death penalty. And, in a case heard in Tennessee, the court recognized the possibility that genetic testing of the MAOA locus and the serotonin transporter *'might have influenced the jury's decision in the penalty phase of the trial as to whether to select death as the proper punishment. ... The Court finds, as a matter of law, that the expert services sought are necessary to ensure that the constitutional rights of the Defendant are properly protected.'*

Genetic testing can save your life, and there is more good news on the way:

> **Our genetically enriched descendants may view us as little more than sociopaths. For with enlightened gene therapy the role of, say, key receptor sub-types of the 'civilizing neurotransmitter' serotonin, the 'hormone of love' oxytocin and the 'chocolate amphetamine'**

phenylethylamine, can be radically enhanced. When naturally loved up and blissful on a richer cocktail of biochemicals than anything accessible today, our post human successors will be able not just to love everyone but to be perpetually in love with everyone as well... our deficiencies in love are only another grim expression of selfish DNA... but a predisposition towards loving each other to bits can also be genetically pre-programmed. The capacity can become innate. Empathetic bliss needn't be a drug induced aberration.

http://www.oxytocin.org.

If you cannot wait to be genetically engineered to correct your behavioral deficiencies, at least you can find out what they are. You can have your current DNA configuration analyzed with the help of 23andMe (http://www.23andme.com): *'...after producing a saliva sample using an at-home kit.'* You can check out your serotonin transporter status, your MAOA genotype, and indeed check for the presence of all the genetic characters we have introduced to you in the course of this book. With this information, *'... you can use our interactive tools to shed new light on your distant ancestors, your close family and most of all, yourself.'*

All of these claims rest on the idea that genes cause behavior, in a linear pathway from genetic variant, cellular components, neural circuitry to behavior. In the same way that alcohol disinhibits, cocaine produces euphoria, and LSD induces hallucinations, genes cause our behavior to change. The same assumption lies behind the broadsheet announcements that a 'gene for behavior' has been discovered. It is the hope of the murderer, the promise of the website, the lawyer's check, and the unquestioned, beloved of journalists. Academic journals take pains to disavow it, but don't deny that it may exist: *'Much research has focused on genes*

involving major neurotransmitters such as serotonin and dopamine and proteins that affect these neurotransmitters. No research has yet to isolate a specific "crime gene" and probably none ever will. Some of the reasons this is unlikely are incomplete penetrance, genetic heterogeneity, and the complex interaction among environmental factors, development, and gene expression' (Bernet et al., 2007). In other words, the gene for crime is there, but it's hidden. Is this true?

Two ways of explaining genetic effects

In this book, we have taken two quite different approaches to studying the inter-relationship between genes and behavior. On the one hand, we have reviewed many studies that examine individual differences as they exist in natural populations (like humans). These studies work only with what nature provides. On the other hand, we have reported many investigations that examine the impact of genes on behavior by mucking about with the genes in the laboratory, mutating them and in other ways perturbing their function, and then seeing if this process changes behavior.

These two approaches toward studying genes and behavior can give very different results. Let us illustrate this. Imagine gene X plays a critical role in producing behavior Y. However, gene X is so important to the organism that even very slight changes in the function of gene X are so poorly tolerated that they are quickly removed from the population by selection. While there are likely to be genetic variants in unimportant parts of this gene, with respect to the workhorse part, the gene is *monomorphic*—there is

no variation. What would happen if we were to study this gene in natural populations by linkage or association studies? We would find that variants in this gene were *not* associated with the behavior. However, if—in an experimental organism—we knocked out the function of that gene, we could get a dramatic change in the behavior.

So, can we conclude that gene X influences behavior Y or not? It is correct to say that 'Variants at gene X in population Z do not influence behavior Y' and to say 'Knockouts of gene X in laboratory Z demonstrate a large effect on behavior Y.' This might be confusing but it is none the less true. One study is not more right than the other; rather, the difference is that the experiments are asking different questions.

These two contrasting approaches, studying naturally occurring variants versus inducing mutations in the lab, began from different premises and, despite the fact that they had the same ultimate goal—an understanding of the genetic underpinnings of behavior—they necessarily had different proximate goals.

The focus of the first or 'quantitative genetic' approach, working with naturally occurring variation, either in the wild or in laboratory selection experiments, asked questions about the effect of all of the genetic variants available in a population on a phenotype. Quantitative genetics investigated how phenotypic variation could be explained by its environmental and genetic components and how evolutionary forces acted on those constituents. Much of quantitative genetics is statistical in nature and is based on the theoretical work of the statistician Ronald Fischer (Fischer, 1930). Throughout most of the field's history, the individual genetic factors responsible for such naturally occurring, continuously varying traits were unknown and the analysis consisted largely

of estimating the number of contributing loci and the independence (additivity) or non-independence (epistasis) of their interactions. Often, these results followed from artificial selection experiments in the laboratory.

By contrast, single-gene mutant analysis traces its origins to microbial genetics, which concentrated on cellular mechanisms to the virtual exclusion of all evolutionary or environmental questions. It consisted of the induction of mutants to identify relevant genes and the direct demonstration of biochemically definable roles and interactions between them. A particular strength of the approach is the theoretical ability to produce at least one mutation in every relevant gene for a particular trait (saturation mutagenesis) and thereby, presumably, identify all of the genes that are mutable to produce alterations in the selected phenotype.

Initially worked out on such prokaryotic phenomena as phage assembly (Wood *et al.*, 1968), saturation mutagenesis was later applied to more complex multicellular phenotypes such as embryonic pattern formation (Nusslein-Volhard and Wieschaus, 1980) (recent genome-level analysis suggests that saturation mutagenesis is actually quite difficult to achieve in practice; Giaever *et al.*, 2002). The single-gene, induced-mutation school was not interested in whether a gene would exhibit natural variation. Instead, the interest lay in which genes contributed to the behavior and which neural or biochemical components were selectively altered.

A measure of the past separation between single-gene mutagenesis advocates and the quantitative geneticists focusing on natural variation can be seen in their criticisms of each other. The genetic architecture camp criticized their single-gene counterparts (whom they sometimes derisively call 'gene-jocks') for their

failure to take into account the subtlety of the various contributions of the genetic background on the phenotype. The mono-geneticists disparaged the architecturists for their softheadedness and their failure to be able to say anything about which genes might be involved, as well as for the lack of relevance of small-effect genes to underlying mechanism. One particularly potent put-down is, 'They just care about statistics, not real genes.'

We are oversimplifying here. There are also those who study single gene effects in natural populations (by linkage analysis) and they in turn deride twin and other quantitative genetic approaches. This is part of the endless effort among scientists to distinguish themselves from each other, and to assert that 'mine is better than yours.'

The single-gene perspective ignores background effects

The severity of a mutant phenotype is a complex function of many factors. It depends, among other things, on the nature and extent of inactivation or alteration of the gene in question, on the gene's role in development and behavior, and on the genetic background in which it is expressed.

Behavioral mutants are notoriously sensitive to variations in genetic background—the natural, genetic heterogeneity in laboratory stocks (also known in the classical genetics literature as 'modifiers'). Whereas quantitative geneticists have long been aware of this problem, in general single-gene practitioners have not, sometimes to their embarrassment.

A case in point is the erroneous identification of the temperature-sensitive paralytic mutation *shibire* as the voltage-sensitive sodium channel (Kelly, 1974), based on the greater resistance to tetrodotoxin of the mutant relative to a control strain. The control, however, was not of the same genetic background as the mutant. As it turned out, the 'control' strain was exceptionally sensitive to tetrodotoxin (Gitschier *et al.*, 1980) whereas the *shibire* mutant was as resistant to it as most other fly strains (mutant or normal). The genetic basis of resistance in this control strain has never been properly determined.

Mutant phenotypes can fade with time. Their spontaneous disappearance has been reported for mutants affecting learning and brain development in flies (de Belle and Heisenberg, 1996). The ubiquity of the problem has bedeviled mutant studies all along. In a legendary incident at a *Drosophila* meeting in the early 1970s, one investigator began his talk by saying, '*I would like to announce that Hyperkinetic is now a recessive*' (J.C. Hall, personal communication, but not the speaker). In other words, the strain no longer showed a dominant mode of inheritance for the mutation, as reported originally.

Such phenomena are presumed to be the result of spontaneous selection for modifying alleles that are present in the population—a distinctly quantitative genetic problem! Moreover, the potency with which a given background can mask or exacerbate the phenotype of a mutation underlines its relevance to the issue of genetic mechanism. A graphic example of the range of these effects was shown in a study of modifiers of the *sevenless* mutation in *Drosophila*, a mutant originally isolated as part of a genetic dissection of phototaxis behavior (the tendency to approach light) (Harris *et al.*, 1976) and subsequently studied in great depth for its role in cell fate determination in photoreceptors (Brennan and Moses, 2000). When a moderate allele of *sevenless*

(roughly midway between the most severe mutation and the wild type) was placed on a range of different genetic backgrounds, phenotypes were found that ranged from fully wild type to more severe than the most effective enhancer mutations isolated previously (Polaczyk *et al.*, 1998). Clearly, genetic mechanisms cannot be properly understood without paying attention to such background effects; that is, single-gene effects fade into quantitative genetics at the margins.

Small-effect genes will tell us little about mechanism

Two mouse geneticists, Joe Nadeau and Wayne Frankel, argued strongly against QTL approaches to finding genes in complex phenotypes (Nadeau and Frankel, 2000). They started by pointing out the disappointing record of QTL methods for identifying genes and argued that alternatives needed to be considered. One problem was that, at least in mouse genetics, most mapping experiments sampled genetic variation segregating in about half a dozen strains so that '*the number of naturally occurring allelic variants that can be evaluated in practice is a relatively small proportion of the total number of genes essential for pathway functions and systems biology.*' By contrast '*potentially every gene in the genome that affects the trait of interest is a target for mutagenesis.*' QTL methods would, even if they worked, only give a partial insight into the biology of a complex phenotype such as behavior. Suppose 100 genes are necessary for the expression of a behavioral phenotype. Mutations in any of these could potentially affect the behavior, but in any natural population, genetic variants will only exist in a subset of those 100 genes, and maybe in only a small subset.

Nadeau and Frankel reserved their strongest argument in favor of mutagenesis for the end: '...it is *the successful identification of the genetic lesions that give rise to mutant phenotypes, compared with the ability to identify the variant that underlies naturally occurring QTLs, which makes mutagenesis the road of choice.*' Mutagenesis produces changes in coding sequence, mutations that truncate genes, mutations that result in null alleles where no functional protein is produced, or proteins of monstrously aberrant function, so obviously deranged that they cannot be missed by even the most sleepy post-doc (this is not quite true as J. F. recently found out, but let that pass).

But it is not just clonability that excites mutagenesis aficionados. There is the additional assumption that large-effect mutants are large for a reason: they disrupt key processes. By contrast, mutations with small effects do not and they are more likely to represent peripheral, non-informative processes. However, as we have seen throughout this book, there is little evidence that single-gene mutations directly and specifically influence behavior. Why is that?

Single genes in genetic architecture terms

Finding genes with a specific role in behavior turns out to be very hard. Genes for behavior, genes that carry a label saying 'my job is to make sure you don't become autistic/murder people/eat too much food' are thin on the ground. Three fly geneticists in an article entitled 'Are complex behaviors specified by dedicated regulatory genes? Reasoning from *Drosophila*' could identify only one example in the fly: the *fruitless*

gene, which is involved in courtship and related sexual behaviors (Baker *et al.*, 2001). To be clear, it is not that genes don't influence behavior, it's that they don't do it specifically.

Recall the work on geotaxis described in Chapter 8, which made us rethink our ideas about how genes influence behavior—that perhaps there were no such things as 'genes for geotaxis,' and that instead genes are versatile and participate in many different processes. We found that *cyrptochrome* and *pigment-dispersing factor* are not circadian rhythm genes, but genes that can affect many functions, two of which are circadian rhythms and geotaxis. As for *importin-α*, the fact that it can exert such a selective effect while being so widely used for other biological functions provides an important insight into the subtle way gene activities intertwine to affect behavior. It tells us that modest alterations in such widely acting genes, in combination with other similarly altered genes, can produce very specific behavioral effects.

As we noted, a corollary of this non-specificity is that genetic effects on behavior are pleiotropic; that is, a gene has multiple effects on many phenotypes. Look at Table 11.1, compiled from screening about 250 mouse knockouts, all screened for the same phenotypes, both physiological as well as behavioral. The table gives the percentage of cases where there is a significant difference between mutants and wild types for each of the phenotypes listed. The behavior open-field activity is the same measure described in Chapter 7 where it was presented as a model for fearful or anxious behavior. What is remarkable is that almost 20% of mutations impact on the level of anxiety displayed in this test.

Open-field activity can be disrupted by many processes that have nothing to do with the brain, so this result does not necessarily mean

Table 11.1 The effect of knockouts on a range of phenotypes: percentage of mutants whose phenotypes are significantly different from controls

Phenotype	%	Total no. of Mutants Analyzed
Open-field activity	18.9	206
Albumin	7.1	254
Alkaline phosphatase	7.1	254
Blood urea nitrogen	9.1	254
Calcium	6.3	254
Cholesterol	10.2	254
Glucose	3.9	254
Hemoglobin	4.5	243
Phosphorous	7.1	254
Platelets	5.8	243
Triglycerides	6.7	254
White blood cells	6.2	243

Data from Flint and Mott (2008).

that 20% of the genome is implicated in 'anxiety,' but even if only 5% of the genes show a central nervous system effect, this implies abundant pleiotropy. In flies evidence for pervasive pleiotropy comes from the substantial overlap of the transcripts for which there are correlated responses in expression to selection from the same base population for copulation latency, aggressive behavior, locomotor startle response, and ethanol resistance (Jordan *et al.*, 2007).

Pleiotropic action, on the scale we've just described, makes the idea of 'a gene for' behavior impossible to maintain. Single genes do not specify behavior, but in combination with each other and with the environment, they may. Some years ago, Sanes and Lichtmann observed that about 100 genes had been implicated in long-term potentiation,

a cellular phenomenon believed to underlie memory processes in the hippocampus (Sanes and Lichtman, 1999). Explaining how many, apparently unrelated, molecules are involved in a complex phenomenon is difficult within the causal model adopted from biochemical genetics, in which genes are arranged in linear pathways. Instead it may be more appropriate to examine genes in networks and assign function to combinations of genes, rather than individual entities.

Genetic architecture in single-gene terms

In populations, the pleiotropic and network attributes of genes have consequences for how genetic variation can produce behavioral variation. Each allele of a gene can potentially contribute in several ways to a phenotype. These contributions, in turn, depend on the partners with which that gene interacts. Variation can thus occur in a restricted portion of a gene's range of activities, if its interacting partners are more sensitive to perturbation in one place than in another. If its interacting partners also come in allelic variants, a further dimension is added.

Phenotypic variation in a population, which is what one measures, is thus not a monotonic function of allelic variation. Instead, it may well represent a more complex fabric than the distribution of alleles alone might suggest. This may seem to present an even more bewildering picture than the traditional view. Its saving grace, however, is that knowing the network nature of a gene's interactions ultimately makes its contributions to phenotype more comprehensible. Further study of the interacting nature of one gene's variation with that of another in

turn brings its population genetic architecture within the realms of comprehensibility.

The two perspectives can be distilled into one: many genes for each behavior (*e pluribus unum*) and many behaviors from each gene (*ex uno plura*) (Greenspan, 2004).

How genes influence behavior

One of us (K.S.K.) has proposed criteria that can be used to judge the validity of a claim that 'X is a gene for Y,' where X is a scientist's favorite gene and Y a particular behavior or psychiatric disorder (Kendler, 2005). Four criteria are appropriate in this context: the *strength of the association*, the *specificity of the relationship*, the *non-contingency* of the effect, and the *causal proximity* of X to Y.

We can summarize this as follows: if gene X has a strong, specific association with a behavioral trait or psychiatric disease Y in all known environments and the physiological pathway from X to Y is short or well-understood, then it may be appropriate to speak of X as a gene for Y.

How often might these criteria apply to genes and human behavioral or psychiatric syndromes? The short answer is 'hardly ever.' As we have documented, the strength of the association between the discovered risk genes (and the even fewer that have been replicated) and behavioral phenotypes are quite weak. They account, at most, for a few percentage points of the total liability, and often even less than that.

Do genes have a specific effect on behavior? Almost certainly not. Variation in gene X hardly ever influences trait Y only, because variants in X affect other phenotypes. Almost never are the genetic influences of trait Y restricted to only gene X. Thus, the association between genes and behaviors are not typically one to one, or one to many, or many to one, but rather many to many. Evolution is to blame for this complexity; it is a tinkerer and promiscuous in the use of genes, taking whatever material is to hand to work on.

Will the relationships we find between genetic variants and psychiatric and behavioral traits be robust—that is, not be contingent on other genes or environmental exposures? As we outlined above, this also is rarely the case. Most genes that influence behavior are quite sensitive to the impact of the genetic background and the environment. The causal pathway from gene to behavioral phenotype is rarely direct or imperturbable. Rather, it is commonly indirect and sensitive to genetic and environmental context.

The last criterion, that of causal proximity, is more complex than those we considered previously and is best illustrated by a brief vignette: A jumbo jet contains about as many parts as there are genes in the human genome. If someone went into the fuselage and removed a 2-foot length of hydraulic cable connecting the cock-pit to the wing flaps, the plane could not take off. Is this piece of equipment then a *cable for flying*?

Most of us would be uneasy answering yes to this question. Why? Because this example violates our conception of *causal proximity*. When we say X is for Y, we expect X to be, to a first approximation, directly and immediately related to Y. That is not the case for the cable and flying. There are many mechanical steps required to get from the function of that cable to a jumbo jet rising off the runway. Saying that the hydraulic cable on a jumbo jet is a cable for flying is probably a lot like saying a particular gene (X) is 'for' behavior. The association is very indirect and will involve many other indirect steps. The 'genes for' behavior hypothesis fails the causal proximity test.

So, in aggregate, this thought experiment indicates that we are almost never justified in using the language or concept of a 'gene for' a behavior or psychiatric trait. The relationship between genes and behavior is too contingent and indirect for such language to be appropriate.

The relative contributions of genes differ

We've reviewed evidence that throughout the animal kingdom, individual differences in behavior are, almost without exception, influenced by genetic factors. Most commonly, these genetic effects are of moderate rather than overwhelming importance, and sometimes genetic influences are even more modest than that. Across a wide variety of species, including humans, the genetic influences on behavior are typically the result of a moderate to large number of individual genes, each of which, on its own, has a small effect on the behavior. In both humans and simpler organisms, the inter-relationship between genes and the environment in their impact on behavior is, at least for a number of traits, likely to be complex. Gene–environment interaction, while still much under-researched, may be widespread in its effects. It is equally likely that genes, through 'outside the skin pathways,' play critical roles in influencing important aspects of the social or physical environment to which the organism is exposed.

It is possible to explain this complex picture of genetic action from the action of networks of genes. The recognition of the ubiquity of pleiotropy means that each gene has, in effect, its own architecture—a distributed pattern of action through the various stages and tissues of the organism (and even potentially reaching outside the organism in its effects on the environment—think of beavers' dams). In this sense, the summed action of the genes is not so much a jigsaw puzzle in which each piece fits together with its immediate neighbors in one spot, but rather a flexible, multilayered network—a viewpoint that was implicit in quantitative genetics and that single-gene genetics has been slowly approaching.

Synergism and network flexibility make it easier to conceive how new properties in behavior can emerge: tune an allele up here, tune another one down there, combine them with some other pre-existing variants, allow it all to ripple through the networks, and boom! You have a new behavior. Although no one is yet at the point of being able to demonstrate this in the lab, the threshold effects that are frequently seen in selection experiments, in which the phenotype does not move at all for many generations and then diverges rapidly, or in which the phenotype fluctuates dramatically before diverging consistently, suggests that such effects can occur in the laboratory, where they can be studied in the ways exemplified above. (Note that this discussion does not add the extra layer of complexity that these gene pathways are likely interacting with a range of important environmental influences.)

At the same time, it is also easy to imagine that the number of ways for genes to influence behavior will be manifold. It will depend on the context of other alleles present (i.e. genetic background), as well as on the actual role (s) a given gene plays in that behavior. The impact of one level, an individual gene, on the other, the gene system, is reciprocal: individual genes influence the network, and the network properties, in turn, influence the action of individual genes.

At the beginning of the single-gene era of behavioral studies, Sydney Brenner remarked, '*Understanding the genetic foundations of behavior may well require solving all of the outstanding questions of biology*' (Brenner, 1974). The years that have passed since then suggest that this may not quite be true. But to the extent that we must understand the nature and principles of how gene networks influence complex phenotypes, the synthesis of quantitative and single-gene approaches that is currently under way would seem to be a prerequisite.

How to understand an explanation

The goal of science is explanation. Scientists want to understand how things work. In this book, our focus has been on behavior. What can we conclude about what controls behavior? In the last sections we've contrasted two ways of explaining genetic action, a single-gene versus a quantitative-genetics approach and we've pointed to the need for their reconciliation, the need to take into account network effects. But a major objection will be, what can a network explain? I understand how a mutation can cause behavior, but a network? This spidery figure of interconnecting lines, what has that ever explained? This problem is the difference between reductionist and systems approaches to biology.

One of the deep debates in philosophy is between reductionism and emergentism.

Reductionism argues that the real causes in our world happen at very basic levels and then work their way upward through increasing levels of complexity. Emergentism takes the position that real causes in our world are more distributed. Some happen at basic levels but others *emerge* from systems that form out of these more basic constituents. Reductionists see true causes as coming from individual parts, the smaller the better. Emergentists see causes as often arising from interactions between these parts. Reductionists like to think in terms of parts. By contrast, emergentists are 'systems thinkers.'

Reductionism views the behavior of complex things as predictable from the behavior of the individual components. So if you understand the little bits, you can predict how the whole thing works. Emergentism disagrees and believes that the behavior of complex things typically does not arise from simply understanding what the parts do in isolation. This is because, as parts interact, new causal effects arise that cannot be simply predicted from the bits themselves.

This is pretty abstract. Let's try to illustrate this with a question about an ecosystem. Imagine a pond with fish, algae, a variety of insects, sunshine, some frogs, and a fisherman or two. A reductionist biologist would examine each individual organism—one at a time—and determine its needs, the waste it produces, what it might eat and what eats it. He would then measure all of the physical properties of the system—the water temperature, pH, degree of sunshine, amount of pollution run-off, etc. The reductionist would then construct a model of the pond ecosystem putting in all of this individual information. He would hope that this model would accurately describe how the pond ecosystem works. The emergentist biologist, by contrast, would argue that this model would be inaccurate because it leaves out important features of the ecosystem. In particular, it does not incorporate the interactions between organisms or between organisms and physical aspects of the environment. Importantly, the emergentist would argue that many of these interactions—which could become quite complex—cannot be predicted from the individual features of the creatures or their physical environment.

How do we come down on this question? We are sympathetic to many of the impulses of reductionist thinking. After all, we really do feel that studying twins and 'heritability'—while a great start—is not the be-all and end-all of the questions that you can ask in the genetics of behavior. You can learn a lot by looking at the parts of these systems—like individual genes or even individual tinier bits like the base pairs of DNA within genes. But, if you pushed us to the wall, we are more sympathetic to emergentist position. That is because, after you go down and study the bits, we are quite convinced that you have to come back up and study systems to understand the way genes really work on behavior. This means not only studying the systems of other genes (although this is quite critical), but also studying the physiological system in which they sit (i.e. nerve cells and pathways), the developmental history of the organism, and the environment in which this organism sits.

One feature of the emergentist position with which we are particularly sympathetic is that it is multilevel. While reductionists always think that the best science studies the smallest of the bits, emergentists see value in many perspectives on complex systems. For example, we don't see that molecular genetic studies are inherently superior to twin or adoption studies. They are asking different questions and provide us with distinct but complementary views on how genes relate to behavior. Sometimes you have to study small bits of the system to

understand how they work. Other times you need to look at whole systems and how they interact with the environment or development. Our job, eventually, is to put all of these perspectives together.

The world of genetics in general and behavioral and psychiatric genetics in particular is, in our view, too 'gene-centric.' If you wanted to be less polite, you could call it 'gene-crazy.' While important, the key issue is how genes actually influence behavior. One important step in this process is identifying the genes that can make a difference, but this is only a start. The real action begins when we try to put these genes back into their gene networks, into nerve cells and nerve networks, and finally into organisms who sit in and interact with their environment. It will not work, we believe, to assume that the little 'bits' of this puzzle all just add together. We know already that they do not.

One of us (R.J.G.) has publicly spoken out about the excess 'gene-centrism' in our field. At a major meeting on genes and behavior, he began the concluding talk of the conference with the memorable phrase, '*Hello. My name is Ralph Greenspan and I am a former gene-holic.*' He went on to outline his own serious study of how genes fit into networks, demonstrating the important limitations of our world view of taking one gene at a time.

Ethics: should I write back to the prisoners?

Before we conclude, we need to continue the discussions we started above about the relationship between genes and moral responsibility. Many people associate strongly the idea of 'genes' and 'determinism.' If something is 'in your genes' then 'God help you,' because there is nothing you can do about it. As shown by the science we have reviewed in this book, that is not how the world works for most of the behaviors we care about. Yes, there are what we call Mendelian genes: for some genes, if you have a defective copy you will inevitably develop dementia or another neurological disease that alters behavior. But if you look at our ability to learn, our risk for depression, schizophrenia, or alcoholism, or our personality, genetic influences are probabilistic and not deterministic. The idea that genes 'seal your fate' might be popular in the public imagination, but it is not science.

That said, it is also true that individuals really differ—as a result of the genes they inherit from their parents—in their personalities and their propensity for many behaviors and (at least for people) their risk for psychiatric and drug-use disorders. Genes do matter and, even though we might wish it, we are not all born equal with respect to these vulnerabilities.

Now comes the hard part. How do genetic influences relate to moral responsibility? Assume you are a judge and someone is brought before you for drunk driving because they injured another individual in a resulting car crash. The accused has a strong genetic risk for alcoholism. Is such an individual less culpable for this injury than someone who had little genetic risk?

We do not have a good answer to this question. There are two thoughts we want to leave you with. Firstly, this is fundamentally not a scientific question but an ethical one. The system of English common law with which the authors are most familiar is generally intolerant of such justifications. After all, no one forced the suspect to consume the alcohol that made

him intoxicated. He should have known about his inability to stop drinking once he started. Secondly, however, it is naïve to think that we are all born with equal risks for alcoholism or criminal behavior. That is a scientific fact that our judicial system may or may not wish to pay attention to. But the question is not a simple one. We know that antisocial personality disorder—which substantially increases the risk for criminal behavior—is moderately influenced by genetic factors. Imagine an individual with a strong genetic propensity toward this disorder who has committed a crime. On the one hand, you could argue that because of this high genetic liability, this individual has reduced culpability and therefore ought to receive a shorter sentence. But you could also argue that, because of this same liability, he would be at especially high risk for a repeat offense and therefore should receive a longer sentence. These and related issues suggest that we should utilize considerable caution in introducing genes into our courtrooms.

We end on a sobering note introduced by the following quotation from Friedel Weinert, a philosopher of science: '*Animals are rigidly controlled by their biology (instincts). But human behavior is largely determined by culture, albeit within limits of biological constraints.*' (Weinert, 2004).

Weinert expresses a common sentiment. The behavior of animals is highly constrained and largely instinctual. By contrast, we, with our big brains, are much freer of our biological roots. This widely held idea has a simple empirical prediction. The degree of genetic influence on animal behavior—that is the heritability—ought to be much higher than what we see in humans. While perhaps commonsensical, this belief is not supported by the facts. As part of a review article written by two of us (K.S.K. and R.J.G.), we reviewed the relevant literature in this area—studies comparing the heritability of a wide range of behaviors in humans and experimental organisms (Kendler and Greenspan, 2006). We here paraphrase our conclusion (which provides a short summary of some of the research we have reviewed in this book).

Genetic risk factors have been found for every psychiatric condition that has been seriously studied and significant genetic influences have also been found for more 'normative' human traits such as personality. Heritability varies meaningfully between psychiatric disorders, with relatively consistent results across studies: from 20 to 30% for most anxiety disorders, 30 to 40% for major depression, 50 to 60% for alcoholism, and 80% or higher for schizophrenia, bipolar illness, and autism. Genetic variation appears to be present for nearly every behavior ever systematically examined in non-human animals. In a review of 57 studies of animal behavior, the mean heritability was reported to be 38% (Meffert *et al.*, 2002). These figures are not precisely comparable, as most of the animal studies were done on laboratory strains under artificial conditions while the human studies were, actually, done under more 'natural' conditions; that is, in natural populations in real environments. However, the available evidence does not support our pre-supposition that our big brains and highly developed culture have freed us and our behavior from the effects of genes. The heritability of human behaviors looks to be at least as high as typical behaviors in other animals. This might be an uncomfortable revelation for our readers. Unlike all other creatures on earth, we have the wonderful gifts of language and advanced culture, art and science, poetry and story-telling. But in our personalities, and our risk for psychiatric and substance-use problems, we are still shaped in important ways by the genes carried in that tiny sperm from our father, swimming for all it is worth, and those waiting in our mother's egg, the target of its ardent quest.

Summary

1. Studies of genes and behavior have traditionally fallen into one of two categories: studies of natural variants or studies of mutations induced in the laboratory. The dichotomy also generally corresponds to small versus large effects of individual genes on a behavioral phenotype.

2. Studies of induced mutations have tended to ignore the role of genetic background, assuming it to be irrelevant to fundamental mechanisms.

3. Studies of natural variants have broadened our picture of how wide an array of genes is capable of affecting a given behavior and how pleiotropic those genes are.

4. The dichotomy can be resolved by recognizing that there is a wide spectrum of gene effects, from small to large, and that behaviors can be affected significantly by many of them.

5. A further resolution comes from the realization that genes do not act in isolation but as part of networks with emergent properties. Thus, genetic influences on behavior work through the organism's system of gene interactions, neuronal interactions and environmental exposures.

6. Saying that genes influence behavior is not equivalent to saying that genes determine behavior. Thus, the study of genes and behavior will not make obsolete the idea of morality.

References

Baker, B.S., Taylor, B.J., and Hall, J.C. (2001). Are complex behaviors specified by dedicated regulatory genes? Reasoning from *Drosophila*. *Cell* **105**:13–24.

Bernet, W., Vnencak-Jones, C.L., Farahany, N., and Montgomery, S.A. (2007). Bad nature, bad nuture and testimony regarding *MAOA* and *SLC6A4* genotyping at murder trials. *J Forensic Sci* **52**:1362–1371.

Brennan, C.A. and Moses, K. (2000). Determination of *Drosophila* photoreceptors: timing is everything. *Cell Mol Life Sci* **57**:195–214.

Brenner, S. (1974). The genetics of *Caenorhabditis elegans*. *Genetics* **77**:71–94.

de Belle, J.S. and Heisenberg, M. (1996). Expression of *Drosophila* mushroom body mutations in alternative genetic backgrounds: a case study of the mushroom body miniature gene (*mbm*). *Proc Natl Acad Sci USA* **93**:9875–9880.

Fischer, R.A. (1930). *The Genetical Theory of Natural Selection*. Oxford: Oxford University Press.

Flint, J. and Mott, R. (2008). Applying mouse complex-trait resources to behavioral genetics. *Nature* **456**:724–727.

Giaever, G., Chu, A.M., Ni, L., Connelly, C., Riles, L., Veronneau, S., Dow, S., Lucau-Danila, A., Anderson, K. *et al.* (2002). Functional profiling of the *Saccharomyces cerevisiae* genome. *Nature* **418**:387–391.

Gitschier, J., Strichartz, G.R., and Hall, L.M. (1980). Saxitoxin binding to sodium channels in head extracts from wild-type and tetrodotoxin-sensitive strains of *Drosophila melanogaster*. *Biochim Biophys Acta* **595**:291–303.

Greenspan, R.J. (2004). E pluribus unum, ex uno plura: quantitative and single-gene perspectives on the study of behavior. *Annu Rev Neurosci* **27**:79–105.

Harris, W.A., Stark, W.S., and Walker, J.A. 1976. Genetic dissection of the photoreceptor system in the compound eye of *Drosophila melanogaster*. *J Physiol* **256**:415–439.

Jordan, K.W., Carbone, M.A., Yamamoto, A., Morgan, T.J., and Mackay, T.F. (2007). Quantitative genomics of locomotor behavior in *Drosophila melanogaster*. *Genome Biol* **8**:R172.

Kelly, L.E. (1974). Temperature-sensitive mutations affecting the regenerative sodium channel in *Drosophila melanogaster*. *Nature* **248**:166–168.

Kendler, K.S. (2005). 'A gene for...': the nature of gene action in psychiatric disorders. *Am J Psychiatry* **162**:1243–1252.

Kendler, K.S. and Greenspan, R.J. (2006). The nature of genetic influences on behavior: lessons from 'simpler' organisms. *Am J Psychiatry* **163**:1683–1694.

Meffert, L.M., Hicks, S.K., and Regan, J.L. (2002). Nonadditive genetic effects in animal behavior. *Am Nat* **160** (Suppl. 6):S198–S213.

Nadeau, J.H. and Frankel, W.N. (2000). The roads from phenotypic variation to gene discovery: mutagenesis versus QTLs. *Nat Genet* **25**:381–384.

Nusslein-Volhard, C. and Wieschaus, E. (1980). Mutations affecting segment number and polarity in *Drosophila*. *Nature* **287**:795–801.

Polaczyk, P.J., Gasperini, R., and Gibson, G. (1998). Naturally occurring genetic variation affects *Drosophila* photoreceptor determination. *Dev Genes Evol* **207**:462–470.

Sanes, J.R. and Lichtman, J.W. (1999). Can molecules explain long-term potentiation? *Nat Neurosci* **2**:597–604.

Weinert, F. (2004). *The Scientist as Philosopher: Philosophical Consequences of Great Scientific Discoveries*. New York/Berlin/Heidelberg: Springer.

Wood, W.B., Edgar, R.S., King, J., Lielausis, I., and Henninger, M. (1968). Bacteriophage assembly. *Fed Proc* **27**:1160–1166.

Appendix *Molecular methods*

The writing-up of an experiment is the hardest thing. It is particularly hard when you haven't done it before, as is the case with the undergraduates and most of the graduates who pass through a molecular biology laboratory, for whom the real excitement lies in what they can do with their hands: the chopping and changing of DNA and the fun of playing with really big machines labeled 'DANGER LASER.' When students write up their experiment, their thesis, the part they like to do first is the bit they understand most, the methods section—possibly the least interesting section of any paper and certainly the least interesting section of any thesis. Here's a typical example of the genre:

> A full-length cDNA encoding mouse Tuba1 (Villasante *et al.*, 1986) or a mutated form (S140G) generated by PCR and checked by DNA sequence analysis was subcloned into a pET23 vector (Novagen). These plasmids were used to express the corresponding unlabeled or ^{35}S-methionine-labeled recombinant protein in host BL21(DE3) *E. coli* cells (Studier *et al.*, 1990). Insoluble inclusion bodies were purified, unfolded in 7M urea (Gao *et al.*, 1992), and quantitated by staining with Coomassie blue following resolution by SDS-PAGE.

> Keays *et al.* (2007).

Obviously this is completely incomprehensible. Yet understanding how experiments are done is essential if you are to have any idea of the validity and robustness of the results. Although we'd like to have you in the lab to show you how things are done, unfortunately health and safety won't allow it. Instead, we have to tell you what it's like to carry out the experiments, what sort of problems you would face, and how challenging it can be.

Nucleic acid biology

Here is a small piece of information that one day may save you severe embarrassment and save the laboratory in which you work a lot of money. One of the laboratory chores given to new arrivals is to design oligonucleotide primers. The task sounds simple. You are given a piece of DNA sequence (usually much longer than this):

CCCCCGGGATATGGGCCCAAGGCCTTAACCGG

Given the rule that the complementary letter of A is T and of C is G, write down the complementary sequence of the last six base pairs of the sequence above (i.e. AACCGG). The answer is CCGGTT. Not, as you would have thought, TTGGCC. The explanation lies in the structure of DNA.

Genetic information is carried in two molecules, deoxyribonucleic acid (DNA) and ribonucleic acid (RNA). Both molecules consist of linear chains of nitrogenous bases bound to a sugar (ribose) and a phosphate backbone (see Figure A.1).

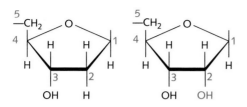

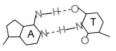

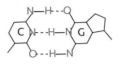

The pentose sugars: deoxyribose on the left is used in DNA; ribose on the right is used in RNA. The five carbon atoms are numbered. Bonds at carbon atoms 3 and 5 give rise to the chain of phosphates and sugars that forms the backbone of DNA, and is responsible for the naming convention. 5′ and 3′ (five prime and three prime)

Two nitrogenous bases: adenine (A) bound to thymine (T)

Two more nitrogenous bases: guanine (G) bound to cytosine (C)

The phosphate group that joins the sugars

Figure A.1 Chemical components of nucleic acids.

DNA contains four nitrogenous bases: adenine (A), guanine (G), cytosine (C), and thymine (T). RNA differs in that it has uracil (U) instead of thymine. The combination of a base, sugar, and phosphate is called a nucleotide, the basic unit of the DNA molecule, a chain (a polymer) of nucleotides (in short, a polynucleotide).

The critical piece of information, and the one everyone forgets, is the following: because of the way the sugars are joined together, one end of each nucleic acid strand will have a terminal sugar residue in which the carbon atom at position number 5 of the ribose molecule is not linked; the carbon atom at the other end of the polynucleotide is at position 3 (look at Figure A.2). The two ends are called 5′ (5 prime) and 3′ (3 prime), respectively. DNA and RNA sequences are written so that the order of bases in a single strand is in the 5′ to 3′ direction.

DNA is a double helix in which two strands are held together by weak hydrogen bonds between opposed base pairs, C pairs to G and A pairs to T (Figure A.2). This is called Watson–Crick pairing because it was discovered by Francis Crick and James Watson, and it explains the rule given above for the complementary letters (A for T, and C for G). Watson–Crick pairing means that the sequence of one strand can be inferred from the other. The two strands are said to be complementary to each other, and this property is exploited whenever DNA is copied.

Because of 5′ and 3′ ends, complementary DNA sequences, written in the standard format from 5′ to 3′, are deeply confusing. The difference between 5′-AACCGG-3′ and 5′-CCGGTT-3′ is the difference between DNA sequencing or a polymerase chain reaction (PCR) working or not working. And making this mistake, ordering the wrong primers, costs laboratories lots

5′ beginning

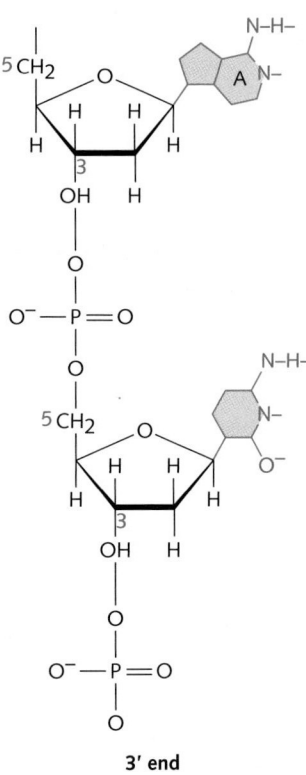

3′ end

DNA put together: a dinucleotide. Sugars are joined at carbon atoms 5 and 3 to phosphates; bases are joined to carbon atom 1 of the sugar.

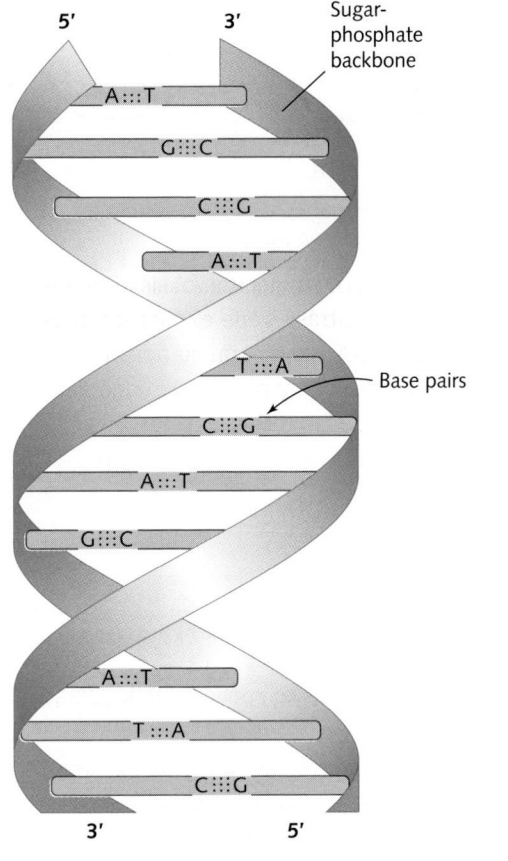

The double helix. Two sugar phosphate backbones hold the bases in position. The strands are not simply reflections of each other, because the molecule has polarity, as indicated by the 5′ and 3′ strands.

Figure A.2 The structure of DNA.

of money. Just for completeness, work out the six base pairs that are complementary to the start of the sequence given previously. If you get it right, you have two primers that can be used to amplify the target DNA by PCR.

There are two structural differences between DNA and RNA that are also worth knowing, because they explain much of the biology. Firstly, RNA has a hydroxyl group on part of its sugar constituent whereas DNA has a hydrogen atom (Figure A.1). The result is that, in most biological environments, RNA is much more unstable than DNA. This makes sense as RNA mediates the expression of genetic information; its production and degradation are tightly controlled. RNA is translated into a linear order of amino acids in proteins according to a three-letter code (e.g. GAA encodes the amino acid glutamine).

Secondly, RNA normally exists as a single molecule, whereas DNA is a double helix. DNA acts as a template for its own production and for the production of RNA in a process called transcription. But DNA is more than a stable repository of encoded protein sequence information; it also contains information that controls the transcription of RNA. Disorder of the template function of DNA is the molecular basis of inherited disease. By contrast, gene expression (the transcription of DNA and the translation of RNA) is not entirely genetically pre-determined. It is highly regulated, but in response to changes in the cellular environment, which in turn reflect changes in the state of the organism.

Key papers

Alberts, B., Johnson, A., Lewis, J., Raff, M., Roberts, K., and Walter, P. (2007). *Molecular Biology of the Cell*. New York: Garland Science, Taylor & Francis Group.
Strachan, T. and Read, A.P. (2003). *Human Molecular Genetics*, 3rd edn. Oxford: Bios Scientific Publishers.

Two classic textbooks to introduce molecular biology. *Molecular Biology of the Cell* is also available online, for free, at http://www.ncbi.nlm.nih.gov/books.

DNA sequencing

DNA sequencing has now become so routine and is becoming so cheap that it will not be long before we think nothing of sequencing whole organisms, and before the basic unit of biology becomes the genome. Until recently, all DNA sequencing was carried out by one of two methods, although only one, chain termination using dideoxynucleotides or Sanger sequencing, after its inventor the Cambridge scientist Fred Sanger, is commonly used (Figure A.3).

Sanger sequencing works by exploiting the cell's ability to copy DNA using an enzyme called a polymerase. In DNA synthesis in the cell, the polymerase uses one strand as a template to construct the other, but it does so only from one end of the molecule: it adds bases to the 3' end of a chain. As stressed above, the idea that a molecule has polarity, that one end is different from the other so you can't just flip it around and expect it to be the same, is critical for understanding many processes in molecular biology.

The enzyme has another important characteristic: it won't work on single-stranded DNA, which makes it difficult to imagine how it could be any use for copying DNA at all. The polymerase needs some help. It operates at the junction between double- and single-stranded DNA, at a place where one strand stops and the other continues. This characteristic means that the action of the polymerase can be targeted to any region in the genome by the simple expedient of using a small piece of single-stranded DNA to define the start site.

It is now straightforward to have chemists synthesize a DNA molecule of about 20 base pairs (lots of companies offer this service), often referred to as an oligonucleotide or oligo. By heating double-stranded DNA so that the two strands break apart, and adding oligonucleotides to the solution (Figure A.3), Watson–Crick pairing means that, as the DNA cools, the oligonucleotides attach, or anneal, to their complementary sequence in the genome (assuming there is one; sometimes you write the sequence down incorrectly when you send off the order, or the company screws up and sends you the wrong oligo). Oligos bound to the template DNA form the structure upon which the polymerase can act. The oligo primes the polymerase to start the job of synthesizing the DNA and the

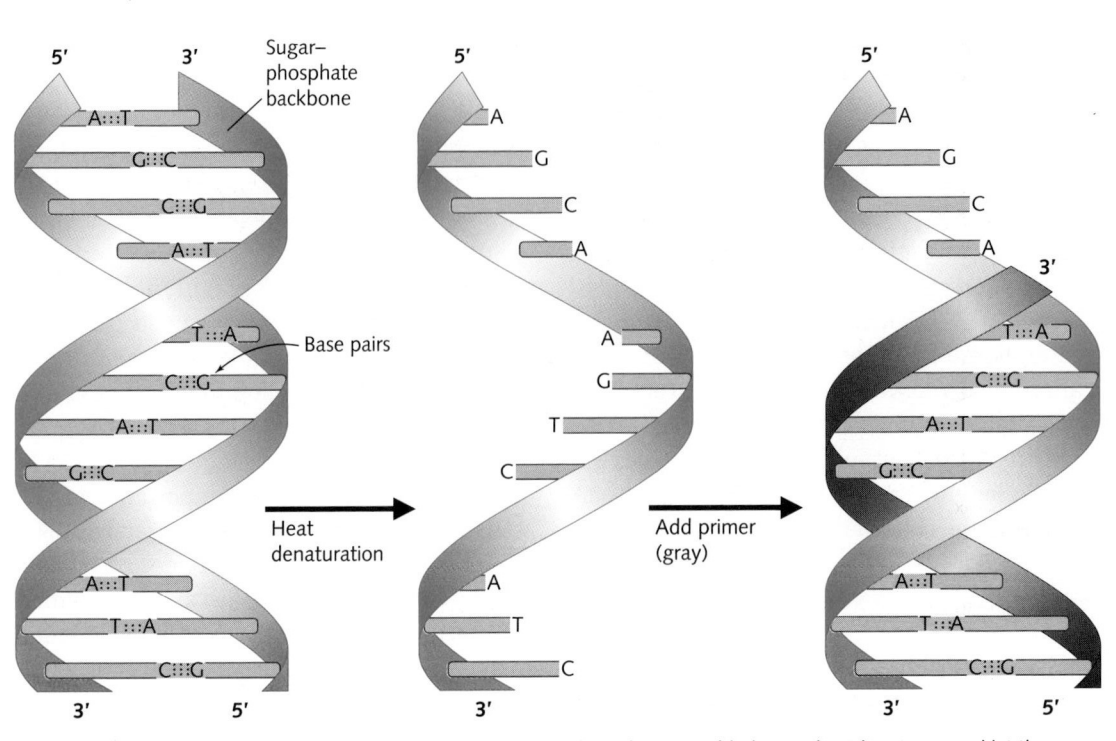

Heat a solution of DNA for a few minutes so that the two strands peal apart. Add oliognucleotide primers and let the mixture cool. The primers (in gray) bind to their complementary sequence.

Figure A.3 DNA sequencing: primer binding.

oligonucleotides used for this purpose are thus often called primers.

Sanger sequencing requires you to add all the ingredients for DNA synthesis, all the components of DNA, the phosphates, sugars, and bases, the oligonucleotides as well as the polymerase and whatever it needs to keep happy, but with one twist: some (but not all) of the bases are chemically altered so that the polymerase can't add anything more to them (Figure A.4). These altered bases are called chain terminators and in their presence the reaction products contain a mix of different-sized molecules. By carrying out the reaction four times, with terminators for each of the four bases, it is possible to create

a set of molecules that have stopped at every base in the sequence. Label the molecules with radioactivity, or fluorescent dyes, and the DNA sequence can be read by measuring the difference in size of the reaction products (Figure A.5).

The practice of DNA sequencing is, however, a little harder than the theory. When the techniques were first introduced, in the late 1970s and 1980s, you could get a PhD for sequencing a gene. Sanger sequencing requires you to add four reagents into four separate tubes at exactly the same moment. You can just about do this by placing the tubes in a benchtop centrifuge, pipetting a drop of reagent onto the edge of each, and then (assuming

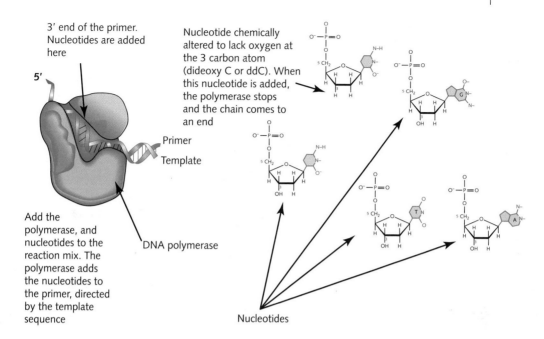

Figure A.4 DNA sequencing: components added.

you had managed to get everything ready in time) briefly press the spin button on the centrifuge (preferably not the button that set the machine spinning for half an hour, which was annoyingly placed next to the brief spin button). You then have to run the reagents out on an acrylamide gel in order to measure their size.

Template sequence ACCGTTGAAGAGT

Reaction 1 (ddA)	A* ACCGTTGA* ACCGTTGAA* ACCGTTGAAGA*
Reaction 2 (ddC)	AC* ACC*
Reaction 3 (ddG)	ACCG* ACCGTTG* ACCGTTGAAG* ACCGTTGAAGAT*
Reaction 4 (ddT)	ACCGT* ACCGTT*

DNA sequencing products from a chain terminator reaction (Sanger sequencing). In each reaction a different chain terminator is added (A* is dideoxy A, C* is dideoxy C, and so on). The reactions produce different size molecules, which can be visualized by incorporating radioactivity into the reaction (such as ^{32}P) and running out the reactions on an acrylamide gel.

An electric current is passed through the gel so that the DNA migrates through the acrylamide, in a process known as electrophoresis: large molecules move more slowly than small molecules, with the result that the DNA is fractionated by size. Acrylamide can resolve differences of a single base pair, a level of resolution necessary for sequencing.

Acrylamide in its liquid form is noxious, but by adding a couple of reagents it polymerizes and turns into a jelly. The trouble is

Figure A.5 DNA sequencing products from a chain terminator reaction (Sanger sequencing).

that it sets within a few minutes, which is all the time you have to pour the liquid between two glass plates that are only a millimeter apart. Pour too slowly and it sets in the flask; pour too quickly and you have neurotoxin running over the bench. And, while pouring, you need to check that the yellow tape you used to bind the two glass plates together doesn't have any leaks. Otherwise, while you're congratulating yourself on your pouring abilities at one end, at the other the stuff is dribbling out onto the floor. Finally, you have to squeeze a thin piece of plastic between the two glass plates so that the gel sets in a horizontal line at the top.

Loading the gel is just as traumatic as making it. Try pulling out the plastic at the top without tearing the gel. If you manage that, you have to insert a thin plastic comb, again without damaging the trembling jelly. When the jelly has set, you pull out the comb (preferably without tearing the acrylamide, otherwise you're back at the beginning) to leave a set of tiny wells ready to receive a few microlitres of highly radioactive DNA. It takes a steady hand to get the solution into the right place; most people give up at the first attempt. But persist, run the gel (you have to wire it up to a high-voltage source and leave it for a few hours), and then face the last challenge: slice through the plastic tape, expose the flank of the gel, insert a knife between the glass plates, and pray that when you lever them apart the gel stays on one plate, rather than tearing down the middle and breaking up into gelatin fragments (some desperate post-docs have been known to collect up these fragments and try to reassemble them, like a sort of radioactive jigsaw puzzle).

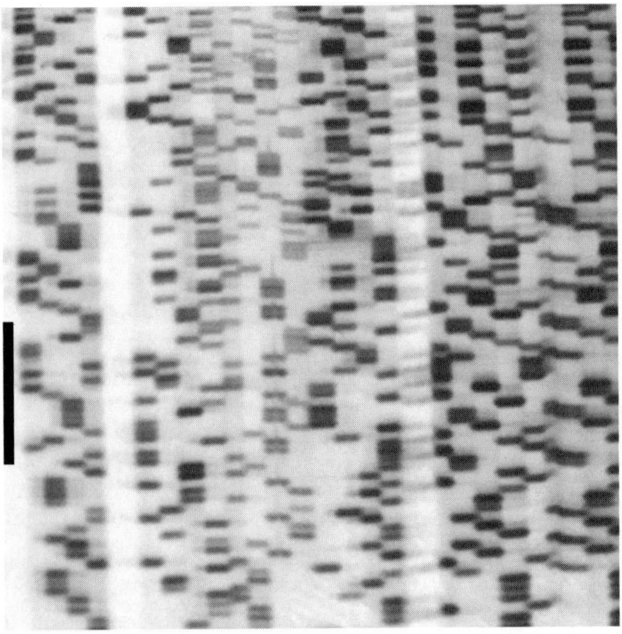

The last part is possibly the worst. Prepare a mixture of methanol (moderately toxic) and acetic acid (highly corrosive). Leave the gel on the glass plate in the liquid for about half an hour (most people put the whole thing into a plastic tray big enough to hold the liquid and gel apparatus)—enough time for the whole lab to reek of vinegar. Then take a piece of blotting paper, place it over the gel so that the gel sticks to the paper and leaves the glass plate behind. Triumphantly, pull out the gel on the paper, dry down for an hour, and leave overnight on film to visualize the neat bands of radioactive DNA (Figure A.6).

Figure A.6 An acrylamide gel showing a DNA sequence. Each lane contains the reaction products with one chain terminator, which in this case have been added in the order A, C, G, and T. The DNA sequence is read from top to bottom so that in the marked region (black bar) the sequence is GAATATACGGGGTCA. Not every reaction works as well as this, as shown by the smeary results on the right of the gel.

Actually, this is not what happens. Instead, part of the gel decides to remain sticking to the glass plate and won't dislodge. However, the blotting paper also won't be parted from the gel, and turns into a sort of mush of acrylamide, radioactive DNA, acetic acid, and methanol, which you have to dispose of in the radioactive waste area quickly, before your laboratory head notices. (This can be difficult if the waste area is already stuffed with your previous efforts.)

One of the great inventions of the 20th century was the creation of automated DNA sequencing machines, machines that did away with the acrylamide gel, thus liberating thousands of postdocs from the chains of DNA sequencing (and genotyping, for acrylamide gels were the standard method to detect small size differences in PCR products, for which see more below).

The introduction of automated sequencing, with the massive increase in data it enabled, meant for the first time that analyzing DNA-derived data was more time-consuming (for a scientist) than creating it, so that a new profession came into existence, the bioinformatician (a post-doc who cannot get experiments to work in the lab but likes playing with computers). That trend has only continued, with the development of ever-faster sequencing machines (Figure A.7). The first machine we had could run a couple of dozen samples; the next ran 96, the one after that could take 384 at a go.

Since 2005, there has been another revolution, a change whose impact on genetics, and biology in general, we are still experiencing. New ways of sequencing DNA, using alternatives to Sanger sequencing have appeared: for example, the use of reversible terminators and pyrosequencing, in which small quantities of nucleotides are provided to the DNA polymerase so that it pauses and the addition of each base is registered by the emission of light. But it is not the novel biochemistry that makes the most difference: it is the scale of data collection.

Figure A.7 Typical sequencing machines available in 2009.

Two landmark papers in 2005 showed that sequencing reactions could be performed on such a small scale that several hundred thousand sequencing templates could be analyzed in parallel. The cost of genome sequencing plummeted and continues to fall, so that we are in sight of the US$1,000 genome. To put this in perspective here is a summary from the US government of the genome sequencing costs using conventional technology:

> The total cost for the working draft [of the human genome] is approximately $300 million worldwide, with roughly half ($150 million) being funded by the US National Institutes of Health. The cost of sequencing the human genome is sometimes reported as $3 billion. However, this figure refers to the original estimate of total funding for the Human Genome Project over a 15-year period (1990–2005) for a wide range of scientific activities related to genomics. These include studies of human diseases, experimental organisms (such as bacteria, yeast, worms, flies and mice), development of new technologies for biological and medical research, computational methods to analyze genomes, and ethical, legal and social issues related to genetics.
>
> http://www.nih.gov/news/pr/jun2000/nhgri-26.htm

Genome sequences can be found on the web: try http://www.genome.ucsc.edu or http://www.ensembl.org, though be warned, it's daunting even for the initiated.

What this will mean for biology is still not clear. When it becomes cheaper to sequence than to genotype, then sequencing will be the way to perform all genetic studies. How we will make sense of that amount of information is not known.

Key papers

Margulies, M., Egholm, M., Altman, W.E., Attiya, S., Bader, J.S., Bemben, L.A., Berka, J., Braverman, M.S., Chen, Y.J. *et al.* (2005). Genome sequencing in microfabricated high-density picolitre reactors. *Nature* **437**:376–380.
Shendure, J., Porreca, G.J., Reppas, N.B., Lin, X., McCutcheon, J.P., Rosenbaum, A.M., Wang, M.D., Zhang, K., Mitra, R.D., and Church, G.M. (2005). Accurate multiplex polony sequencing of an evolved bacterial genome. *Science* **309**:1728–1732.

The papers that introduced the next generation of sequencing technology, already classics in the literature.

Polymerase chain reaction

PCR is a central part of molecular biology. Compared with many molecular techniques, it is relatively straightforward, which means that scientists with scant or even no background in molecular biology can do it, thus democratizing molecular techniques (see Figures A.8 and A.9). PCR explains why genetics has become so pervasive: it is currently easier to look at genes than at any other cellular component.

PCR was introduced to science in the 1980s. For its discovery, Kary Mullis was awarded the 1993 Nobel Prize in Chemistry. This is from his Nobel acceptance speech:

> One Friday night I was driving, as was my custom, from Berkeley up to Mendocino where I had a cabin far away from everything off in the woods. My girlfriend, Jennifer Barnett, was asleep... As I drove through the mountains that night, the

Polymerase chain reaction

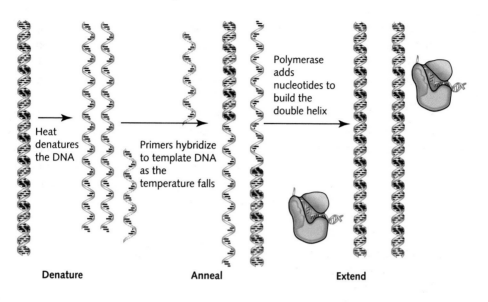

Heat denatures the DNA

Primers hybridize to template DNA as the temperature falls

Polymerase adds nucleotides to build the double helix

Denature　　　　**Anneal**　　　　**Extend**

Figure A.8 Principles of the polymerase chain reaction. The reaction proceeds in three steps: denaturation, annealing and extension, leading to a doubling of the DNA template.

stalks of the California buckeyes heavily in blossom leaned over into the road. The air was moist and cool and filled with their heady aroma. I was thinking ... what if the oligonucleotides in the original extension reaction had been extended so far they could now hybridize to unextended oligonucleotides of the opposite polarity in this second round. The sequence

which they had been extended into would permit that. What would happen? EUREKA!!!! The result would be exactly the same only the signal strength would be doubled. EUREKA again!!!! I could do it intentionally, adding my own deoxynucleoside triphosphates, which were quite soluble in water and legal in California. And again, EUREKA!!!! I could do it over and over again. Every time I did it I would double the signal. ... I stopped the car at mile marker 46.7 on Highway 128.

Kary Mullis is an interesting person: *'The word "eccentric" seems to come up often in connection with Mullis' name: His first published scientific paper, in the premier scientific journal Nature in 1986, described how he viewed the universe while on LSD—pocked with black holes containing antimatter, for which time runs backward. He has been known to*

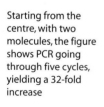

Starting from the centre, with two molecules, the figure shows PCR going through five cycles, yielding a 32-fold increase

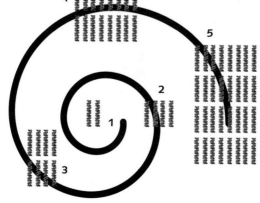

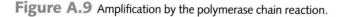

Figure A.9 Amplification by the polymerase chain reaction.

show photographs of nude girlfriends during his lectures, their bodies traced with Mandelbrot fractal patterns. And as a side project, he is developing a company which sells lockets containing the DNA of rock stars' (http://aids-info.net/micha/hiv/aids/mullisspn.html).

Mullis might be strange, but not as weird as PCR. PCR is a biological chain reaction, a way of generating millions of copies of a piece of DNA from as little as a single molecule. It amplifies small pieces of DNA, usually a thousand or fewer base pairs in length (Figure A.9), allowing a scientist to make a solution that contains only the piece of DNA of interest. The template DNA that is copied is of such low concentration that for most purposes it can be ignored. With PCR, it's possible to isolate one tiny fragment from the billions of bases in the genome, and to get sufficient quantities to measure it, to calculate its size (DNA fragments can differ in length as well as base composition), and of course to sequence it.

Heat and alkali are good at separating, or denaturing, the two strands of DNA. Heating up DNA to near boiling point and then cooling it will allow small, single-stranded DNA fragments (oligonucleotides) the opportunity to find their complementary sequence (complementary in the way defined above in the description of DNA structure; see Figure A.2).

PCR needs a pair of oligonucleotides that match opposite strands of DNA on either side of the region we want to amplify (Figure A.8). An enzyme (a polymerase) combines DNA constituents to fill in the gap between the two oligonucleotides, thereby creating a copy of the target DNA. Having a single copy does not help much, but Kary Mullis realized that you could simply repeat the process, starting a chain reaction that doubles the amount of target in each reaction cycle.

That's the theory. In practice, PCR is possibly the most frustrating technique ever invented. You mix together some DNA (colorless fluid), the ingredients of DNA (colorless fluid), some oligonucleotides (colorless fluid) that contain the sequence you want to amplify, an enzyme (colorless fluid), some salt solution (colorless fluid) and some water (colorless fluid). You put the small tube containing all of these colorless ingredients into a machine that repeatedly heats up and then cools down the mixture. At the end, you are supposed to have amplified a small stretch of DNA.

PCR is frustrating not because it is difficult. It's frustrating because it will suddenly decide not to work for no reason that you can think of other than to be deeply frustrating, in an almost personal way. I say this because everyone gets their first (alright sometimes their second) PCR to work, making them feel so happy and confident in their abilities as a molecular biologist that they find it hard to understand why the next time they try it, it doesn't work. And when I say it doesn't work, I mean exactly that. PCR rarely, if ever, almost works: either it works or it doesn't.

In order to know whether PCR has worked, you have to visualize the reaction products (remember the ingredients are all colorless fluids). To do so, you add a dye that binds to the DNA and fluoresces under ultraviolet light (the dye is highly carcinogenic and comes as a deep orange solution; ultraviolet light is also not too good for you). You place the reaction products into the well of an agarose gel (a sort of thick gelatin) through which an electric current is passed. This method, electrophoresis, works on the same principle as the sequencing gels described above: the large molecules move more slowly through the gel than small molecules so the DNA is size fractionated. Acrylamide has a high resolution, separating DNA that differs by a base pair; agarose is used for larger size differences (up to kilobases, or even more).

Agarose gels are a central part of the life of any molecular biology lab. Agarose is a white powder that comes in large plastic tubs. Add water, boil, let it cool, and it turns into a slightly opaque jelly whose consistency depends on the amount of agarose added: at 4% it's like rubber; at 0.5% almost water. Agarose gels are not as difficult to make as acrylamide gels, but they have their own problems. Boiling low concentration solutions, less than 2%, is easy: stick the flask in the microwave, blast it for 2 minutes, and let it cool. For genotyping, where we have to see small fragments of DNA about 300 to 400 base pairs in length, we need to make 4% gels. Boil a 4% gel for 2 minutes and the contents of the flask spew out to cover the interior of the machine with a sticky fluid that rapidly burns to an unpleasant brown color.

Once you've worked out how to coax the microwave into gently heating the fluid, you then have to pour molten agarose into a gel tray, a square plastic tray whose opposing ends are sealed by sticky tape so that when the gel is set, you peel off the tape, allowing an electric current to flow through the exposed gel. The difficulty is in the pouring. If you wait too long, the gel begins to set in the flask, so that when you pour it, lumps fall out, splashing hot molten gel over you and the bench, and lie in the middle of the gel so that, once the gel is set and you try to use it, the electric current (and DNA) won't run smoothly. If you pour too quick, the heat of the gel bends the plastic tray, disrupts the sticky tape, and you have hot gel pouring out onto the bench and onto the floor (excitingly, it may also pour down the cracks at the back of the bench to short out the electrical supply to the whole laboratory).

Most frequently, when you view it under ultraviolet light, there is absolutely nothing at all on the gel. The picture is black, apart from the size marker lane. Occasionally, to add some variety, the entire lane lights up, as if you've generated DNA sufficient to make an entire organism, but no trace of a band. What you're supposed to do when things don't work is to test each of the reagents in turn and find out which is at fault. Is it the DNA, the enzyme, the DNA constituents, or the water you've used? You can spend hours, days, weeks checking each one, ordering in new reagents from company representatives (you know things are not going well when you are on first-name terms with the reps). Laboratory myths speak of methods that yield reliable PCR results and every molecular biologist has her or his favorite additional ingredient. My own advice is to throw everything away, order in fresh material, and start again.

Genotyping microsatellites

Before the advent of PCR it was possible to sequence and to genotype, but by the 1990s PCR-based methods replaced the earlier techniques. And while PCR will in its turn be overtaken by new genotyping assays and new sequencing methods, most of the single-nucleotide polymorphisms (SNP) assays used in linkage, candidate gene, and whole-genome association studies still depend on it.

For many years, genotyping using PCR meant amplifying small repetitive sequences in the genome that are polymorphic between individuals. While this approach has been largely superseded by SNP assays, it is not yet defunct and it provides a simple introduction to genotyping methodology.

Many species, including ours, have stretches of repetitive DNA that looks like this—CACACACACACACAC—dispersed throughout the genome. No one knows what they do or why they are there. Most of them differ in size between individuals, so think of them as God's gift to molecular geneticists: a molecular tag for each segment of every chromosome.

Such tags are tremendously useful because, for genetic mapping, using linkage for example, we need to determine whether a segment of chromosome comes from the mother or father of a subject (or when mapping using crosses between two inbred strains of laboratory mice, whether the segment comes from strain A or strain B). Measuring the repeats would give us this answer, but how do we measure the size of part of a molecule? Any genotyping method has to get over two seemingly insurmountable problems: the vanishingly small amounts of DNA we want to detect, and the fact that those bits of DNA are such a minute part of a much larger structure; the target might be just 20 base pairs in a human genome that measures 3.3 gigabases ('giga' here means 10^9, so that is less than one part in 1,000,000,000). PCR deals with both of these problems at once. The sequence specificity of PCR makes it possible to analyze just the region of interest: primers are designed to sequences that flank the repeat so that the amplification reaction works uniquely on that location in the genome (see above description of PCR, and Figures A.8 and A.9). PCR produces sufficient DNA from that locus for it to be visible as a band on a gel. As both alleles are amplified, it is then possible to tell them apart by determining which is larger: larger fragments run more slowly on the gel.

Assume there are two alleles—generally true in mouse studies but not generally true in human studies where there could be a dozen or more alleles in any given population (but never more than two in any one individual!). We will call *a* the smaller allele containing ten repeats of the dinucleotide CA, and *b* the larger allele containing 20 repeats. We determine whether the genotype is *aa*, *bb*, or *ab* by comparing the size of the amplified DNA. At the end of the experiment (a couple of hours for the PCR, an hour to run the gel), you can take a photograph of a set of neat bands (Figure A.10).

The DNA in the gel is bound to a dye which fluoresces under ultraviolet light, allowing the products of PCR to be photographed, as shown in Figure A.10. In this example, fluorescent bands appear black, but often gel photos are printed with white bands, just as you would see them under the UV source. There are eight lanes in this gel, one for each individual analyzed by PCR. At the bottom, where the smallest pieces of DNA run, in every lane are some black blobs. These are the detritus of PCR, mostly the excess primers, which may have bound to each other. At the top of the gel are the bands that tell us the genotypes of the eight individuals.

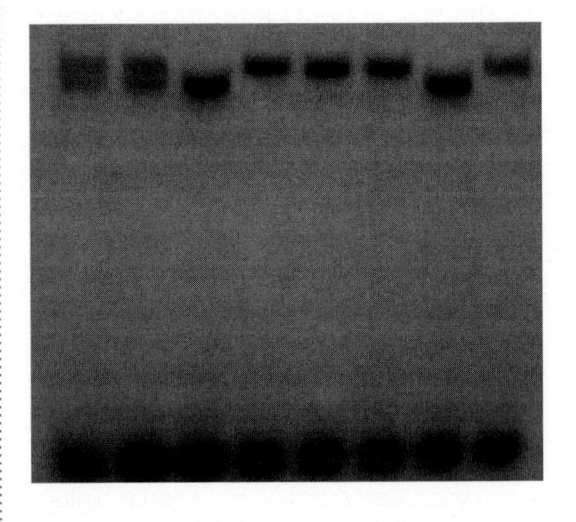

Figure A.10 Example of an agarose gel showing the results of a PCR amplification.

There are two band sizes, corresponding to the two alleles, *a* and *b*. Individuals with two bands have the genotype *ab*, while the others are homozygotes, *aa* or *bb*. It's quite easy to genotype individuals from this gel. The first individual is *ab*, the second is *ab*, the third *bb*, the fourth *aa*, and so on. Things are more difficult with multiple alleles; they are harder to tell apart, and usually they are analyzed not on agarose but on acrylamide (the same noxious substance used in sequencing reactions) or another form of polymer that can resolve small size differences (the high-throughput capillary machines, able to run 96 samples at once, used this approach).

The short lengths of CA repeats used as markers are known as microsatellites (there are blocks of much larger repeats (although not of CA motifs) near the centromeres of chromosomes called satellites and there are slightly larger repeats spread across the genome called mini-satellites). Microsatellite genotyping was largely replaced by typing single base-pair changes (SNPs) when it became possible to type these in a high-throughput and reliable fashion.

Genotyping SNPs

'1993 *and still kit free*' is graffiti I found in a lab on the east coast of the USA. If you were working in a molecular biology in the 1980s, you made everything yourself, buying only chemicals from chemical companies like Sigma and otherwise making up the reagents from scratch, purifying from bacteria the enzymes needed for cutting up and joining DNA. Only amateurs bought kits to carry out their molecular biology. As molecular biology grew, with more grant money available and more demand for reagents, biotech companies

began to sell what any post-doc could easily make. For example, by suspending bacteria in cold water you can make them competent to take up DNA and grow it in sufficient quantities for sequencing. The process takes a few hours and costs a few pennies. Nevertheless, you can, and many people do, buy such bacteria from companies.

By 2003, I doubt if any lab was kit free. Scorned by purists, kits were just one sign of ever closer penetration by industry into molecular biology. Nowhere has this been more obvious than in the way genotyping is carried out. All the theoretical and available empirical evidence pointed to the need to carry out genotyping on an industrial scale, and that is exactly what eventually happened.

The invention that made this possible was '*light-directed, spatially addressable parallel chemical synthesis*,' a suitably intimidating description of a technology that relegated hand-made genotyping to history, and one that was published 4 years before Risch and Merikangas asked for the development of novel technologies (Fodor *et al.*, 1991). The genotyping principle is nothing new, based on hybridization, the ability of one strand of DNA to recognize, and bind to, its complementary partner, on the basis that A binds specifically to T and C binds specifically to G. So the sequence ACTGGCTGGC would bind to TGACCGACCG (there's a slight complication in that the strands have polarity, so that the complement of ATCGGCTGGC is, chemically speaking, GCCAGCCCAGT, a mistake that most of us make once—or dare I admit it—even twice in our laboratory lives). Hybridization between DNA strands is fussy enough to complain about a single mismatch so ACTGGCTGGC won't bind as well to TGACCG**T**CCG. This perfectionism can be exploited to detect polymorphisms, as had been known for many years. The problem was that synthesizing oligonucleotides is expensive and time-consuming (and in the method we use, fairly smelly). So making hundreds of thousands seemed out of the question, until along came photolithography.

Photolithography is the process used to manufacture electronic circuits on silicon. It uses light to activate a reaction on a solid surface and its advantage is that thousands of reactions can be independently controlled by determining which molecules on the surface are exposed to light, for example by using a mask to obscure a proportion of the reactions from the light source. Extraordinarily high resolution can be achieved; for example, with electron beam lithography, patterns at a density of 10^{10} cm^{-2} are possible. Applying photolithography to synthesize oligonucleotides directly onto glass means that hundreds of thousands can be made, and, because the manufacture is on such a small scale, using so few reagents, it's relatively cheap.

Here is one method now currently used to detect SNPs. Suppose the two alleles of a SNP are embedded in a sequence as follows, an A allele ACTGGCTGGC**A**CGGTCCTAAA and a T allele ACTGGCTGGC**T**CGGTCCTAAA. Oligonucleotides are synthesized that correspond to a perfect match of both the A and T alleles. But, in addition, to determine specificity in binding, mismatch probes are synthesized for each allele, differing from the perfect match by one nucleotide. In fact, for each SNP, many oligonucleotides are made with slight variations in matches, mismatches, and length of flanking sequence around the SNP. Genomic DNA, purified and labelled with a fluorescent dye, is then hybridized to the array of oligonucleotides and the intensity of hybridization—a measure of how well the genomic DNA sticks

to the oligonucleotides—is measured by the amount of fluorescence seen at each probe.

An example of a result from genotyping a single SNP is shown in Figure A.11, taken from one of the first papers to demonstrate that hundreds of thousands of SNPs could be genotyped in this manner (Matsuzaki *et al.*, 2004). The measure plotted on the two axes reflects the hybridization intensity of one allele compared with signals from both alleles. The three circles points indicate the positions of the three genotypes, homozygote for an A allele (A/A), heterozygote (A/T) in the middle, and homozygote for T (T/T). Now it's easy viewing this plot for us to see this pattern, but we're not going to look at hundreds of thousands of these. There are far too many for manual (i.e. human) genotyping; the process has to be automated. The computer algorithm used in this case decided that one of the heterozygote genotypes was not clear (marked with a cross in the centre of Figure A.11). As the methods developed, better quality control and automation came to be a priority, work for ever more computational biologists.

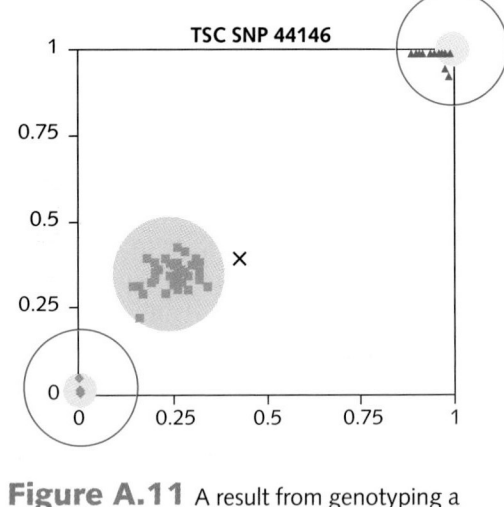

Figure A.11 A result from genotyping a single SNP.
Source: Matsuzaki *et al.* (2004).

Geneticists now had a choice. They could buy the arrays and the expensive machinery that reads them (remember the arrays have hundreds of thousands of individual spots) and then perform the DNA purification, labeling, and hybridization reactions themselves, although, as Affymetrix, one of the leading manufacturers of genotyping technology, points out in their GeneChip Mapping 100K Assay manual (© Affymetrix, 2004), some of the components involved can be hazardous.

Alternatively, you can just send off the DNA to the company and they do the whole process for you, sending back terabytes of data. Academic genotyping laboratories began to be outnumbered by computer scientists, bioinformaticians, and statistical geneticists.

Cloning and sequencing: methods to find disease mutations

Before the completion of the human genome project, the work needed to identify a causative mutation consisted primarily of cloning DNA. DNA sequencing by hand is challenging (see the above section on sequencing), but it is child's play compared with cloning DNA. Frequently the steps are described with helpful diagrams of fragments of human DNA (usually portrayed as wavy lines) joining up with other wavy lines (DNA sequences that can grow in bacteria) (see Figure A.12 for an example).

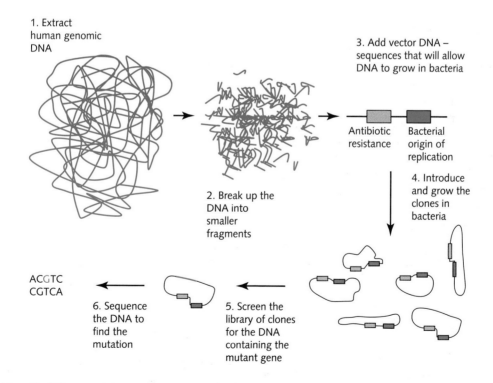

Figure A.12 Outline of the process of cloning DNA.

The result is a set of (usually) circular pieces of DNA, part human, part bacterium. A human genome is thus turned into a library of overlapping fragments, clones that are propagated in bacteria, one of which contains the mutation giving rise to disease. Once the correct clone is found, and sequenced, the mutation that causes the disease will be discovered. This, in brief, is positional cloning (Collins, 1995).

Rarely, however, does cloning proceed smoothly. Preparing human DNA alone can take a week; it's too big, too small, too dirty or too mixed up with the other reagents in the freezer (all DNA samples are the same colorless liquid; unfortunately, there is no easy way of knowing what is in a tube if things get mixed up). The bacteria either won't grow, or they get infected with some horrible virus that keeps killing them, or they won't take up the human DNA. And then the critical sequence, the one most likely to contain the mutation, turns out to be toxic to bacteria so some other way of growing it has to be found (it is a generally acknowledged truth that the disease gene is always in the region you could not clone).

After cloning the DNA and using markers to map the mutation, the causative mutation has to be found. Even the complete DNA sequence doesn't guarantee success because a DNA sequence doesn't come with the genes annotated. The presence of a gene has to be proven, for example by finding regions that are transcribed into RNA. Unlike DNA, which, in some circumstances, can stay around for millions of years, RNA disappears at the first opportunity. For some reason I've never understood, the only thing in a molecular biology laboratory that does not immediately destroy RNA is tissue paper. Everything else (particularly your fingers) is coated with enzymes that break down any RNA that hasn't already disintegrated of its own accord (never touch the laboratory benches of those working with RNA; their life is hard enough as it is).

Because it's so unstable, the only easy way to keep RNA is to turn it into DNA. Again, this is easier said than done: the enzyme that converts RNA to DNA has a tendency to be lazy and give up half way through the job, so getting full-length transcripts requires a lot of skill and patience. Having the transcript, you then have to sequence it, determine its structure, and, ideally, find a mutation in the DNA that produces it. Sequencing the transcript is difficult: one end of the transcript, the tail, which is almost always the only bit you have, consists of a string of A residues (i.e. the sequence is AAAAAAAAAA, etc.). The sequencing enzyme, a polymerase that has to copy the DNA, gets confused by the repetitive string and produces different lengths. These make the sequence unreadable.

Supposing that these technical problems are overcome, which eventually they will be, and the sequence of all of the genes in the region containing the disease-causing mutation is available, what happens next? In a condition like Huntington's disease or cystic fibrosis, when you know without argument who has the disease and who has not, proving that a sequence variant is the causative mutation requires demonstrating two things: that the sequence variant is only present in the sick, and that it does something terrible to the protein that is translated from the RNA sequence. The first candidate genes for Huntington's disease had features that made them seem plausible (expressed in the brain, for instance), but there was nothing in the sequence of affected individuals that marked them out. Mutation analysis was primary evidence that the gene associated with cystic fibrosis had been found: part of the gene's DNA was missing in patients, never in controls. The deletion altered the protein. The Huntington's gene mutation, true to form, was more complicated: a tandem

repeat of three base pairs that was longer in patients than controls. The repeat altered the protein (it increased its size), but exactly what that did to cause disease took a long time to establish.

Key papers

Collins, F. (1995). Positional cloning moves from perditional to traditional. *Nat Gen* **9**:347–350.

Lander, E.S., Linton, L.M., Birren, B., Nusbaum, C., Zody, M.C., Baldwin, J., Devon, K., Dewar, K., Doyle M. *et al.* (2001). Initial sequencing and analysis of the human genome. *Nature* **409**:860–921.

Venter, J.C., Adams, M.D., Myers, E.W., Li, P.W., Mural, R.J., Sutton, G.G., Smith, H.O., Yandell, M., Evans, C.A. *et al.* (2001). The sequence of the human genome. *Science* **291**:1304–1351.

Waterston, R.H., Lindblad-Toh, K., Birney, E., Rogers, J., Abril, J.F., Agarwal, P., Agarwala, R., Ainscough, R., Alexandersson, M. *et al.* (2002). Initial sequencing and comparative analysis of the mouse genome. *Nature* **420**:520–562.

The first paper gives a brief description of positional cloning, just before the publication of genome sequences made the technology (almost) redundant. The last three—the genome papers—describe the first mammalian genomes sequenced, human and mouse. They include an historical introduction, as well as detailed and accessible descriptions of the terminology. Together, these papers are a good place to start for an introduction to the relevant molecular biology.

Genetic engineering

The mouse is genetically normal except for a select group of novel genes that are added to the genome. A DNA clone of these genes is injected into the fertilized mouse egg, thus linking them to the chromosomal DNA in the zygote, which is subsequently inherited by cells of the resulting embryo. Before injection into the germ line, these genes are custom designed so they can be 'turned on' and expressed only in specific mouse tissue and along a predictable timetable.

This quote doesn't come from a scientific article, nor from a text book, nor a news report. It's from a novel, *White Teeth* by Zadie Smith. And, as the character dealing with this information points out, it is 'scary shit.' Few advances in biology have captured the imagination more than genetic engineering, the ability to change the genome of an organism that confers almost divine attributes on the scientists who do this kind of work. To delete or insert genes, to make changes that take away abilities or improve them, or even endow animals with new facilities, were all impossible aims in the 1980s. By the turn of the century, the methods had become routine and introduced a completely new way of using genetics to understand physiology and, more recently, behavior.

On 8th October 2007, the winners of the Nobel Prize in Physiology or Medicine were announced, for the discovery of how to genetically engineer mice. There were three winners: Mario Capecchi, born in 1937 in Verona and now at the University of Utah, Salt Lake City; Martin Evans born in 1941, now working in Cardiff, UK; and Oliver Smithies, born in Yorkshire in 1925 and now at the University of North Carolina at Chapel Hill. Of the three, Mario Capecchi's pathway to a Nobel Prize is the most unusual. His mother Lucy Ramberg was a poet and his father, Luciano Capecchi, an Italian air-force pilot. The Nazis interned his mother in the Dachau concentration camp when he was four and a half, leaving him to

fend for himself. Living on the streets, with other children, he survived by begging and stealing until his mother found him in a hospital, when he was nine, and took him to live with his uncle in a Quaker community north of Philadelphia. Capecchi started school in the USA knowing no English and unable to read or write in any language. Not surprisingly, his teachers said he would never go to college. Instead, he contributed to one of the key developments in biology.

The first ingredient: embryonic stem cells

Genetic engineering in the mouse had its roots in two lines of basic investigation: homologous recombination (in which DNA is exchanged between two similar or identical sequences) and embryonic stem cells (stem cells derived from the inner cell mass of an early-stage embryo known as a blastocyst). The former made it possible to target a gene; the latter made it possible to grow an entire animal from a single cell. One of the critical early steps towards finding mouse stem cells was taken when Leroy Stevens developed a strain of mice (129Sv) that spontaneously developed a form of testicular cancer known as a teratoma. Teratomas are derived from the germ line, from the ovaries for example, and are famous for containing a complex mixture of tissue types, in different stages of differentiation. As eggs in the ovary can turn into any cell type (they are 'pluripotent'), an ovarian teratoma can, and will, contain all sorts of tissue.

Teratomas from the 129Sv mouse strain can be grown from a single transplanted cell, and can be made to differentiate relatively easily into a diverse array of tissues: they give rise to beating heart muscle, nerve, skin, cartilage, tooth, and bone. The fact that a single cell could turn into all these tissues indicated the potential that teratoma cells, or rather embryonal carcinoma cells, had. Could this ability be exploited? Could they be used to grow an entire animal?

Many investigations had shown a close relationship between embryonal carcinoma cells and an early embryo, but there appeared to be no way to grow cells in the laboratory that had the potential to turn into a complete mouse: a pluripotential stem cell line was needed. Achieving this was the breakthrough that led eventually to Martin Evans' Nobel Prize. To do so Evans turned to investigating the blastocysts of strain 129Sv mice. A blastocyst is at a stage of development between the fertilized egg cell and the embryo, a small mass of dividing cells that has not yet implanted into the wall of the womb. Blastocysts were a likely source of pluripotent stem cells, but they are very small, very difficult to isolate, and the cells are programmed to turn into mice, not to sit about in plastic Petri dishes waiting to be tampered with by embryologists.

Evans worked with Martin Kaufman, who had shown that it was possible to stop blastocysts developing by removing the ovaries of mothers just after they had become pregnant: without the hormonal cue, blastocysts seemed not to know what do. Rather than implant in the uterine wall and continue developing, they would grow a little, but remained freely floating in the womb. After isolating artificially arrested blastocysts, Evans and Kaufmann were able to show that a proportion of the cells in the blastocyst behaved like embryonal carcinoma cells: they could be made to differentiate and they formed teratomas. These proved to be the pluripotent stem

cells Evans was after and he showed that, under the appropriate conditions, they could be grown in the laboratory without undergoing further differentiation. In the publication in *Nature* in 1981 announcing their discovery, the cells were called EK cells (based on the authors initials, Evans–Kaufman) but the name that stuck, ES cells (embryonic stem cells), was introduced a year later (by Gail Martin). The 129Sv mouse strain, from which the first ES cells were derived, was to become famous the world over as the strain in which genetic engineering is carried out.

The next step was to show that ES cells could form a mouse. Evans, working with Liz Robertson and Allan Bradley, injected between 8 and 12 ES cells into the cavity of blastocysts from an albino mouse. The ES cells mixed with the host blastocyst cells and when re-implanted into the uterus were capable of developing to term. The resulting mouse contained a mix of genetic material, differentiated by coat color: skin derived from the ES cells was black; skin derived from the host blastocyst was white. An animal in which cells have different genetic constitutions (in this case, some from the blastocyst and some from the ES cells) is called a chimera. Figure A.13 shows the results from their publication showing that the technique worked.

Key paper

Bradley, A., Evans, M., Kaufman, M.H., and Robertson, E. (1984). Formation of germ-line chimaeras from embryo-derived teratocarcinoma cell lines. *Nature* **309**: 255–256.

The paper describing the production of chimaeras.

This bald summary of the work ignores the fact that, at the time, the outcome of the experiments

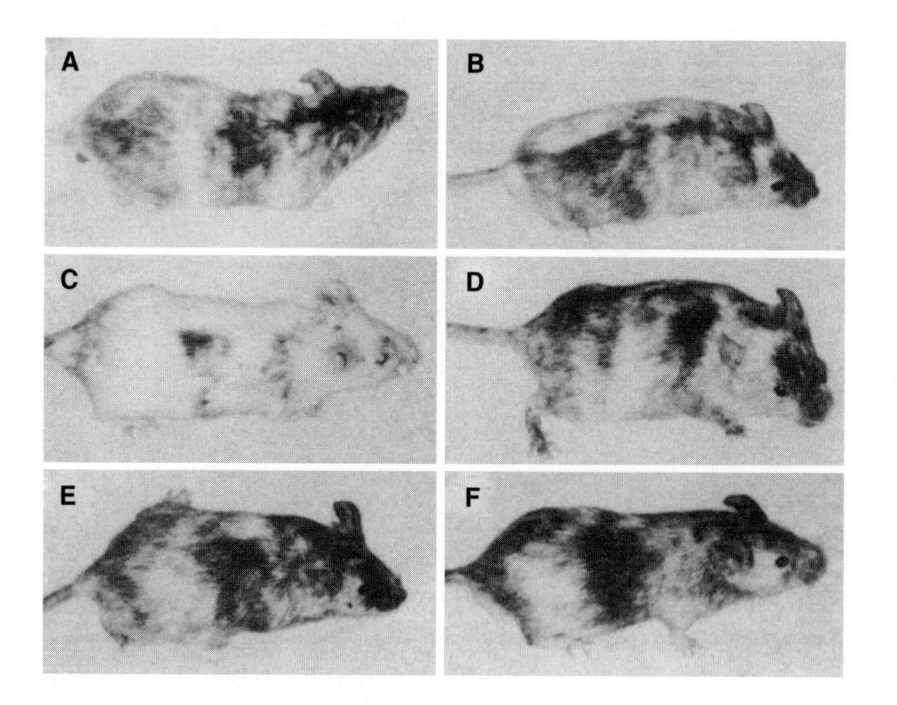

Figure A.13 Germ line chimaeras as shown by coat colour variation.
Source: Bradley *et al.* 1984.

was uncertain and the value unknown. The seemingly dry developmental experiments using tissues with unpronounceable names doesn't immediately strike one as an obvious candidate for a technology that would transform biology. And Evans' success was not won easily:

> There have been numbers of times when the funding's been very difficult... I had some really nice people with me... Liz Robertson, Allan Bradley, Alan Clark, among others. And really because of the funding situation, all of them had to leave and go elsewhere, and I was left really all by myself to start it all over again. And I remember one of my colleagues saying to me on one of these miserable sort of pessimistic approaches, saying, okay Martin, you've done it once. You'll never do it again. You're finished.

> http://www.laskerfoundation.org/awards/2001_b_interview_evans.htm

It's hard to imagine this sort of admonition ever occurring in the USA, where work on homologous recombination, the second component of genetic engineering, was going on.

The second ingredient: homologous recombination

British and US approaches to failure may differ, but on neither side of the Atlantic was there much optimism that homologous recombination would lead anywhere. Harold Varmus, himself already a Nobel Laureate, was to remark later in conversation with Capecchi,

'*I remember actually our labs had some collaborative activity in those early stages. And I frankly could not have said then that I would have been able to foresee that this method would transform the way we did biology.*'

Interest in recombination grew out of work into how to incorporate DNA into the genomes of mammalian cells. Using a fine glass pipette it's possible to inject DNA into the nucleus of a cell. In so doing, occasionally the DNA gets taken up and becomes part of the cell's DNA. The exogenous DNA integrates into the host cell. With foreign DNA the cell can produce foreign protein, in fact any protein that the DNA encodes. For example, inject DNA that encodes for antibiotic resistance and cells that take up the DNA will grow in the presence of an antibiotic that would otherwise kill the cells.

In 1980 came the first report that DNA injected into eggs could produce a mouse with a heritable alteration of its germ line. Gene expression by this injection method, giving rise to what became known as a transgenic mouse, was variable. When linear DNA is injected into fertilized eggs, about 25% of mice are born carrying one or more copies of the transgene. About 70% of the mice have the transgene in all cells, including the germ cells, so that the inserted DNA is inherited. In the other 30%, transgenes are present in only a fraction of cells (the mice are chimeras, because, like the mice generated by mixing ES and blastocysts described above, they contain cells of two different genetic constitutions).

Capecchi was struck by something that happened to the DNA in this process: '*We were using very fine glass needles and put them [DNA molecules] right into the nucleus. And what we found was that indeed they were randomly inserted into the genome.*' But although the site of integration might be random, what happened at that site did not look random. Multiple copies of the

DNA molecules integrated into the same position. '*The molecules were all head to head—that is, they all had the same orientation. That meant one of two possibilities. One was that all those molecules were being synthesized in the cell that way—we would inject one molecule and it was acting as a template to make a lot more. We were able to rule out this so called synthesis model. The other possibility was that there was a machinery in the cell which recombined or put things together according to the same sequences. This is called homologous recombination, and these are homologous sequences.*'

Everyone had assumed that homologous recombination only occurred in the sex cells, as a way of exchanging material between maternal and paternal chromosomes. What Capecchi and Smithies suggested was that homologous recombination might be going on in cells that had nothing to do with sex, such as skin cells or cells grown in tissue culture. If all cells had this machinery, then researchers could exploit it by tricking cells into carrying out homologous recombination using the DNA they added. So, for example, Smithies showed that he could add two bits of DNA into cultured mammalian cells and the cell's machinery would recombine the two pieces to generate a new DNA structure. As Capecchi saw it, '*If all cells have that machinery we could actually exploit it to do what we wanted. And what we were interested in doing with this machinery was to use it to perform exchanges between an exogenous, newly added DNA sequence, and the same DNA sequence of the chromosome of a living cell. That would allow us to modify the whole program involved in specifying cell function.*'

At the time, many people were trying to use viruses to introduce DNA into cells; the idea was that the virus could deliver DNA into the nucleus, where it would integrate, and that if this process could be controlled and carried out early in development, by infecting pre-implantation embryos, then a germ-line

alteration of the mouse genome might be possible. Capecchi and Smithies tried using homologous recombination rather than a virus to get the DNA into the cell; as Smithies showed, you could do this in cell culture, but to get the integrated DNA into an entire mouse the process would have to happen in a germ-line cell that could develop into an embryo.

The third ingredient: homologous recombination in ES cells

Both Capecchi and Smithies recall a conference where they heard about Martin Evans' work on ES cells. Clearly, if homologous recombination could be carried out in ES cells, and if ES cells could be made to form a chimeric embryo, there was the possibility for the first time of engineering a mutation in a mammal.

Capecchi describes what happened:

> It was both exciting and also a disaster. I mean we actually, we had made the mice. And then we found out our mouse colony was infected. With a virus, a hepatitis virus. And I called Bar Harbor [a mouse laboratory] up, and they said, 'The best thing to do is just to start over, eliminate the colony.' ...We actually had to get money to rebuild a new facility in order to shut ourselves off from the other people and then start all over again. So that, you know, I had a peak and a real drop, because we never found out whether we were getting germ-like chimeras. When we had the chimeras and then had to quit...

With a new, clean, mouse house, an efficient method of delivering the DNA into the nucleus (Capecchi added the DNA to cultured ES cells and passed an brief pulse of electricity through the mixture, sufficient to disrupt the membranes briefly), and a technique to identify the correctly targeted cells (antibiotic selection), genetic engineering finally worked. By the end of the century, the technology was making a considerable impact on behavioral research.

Key paper

Capecchi, M.R. (1989). Altering the genome by homologous recombination. *Science* **244**: 1288–1292.

A description of homologous recombination from one of its pioneers.

Lots of things can, and do, go wrong in making a mutant mouse. Usually the job entails making a construct. 'Construct' is one of those lapidary terms that makes the work of molecular biologists sound important. It means a piece of DNA that has been constructed in the laboratory, usually by sticking together other pieces of DNA. Targeting constructs have to have a selectable marker, an antibiotic resistance gene whose incorporation into the DNA of the ES cells means we can select those cells that have taken up the DNA. They also have to have a piece of DNA homologous to the DNA in the mouse so that homologous recombination can take place. And they need sequences that allow the DNA to replicate in bacteria (the molecular biologist's favorite organism for making constructs).

There are a host of other things you can put in, to track the changes made, delete sequences, add things in later, and so on. The simplest design is to make a mutant by removing a critical part of a gene, for instance by replacing the first part

of a gene with an antibiotic resistance gene. In essence, make a construct that contains about a couple of thousand base pairs of the sequence leading up to the bit you want to delete, followed by the antibiotic resistance gene sequence and then followed by another couple of thousand base pairs of sequence identical to that immediately after the bit you want to delete. In the ES cells, the two matching regions will line up and homologous recombination will occur, swapping the entire segment so that the ES cell ends up with the antibiotic resistance gene instead of the critical piece of gene.

In fact, this is only one of several outcomes (which include nothing happening at all, the most likely event, but one we can ignore as cells in which that happens die when exposed to the antibiotic because they don't have the resistance gene). Much of the work in designing the construct goes into making sure we get the outcome we want, and that we can check it has actually happened. And designing and building mice is now a whole new career option, requiring a mastery of splinkerettes, floxing, recombineering, and more neologisms than Lewis Carroll ever thought up.

In the days before genome sequences were available, the most onerous job was getting the homologous sequence. In the worst case, the gene might not have been cloned. In other cases only the RNA had been cloned (turned into a DNA copy using a reverse transcriptase enzyme) so that the structure of the gene still had to be worked out and the flanking sequences suitable for targeting to be found. The sort of problem to avoid was having the targeting sequences point in the wrong direction, or coming from the wrong mouse strain so that they wouldn't match the DNA in the ES lines. Nowadays, the necessary information is available on the genome websites. That makes the task easier, but not easy.

The next hard part was putting the pieces together. There are many ways to do this, mostly involving some PCR and now also exploiting homologous recombination in bacteria. Whatever method you employ, it almost always takes much longer than ever anticipated. When you finally give your construct to whoever is putting it into cells for you, you have more months of waiting to see whether the targeted cells will be incorporated into the germ line of a mouse (and therefore become inherited). Once it has gone into the germ line, two mutant mice have to be mated to produce a homozygote (targeting only hits one chromosome, so the mutants produced by homologous recombination are heterozygotes). Finally, there is always the chance that the mutant mouse might not be viable (a polite way of saying they all might end up dead before or shortly after birth). A classic problem with gene targeting is that the absence of the gene leads to absence of mouse because the gene makes a product vital to life (Then, there is also the equally vexing outcome of three or more years of hard work when the mutant turns out to have nothing wrong at all.)

Mutagenizing flies

Fly geneticists have for years used transposable elements to introduce DNA into flies. Transposable elements (or transposons) are DNA segments capable of changing their positions within the genome of a cell. Gerry Rubin and Allan Spradling introduced this approach in the early 1980s and it has been a basic technique since that time for inducing mutations and introducing exogenous DNA (Rubin and Spradling, 1982; Spradling and Rubin, 1982). Most laboratory strains do not have a class of transposons called P elements nor the repressor that prevents the P elements from jumping around the genome and introducing mutations wherever they land. Spradling and Rubin showed how this naturally occurring mutagenesis system could be harnessed; by injecting P elements into fly embryos it proved possible to mutagenize the genome, and, critically, leave a molecular tag (the P element) at the site. Chemical mutagenesis for example just changes a base pair at random so there is no way to find out what has happened other than resort to positional cloning. The P element sequence is known, and its presence can be detected by hybridization and PCR strategies.

P element mutagenesis does not allow an investigator to target a specific genomic region in the fly. Homologous recombination would achieve this and it has been made to work in *Drosophila* (Rong and Golic, 2000), but it is difficult, slow and very few labs use it. Instead, fly geneticists now use a modification of the P element protocol. An enzyme called an integrase (φC31) mediates recombination between two DNA sequences called *attB* and *attP* recognition sites. By integrating these sites into the genome with a P element, subsequent targeted insertions can be made (Groth *et al.* 2004). This does not however give fly geneticists the genetic engineering capabilities that currently lie in the hands of mouse geneticists. Recent advances with human stem cells may also confer those powers on human geneticists.

References

Bradley, A., Evans, M., Kaufman, M. H., and Robertson, E. (1984). *Nature* **309** (5965): 255–256.

Collins, F. (1995). Positional cloning moves from perditional to traditional. *Nat Gen* **9**:347–350.

Fodor, S.P., Read, J.L., Pirrung, M.C., Stryer, L., Lu, A.T., and Solas, D. (1991). Light-directed, spatially addressable parallel chemical synthesis. *Science* **251**:767–773.

Groth, A.C., Fish, M., Nusse, R., and Calos, M.P. (2004). Construction of transgenic *Drosophila* by using the site-specific integrase from phage φC31. *Genetics* **166**:1775–1782.

Keays, D.A., Tian, G., Poirier, K., Huang, G.J., Siebold, C., Cleak, J., Oliver, P.L., Fray, M., Harvey, R. J. *et al.* (2007). Mutations in alpha-tubulin cause abnormal neuronal migration in mice and lissencephaly in humans. *Cell* **128**:45–57.

Matsuzaki, H., Loi, H., Dong, S., Tsai, Y.Y., Fang, J., Law, J., Di, X., Liu, W.M., Yang, G. *et al.* (2004).

Parallel genotyping of over 10,000 SNPs using a one-primer assay on a high-density oligonucleotide array. *Genome Res* **14**:414–425.

Rong, Y.S. and Golic, K.G. (2000). Gene targeting by homologous recombination in *Drosophila*. *Science* **288**:2013–2018.

Rubin, G.M. and Spradling, A.C. (1982). Genetic transformation of *Drosophila* with transposable element vectors. *Science* **218**:348–353.

Spradling, A.C. and Rubin, G.M. (1982). Transposition of cloned P elements into *Drosophila* germ line chromosomes. *Science* **218**:341–347.

Index